D1477813

Women Humanitarians

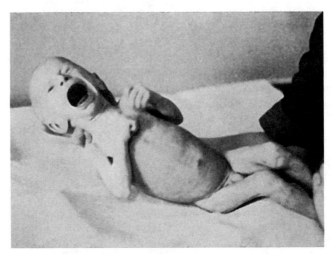

A displaced person, Germany, 1946
(From Ella Jorden, *Operation Mercy*, Frederick Muller, 1957)

Women Humanitarians

A Biographical Dictionary of British Women
Active between 1900 and 1950

Sybil Oldfield

'Doers of the Word'

CONTINUUM

London and New York

First published 2001 by

Continuum
The Tower Building, 11 York Road, London SE1 7NX
370 Lexington Avenue, New York, NY 10017–6503

British Library Cataloguing-in-Publication Data
A catalogue record for this book is available from the British Library.

ISBN 0–8264–4962–X

Library of Congress Cataloging-in-Publication Data
Oldfield, Sybil.
     Women Humanitarians : a biographical dictionary of British women active between 1900 and
1950 / Sybil Oldfield.
          p. cm.
     Includes bibliographical references and index.
     ISBN 0–8264–4962–X
          1. Women—Great Britain—Biography—Dictionaries. 2. Women social reformers—Great
Britain—Biography—Dictionaries. I. Title.

  HQ1595.A3 O43 2001
  305.4'092'241—dc21
  [B]   00–034573

Designed and typeset by Ben Cracknell Studios
Printed and bound in Great Britain TJ International Ltd, Padstow, Cornwall

Contents

To the girls – Milena, Tamara and Alexandra

Acknowledgements

I am grateful to the following:

The Library Committee of Britain Yearly Meeting of the Religious Society of Friends (Quakers) for illustrations to entries for Florence Barrow, Edith Bigland, Bertha Bracey, Ruth Fry, Mary Higgs, Mary Hughes, Kathleen Lonsdale, Priscilla Peckover, Violet Tillard and Elizabeth Spence Watson;

Anti-Slavery International, London, for illustrations to entries for Alice Harris, Clara Haslewood and Dame Kathleen Simon;

The Salvation Army International Heritage Centre, London, for illustrations to entries for Mary Booth, Olive Booth and Motee Booth-Tucker Sladen;

The National Portrait Gallery, London, for illustrations to entries for Kate, Lady Courtney of Penwith, and Sybil Thorndike, and particularly to Terence Pepper of the NPG Photographic Department for advice on copyright;

The Contemporary Medical Archives, Wellcome Institute History of Medicine, London, for permission to reproduce photographs from the *British Medical Women's Federation Journal;*

Harcourt, Inc. and Faber and Faber for permission to publish an excerpt from 'The end and the beginning' in Wisława Szymborska's *View with a Grain of Sand* (1993). English translation by Stanisław Barańczak and Clare Cavanagh (1995);

The Women's Library, Calcutta House, Old Castle Street, London (formerly Fawcett Library), hereafter referred to as Women's Library, London, for their magnificent collection of biographical cuttings and for the courteous patience of David Doughan;

Dr Pat Starkey, Department of History, University of Liverpool, for the entry for Margaret McNeill, and Tim Evens for his contributions of background knowledge to that entry;

Fiona Watson of the Northern Health Services Archives, Aberdeen, for her help at the Scottish end;

Reading University Archives, for permission to quote from Edith Morley's unpublished reminiscences;

All those who answered my request for nominees for inclusion in this dictionary and Lorna Watson for her help in Oxford archives;

For well-informed and good-humoured help, as always, from the Interlibrary Loan colleagues at the University of Sussex Library, from the University of Sussex Photographic and Design Unit and from my secretary, Pat Mounce;

Finally, my commissioning editor, Veronica Higgs, for believing in the project from the first, and Fiona McKenzie for her meticulous copy-editing.

Every effort has been made to contact holders of copyright; any further queries in that regard should be addressed to the publishers.

'The end and the beginning'

After every war
someone has to tidy up.
Things won't pick
themselves up, after all.

Someone has to shove
the rubble to the roadsides
so the carts loaded with corpses
can get by.

Someone has to trudge
through sludge and ashes,
through the sofa springs,
the shards of glass,
the bloody rags.

Someone has to lug the post
to prop the wall,
someone has to glaze the window,
set the door in its frame.

No sound bites, no photo opportunities,
and it takes years.
All the cameras have gone
to other wars . . .

From Wisława Szymborska,
View with a Grain of Sand: Selected Poems,
trans. Stanisław Barańczak and Clare Cavanagh (Faber and Faber 1995)

Introduction

The pre-requisite for conscience: the possibility to be sensitive toward people who don't belong to one's own narrow circle.

Christa Wolf, *A Model Childhood* (1976), English translation (1980), p. 327

Most dictionaries of twentieth-century biography include the mass killers of our time – crazed despots, their perverted henchmen, their army chiefs; but hardly ever do any of their opposites make an appearance. By their opposites I mean the healers who spent themselves in trying to prevent or reduce or redress the deliberate inhumanity of those with the power to hurt. Therefore I set out to compile a volume of *counter*-history to retrieve the memory of some of the outstanding but forgotten humanitarians in the first half of this century. Why only women humanitarians and why only British? I have been constrained by the limitations of my own ignorance. Nothing would make me happier than to see other people attempting to do biographical justice to the heroic humaneness of both men and women in every society on earth.

'Humanitarian' is a concept that is 'maddeningly imprecise'.[1] It embraces people who relieve life-threatening suffering wherever it occurs, or who attempt to prevent mass suffering, or who rescue helpless civilians in imminent danger; they almost always work independently of governmental authority and, ideally, in a totally nonpartisan mode. For the purposes of this work I define a humanitarian as one who puts the desperate needs of *humanitas* first, above the claims of his or her own immediate group – whether of nationality, religion, gender, race or class – and at whatever personal cost. 'Those', as Keats said in *Hyperion*, 'to whom the miseries of the world are misery and will not let them rest.' For all their immense diversity – 'The good are not alike: they differ from one another as much as other people'[2] – the one allegiance that all these women shared was their lived-out commitment to our common humanity. Long before Eleanor Roosevelt and others drafted the Universal Declaration of Human Rights in 1946, long before the founding of Oxfam, Amnesty International or Médecins sans Frontières, these women crossed huge physical, social and psychological barriers to reach out to rescue strangers, including their 'enemies'.

Thomas Haskell has spelt out the four historical prerequisites for humanitarianism in relation to the emergence of the mid-eighteenth-century anti-slavery movement in America and Britain:

> First and most obvious, we must adhere to ethical maxims that make helping strangers the right thing to do before we can feel obliged to aid them . . .

[Secondly] we must perceive ourselves to be causally involved in the evil event . . . [Thirdly] we [must] see a way to stop it. [Fourthly] *some* of us will feel compelled to act [if] the recipes of intervention available to us [have] such sufficient ordinariness, familiarity, certainty of effect, and ease of operation that our failure to use them would constitute . . . an intentional [evil] act in itself.[3]

We may not agree with the 'ease of operation' part of the recipe, but certainly all the women in this dictionary shared a sense of moral obligation to intervene to help people they did not know and who, in many cases, were suffering, directly or indirectly, as a consequence of British policies. Some of the women were war-resisters in wartime, responding to the needs of stranded 'enemy' civilians or prisoners of war and supporting British conscientious objectors and their families, no matter what it cost them. Some were champions of unpopular, persecuted refugees seeking asylum in Britain. Others were international rescue workers and nurses in famine or disaster areas, whether in war zones or in the aftermath of war. Still others were medical missionaries, nurses, doctors and medical researchers risking their own lives to combat disease and premature mortality worldwide – but particularly in areas colonized under the British Empire, about which they felt a particular moral responsibility. In one way or another they all reached out to touch the untouchable, including on occasion untouchables within Britain itself: delinquent youths, homeless tramps, convicted murderers, the incurable old.

But am I not being a naïve sentimentalist to take these women so on trust? After Marx, Freud and the post-modernists, how can anyone believe in authentic altruism at all? Are we not all driven by our own deepest *self*-interest, our will-to-power, and our alleged, still more unsavoury, subconscious psychological needs – including the need that others should suffer in order for us to feel good about helping them? Clearly there have been instances where 'humanitarianism' has been the cover for a domineering ego-trip. Marie Stopes believed that she had a unique mission to save the world; but it is also arguable that she did help to save it, and so has to be forgiven. For the rest, it is remarkable how very many of the women included here did not believe that they had done anything out of the ordinary; they insisted that others did far more than they; they were embarrassed on the rare occasions when they were given any recognition. It was not that they wanted to feel good about themselves, rather that they could not bear to feel badly about the intolerable situation of others without trying to do something to help. Were they masochists? In my view not one of these women actually enjoyed facing violently hostile crowds, private mockery, public abuse, extreme cold and hunger, unpleasant, potentially fatal diseases, prison and even execution, any more than do non-humanitarians. They were unusually tough, but they were not in love with pain. Just *why* these particular women should each have had such a sensitive, compassionate self in the first place, a personality with so imperious a conscience that compelled them, unlike the rest of us, to try to alleviate the suffering of people outside their own circle, has yet to be explained. We are on the threshold of understanding much more about the neurobiological/socio-economic formation of the *anti*-social personality than we are about the altruist.[4] Perhaps we shall discover that Samaritans cannnot help but be Samaritans, any more than their damaged opposites can help their compulsion to hurt and destroy. Thomas Haskell 'does not pretend to plumb the mysteries of individual sensitivity or compassion . . . moral insight, . . . courage in the face of adversity . . . tenacity in uprooting entrenched institutions'.[5]

How did I discover the women included in this dictionary? Twenty years ago, while researching the life of the pacifist feminist Mary Sheepshanks for my book *Spinsters of This Parish* (1984), I came upon two documents from the First World War, both dated April 1915. The first was an Open Letter from the pioneer Dutch doctor and feminist Aletta Jacobs, calling women of all nations to an International Congress of Women in order to protest against the world war and to prevent its recurrence. The second document was a list of 156 names[6] of the British Committee of women publicly supporting that Women's International Congress at The [neutral] Hague whose aims were:

1. To demand that international disputes shall in future be settled by some other means than war.
2. To claim that women should have a voice in the affairs of the nations.

Impressed by their moral courage in being political dissidents even in wartime, I then spent many years trying to identify the British women both on that list and on a second, annotated, list, held among the Catherine Marshall Papers in Cumbria Public Records Office, Carlisle, that gave the names of all those women applying to the British Home Secretary for exit permits to attend that Congress at The Hague.[7] I learned of so much life-saving, life-enabling, life-enriching work done by these women – and also by their even less well-known colleagues – that I felt I must attempt to record that work by compiling this dictionary of biography. In the course of my research I also felt increasingly impelled to look still further and discover and chronicle the work not merely of *bien-pensant* anti-militarists but of 'hands-on' nurses, relief workers and medical women. Therefore I advertised in *The Nursing Times* and *The Friend* and on the Women's History site on the Web for more nominees for inclusion. I read through women's obituaries in the rich collection of cuttings, dating back to the mid-1920s, held in the Women's Library, London, formerly the Fawcett Library; I searched the archives of the Salvation Army, Anti-Slavery International, the British Red Cross, the Church Missionary Society, the Contemporary Medical Archives of the Wellcome Institute's History of Medicine, the Save the Children Fund, Friends' House Library, the Middle East Archives at St Antony's College, and African and Indian materials at SOAS, University of London. What I discovered was that humanitarian intervention by British women in the first half of the twentieth century reached out to almost every part of the world where horrors were perpetrated: the South African concentration camps, the Belgian Congo, the war-devastated Balkans, famine-ravaged Russia and India, colonized Africa, China invaded by Japan, Civil War Spain, stateless Jewry, alienated Arab Palestine, fire-bombed German cities, Japanese prisoner-of-war camps, not to mention all the other places on earth made desolate because of the Second World War.[8]

Naturally I have encountered dilemmas regarding inclusion or exclusion. One could – and should – compile a whole biographical dictionary of Quaker humanitarians, another one of nurses, another of women doctors, yet another of women medical missionaries. I have only been able to offer a personal selection of those I believe to be exemplary representatives of the multifarious humanitarian effort by British women active between 1900 and 1950. This dictionary has no pretensions, therefore, to comprehensiveness; on the contrary, its compiler is haunted by the ghosts of those not in it.[9]

Is it possible to generalize about the women in this dictionary? What they do seem to have had in common was exceptional, problem-solving intelligence and the will and the ability to co-operate in the field. Of the over 150 entries more than two-thirds were single women or childless. Of the 43 women with children, seven had only one child, and most had children who were grown up or, necessarily, looked after by others, including their fathers or other relatives, during their mothers' period of greatest humanitarian activity. Alice Harris, Nan Green, Muriel Paget and Janet Vaughan stand out as mothers faced with the terrible choice of either caring for their own young children or else leaving them in order to care for even more desperately needy others.

A socio-economic analysis of the women's origins reveals that 25 of the 150 came from very modest backgrounds, 25 from upper-class and/or very wealthy backgrounds, while over 100 came from the educated professional, prosperous, middle class.[10] Of their political allegiance, perhaps not surprisingly, the huge majority were on the left/liberal side of the spectrum, but staunch Conservatives like the Duchess of Atholl, Mother Kevin and Mavis Tate should not be forgotten either. *All* the women were *de facto* feminists in that they all transgressed psychological and societal gender constraints in order to speak and act in the public world outside the home; some, like Emily Hobhouse or Mother Kevin, daring to speak truth to the very citadels of male power, whether in the Cabinet, the Army or the Vatican itself. Half of the women here declared themselves as feminists and many were in fact the outspoken leaders of the various sections of the British women's movement of their time who saw women's rights as human rights.

Although it is difficult to know of these women's most private religious beliefs, and in many cases these changed over a long lifetime, only around 30 were definite non-believers in anything called 'God'. The overwhelming majority defined themselves in relation to some kind of Christianity, ranging from Roman Catholic to Quaker and Unitarian; most of them if challenged would have agreed with Muriel Lester's definition of their religion: 'Trying to be Christian'. Were they then motivated by a wish to serve God rather than Man? It is my belief that the women in this dictionary who were Christian were not great, practising humanitarians because of their Christianity – even if they thought that to be the case – but rather that their Christianity was the religious manifestation of their humaneness. For, as Feuerbach wrote: 'He . . . who loves man for the sake of man, who rises to the love of the species, to universal love, adequate to the nature of the species, he is a Christian, is Christ himself. He does what Christ did, what made Christ Christ.'[11] And so does she. Similarly, the Communists among these women were not practising humanitarians because they were Communists, but Communists because they were humane.

It has been a joy and a privilege to compile this dictionary, inadequate to its great subjects though I know it to be. 'We can find something better than ourselves in the . . . past.'[12]

1. Larry Minear and Thomas G. Weiss, *Mercy under Fire: War and the Global Humanitarian Community* (Boulder, CO, Westview Press, 1995), p. 18; see also their chapter 'Guiding principles', pp. 60–75.
2. Julia Kavanagh, *Women of Christianity* (London, 1852), Preface.
3. Thomas Haskell, 'Capitalism and the origins of the humanitarian sensibility', *American Historical Review* **90**(3) (1985), pp. 357–8.
4. For two works on the roots of human altruism see S. P. Oliner and P. M. Oliner, *The Altruistic Personality: Rescuers of Jews in Nazi Europe* (New York, Free Press, 1988); and Nancy Eisenberg, *The Caring Child* (Cambridge, MA, Harvard University Press, 1992).

5. Haskell, *op. cit.*, p. 361.
6. See Appendix I.
7. I am grateful to Dr Hilary Francis, Harrogate and the University of York, for alerting me to this list.
8. For the devastation and despair in Europe after 1945, especially in Germany, see Alfred Grosser, *Western Germany, from Defeat to Rearmament* (London, George Allen and Unwin, 1955); and Douglas Botting, *In the Ruins of the Reich* (London, George Allen and Unwin, 1985).
9. Among such 'ghosts' are Miss M. C. Albright, Lady Barlow, Henrietta Barnett, Eleanor Barton, Dr Mary Blacklock, Lily Boileau, Margaret Bondfield, Phyllis Bottome, Dr Helen Boyle, Stella Browne, Bryher, Elizabeth Cadbury, Amy Carmichael, Dr Harriette Chick, Dr Catherine Chisholm, Helen Crawfurd, Rhoda Dawson, Lady Denman, Annie Dickinson, Dr Ethel Douglas, Marian Fox, Judy Frydd, Eva Gore-Booth, Mary Agnes Hamilton, Margery Edge Harris, Rosalie Harvey, Elizabeth Fox Howard, Joan Howson, Dr Elizabeth Hurdon, Dr Isabel Emslie Hutton, Dorothy Jewson, Dr Ivy Keess, Angela, Countess of Limerick, Joice Loch, Margaret Macmillan, Frances Melville, Muriel Monkhouse, Olga Nethersole, Dr Innes Pearse, Dr Kate Platt, Edith A. Roberts, Gladys Schütze, Amelia Scott, Shena Simon, Sarah Jane Tanner, Dr Barbara Tchaikowsky, Grace Vulliamy, Rosa Waugh, Alice Wheeldon, Jane Wicksteed, Irene Cooper Willis, Theodora Wilson-Wilson, Dr Ruth Young and Alice Zimmern. Had I but world enough, and time . . .
10. Cf. my socio-political analysis of the background and beliefs of the women on the two lists in my article 'England's Cassandras in World War One' in Sybil Oldfield (ed.), *This Working-Day World: Women's Lives and Culture(s) in Britain 1914–1945* (London and Bristol, PA, Taylor and Francis, 1994), pp. 90–1.
11. Ludwig Feuerbach, *The Essence of Christianity*, translated by George Eliot (first published 1843; reissued London and New York, Harper Torch Books, 1957), p. 269.
12. Simone Weil, *Selected Essays, 1934–1943*, edited and translated by Richard Rees (Oxford, Oxford University Press, 1962), p. 44.

The Dictionary

Names in SMALL CAPITALS
within an entry indicate that
there is an entry for that person
in the dictionary.

A

ASHBY, MARGERY CORBETT, DBE
(19.4.1882–9.5.1981)

INTERNATIONALIST FEMINIST, WORKER FOR DISARMAMENT

Father: Charles Corbett, barrister, Liberal MP, squire
Mother: Marie, née Gray, feminist philanthropist

Anglican

The most engaging and alert 97-year-old this writer has ever encountered, Dame Margery Corbett Ashby put together her memoirs at the very end of her life, but unfortunately she did not do full justice to her own most radical attempts at humanitarian political intervention. She came from an immensely privileged, prosperous background but her father's radical Liberalism prohibited complacent acquiescence in injustice and inequality. A committed feminist, she held a leading position in the pre-war National Union of Women's Suffrage Societies and faced all the mockery and hostility that entailed, including from within her own social circle. As a quite outstanding linguist (fluent in French and German, able to speak Italian and Turkish as well as read Norwegian), it was natural for her to serve the *International* Alliance of Women, first as Secretary and then as President (1923–46).

As a young wife and mother, Margery Corbett Ashby had known what it was to have her husband ordered out to the trenches in France: 'Often, I remember, I used to wake at 4 a.m., the time at which the troops were liable to go over the top, with a dreadful feeling of foreboding, and I used to bicycle daily to St Michael's Church to pray for Brian's safety.'[1] As soon as possible after the war she tried to bring the International Women's Suffrage Association (later the International Alliance of Women) back to life, starting by making renewed contact in Germany. In Cologne she discovered a total breakdown of civil society, not helped by the British servicemen of the Occupation, who were both infecting the starving girl prostitutes with syphilis and being infected by them. She successfully negotiated an agreement between the Mayor of Cologne and Commandant Allen of the Volunteer Women's Police that women police should be sent out to help control the situation, that the British soldiers' pay be taken from them and put into savings accounts, and that unprotected girls arriving at Cologne railway station should be met and taken back home. Her next intervention was at the formation of the League of Nations in Paris in 1919, where she succeeded in getting at least lip-service paid to gender equality within the League apparatus itself and as part of the policy of the International Labour Organization.[2] At the Rome IWSA Congress of 1923 she had to watch while 'Mussolini's young fascist toughs pushed our members off the platform' and she herself headed a suffrage deputation to Il Duce: 'Mussolini was seated at the far end of a vast room doing his Napoleonic act, scowling at us with head resting on folded arms.'[3] In 1929 she presided over the International Alliance of Women Congress in Berlin:

The memory of those . . . ardent young men and women longing to be brought into the community of nations haunted me as the post-war policy of France and the Lloyd George attitude of 'squeezing them until the pips squeaked' made the second war seem inevitable . . . I still think better treatment . . . would have avoided further war and woe.[4]

Margery Corbett Ashby deliberately, and against much opposition, put campaigning for peace on the agenda of the International Alliance of Women – the 'greatest freedom won by women is surely precisely [the] right with men to effective interest in the whole of life'.[5] One aspect of peace was peace within the new multi-ethnic nation states of Europe. After visiting Greece, Bulgaria, Yugoslavia, Hungary and Czechoslovakia, she enunciated the three basic demands among all minorities in 1929: (1) the right to land; (2) the right to primary education in one's mother tongue; and (3) religious freedom in one's own tongue.

The years 1932–34 were the most depressing period in Margery Corbett Ashby's life because, as substitute British delegate at the League of Nations Disarmament Conference in Geneva,[6] she had apparent responsibility but no power and had to witness her own country's deliberate frustration of the world's last chance to control and reduce a fatal rearmament race. She was exasperated by British incompetence and lukewarmness, and the abuse of the technical commissions, constantly lobbied as they were by the Royal Air Force and the Naval High Command, among others, as they hindered any and every practical disarmament proposal. She was present when von Neurath warned Sir John Simon, in vain, that the absence of concessions to Germany was about to cause the defeat of Brüning and the triumph of the Nazis. Finally, in March 1935, Margery Corbett Ashby sent the Prime Minister her resignation.

For nearly three years I did my utmost to urge HM Government to support any practical scheme for mutual security and defence, since almost every European country considered mutual protection the indispensable basis for any reduction in armaments. [But Britain] consistently opposed every suggestion put forward by the political commission . . .

In face of such a policy, if I left the delegation, I should feel less useless to the cause of peace.[7]

After the Munich agreement (October 1938) she tried to resign as President of the International Women's Alliance because of the painful conflict between her beliefs and British government policy. She was on Hitler's black list and three of her dearest colleagues, Rosa Manus from the Netherlands, Senator Plaminkova in Czechoslovakia and Mme Siminska in Poland, were murdered in the Second World War by the Nazis.

Ironically, she was also placed on Stalin's black list after the war. In the winter of 1947 she visited the cold, hungry British Zone of defeated Germany and reached out a hand to 'the shining courage and faith of the leaders of the new women's movement [there]'.[8]

Perhaps her most radical initiative of all was the appeal for prominent British women to sign a public declaration in March 1945 asking the British government to release from prison 90 Indian national leaders. She was responding to the urgent concern of the Indian members of the International Women's Alliance.[9] In 1946, at the United Nations in New York, Margery Corbett Ashby was asked by Professor

Lemkin of the Nuremberg Tribunal to put her weight behind defining a newly identified crime: 'genocide'. This she did, swinging the women members of the British delegation behind her and also enlisting the support of the leader of the delegation from India. 'The resolution was passed [by the General Assembly presided over by Mrs Pandit] and genocide is a recognised international crime – at least in theory.'[10]

It may be too much to claim, as *The Times* obituarist did, that 'Probably no-one has done more for the emancipation of women during the century than Margery Corbett Ashby',[11] but she was undoubtedly herself a very fine example of emancipation.

1. Dame Margery Corbett Ashby, *Memoirs* (privately printed, 1996), held in the Women's Library, London, pp. 94–5.
2. *Ibid.*, pp. 105–6.
3. *Ibid.*, p. 117.
4. *Ibid.*, p. 133.
5. *Ibid.*, p. 137.
6. In 1930 she had led a deputation of American, British, French and Japanese women to the London Naval Conference to urge a substantial reduction in naval armaments.
7. Ashby, *Memoirs*, pp. 159–60.
8. Margery Corbett Ashby, 'A fortnight in Germany', *International Women's News* (December 1947), p. 35.
9. See Ashby papers, Women's Library, London, for interesting manuscript lists of British women appealed to and of women signatories.
10. Ashby, *Memoirs*, p. 205.
11. *The Times* (16.5.1981).

See also Brian Harrison's essay on Margery Corbett Ashby in his *Prudent Revolutionaries: Portraits of British Feminists between the Wars* (Oxford, Clarendon Press, 1987).

ASHTON, MARGARET
(19.1.1856–15.10.1937)

PIONEER WOMAN IN LOCAL GOVERNMENT; SUFFRAGIST; ANTI-WAR WITNESS

Father: Thomas Ashton, Manchester cotton magnate, Liberal
Mother: Elizabeth, née Gair

Unitarian

Margaret Ashton, c. 1930

Margaret Ashton was 42 when, on her father's death, she became free to lead an independent political life of active social intervention. Her early involvement with the Women's [Poor Law] Guardian Association and the Women's Trade Union League in Manchester had educated her in the facts of women's poverty and their imperative claim to the weapon of the vote. In the first decade of the twentieth century she became a leading figure in the National Union of Women's Suffrage Societies and was elected the first woman councillor on Manchester City Council (in 1908), where she concentrated on the areas of education and public health. In 1910 she said she had 'a "watching brief"' for all women's questions, from municipal milk and midwifery to public lavatories and lodging houses.[1] She helped found – and fund – the Manchester Babies' Hospital and the first municipal lodging house for women. It took great moral courage for a woman to stand for public office, risking both ridicule and humiliation at the polls, not to mention alienating her own respectable family, when, like Margaret Ashton, she also faced hostile, jeering crowds on the subject of votes for women. Margaret Ashton's mother, who lived with her MP son in London, was not pleased when her daughter sold her large Manchester home and moved into 'a hovel' in order to give money to the women's movement. She had left the Liberal Party for the Labour Party in 1906 because the former would not back women's suffrage.

The true extent and depth of Margaret Ashton's dogged moral courage was made plain in the First World War. Not only did she sign EMILY HOBHOUSE's Open Christmas Letter to the (enemy) women of Germany and Austria in December 1914,[2] but in 1915, after very painful heart-searching, she, together with other leading British feminists who prioritized the ending of the war by negotiation and who, to that end, had supported the Women's International Congress at The Hague in April 1915, resigned from the National Executive of the Women's Suffrage Societies led by Mrs Fawcett.[3] Margaret Ashton, then 60 years old, led the strongest branch of the British section of the Women's International League for Peace and Freedom (in Manchester), chairing its public meetings, which were raided by police. She would then lead the silent, non-violent protest against the police arrests of conscientious objectors present at the meeting.[4] She was spied on by the Home Office for over a year.[5] In 1917 she attempted to speak at a Women's Peace Crusade meeting in central Manchester only to find it banned by police and a hostile crowd confronting her and threatening violence.[6] At the end of the war she 'was removed from the education committee of [Manchester] City Council on the grounds that she was unfit to be concerned with young people'.[7] Her portrait by Henry Lamb was not allowed to hang in Manchester City Art Gallery on the grounds of her pacifist position in 1914–18.

Margaret Ashton's 'tiresome conscience'[8] had led her to leave the conventional upper-middle-class women's domestic world and to take on the unpopular radical causes of unenfranchised women, of the exploited and wretched poor and of resistance to war, to all of which she remained true until her death. At her memorial service in Manchester Cathedral it was said of her: 'Like all really great people, she never put herself in the centre of the picture; the cause was everything and she was nothing.'[9]

1. See Patricia Hollis, *Ladies Elect: Women in English Local Government 1865–1914* (Oxford, Clarendon Press, 1987), pp. 430, 419–20.
2. See entry for EMILY HOBHOUSE for extracts; and *Ius Suffragii* (January 1915) for the whole text of the Open Letter and the initial list of signatories.
3. See Appendix I for the list of British pacifist feminist supporters of The Hague Congress; see also Sybil Oldfield, *Spinsters of This Parish* (London, Virago, 1984), ch. 9; and Anne Wiltsher, *Most Dangerous Women: Feminist Peace Campaigners of the Great War* (London, Pandora, 1985).
4. See Jill Liddington, *The Long Road to Greenham: Feminism and Anti-Militarism in Britain since 1820* (London, Virago, 1989), chs 5 and 6.
5. *Ibid.*

6. *Ibid.*
7. Olive Banks, *The Biographical Dictionary of British Feminists*, vol. 2 (New York, New York University Press, 1990), p. 10.
8. Shena Simon, *Margaret Ashton and Her Times*, Margaret Ashton Memorial Lecture for 1948 (Manchester University Press, 1949), p. 14.
9. *Manchester Guardian* (21.10.1937).

There will be an entry for Margaret Ashton in the *New Dictionary of National Biography*.

ATHOLL, DUCHESS OF, *see* Stewart-Murray, Katharine

AYLWARD, GLADYS
(24.2.1902–1.1.1970)

CHILD RESCUER, CHINA

Father: Thomas Aylward, postman
Mother: Rosina Florence, née
  Whiskip, bootmaker's daughter

Nonconformist

Gladys Aylward with grown-up 'Ninepence' and son (From Alan Burgess, The Small Woman, *Reprint Society, 1957)*

Despite failing her examination in theology as a probationer at the China Inland Mission Centre, Gladys Aylward became an immensely effective missionary and social worker in north China in the 1930s and 1940s, a time of bandit attacks, civil war and brutal invasion by Japan. She had set off for China in October 1930, after having been a London parlourmaid and in her spare time an evangelical preacher on street corners since leaving school at 13. She had only £2 and 9 [old] pence (roughly the equivalent of a fortnight's wages) and her rail ticket with which to cross Stalin's Soviet Union to Siberia before sailing from Vladivostok to Kobe and then travelling from Japan to Tientsin (Tianjin) in China. All this without knowing a word of Russian, Japanese or Chinese – or having any official backing. Her eventual goal was to join a Scottish missionary, Mrs Jeannie Lawson, in Yangcheng, a mountainous citadel in north China reached only by mule and so hostile to unfamiliar 'white devils' that she was spat on and pelted every time she went out of doors.

After that unpropitious start, Gladys Aylward set to with a will to learn to speak the local languages in order to tell the Gospel story, and to understand spoken Mandarin Chinese. She wore Chinese dress and eventually became a Chinese citizen; her short stature, dark hair and eyes helped her to be accepted, as did her sharing in the poverty of the hard life around her. She opened an inn for muleteers crossing the mountain pass and in 1931 was ordered by the local mandarin to become the official foot inspector throughout Yangcheng province, ensuring that every infant girl's feet were unbound, on pain of a prison sentence.

She was also ordered to stop a local prison riot, out-facing a crazed axeman who had already killed several prisoners. Her humanitarianism was proved not by these two activities into which she had been conscripted but by what she did without compulsion. She insisted that the prison governor start work projects for the sake of the prisoners' sanity: cotton weaving, shoemaking, rabbit breeding. She also used her first-hand knowledge of women's miserable domestic lives to intervene on their behalf, challenging the local mandarin to take action to stop the endemic wife-beating, girl-child-selling and general treatment of females as mere chattel-slaves in his province. Christian conversion brought with it human status for wives and daughters of the converts. She herself became the adoptive mother of five abandoned children, including a brutally maltreated 2-year-old girl whom she bought for 9 pence.

In spring 1938 the Japanese attacked north China by air. Gladys Aylward was buried alive by bomb rubble but was dug out and went on to organize the rescue/relief operation in Yangcheng. She left the city to start a primitive cave hospital in the mountains and then had to see the ghastly aftermath of the occupation of Yangcheng by Japanese infantry, who had bayoneted every man, woman and child found there. She and her adopted children became refugees, moving on to work in the mission orphanage in Tsehchow. When the Japanese took over Tsehchow, she was hit on the head by a rifle butt and kicked unconscious by a soldier. The cycle of carnage, flight, nursing the injured, hiding with her children in the mountains, living in a cave on millet porridge and twig tea with wolves outside, reporting to the Nationalists where Japanese were billeted – all this continued until she learned that the Japanese had put a price on her head. During one flight from the advancing occupation she was shot in the back. She realized that her children and all the other orphans left in the Tsehchow mission were at risk as possible hostages and determined to take them across the mountains to safety.

That epic journey shepherding nearly 100 children – twenty girls aged 13 to 15, seven boys aged 11 to 15 and 65 other children between 4 and 8 – sleeping over twelve nights in the open, with very little food, steering south by the sun, the children at last whimpering with hunger while she herself was near despair and guilty over what she had brought upon them, seemed to have reached a hopeless end when they finally reached the Yellow River to find it closed to all water traffic by the war. Even after an illegal river crossing was made to Nationalist-held Shansi province, she and the children still had many days and nights on a train followed by yet another mountain range to cross, again sleeping in caves or in the open, until finally they could be transported secretly by night on an open coal truck to the city of Sian (Xi'an) – only to find it locked against them. Not another refugee was allowed to enter, overpacked as it was with refugees already. Instead, therefore, she got the children to a refugee centre in nearby Fucheng, and collapsed.

On recovering from the after-effects of exhaustion, privation and the internal damage done by her war wounds, Gladys Aylward had to earn her living again, which she did by helping with a mission to lepers in Szechuan. She returned to England in 1949, but left in 1953 to work for 17 years as head of a mission orphanage in Taipei, Taiwan. Her biographer Alan Burgess could be excused for claiming that she was 'one of the most remarkable women of our generation'.[1]

1. Alan Burgess, *The Small Woman: The Heroic Story of Gladys Aylward* (London, Evans Bros, 1957; Reprint Society, 1959). See also G. Aylward, *Gladys Aylward: Her Personal Story as Told to Christine Hunter* (London, Coverdale House, 1971).

Gladys Aylward was later portrayed by Ingrid Bergman in the film *The Inn of the Sixth Happiness*. Gladys Aylward commented that had she looked anything in the least like Ingrid Bergman the Chinese would never have accepted her.

See also article in *Daily Telegraph* (14.11.1962); and obituary in *The Times* (5.1.1970).

AYRTON, HERTHA (née **SARAH MARKS**)

(28.4.1854–26.8.1923)

SCIENTIST; INVENTOR OF
ANTI-POISON-GAS FAN

*Father: Levi Marks, Polish refugee
    watchmaker/hawker*
Mother: Alice, née Moss

*Brought up Orthodox Jewish, became humanist
agnostic*

Hertha Ayrton

Brought up in Portsea as one of eight fatherless children, Sarah Marks helped her remarkable mother to sew and care for the family until, at the age of 9, she left home for seven years in London to attend the school run by her clever maternal aunt, Marion Hartog. Sarah's exceptional intelligence had been recognized and cultivated as far as was then possible for a poor Jewish girl in England. At 16 she went out to work as a governess and visiting coach in mathematics in order to support her family. She had by this time become a convinced rationalist, rejecting all religious dogma. In 1873 she taught herself all the subjects, including Greek, for the Cambridge Higher Local Examination. By great good fortune she was introduced to Barbara Leigh Smith Bodichon, the free-spirited campaigner for the liberation of women and founder of Girton College, Cambridge, who became in effect a second parent to her as well as an amazingly candid, affirming, lifelong friend. Hertha (as she now called herself) Marks finally reached Girton in 1876. After completing the Tripos in mathematics she again went to work as a tutor of mathematics to repay her debts and support her dependent relations; she also started a club for very poor working girls in her part of London. Three years later, again supported by Barbara Bodichon, she started her career as an experimental physicist and inventor, eventually making important discoveries about the electric arc, the right sort of carbon for searchlights, and the nature of wave motion, and becoming the loved and respected friend of Marie Curie. In 1885 she married Professor W. E. Ayrton, FRS.

Her passion for basic democratic justice made Hertha Ayrton a convinced, ardent suffragist; she gave money and support between 1906 and 1912 to the militant Women's Social and Political Union. On 18 November 1910, 'Black Friday', she was one of the twelve distinguished women in a deputation to the Prime Minister who were violently mistreated by the police: 'Twice, policemen seized me by the throat and jerked my head back till it felt as if my neck would break.'[1] She gave her own home for use as a 'safe place' where released hunger-striking suffragettes, including Mrs Pankhurst, could be nursed and concealed from the police. Her other humanitarian cause at this period was her support for the Humanitarian League's attempt to abolish flogging as a judicial punishment in Britain.

During the First World War Hertha Ayrton applied her knowledge of vortices in water and air to the invention of a fan which, if vibrated correctly, could clear away noxious gases, replacing them with currents of fresh air. She offered the invention free to the War Office for use in the trenches against poison gas, only to be met by indifference, obstruction, incompetence and fatal delay. 'I suppose, if I had invented something to destroy life instead of saving it, it would get taken up at once as a military proposition!'[2] The pain of her conviction that men and boys had coughed their lives out when they might have been saved by her fans never left her.

Incurably compassionate and charitable in private life – she preferred always to risk being cheated rather than distrust someone – Hertha Ayrton remained a political idealist, taking humanity on trust and backing the pacifist, internationalist and socialist hopes of the young Labour Party. 'She was physicist, suffragist, democrat, humanitarian and very human woman – but never any of these things in a water-tight compartment . . . her lasting monument will be found . . . in the laboratories where science is brought to the aid of humanity.'[3]

It was particularly fitting that her only child Barbara (named after Barbara Bodichon) Ayrton Gould should become a co-founder of the Save the Children Fund, an anti-militarist, a co-organizer of relief for refugees from Nazi Germany, a champion of deprived women and children in the depressed coalfields, an investigator of domestic violence against children, and Labour MP for Hendon North in 1945.[4]

1. Unpublished letter to the editor of *The Times*, quoted in Evelyn Sharp, *Hertha Ayrton: A Memoir* (London, Edward Arnold, 1926), p. 223. See also entry in Olive Banks, *The Biographical Dictionary of British Feminists*, vol. 1 (New York, New York University Press, 1985).
2. Sharp, *op. cit.*, p. 256.
3. *Ibid.*, pp. viii and 300. See also Anna Ford, 'First Lady: Hertha Ayrton, first woman member of the Institute of Electrical Engineers', *IEE Review* (July 1999), pp. 155–8.
4. See obituaries for Barbara Ayrton Gould in *The Times*, *Manchester Guardian*, *News Chronicle* and *Daily Herald* (all 16.10.1950). 'I believe that the only way to prevent war is to have an educated body of public opinion which is so large and definitely opposed to all war, that it is able to check the great surge of hysterical feeling which sweeps over the people, when a calculating Government, backed by a jingo press, calls upon the patriotism of the nation to save the country by a bloody war': Barbara Ayrton Gould's declaration in W.T. Chamberlain, *Fighting for Peace* (London, 1928).

B

BALFOUR, MARGARET, CBE, MB, MD, FRCOG
(1866–1945)

PIONEER OF MEDICAL CARE FOR WOMEN AND CHILDREN IN INDIA

Father: Robert Balfour, chartered accountant, Edinburgh

Christian

Immediately on qualifying MB, CM at Edinburgh and London in 1891, Dr Balfour sailed for India in 1892 to become the Medical Officer in Charge of the Zenana Hospital in Ludhiana. 'Zenana' (meaning 'women's quarters') hospitals were established by Christian women missionaries[1] for Indian women in purdah, whether Muslim, Hindu or Sikh, whose religion forbade them to be treated by male doctors or nurses. After three years at Ludhiana, Dr Balfour was promoted to Medical Superintendent of the Women's Hospital at Nahan (1899–1902) and then Medical Superintendent of the Lady Dufferin Hospital in Patiala (1903–13). She later became Assistant to the Inspector-General of Civil Hospitals in the Punjab, and finally Chief Medical Officer of all the Women's Medical Services in India (1920–24). She was awarded the CBE on her retirement.

The long list of Margaret Balfour's publications on midwifery, infant mortality and maternal mortality in childbirth in India testifies to her dedication to improving the life-chances of Indian women and babies. She was an expert witness called in 1928 by the Joshi Committee Enquiry into child marriage in India which concluded, a year later, that over 42 per cent of Indian girls were married before the age of 15, and commented:

> Early maternity is an evil and an evil of great magnitude. It contributes very largely to maternal and infantile mortality, [and] in many cases wrecks the physical system of the girl . . . After going through the ordeal, if a woman survives to the age of thirty, she is in many cases an old woman . . . Her life is a long lingering misery.[2]

Dr Balfour laid particular stress in her testimony on the incidence of osteomalacia, a disease suffered by girls and women in purdah which was caused by the absence of sunlight and resulted in a softening of the bones that made natural labour impossible. She was still more concerned by the even greater prevalence of anaemia in pregnancy, also associated with conditions in purdah.[3] Even after her 'retirement' after over 30 years' service in India, she continued to research in India and publish, e.g., *Anaemia of Pregnancy* (1927) and *Maternity Conditions of Women Millworkers in Bombay* (1930).

'I think it was her singleminded devotion to the medical and health needs of Indian women and children that carried her through all difficulties and obstacles . . . [She] was a believer in "making a beginning". She did not wait for perfect conditions or lots of money before starting new schemes.'[4] Therefore, despite the official and professional misgivings of her colleagues, Dr Balfour made a determined start on training Indian women as health visitors, beginning with the teaching and supervision of traditional midwives or *dais*, whose earlier lack of medical training and of access to hygiene had caused them all too often to be the inadvertent causes of maternal and infant death.[5] 'Beneath her quiet manner and gentle voice there was a core of steel.'[6]

When her last GP called to see Margaret Balfour as a patient of nearly 80 in wartime London, she found the white steel helmet of an ARP Medical Officer hanging in the hall and learned that her patient and the ARP Medical Officer were one and the same.

1. See Mrs Weitbrecht, *The Women of India and Christian Work in the Zenana* (London, James Nisbet, 1875); Mrs E. R. Pitman, *Missionary Heroines in Eastern Lands* (London, S. W. Partridge, 1893); J. C. Pollock, *Shadows Fall Apart: The Story of the Zenana Bible and Medical Mission* (London, Hodder and Stoughton, 1958).
2. *Report of the Age of Consent Committee (called the Joshi Report)*, (Government of India Central Publication Branch, Calcutta, 1929), ch. 1, quoted in Eleanor Rathbone, *Child-Marriage: The Indian Minotaur* (London, George Allen & Unwin, 1929), pp. 21–2.
3. Rathbone, *op. cit.*, pp. 127–8.
4. Dr Ruth Young in *Medical Women's Federation Quarterly Review* (January 1946), pp. 29–30.
5. See Rathbone, *op. cit.*, *passim*. And note the tribute to her from an Indian woman doctor in the obituary in *The Lancet* (15.12.1945), p. 799: 'Dr Balfour is remembered with love and gratitude by countless women, in a country where polygamy, early motherhood, and sad widowhood create so much unhappiness.'
6. Dr Agnes Scott in *Medical Women's Federation Quarterly Review* (January 1946), p. 31.

BAMBER, HELEN
(1.5.1925–   )

REHABILITATOR OF
CONCENTRATION CAMP
SURVIVORS; CAMPAIGNER
AGAINST TORTURE

Father: Louis Balmuth, accountant,
*   London*
Mother: Marie, née Bader

Humanist

Helen Bamber with Jewish Relief Unit in Belsen,
1946 (courtesy of Helen Bamber)

Helen Bamber was only 19 when she volunteered to join the Jewish Relief Unit set up by the British Jewish Committee for Relief Abroad to work with Jewish survivors of concentration camps. At 20, in early autumn 1945, she was inside Belsen. Helen Bamber never had any illusion that every survivor could be healed; she could only try '*to save what could be saved. I know we can't save everybody, but I believe that we can save some*' (original italics).[1] She was neither a nurse nor a member of the Red Cross Search Bureau reuniting remaining family members; at first all she could do was negotiate for food and clothing for the Jewish 'displaced persons' stranded in Belsen for month after month as no country would take them and it was illegal to emigrate to Palestine. But she quickly discovered that there was something else she could do: she could listen. The women survivors

> would need to tell you *everything*, over and over and over again . . . They would need to hold onto you . . . and it was important that you held them, and often you had to rock, there was a rocking, bowing movement, as you sat on the floor.[2]

> [What mattered was] to receive the horror so that they did not hold it alone, to hold it with them.[3]

She was often the target of the distraught anger of these people tormented, brutalized and bereaved beyond bearing. 'Nobody was liked; nobody was good enough; nobody could do enough.'[4]

On her return to England, Helen Bamber worked for seven years for the Committee for the Care of Children from Concentration Camps (see BERTHA BRACEY). When she was 61, in 1985, after many years of working for Amnesty International, she founded the Medical Foundation for the Victims of Torture in two rooms in the National Temperance Hospital, London. In 1993 she went to Israel to testify on behalf of a tortured Palestinian; it was an ordeal to have to declare that the Jewish state was a torturing state.

> The world has paid a terrible price for the Holocaust . . . There is no clearer message for me than the sequence of perpetration . . . What interests me is what we can learn, what the second generation can learn. The sequence has to be broken.[5]

Helen Bamber's own life is testimony to the possibility of breaking that sequence. Herself the child of an unloving marriage, bleakly exposed to parental war and to her father's obsession with the fate of Europe's Jews that always dwarfed and invalidated any childhood suffering of her own, she also suffered the death in the Blitz of her maternal aunt Mina, the only warm, supportive, outgoing member of the family who had made her laugh and want to live. But instead of nursing her own inner wounds for ever, seeking private therapy, she has done what she can to heal herself by doing what she can to heal others whose suffering has been so immeasurably worse. She 'will go down in history as a great humanitarian'.[6]

1. Neil Belton, *The Good Listener – Helen Bamber: A Life against Cruelty* (London, Weidenfeld and Nicolson, 1998), p. 69.
2. *Ibid.*, p. 89.
3. Mavis Nicholson, *What Did You Do in the War, Mummy? Women in World War II* (London, Pimlico, 1995), p. 234.
4. Belton, *op. cit.*, p. 102.
5. *Ibid.*, p. 347.
6. Terry Waite, 'Goodbye cruel world', review of Neil Belton, *The Good Listener*, *Observer* (3.1.1999), p. 13.

See also *Guardian* (26 October 1999), p. 21 for Helen Bamber's protest against internment of asylum seekers in Britain; and *Guardian* (29 October 1998), p. 13, for her outrage at the initial High Court ruling that General Pinochet was immune from prosecution, saying that it made a mockery of the Universal Declaration of Human Rights: 'The High Court has made England a safe haven for dictators and former dictators acting in their official capacity as heads of state, undermining the absolute nature of the prohibition against torture in international law.'

BARK, EVELYN, OBE
(26.12.1900–7.6.1993)

BRITISH RED CROSS RELIEF AND
INTERNATIONAL TRACING SERVICE

Father: Frederick William Bark, London
*   clerical worker*
Mother: Nellie Hepzibah, née Layton

Evelyn Bark (Reproduced from her book
No Time to Kill, *Robert Hale, 1960)*

Evelyn Bark was 44 when she began her twenty-year-long commitment to international relief and tracing operations. Her single greatest qualification, in addition to her intelligence, energy and compassion, was her exceptional competence in foreign languages: she was not only fluent in French and German but also knew Swedish, Danish and Norwegian, not to mention Icelandic, and could read Flemish, Dutch and German Gothic script.

After four years' voluntary war work as a VAD in London maternity hospitals and air-raid warning posts, Evelyn Bark was taken on by the British Red Cross for its Postal Message scheme – 25 words in English, French or German – through which relatives living in belligerent or occupied countries, some of them refugees, prisoners of war or even deportees, could manage to communicate their life and/or death messages. By the end of the war, the transmission of nearly 25 million such Red Cross forms had been recorded in Geneva.

Her next project was to evolve and produce a Red Cross language card for doctors, nurses and their wounded or sick patients, consisting of 26 basic medical questions concerning symptoms, in English in one column and translated into the patient's language in the other; on the reverse of the card were the patient's most common questions in the two languages. Such a card proved indispensable not only in wartime but also in disaster relief all over the world.

In response to the thousands of inquiries coming into the office by the end of the war about missing relatives abroad, Evelyn Bark started her file of missing people for a Red Cross 'Tracing Service'. She landed in liberated Belgium and Holland in 1944, looking for the missing and distributing relief to the starving. Then she had to face the single worst revelation of inhumanity she was ever to confront: Belsen. In addition to the tens of thousands of unburied dead and dying, there were still 45,000 people of 22 nationalities desperately sick with hunger typhus, famine diarrhoea, or typhoid. (The liberation of Belsen had arrived too late for Anne Frank, who had died in May 1945.) Everyone in the British contingent of liberators, including Evelyn Bark, together with conscripted German nurses, set to work in turning barracks into 'wards', removing corpses, fetching food, which had to be fed with extreme patience and care to each patient in order not to kill them, emptying overflowing bedpans, administering medicines and injections. It was the hardest work they were ever to do in their lives but by the end of two weeks the death rate from typhus had dropped from 800 a day to zero. The Nazis had destroyed all the records of their captives in the concentration camp, so that Evelyn Bark had an immense task to try to identify the survivors: no one knew who the orphaned toddlers were, and it was impossible at that stage to learn the names and next of kin of the dead.

Evelyn Bark then worked among the defeated Germans for four years (1945–49), organizing Red Cross relief for the homeless and hungry still huddled in the underground bunkers and for the hundreds of thousands of refugees, either deported or in flight from the east, some of them sleeping 80 to a room (cf. DOROTHY ENGLAND, ELLA JORDEN, MARGARET MCNEILL and ELSIE STEPHENSON). She then became head of Red Cross Foreign Relations units in north-west Europe. Once again, in the chaos of mass displacement families had been split; the walls of public buildings in north Germany were covered with photographs of lost children, e.g.:

'Renate Louisa Muller, born 1st July 1943. Brown eyes, straight, reddish hair, dimple on left cheek and a few freckles on nose. Answers to name of Püppchen. Was with her mother on ship which sank in Baltic on 10th April 1945. Both picked up by different lifeboats. Child not seen since. Mother in Refugee Camp No . . .'

Twenty-five thousand mothers were then looking for their children and thirty-six thousand children had not found their mothers.[1]

The Red Cross Tracing Service continues to function to the present day.[2]

After the founding of the state of Israel, Evelyn Bark organized relief for Palestinian refugees in Jordan. In 1956 she was in charge of British relief convoys to Hungary, and in the early 1960s she was in charge of the Red Cross contribution to earthquake relief in Agadir and Iran. Looking after the casualties of the civil war in the Yemen in 1964, she had to sleep in caves. Only 4 feet 11 inches tall, she was known within the Red Cross as 'The Mighty Atom'.

How does one spend the rest of one's life after years of continuous exposure to much of the world's most terrible suffering? Evelyn Bark played the piano and taught foreign languages.[3]

1. Evelyn Bark, *No Time to Kill* (London, Robert Hale Ltd, 1960), pp. 62–3.
2. See obituary for Muriel Monkhouse, OBE (1910–96), *The Times* (2.1.1997). Muriel Monkhouse worked for the Red Cross Tracing Service for 50 years after 1940, tracing relatives forcibly separated during the Second World War and during later conflicts in Biafra, Pakistan, Cyprus, the Lebanon and elsewhere.
3. See also *Guardian* (1.6.1960); and obituaries in *Independent* (24.6.1993) and *The Times* (26.6.1993).

BARRETT, FLORENCE, LADY, CH, CBE, MD, MS, B.Sc
(1867–7.8.1945)

OBSTETRICIAN; GYNAECOLOGIST; PIONEER OF SOCIAL MEDICINE

Father: Benjamin Perry, gentleman
Mother: Elizabeth Perry

Spiritualist

The foremost woman gynaecologist of her time, Florence Barrett's chief interest outside her clinical work was in improving the living conditions of working-class mothers and babies. She diagnosed their inadequate food, abominable housing, tiredness and the lack of contraception as of first importance in their health problems. Her work in the King's Cross area and at the Salvation Army Mothers' Hospital served some of the poorest women in London. Her writings include *A Plea for the Feeding of Nursing Mothers as a Means of Preventing the Waste and Maiming of Child Life*. She was ambitious to raise the status of women everywhere, not just in Britain, and to that end she did all she could to advance women in the medical profession.

Despite all the distinctions heaped on her, Lady Barrett remained easy to approach by those who needed her: 'She gave herself and her help so generously and adequately. It was good to see her arrive, perhaps late at night, in some out of the way place to take over a difficult midwifery case, and to feel so confident that all would go well.'[1]

1. Dr Mary Blair in *Medical Women's Federation Quarterly Review* (October 1945), p. 39. See also *The Times* (9.8, 11.8 and 16.8.1945); *Who Was Who, 1941–1950*; and *The Lancet* (1.9.1945).

BARRETT, ROSA
(1855–28.8.1936)

CHILD RESCUER; JUVENILE PENAL REFORMER; PACIFIST

Father: William Garland Barrett, Congregational minister, missionary in Jamaica
Mother: Martha, née Fletcher

Congregationalist, then Spiritualist towards the end of her life

In her early twenties Rosa Barrett began her lifetime commitment to the children of the poorest in the community by founding the first crèche in Dublin at Kingstown (now Dun Laoghaire) in 1878. For 50 years she acted as Hon. Secretary for that Cottage Home for Little Children, which was still in operation at the end of the twentieth century. Most of its original intake of children under 8 were admitted as the result of a family crisis, usually the father's death, desertion or drunken violence, which necessitated the mother's going out to work. For a penny a day, or even less, not only could the mother leave her small children safely supervised but she also knew that they were given a 'headstart' of proper feeding and proper care.[1]

In 1899 Rosa Barrett founded the Irish section of the National Society for the Prevention of Cruelty to Children, having discovered pauper children 'sleeping in orange-boxes, underfed and sickly'[2] in a 'home' in Tuam; she called over an NSPCC inspector from London to investigate, and the person responsible for the child neglect was arrested, tried and imprisoned. Unfortunately, as a Protestant, she was not able to gain the confidence of Dublin's Catholic clergy in her campaign against cruelty to children.

Her detailed, global, study of 'The treatment of juvenile offenders' for *The Journal of the Royal Statistical Society* (1900), advocating separate juvenile courts to try young offenders, and trade schools rather than imprisonment for their rehabilitation, was awarded the Howard medal.[3]

Rosa Barrett also worked for Temperance, the rescue of girl prostitutes, women's suffrage and world peace. In 1907 she was a co-founder, with Lady Aberdeen, of the National Women's Health Association for Ireland, which mounted a public education campaign to help prevent the spread of tuberculosis. In 1915 Rosa Barrett, a well-travelled internationalist, publicly supported the unpopular, because 'unpatriotic', Women's International Congress at The Hague.[4]

For all her lifelong deeply serious commitment to social reform, in her private life Rosa Barrett 'had a keen sense of humour, gathered interesting people round her, and charmed all who came in contact with her'.[5]

1. See R. Barrett, *The Cottage Home for Little Children: A Retrospect* (Dublin, *c.* 1905); and Maria Luddy, *Women and Philanthropy in Nineteenth-Century Ireland* (Cambridge, Cambridge University Press, 1995).
2. Anonymous correspondent in *The Times* (2.9.1936).
3. See also R. Barrett, *The Rescue of the Young* (16 pp.; Dublin, 1899).
4. See Introduction and Appendix I.
5. *The Times, loc. cit.*

BARROW, FLORENCE MARY

(27.1.1876–3.3.1964)

INTERNATIONAL RELIEF WORKER;
HOUSING REFORMER

Father: Richard Cadbury Barrow, Quaker businessman and Mayor of Birmingham
Mother: Jane, née Harrison

Quaker

Florence Barrow, c. 1914

After her education at Edgbaston High School and Mason College, Birmingham, Florence Barrow started a class in adult literacy for Birmingham women in 1894, thus pioneering the adult schools movement there. She went on in 1900 to train as a social worker at St Hilda's Settlement in Bethnal Green. August 1914 found her already in Marseilles, working in a quarantine department with Serbian refugees from the Balkan War of 1912.

In 1916 Florence Barrow was sent from Newcastle by sea to Murmansk in order to do Quaker relief work in Buzuluk, western Russia (now in Ukraine), helping what would later be termed 'displaced persons': two and a half million Poles, Jews and Byelorussian refugees from the Eastern Front who were in a desperate situation. She helped set up nurseries for abandoned children, feeding centres, co-operative craft workshops, pharmacies, even a circulating library. She witnessed the Russian Revolution in 1917–18 and noted that there was already a threat of famine: 'Men work for the common good but find it harder than they thought; . . . the rich are robbed of their spoils but selfishness appears under new forms.'[1] She had to cross

Russia eastwards by Trans-Siberian railway, reaching Japan, then America, and finally crossing the U-boat-infested Atlantic in a camouflaged vessel in order to report back to London Friends.

In 1919 she was sent by the Friends' War Victims' Committee to distribute Quaker food relief in a starving Germany still punished by the Allied blockade. '[German] feeling very bitter in Breslau, . . . and as [the doctor] showed us one tiny distorted form after another it was almost more than one could bear.'[2] From 1921 to 1924 she was head of Quaker relief operations among repatriated Poles in devastated Brest Litovsk: 'I think that she must be an ideal head; she is evidently very capable, . . . and seems only to be head by reason of her extra care for everyone.'[3] She oversaw the distribution of seed and tools and the ploughing of land as well as the rebuilding of whole villages. Her monument was the orphanage she left behind.

Florence Barrow was the kind of Quaker one expects to find in the Society, but who is, in fact, rare, like everything near perfection. She had large, quiet, grey eyes, a quiet, unhurried manner, sympathy that was profound and genuine, but unsentimental and practical, and the kind of selflessness and appreciation of other people that had impressed me in Dr HILDA CLARK. I was not surprised that the Unit was doing a living work under her leadership.[4]

On her return to Britain in 1924 Florence Barrow co-founded the Birmingham Conference on Politics, Economics and Citizenship (COPEC) House Improvement Society that pioneered municipal slum clearance and the regeneration of inner-city housing there. She was the driving force for over 37 years behind 'practical schemes of reconditioning, reconstruction, conversion and rebuilding'.[5] At the age of 56, in 1932, she left Birmingham for Syria, Salonika and Egypt to work once more with refugees. During the later 1930s the Quakers sent her as a secret agent to Nazi Germany and Austria, taking messages to and from endangered Jews. She later said she had found it 'very trying to know that every conversation might be overheard' and reported to the Gestapo.[6]

Back in Birmingham at the start of the Second World War, Florence Barrow continued to work on inner-city housing reform as Hon. Secretary of COPEC and to organize the reception of Jewish refugees from Nazism. In 1958 the City of Birmingham gave her its Civic gold medal for services to its urban housing programme, including the provision of low-rental accommodation for single working women and 'sheltered housing' for the elderly and the handicapped. They regretted to report that her active days as a social worker were almost finished – at the age of 82![7]

Florence Barrow was very gentle, almost timid in manner, and only 4 feet 6 inches tall; her 'outward appearance gave little indication of the power within'.[8]

1. Florence Barrow, 'Stray memories of Buzuluk', unpublished typescript, held in Friends' House Library, London.
2. Florence Barrow, unpublished letter, held in Friends' House Library, London.
3. Joan Fry, unpublished letter to Friends' House (23.1.1922).
4. Francesca Wilson, *In the Margins of Chaos: Recollections of Relief Work in and between Three Wars* (London, John Murray, 1944), p. 140.
5. *The Friend* (13.3.1964). See also F. Margaret Fenter, *COPEC Adventure: Birmingham House Improvement Society* (Birmingham, COPEC, c. 1980).
6. *Birmingham Mail* (4.3.1964).
7. *Birmingham Post* (3.11.1958 and 4.3.1964).
8. Warwickshire Monthly Meeting (14.11.1964), printed in *London Yearly Meeting Proceedings* (1965).

BELL, JULIA, FRCP
(28.1.1879–26.4.1979)

MEDICAL RESEARCHER

Father: James Bell, Nottingham printer and
*   publisher*
Mother: Katherine, née Heap

Rationalist

Julia Bell, c. 1908 (Courtesy of her niece
Margaret Brentall)

The tenth of fourteen children, Julia Bell was encouraged by her gifted and enterprising father to become highly educated. She went to Girton College, Cambridge, in 1898 to read mathematics, working as a postgraduate with A. R. Hinks in 1901 in the Cambridge Observatory, studying the solar parallax. In 1908 she started working as a statistical assistant to Karl Pearson, Professor of Applied Mathematics and Mechanics at University College, London. She became increasingly interested in the biological implications of statistical measurement; in order to work with Pearson on the genetics of inherited disease and other pathological conditions, she decided to study medicine. In 1914, at the age of 35 she entered the Royal Free Medical School, qualifying as MRCS, LRCP at the London School for Medicine for Women in 1920. It is significant that she should have testified to her radical, humane political stance in this period by joining in suffrage marches and by being one of the signatories of the British Committee supporting the Women's International Congress at The Hague in April 1915.[1]

Julia Bell, together with her team-workers in the Biometric Laboratory, was largely responsible for volumes II, IV and V of *The Treasury of Human Inheritance*, founded and edited by Pearson.[2] Volume II (1931) covered anomalies and diseases of the eye. Regarding Leber's hereditary optic atrophy, she anticipated 'the phenomenon of mitochondrial inheritance by 60 years'.[3] Volume IV (1948) demonstrated and analysed the hereditary aspect of Huntington's chorea, hereditary ataxia and spastic paraplegia, and progressive muscular dystrophy. Volume V (1958, completed when she was 79), described hereditary digital anomalies. Julia Bell's motivation was the eradication of disease; she quoted Donne: 'To cure the sharpe accidents of diseases is a great work; to cure the disease itself is greater.'[4] In 1932 she was appointed a member of the MRC Human Genetics Committee to advise on research into 'the part played by inheritance in the causation of disease'. In 1936 she also became attached to the MRC Neurological Research Unit at the National Hospital, Queen Square, helping with clinical assessments of patients. Julia Bell's work with J. B. S. Haldane (1937; republished 1986) on 'The linkage between the genes for colour-blindness and haemophilia in man' was the first demonstration of genetic linkage in humans, foreseeing the development of predictive genetics in embryology in the 1980s.[5]

It is largely thanks to the pioneering work in human genetics of Julia Bell and her co-workers that pregnant women are now able to make an informed choice about whether or not to continue with their pregnancy once a serious inherited pathological condition has been diagnosed in the foetus. She recognized that the ethical dilemmas involved in therapeutic abortion, real as they are, must always be distinguished from the criminally unethical practice of 'eugenic euthanasia'.

Julia Bell was a dedicated, brilliant polymath. Her scientific work, spanning more than 50 years, much of it unpaid and under-acknowledged,[6] has a real claim to be considered a significant humanitarian achievement.

1. See Introduction and Appendix I.
2. See M. Eileen Magnello, 'The non-correlation of biometrics and eugenics: rival forms of laboratory work in Karl Pearson's career at University College London', *History of Science*, **37**: Part One (March 1999), pp. 79–106; Part Two (June 1999), pp. 123–50. I am grateful to Eileen Magnello for looking through this entry.
3. The late Sarah Bundey, FRCP, Department of Clinical Genetics, Birmingham Maternity Hospital, 'Julia Bell MRCS LRCP FRCP (1879–1979). Steamboat lady, statistician and geneticist', *Journal of Medical Biography*, **4** (February 1996), p. 11.
4. *Ibid.*
5. *Ibid.*, p. 12. See also *The Treasury of Human Inheritance*, vols 2 (1933), 4 (1948) and 5 (1953 and 1958) (Cambridge, Cambridge University Press).
6. After her first retirement Julia Bell worked for over twenty years (1944–65) as an Honorary Research Fellow at the Galton Laboratory. Her research notes are held among the Karl Pearson, L. S. Penrose and J. B. S. Haldane collections in the archives of University College, London. Her obituary in *The Times* was not published until 11.11.1979.

BENNETT, LOUIE
(1876–11.1956)

IRISH CHAMPION OF WORKING WOMEN'S RIGHTS, AND OF PEACE

*Father: — Bennett, Dublin auctioneer,
    antiques valuer*
*Mother: Susan, née Boulger, daughter of army
    officer*

Christian Socialist

Louie Bennett's earliest political cause, leading her to leave behind her sheltered life as a cultivated upper-middle-class lady novelist, was the struggle for women's suffrage. In 1911 she founded the Irish-women's Suffrage Federation and became its first Secretary. But the bitter labour disputes in Dublin of 1913 awakened her to the desperate, nearly starving, situation of Irish women workers, 'the slaves of slaves'. Through the Irish Women's Reform League that she then founded, she led

Louie Bennett (From R. M. Fox, Louie Bennett: Her Life and Times, Talbot Press, 1958)

the struggle for economic justice and minimal human dignity via basic trade union rights for the sweated women workers of Ireland. She fought decade after decade, first for the women in the printing trade and next for the laundry workers – not only for better wages but also for better sanitation, ventilation, light and heat, shorter hours and paid holidays. She soon became a familiar sight standing in the rain with the girl strikers on the picket line.

As well as being a Co-operative Socialist, Louie Bennett was a staunch pacifist. She was one of the leading suffragists who had supported the Women's International Congress at The Hague in 1915,[1] although warned that such non-patriotism could destroy general public support for the women's movement. Ireland itself, of course, provided another great test for pacifism; although she supported Irish independence after 1916, she always insisted that the struggle should be non-violent. That commitment to pacifism made her unpopular both with pro-Britons and with Irish Nationalists. She criticized Sinn Fein for its violence as well as for its nationalistic failure to recognize the vital importance of *inter*national *inter*dependence. Like Gandhi, she spelt out that 'No revolution is permanently achieved by violence: such violence, even in the name of freedom, is tyranny'.[2] Between 1920 and 1922, she took part in the efforts to end the Irish civil war by negotiation, and in 1921 she went to Washington to give evidence before the American Commission on the effects of the British military occupation on conditions in Ireland. In 1926 she presided over the Dublin Congress of the Women's International League for Peace and Freedom, of which she had been a founder member since 1915. In 1928 she suppported the Soviet Foreign Minister Litvinov's call to the League of Nations for general and immediate world disarmament. Already in 1932 she was prescient enough to warn the Irish Trades Union Congress of the dangers of fascism in Europe. After Hiroshima she pleaded, in her old age, for the outlawing of nuclear weapons.

After the partition of Ireland into Eire and Ulster, Louie Bennett, herself from a Dublin Protestant background, worked to try to keep open every possible means of friendly, constructive contact between North and South. She argued for the establishment and/or retention of co-operative links of communication, power lines, drainage and transport and hoped, in vain, to see a united, federal Ireland in her lifetime.[3]

1. See Introduction and Appendix I.
2. Louie Bennett, *Ireland and a People's Peace* (published for Irish Section of the Union for the Democratic Control of Foreign Policy; Dublin and London, Maunsel and Co., 1918), p. 16.
3. See R. M. Fox, *Louie Bennett: Her Life and Times* (Dublin, The Talbot Press, 1958).

BENTHAM, ETHEL, MD, JP
(1870–19.1.1931)

DOCTOR TO THE POOR; MAGISTRATE; LABOUR MP

Father: William Bentham, JP, insurance company manager, Dublin
Mother: Mary Ann, née Hammond

Quaker

Ethel Bentham first encountered the suffering entailed by appalling poverty when, as a schoolgirl, she saw the slums of Dublin. Her first job was to share a general medical practice in a deprived area of New-castle upon Tyne (1897–1910) with Dr ETHEL WILLIAMS. A campaigning suffragist and a publicly committed socialist when it was not quite respectable for a woman doctor to be either, let alone both, Dr Bentham founded and supervised the first baby clinic in Britain in North Kensington in 1911, in memory of two Labour women, Mary Middleton and Mary MacDonald. Her indignant awareness of the remediable social cause of much ill-health was confirmed as she was forced to see that 'almost all the [babies'] diseases are those of malnutrition'.[1] That clinic, to which was gradually added an ante-natal department, a dental department and a sunlight department as well as a small children's hospital, pioneered medical services for children.[2] As well as being a Labour Councillor for North Kensington, Dr Bentham became one of the first women magistrates, having a particular concern for children in trouble with the law, and also

Dr Ethel Bentham, MP, JP (courtesy of the Wellcome Institute Library, London)

served on the Metropolitan Asylums Board, supporting the reform of the casual wards.

After three unsuccessful attempts to enter Parliament, Ethel Bentham was elected Labour MP for East Islington in 1929 at the age of 68, being the first woman Friend and the first medical woman to become an MP. Her maiden speech was on the causes of industrial accidents, including the eye disease miners' nystagmus. She served, with EDITH PICTON-TURBERVILL and ELEANOR RATHBONE, on an all-party Parliamentary Committee for the Protection of Coloured Women, which tackled enforced female circumcision in Kenya, child marriage in India, and *mui tsai* or child slavery in Hong Kong and Malaya. She also served on a Select Committee on the Abolition of Capital Punishment.[3]

When Dr Bentham died, with many self-imposed crusades uncompleted, the Prime Minister Ramsay MacDonald wrote of her 'Quaker simplicity and strenuousness'[4] and people 'of all classes and creeds bore testimony to her as a woman and as a worker . . . Dr Ethel Bentham was unforgettable as friend, as colleague and as adversary.'[5]

1. Patricia Hollis, *Ladies Elect: Women in English Local Government 1865–1914* (Oxford, Clarendon Press, 1987), p. 439.
2. Dr Honor Bone, obituary for Dr Bentham, *Medical Women's Federation Quarterly Review* (1931), p. 50. See also Sheila Ferguson, 'Labour women and the social services' in Lucy Middleton (ed.), *Women in the Labour Movement* (London, Croom Helm, 1977).
3. Pamela Brooks, *Women at Westminster: An Account of Women in the British Parliament 1918–1966* (London, Peter Davies, 1967), pp. 87–9.
4. Obituary, *Medical Women's Federation Quarterly Review* (1931), p. 50.
5. Bone, *op. cit.*

See also obituary in *The Times* (20.1.1931); and Olive Banks, *The Biographical Dictionary of British Feminists*, vol. 2 (New York, New York University Press, 1990).

BIGLAND, EDITH

(10.11.1862–5.6.1951)

INTERNATIONALIST; PENAL REFORMER

Father: Thomas Aggs
Mother: Anna, née Christie

Quaker

Edith Bigland, c. 1914

Edith Bigland's nearly 90 years spanned a commitment to humane intervention that stretched from her support for Josephine Butler's controversial crusade against the state regulation of prostitution of girls and women in the 1880s to being President of her local branch of the United Nations Association in 1950. One of her earliest acts of social commitment was to found a club for working girls in the central London district of Westminster, but she was to embrace many wider fields of endeavour, some of them with worldwide application.

During the First World War Edith Bigland's response as a Quaker was intellectual, practical and spiritual. Already in the winter of 1914 she and her husband joined a group of about twenty people, including the MP Sir Willoughby Dickinson, Goldsworthy Lowes Dickinson and Lord Robert Cecil (later head of the League of Nations Section of the British Delegation to the Versailles Conference), to examine the possibility of establishing a Society of Nations for the peaceful settlement of international disputes. She signed EMILY HOBHOUSE's Christmas Open Letter to German Women[1] and supported the British Committee for the Women's International Congress at The Hague in April 1915.[2] She helped to organize the Friends' War Victims' Relief operations for civilian refugees in northern France, Belgium and Holland. And finally she took up the deeply unpopular position of supporting the brutally treated British Quakers, imprisoned for their conscientious objection to killing after the 1916 Conscription Act, by chairing the national Committee that ensured they would be visited regularly by Quaker chaplains, of whom her husband was one.

Once the League of Nations was in existence, Edith Bigland, then in her sixties and seventies, spent a great deal of time promoting both its actual work and its still greater potential in public lectures throughout Britain. She also worked much of the year in Geneva on the League's penal reform programme, in particular its attempt to abolish flogging and capital punishment all over the world. She became Secretary of the Criminal Law Amendment Committee which worked to the same end in Britain and consistently supported the Howard League's advocacy of more liberal measures to treat young offenders.

During the 1930s, Edith Bigland's home became a place of refuge for many fleeing from Nazi persecution. 'The combination of inflexible principles and high ideals with solid common sense which characterised her speaking on public matters and the kindliness, the wisdom, the humility which appeared in her ordinary talk are precious memories.'[3]

1. See *Ius Suffragii* (January 1915) and *The Labour Leader* (January 1915) for the whole text of the letter
   and the list of signatories.
2. See Introduction and Appendix I.
3. *Yearly Meeting Proceedings* (Friends' House, 1952), p. 175. See also obituary in *The Friend* (June 1951).

BISSET, MARY RONALD, MB, ChB, LM
(4.10.1876–20.1.1953)

EYE SURGEON AND OBSTETRICIAN IN INDIA

Father: — Bisset, Nonconformist minister

Baptist

Mary Bisset may stand as an exemplar of all the many devoted British medical women who served the needs principally of women and children in India in the first half of the twentieth century.[1] After training in Aberdeen and Dublin, she went out to the Punjab in 1907 to work at the first Baptist Missionary Hospital. She specialized in eye-surgery and held several village eye-camps for the extraction of cataracts, in many cases succeeding in giving the blind back their sight. She also concentrated on trying to improve maternity conditions, training local Indian midwives. After 30 years' work in Bhiwani, her health broke down. So huge was the crowd of Hindus, Muslims and Christians on the railway platform to thank her when she left that it was difficult to move. The British Government awarded her the Kaiser-i-Hind gold medal for her work for the women of India. After regaining her health in Britain, Dr Bisset became an expert in the treatment of tuberculosis.[2]

1. See Margaret Balfour, *The Work of the Medical Women in India* (1929). See also the entries for Doctors CONSTANCE COUSINS, ELLEN FARRER, ISABEL KERR and CLAIRE THOMSON. Many more medical women in India should be remembered, e.g., Dr Kate Platt, Dr Ruth Young and Professor Harriet Acheson, who died the day after Dr Bisset and whose obituary is next to hers in *Medical Women's Quarterly Review* (1953).
2. See *Memoirs of Ministers and Missionaries* (Baptist House, 1954), pp. 320–1.

BONHAM CARTER, LADY VIOLET, DBE, HON. LLD
(15.4.1887–19.2.1969)

ANTI-TOTALITARIAN INTERNATIONALIST; ANTI-RACIST; CAMPAIGNER AGAINST DEATH PENALTY

Father: Herbert Henry Asquith, Earl of Oxford and Asquith, Liberal Chancellor of the Exchequer 1905–8, Prime Minister 1909–16
Mother: Helen Kelsall, née Melland, doctor's daughter, d. 1891
Stepmother: Margot, née Tennant

Christian

Young Violet Asquith 'was the equivalent of a princess',[1] at least between the ages of 18 and 29, while her father was in power. But what might have been a fatal combination of pride in her ability and the privilege of her plutocratic/aristocratic connections never turned her into an arrogant or frivolous worldling. Instead, Violet

Bonham Carter grew into a steadfast humane campaigner, 'The most effective woman orator I have ever heard'.[2] She was an impassioned opponent of dictators. Already in 1923 she had warned of the fragility of Germany's newborn anti-militarist democracy, and prophesied that the brutality of the French invasion of the Ruhr would have fatal consequences for the children of all the world.[3] Exactly ten years later those fears had begun to be fulfilled, and after only three months of Nazi rule Violet Bonham Carter told the Liberal Party Conference that already in Germany, just in a few terrible weeks, 'a nightmare reign of terror whose horror we can hardly conceive' had begun. In September 1933 she warned in a public speech that Nazism threatened 'not merely the soul of a people, but the peace of the world'.[4] And in December 1933 she seconded an appeal for the resettlement of German Jewish women and children:

> this is not a matter which concerns the Jewish community alone. It concerns all who believe in justice and in our common humanity . . . we wish to stand by your side in taking up this challenge . . . I suppose if this were Germany most of us would be behind barbed wire. I can only say for myself that I should be shamed to be anywhere else.[5]

Throughout the years up to 1939, Violet Bonham Carter was a leading opponent of the British government's policy of appeasement; instead, with Churchill and her fellow members of his Focus in Defence of Freedom and Peace Movement, she urged the backing of Article XVI of the Covenant of the League of Nations in order to impose economic and even military sanctions on an aggressor. She crusaded for the League of Nations from its conception until 1941. In the name of 'Democracy – that great Army that needs no uniform' she urged Britain to 'take the same risks for Justice, Peace and Freedom as . . . the Gangsters . . . are prepared to take for the fruits of aggression'.[6] In 1938 she joined ELEANOR RATHBONE, SYBIL THORNDIKE and ELLEN WILKINSON in petitioning Hitler, in vain, to commute the death sentence for treason on the German pacifist Liselotte Herrmann.[7]

During the Second World War, Violet Bonham Carter was one of the unsuccessful delegation led by William Temple, Archbishop of Canterbury, and other Church leaders, to petition the Home Secretary Herbert Morrison for the admission of 2,000 Jewish children from (Vichy) France into Britain to prevent their deportation to Germany. Morrison 'refused *everything*. I have never seen a deputation so mishandled and so angry.'[8] As a Governor of the BBC, in November 1943, she pressed, like ELEANOR RATHBONE, and equally unsuccessfully, for a broadcast on help to the Jews.[9] Meanwhile she also campaigned in vain to stop the manacling of German prisoners. October 1945 found her with Victor Gollancz and Eleanor Rathbone speaking for the 'Save Europe Now' campaign to feed starving Germany.

The present writer has never forgotten Violet Bonham Carter's electrifying declaration at Victor Gollancz's later 'No More Hanging' rally in 1961: 'I believe in the resurrection of the spirit in *this* world.' Her last speech, at the age of 77 in the House of Lords, was about the starvation following the attempted secession of Biafra from Nigeria in 1964. 'As with all [the] causes she took up, she would never compromise or give up a battle . . . of her passionate care for fundamental freedoms and her sympathy for suffering people in all nations there was no doubt.'[10]

1. John Grigg, Introduction to Mark Pottle (ed.), *Champion Redoubtable: The Diaries and Letters of Violet Bonham Carter 1914–1945*. (London, Weidenfeld and Nicolson, 1998), p. xxii.

2. Roy Jenkins, Introduction to Mark Bonham Carter and Mark Pottle, *Lantern Slides: The Diaries and Letters of Violet Bonham Carter 1904–1914* (London, Weidenfeld and Nicolson, 1996), p. xxi.

3. Pottle, *op. cit.*, p. 180.

4. *Ibid.*, p. 182.

5. *Ibid.*, p. 183.

6. *Ibid.*, p. 189.

7. See S. Oldfield, 'German women in the resistance to Hitler' in S. Reynolds (ed.), *Women, State and Revolution* (Oxford, Basil Blackwell, 1986), pp. 90–1.

8. Pottle, *op. cit.*, p. 244.

9. *Ibid.*, p. 285.

10. William Haley, entry for Violet Bonham Carter in *Dictionary of National Biography, 1961–1970*. See also obituary in *The Times* (20.2.1969).

BOOTH, MARY, COL.
(SALVATION ARMY), CBE
(22.4.1885–30.8.1969)

REFUGEE RELIEF WORKER; SISTER OF
OLIVE BOOTH

Father: Gen. William Bramwell Booth (Salvation Army)
Mother: Florence, née Soper

Salvation Army

Col. Mary Booth, Salvation Army, c. 1935

Awarded the CBE in 1919, when she was only 34, for her outstanding work organizing hospital visiting to the wounded in France (see her book *With the B.E.F. in France*), Mary Booth then served as territorial commander of the Salvation Army in Germany, the West Indies and Denmark. In 1940 she was in German-occupied Belgium, taking over empty houses where she could organize the shelter and feeding of refugees hiding from the Nazis. She refused to leave them and be evacuated to safety from Dunkirk. The German authorities arrested and interrogated her and the Gestapo threatened to have her shot as a suspected spy. She was imprisoned, often in solitary confinement, in a succession of dungeons and internment camps in Belgium and Germany where she suffered near-starvation with the other prisoners. 'It seemed to me then that so much of the Bible had been writen especially for those in captivity.'[1] After many refusals and threats, she was finally allowed to read from the Bible to her fellow prisoners, 'a wonderful comfort to our sorrowful hearts'.[2] She was surprised to be released and repatriated from Germany to Britain in 1942.

A graphic and compelling speaker, Mary Booth was a dynamic, highly cultured personality with exceptional musical and artistic gifts, all of which she subordinated to her service to the Salvation Army. It was she who sculpted the bust of her grandfather, the Army's founder General William Booth, in Westminster Abbey.

1. Mary Booth, 'My Bible in a German prison', *The War Cry* (South Africa) (15.3.1947), held in the Salvation Army International Heritage Centre, London.
2. *Ibid.*

See also obituary, *The Times* (1.9.1969); and Booth family documents in the Salvation Army International Heritage Centre, London.

BOOTH, OLIVE, LT COL.
(SALVATION ARMY)
(14.8.1891–13.12.1989)

POST-WAR OVERSEAS RELIEF CO-ORDINATOR; SISTER OF **MARY BOOTH**

*Father: Gen. William Bramwell Booth
(Salvation Army)
Mother: Florence, née Soper*

Salvation Army

At the age of 57, Olive Booth finished the work begun by her cousin MOTEE BOOTH-TUCKER SLADEN and her husband in directing the Salvation Army's relief work in post-war Belgium, Holland, France, Germany, Poland, Czechoslovakia and Austria:

Lt Col. Olive Booth, Salvation Army (on left with glasses), with her sister Dora

It was in word and deed the mission for which the Army . . . was brought into being. The hungry were fed, the naked clothed, the homeless were given shelter, the oppressed liberated, the abandoned children and the delinquent youth cared for, the aged loved, the Salvation Army in Germany revived and the poor received the good news of the Gospel.[1]

Nurse Ada Rose in Salvation Army home for abandoned children, Germany, 1946

It was said of Olive Booth at her funeral that she was always searching for good in people and leading them out to do greater things than they had ever dreamed of.

> She was at her best opening hostels, made from reconditioned slave worker barracks, for thousands of vagrant youths. She made the young rootless men feel they had new hope, new usefulness, new opportunities to build a nobler world . . . And the home for the abandoned children of rape, housed in a former Poison Gas factory [supervised by Nurse Ada Rose] especially rejoiced her heart.[2]

1. Olive Booth, Foreword to Lt Col. John Dale, 'Overseas Relief Work, 1945–50' (2 vols, 1989), typescript in Salvation Army International Heritage Centre Archive.
2. See John Dale, funeral tribute to Olive Booth (21.12.1989), Salvation Army International Heritage Centre archive.

See also obituary, *The Times* (15.12.1989).

BRACEY, BERTHA LILIAN, OBE
(1893–1989)

RESCUER OF GERMAN JEWISH
REFUGEES, ESPECIALLY
CHILDREN AND OTHER 'ALIENS'

Father: Henry Bracey, journeyman,
*   carpenter, organ-pipe maker, employee at*
*   Cadbury's Bournville factory,*
*   Birmingham*
Mother: Annie, née Miles

Quaker by convincement

Bertha Bracey, c. 1933

Bertha Bracey was 18 when she became a Quaker 'by convincement' in 1911. After her varied experience of teaching, personnel work at Cadbury's and studying literature at the University of Birmingham, she joined a Quaker relief and reconstruction project with young people in Vienna. Once her German was fluent, she went to work full-time for Friends' Council for International Service in Nuremberg and Berlin, combining welfare work and projects aimed at harnessing the political idealism of young people in the Weimar Republic. When the Friends' German Emergency Committee was formed in 1933, in response to the victory of the Nazis,[1] Bertha Bracey was a natural choice for Secretary. Her office at Friends' House was inundated by requests for help from Jewish Germans already in Britain and then by desperate postal applications from Jewish German would-be refugees for assistance with entry permits to the UK and accommodation and employment possibilities (they had to be guaranteed sponsorship and work before they arrived). By 1939 'the staircases at Friends' House were blocked with lines of people waiting to be seen by Bertha Bracey and her [80] fellow-workers'.[2]

Bertha Bracey was always better at seeing the big picture than at individual case-work. Her leadership qualities were seen at their characteristic best at three historic moments. First, she was part of the delegation of five who pleaded successfully to the Home Secretary Sir Samuel Hoare, after the *Kristallnacht* pogroms in Germany and Austria in November 1938, to allow 10,000 Jewish children emergency entry into Britain without their parents on *Kindertransport* trains. Secondly, when thousands of adult refugees were wrongly interned as 'enemy aliens' after the declaration of war on Germany, she became Chairman of the Central Department for Interned Refugees; she had many 'a tough tussle with the head of Military Intelligence, on a matter which seemed to . . . cut at the very roots of our civil liberties'.[3] She herself visited the women's camps on the Isle of Man and successfully persuaded the authorities to employ volunteers to help with the hundreds of depressed and bewildered internees there; she also persuaded the Central Department to release funds to assist destitute released internees. Her final outstanding act of personal intervention was in 1945 when she learned that 300 children had been found alive in Theresienstadt concentration camp, after witnessing and enduring indescribable cruelty and the total destruction of their own families. She went to the War Office and persuaded the authorities to strip the bombing racks out of ten British bomber planes so that the children could be flown out to a reception camp at Lake Windermere.[4]

After the war, Bertha Bracey returned to a totally devastated Germany to work for the Refugee Section of the Allied Control Commission to help sort out some of the chaos there, before finally working as Women's Affairs Officer in Germany. Instead of stigmatizing all Germans with collective guilt, she now addressed herself to the task of enabling German women to take a positive, creative part in post-war social reconstruction, devising courses in discussion methods and public speaking that succeeded in helping numbers of German women to take a responsible part in national and international politics. Her name is found among the Jewish roll of 'righteous Gentiles'.[5]

1. See entry for EDITH PYE.
2. Alex Bryan, 'Bertha L. Bracey: friend of the oppressed', *Friends' Quarterly* (January 1991), p. 238; see also entry for DOROTHY HARDISTY.
3. Brenda Bailey, 'Bertha Bracey', *The Friend* (27.1.1989), p. 104.
4. Bryan, *op. cit.*, p. 237.
5. See *Jewish Chronicle* (January/February 1989).

See also obituaries in *The Times* (15.2.1989); *Daily Telegraph* (11.2.1989); and *Guardian* (16.2.1989); and article 'Rescuer in the dark shadow of Nazi atrocities', *Oxford Times* (22.11.1985).

BRAZELL, SYBIL
(27.1.1919–   )

VOLUNTEER PLAGUE NURSE

Father: electrical engineer, Welsh Baptist
Mother: elementary teacher, Welsh Baptist

Anglican

After training at University College Hospital, London, and Wolverhampton Women's Hospital, Sybil Brazell joined the Queen Alexandra's Imperial Military

Nursing Service during the Second World War. In 1944 she was posted to North Africa where, at the 94th British Military Hospital, Algiers, she nursed German and Italian prisoners of war as well as Allied servicemen. 'Each patient, of course, received the comfort and care appropriate to his medical condition. In hospital there are no enemies.'[1] Most patients were suffering from gunshot wounds, but there was also dysentery, septicaemia and one confirmed and one suspected case of bubonic plague. After volunteering to nurse this patient, 25-year-old Sybil Brazell and a colleague, Peggy Read, were inoculated against the disease, together with a Medical Officer and two orderlies. The 'Isolation Hospital' comprised a few huts surrounded by a yellow cordon, some five miles from the partly tented 94th British Military Hospital.

For protective clothing we wore 'Zoot suits', covering us from head to toe, apart from slits for eyes and nose. These gave us the appearance of the Ku Klux Klan.

Sybil Brazell (right) with nursing colleague outside hospital tent, Algiers, c. 1942 (Courtesy of Sybil Brazell)

Masks soaked in Dettol, and, of course, rubber gloves were used when treating the patient. Clothing was soaked in disinfectant daily, and all waste food placed in a metal bin containing paraffin and burned. All deliveries such as medical equipment, drugs and food were left outside the yellow perimeter cordon to be collected by the orderly.[2]

The two nurses alternated their duty rota and slept in a hut adjacent to the patient.

When the single light was turned on, the concrete floor became a moving carpet of large cockroaches, centipedes and beetles. Huge 'may-bugs' flew in through the open window and got entangled in our hair and our beds invariably contained bedbugs. That was the worst part.[3]

Both the nurses and the patient survived, the latter probably saved by the recently discovered penicillin.

After her service in North Africa, Sybil Brazell was posted to devastated Hamburg a few days after the German capitulation in May 1945. Next she was sent to India, to Lucknow, and nursed mostly British servicemen who were in need of assessment and rest on their way home from Burma and the Far East. Then, after six months in Hanover, she was demobilized at the beginning of 1947. Shortly afterwards, while applying for a civilian post in the Middle East, a chest X-ray disclosed that she had pulmonary tuberculosis. After two years' treatment, she worked as a Sister in casualty and out-patients departments, as an Assistant Matron, health visitor, health education officer and latterly tutor to community nurses.

In her sixties, after retirement, she studied and gained a degree in social sciences from the Open University. She describes her religious affiliation as Anglican and her politics as 'Liberal!' She is an amateur landscape painter.

1. Personal information to the author.
2. *Ibid.*
3. *Ibid.*

BRITTAIN, VERA
(29.12.1893–29.3.1970)

CHRISTIAN PACIFIST CAMPAIGNER AGAINST RIGHTEOUS ATROCITY IN WARTIME

Father: Arthur Brittain, paper manufacturer
Mother: Edith, née Bervon, daughter of a musician

Anglican

It was her nursing of dying German prisoners as a VAD in November 1917 near Passchendaele that planted the seed of Vera Brittain's subsequent absolute pacifism.[1] She had already lost her fiancé to the war and six months later was to lose her beloved brother. It was too early to bear the recognition that Europe's competition in massacring its youth had been futile as well as mad and barbaric, but the universality of the suffering and death she witnessed as a nurse did initiate her into a profound internationalism. Ironically and terribly, her *Testament of Youth*, the most popular anti-war book written by a woman between the wars in its indictment of the betrayal of the idealism of a whole generation sent to die for 'meretricious gods',[2] was published in 1933, when Hitler's accession to power made the next world war a certainty. Vera Brittain refused to believe either that the next war would come or that it must be fought. However mistaken her view of the possibility of effective non-violent resistance to Nazism may have been (see her *Humiliation with Honour*, 1942), she both suffered for her pacifist leadership after war was declared and did her utmost to try to halt Britain and the Allies from descending to the Nazis' depths of callous inhumanity.

Vera Brittain suffered personally in that, as a leading pacifist, she was not allowed to travel abroad for the duration of the war and was thus cut off from her two children, who had been sent to the United States.[3] She also suffered so acutely in her conscience that, despite her weakness for approval and praise, she was driven to speak, both in season and out, knowing how just how unpopular it would make her.

Abominating fascism in general and in particular the Nazis' cruelty towards Jews, Vera Brittain was convinced, like her contemporary Simone Weil,[4] that the one thing needful was that the *anti*-fascists should demonstrate their alternative faith by actions grounded in basic humanity. Hence she wrote in January 1943 in support of Victor Gollancz's pamphlet *Let My People Go*, urging, in vain, the immigration of threatened Jews into British-mandated Palestine and deploring the British refusal to allow 2,000 Jewish children from Vichy France asylum in Britain (they were all deported to their deaths).[5] Moreover, as Chairman of the Peace Pledge Union's Food Relief Campaign, she wrote and lectured tirelessly, urging the British government to relax its economic blockade of occupied Europe sufficiently to permit minimal medical and relief supplies through. Her pamphlet *One of These Little Ones*

(February, 1943), which sold 30,000 copies, declared: 'Remember that just feeling sorry or shocked will achieve nothing . . . *What is wanted is a change of heart on the part of the Government*, so that they will grant the navicerts [allowing cargo past a blockade] required before Europe's starving children can be fed.'[6] The children of Belgium, Greece and Holland were particularly at risk from extreme malnutrition and consequent disease. 'If we say and do nothing, we shall be held as responsible as the Nazis for the sufferings of "these little ones".'[7] She pleaded for navicerts for just one ship a month laden with medicine and vitamins and for neutral ships to be allowed to transport food from the United States for International Red Cross distribution in occupied Europe. But, like EDITH PYE, she failed in her attempt to sway the Ministry of Economic Warfare.

Vera Brittain's other campaign during the Second World War was to join in the attempt by Bishop Bell, Richard Stokes (Labour MP for Ipswich) and leading Quakers to end the indiscriminate saturation bombing of German civilians by the RAF. In 1942 and 1943 hundreds of thousands of Germans had already been burnt, buried alive or suffocated in the day and night raids on their cities. In November 1943 Vera Brittain wrote *Seed of Chaos: What Mass Bombing Really Means*. It was first published as *Massacre by Bombing* in the USA and aroused immense hostility as well as some disquiet in the Roosevelt administration. Published in April 1944 in Britain, it aroused little interest except a hostile review from George Orwell. Vera Brittain's attempt to remind Winston Churchill, the rest of the British

Dresden, 25 February 1945. Soldiers driving commandeered farm carts have brought bodies to the cordoned-off Altmarkt Square. (Reproduced from David Irving, The Destruction of Dresden, *William Kimber, 1963)*

Dresden, 25 February 1945. After final identification attempts the bodies are stacked onto makeshift pyres. (Reproduced from David Irving, The Destruction of Dresden, *William Kimber, 1963)*

government and the military High Command, including 'Bomber' Harris, of the minimal civilized standards of international law regarding warfare proved as ineffective as the efforts of Bishop Bell and Mr Stokes;[8] nevertheless it was vital that some few *did* speak out so that even worse was not perpetrated. (It has recently emerged that in July 1944 Churchill was contemplating dropping poison gas on German cities, but was told by his Chiefs of Staff that it was not necessary 'to start chemical and biological warfare' in order to shorten the war.[9])

> I am not responsible for the cruel deeds done by the Nazis in the name of the Germans, and much as I deplore them I cannnot prevent them. But so long as [there is] breath in me I shall protest against abominations done by my government in the name of the British, of whom I am one. The mercilessness of others does not release us from the obligation to control ourselves.[10]

'Church leaders and politicians denounced her . . . obscenities and dog faeces were put through her letter box.'[11]

In her old age Vera Brittain joined the demonstrators marching against British nuclear weapons and against British collusion with the American war in Vietnam. As her biographers have said, 'the moral courage and clearsightedness with which she took her stand is still deserving of recognition and respect'.[12]

1. Paul Berry and Mark Bostridge, *Vera Brittain: A Life* (London, Chatto and Windus, 1995), p. 121.
2. *Ibid.*, p. 266.
3. *Ibid.*, pp. 402–3.
4. See Sybil Oldfield, *Women against the Iron Fist: Alternatives to Militarism 1900–1989* (Oxford, Basil Blackwell, 1989), pp. 82–7.
5. Vera Brittain, *Letters to Peace-Lovers* (28.1.1943), reprinted in Winifred and Alan Eden-Green (eds), *Testament of a Peace Lover* (London, Virago, 1988), pp. 138–9.
6. Vera Brittain, *One of These Little Ones* (Herts, Andrew Dakers Ltd, 1943), p. 4.
7. *Ibid.*, p. 10.
8. Cf. David Irving, *The Destruction of Dresden* (London, William Kimber, 1963).
9. *Guardian* (2.11.1998).
10. Vera Brittain, *Letters to Peace-Lovers* (17.6.1943), reprinted in Eden-Green, *op. cit.*, p. 154.
11. Shirley Williams (Vera Brittain's daughter), 'Testament to the touchstone of my life', *Independent* (29.12.1993), p. 16.
12. Berry and Bostridge, *op. cit.*, p. 442.

See also Yvonne Bennett, *Vera Brittain, Women and Peace* (London, The Peace Pledge Union, 1987); Paul Berry and Alan Bishop, *Testament of a Generation: The Journalism of Vera Brittain and Winifred Holtby* (London, Virago, 1985); Britta Zangeu, ' "Above all nations is Humanity" – Vera Brittain's painful path to radical humanism', *Women's History Notebooks*, **6**(1) (Winter 1999), pp. 10–17. The obituary in *The Times* (30.3.1970) made no mention of her stand during the Second World War.

BROWN, EDITH, DBE, LRCP, LRCS, MD, MRCOG
(24.3.1864–8.12.1956)

PIONEER MEDICAL MISSIONARY TRAINING MEDICAL WOMEN IN INDIA

Father: George Wightman Brown, bank manager, Whitehaven, Cumberland, d. 1871. Mother: Mary, née Walther. Both parents Plymouth Brethren

Christian

Edith Brown was one of the first girls in England to have a public secondary education, attending Croydon High School for Girls. She then went on to be one of the early women students at Girton College, Cambridge, reading natural sciences. After teaching science for a year, she trained as a doctor at the Royal Free School of Medicine. Her vocation as a medical missionary had been clear to her from the age of 7 when she had first heard accounts of the suffering of Indian women, because of their lack of medical care, from her eldest sister, on furlough from working as a missionary in south India.

Edith Brown sailed to India under the auspices of the Baptist Zenana Missionary Society in 1891 but 'after two years of hard and frustrating effort'[1] she recognized that what she must do was leave the society and train *Indian* women as doctors and nurses rather than hope that British medical missionaries could answer Indian women's needs. 'She toured India, trying to get other missionaries' support; she toured Britain with her idea . . . She [lobbied] the Surgeon-General of India.'[2] With no more than £50 a year donated to her, she rented a school building in 1894 and took in four Christian Indian girl students to train to work in the 30-bed Zenana Hospital in Ludhiana,[3] 200 miles north-west of Delhi – and often 120°F in the

Dr Edith Brown (From her My Work Is for a King. *Photograph provided by Friends of Ludhiana, 157 Waterloo Road, London SE1 8UU – still supporting Christian Medical College, Ludhiana)*

shade. By 1916 the Punjab government had officially recognized her training school as the Christian Medical College and Hospital of Ludhiana, the college by then training more than 300 women of various religions and several Christian denominations in its medical, nursing, pharmacy and maternity schools. Using the income from her own practice among Maharajahs, together with financial support from Britain, Edith Brown 'was able to build slowly and steadily: ward blocks at first, and later theatres, dispensary and patients' quarters; . . . finally a complete preclinical department and large hostels for students and nurses'.[4] The work was for women by women because of 'purdah' restrictions. ' "Miss Brown's Hospital" became a household word throughout India and further afield.'[5] She herself was administrator, lecturer, clinician and surgeon. The maternity department cared for 1,200 cases each year, and there were 30 cots for motherless babies, some of them rescued from becoming temple child prostitutes. Edith Brown was haunted by all that desperately needed to be done for the hundred million women of India's rural villages: 'the women are so bound by custom, weighed down by poverty and debt and depressed by the hopelessness of "Karma".'[6] But she had a far-seeing practical vision for these rural women. She wanted hundreds of trained women volunteers to go to the villages and transform them (not unlike Julius Nyerere's later vision of *ujamaa* for Tanzania):

> The little colony should include a woman doctor and health visitor, a tuberculosis nurse and a woman teacher for the girls' school. There should be three trained midwives, so that the women need never go out alone . . . [Their houses should be] simple village houses but with proper ventilation, a chimney for the smoke,

good corn bins (protected from rats who carry plague), absorption pits (to avoid standing water, which breeds mosquitos), bore-hole latrines, and a good garden to grow their own vegetables . . . The midwives of the district would be called in for regular teaching and prepared for government diplomas. Illiterate women might be taught to read and the work of cooperative banks encouraged in the fight against debt.[7]

It was deemed too expensive a project at £500 a year, but Dr Brown herself staffed and equipped two such centres, including dispensaries, which served the area until 1948.

Edith Brown officially retired as Principal in 1942 at the age of 76, but she was still lecturing in surgery at the age of 81. When the partition of India brought inter-communal massacres to Ludhiana in 1947–48:

Dame Edith, at 81, was a tower of strength in a disintegrating world . . . Through protracted street fighting she would leave the college as usual to walk the couple of hundred yards down to the hospital, bearing as always sun-helmet and umbrella. At her appearance all shooting ceased, and a hush fell until she reached the safety of the hospital door. Later a wild mob demanded that all Muslim women be handed over or everyone would be attacked. Speaking to them gently, . . . she rebuked them and sent them shamefacedly away.[8]

Edith Brown's great humanitarian work was inspired by her worship of Christ the loving healer. To those who ask whether such humane service might not merely be a 'cover' for religious evangelism, an imperialism of the spirit, it may be asked in return whether such lifelong spending of self for others is not, rather, a partial validation, at least, of the beliefs that animated it.

1. Anon., *Preaching through Teaching* (pamphlet, reprinted from *The Witness*, 1965), held in Wellcome Institute, London, Contemporary Medical Archives.
2. Paul Wigmore, 'Missionary found an off-beat answer', *Cambridge News* (10.4.1965).
3. See entry for MARGARET BALFOUR.
4. Obituary, *The Lancet* (22.12.1956).
5. *Preaching through Teaching*.
6. Edith Brown, 'A medical college in the Punjab', *Girton Review* (Lent Term, 1939).
7. *Ibid.*
8. *The Lancet, loc. cit.*

See also Edith Craske, *Sister India* (London, Stanley L. Hunt, 1930); Christine Trilling, *India's Womanhood* (Lutterworth Press, 1935); Francesca French, *Miss Brown's Hospital* (London, Hodder and Stoughton, 1954); Edith Brown, *My Work Is for a King: Meditations, Prayers, Poems* (London, Friends of Ludhiana, 1994). The Cumbria Record Office, Whitehaven, holds a photocopy of a 6,000-word typescript by Dame Edith giving an account of her life for an American Sunday School Union publication.

BUXTON, DOROTHY FRANCES

(1881–8.4.1963)

HUMANITARIAN
RELIEF PUBLICIST;
INTERNATIONALIST;
SISTER OF
EGLANTYNE JEBB

Father: Arthur Trevor Jebb,
barrister and philanthropic
squire
Mother: Eglantyne, sister of Sir
Richard Jebb, MP and Regius
Professor of Greek

Quaker by convincement

Dorothy Buxton and her children, 1922 (From Accrington Labour Party manifesto)

When Dorothy Jebb married Charles Roden Buxton in 1904, the young couple set up house in the poverty-stricken London district of Kennington in order to share those hardships they dedicated themselves as radicals to relieving, if not abolishing. Buxton was an educationist with political ambitions to reform the country via Parliament; Dorothy was a high-minded social activist, a latter-day Dorothea Brooke,[1] who in 1916 joined both the ILP and the Society of Friends.

When the First World War broke out, with its concomitant propaganda war in which each side saw itself as St George and the enemy as the dragon, Dorothy Buxton could not bear the dehumanization of the German people in the British press; like KATE COURTNEY and CAROLINE PLAYNE, she knew this could only worsen and prolong the war and make an eventual genuine peace settlement with Germany impossible. She determined, therefore, to bring before English readers evidence of the common humanity of 'the enemy', and in particular, evidence of the *opposition* to German chauvinism and militaristic imperialism within Germany. Thus she set herself to translate and publish in leaflet form extracts from the foreign press, including 25 'enemy' papers which the Board of Trade allowed her to import from Scandinavia. From October 1915 to early 1920 she published her unpopular but influential 'Notes from the foreign press' in C. K. Ogden's weekly *Cambridge Magazine*. She published the news of German socialist anti-war demonstrations and the evidence that the British hard-line position on the destruction of Germany only increased support for that country's intransigent military leadership. To translate 100 newspapers in all, from French, German, Italian, Russian, Hungarian, Romanian, Finnish and other languages, required a team of scores of expert linguists and translators and shorthand-typists, not to mention specialists in foreign affairs, all supervised and edited by Dorothy Buxton in her own home, which was turned into their daily headquarters. Although she then had two young children, her 'austerity impelled her to make a sacrifice of home-life itself'.[2]

From 1917 onwards, Dorothy Buxton began to receive and disseminate the news of appalling hunger and suffering among German civilians. So intolerable did she consider the Allied Blockade's starvation of Germans and Austrians after they had surrendered in 1918 that she and her sister EGLANTYNE JEBB, together with Lord Parmoor, KATE COURTNEY, MARIAN ELLIS, MARY SHEEPSHANKS and others, founded the Fight the Famine Committee in 1919 to change that retributive economic policy. Out of that committee came the founding of the international Save the Children Fund, whose name was coined by Dorothy Buxton.

Dorothy Buxton was a humanitarian activist all her life. During the 1930s she collected and circulated reports on Nazi concentration camps that she had received from the refugees she was aiding, only to have them pigeon-holed by the Foreign Office until after the Second World War had broken out and they were inefficacious. She even made a quixotic attempt to interview Goering in Germany in 1935 to confront him with the abominations being perpetrated and so shame him out of his Nazism. He only shouted back at her in fury. 'Failure once more.'[3]

Both before and during the Second World War Dorothy Buxton made contact with the *Bekennende Kirche*, the underground Protestant anti-Nazi Christians in Germany, including Dietrich Bonhoeffer, once again publicizing the existence of humane Germans among British readers.

It was said of Dorothy Buxton and Eglantyne Jebb, after Dorothy Buxton's death:

> In both of them the flame of courage and philanthropy burnt brightly, but in the initial laying bare of the tragedy of the famine-stricken children in Central Europe, and its underlying cause, the Allies' blockade policy, Dorothy Buxton's fearlessly critical mind and inflexible determination were specially needed . . . Together the two sisters set the pattern of intelligent understanding and wisdom, of courage and adventure, in the cause of a fuller life for the child which has been the hallmark of our movement.[4]

1. George Eliot's heroine in *Middlemarch*.
2. Victoria De Bunsen, *Charles Roden Buxton* (London, George Allen & Unwin, 1948), p. 49.
3. *Ibid.*, p. 160.
4. Obituaries by Mosa Anderson in *The World's Children*, organ of the Save the Children Fund (1963), p. 46; and in *The Times* (15.4.1963).

C

CADBURY, GERALDINE BARROW

(29.6.1865–30.1.1941)

PIONEER IN REFORMING THE
TREATMENT OF YOUNG OFFENDERS

Father: Alfred Southall
Mother: Anna Strangman, née Grubb

Quaker

Geraldine Barrow Cadbury, c. 1925
(Frontispiece to Janet Whitney, Geraldine
S. Cadbury 1865–1941: A Biography,
George Harrap, 1948)

'I think Elizabeth Fry is my patron saint,' said Geraldine Cadbury at the end of her life, and her whole working life attested to that. 'She might be called the mother of the Juvenile Court movement in this country.'[1] She had studied the precedent of the Children's Courts in Chicago and when the first Juvenile Court was opened in Birmingham in 1905 she was always present and acted as one of the first, unofficial, probation officers of that city. In 1910, she and her husband Barrow Cadbury, with whom she had 'a marriage of true minds', built and equipped the first remand home in England so as not to send children to prison while they were on remand or committed for trial. She opposed the sending of young people to prison under any circumstances and was also an implacable opponent of the magistrate's power to sentence a boy to be birched. 'Her most original contribution to the better care of young delinquents was the building of Copely Hill.'[2] This was a hostel where boys could finish their sentence after a short period at an Approved School and live a nearly normal life, both going out to work and having friends in to visit. As one of the first women Juvenile Court magistrates in Britain, Geraldine Cadbury always tried to keep in touch with the later careers of the children who appeared before her, especially the girls.

Geraldine Cadbury's other 'causes' were adult education for women (she presided over the 400-strong Women's Adult School in Moseley every Tuesday), improved educational provision for children with special needs, and better maternity care for the poor mothers of Birmingham. It was her concern during the bombing of Birmingham in 1940–41 to found and equip an alternative maternity hospital in a safe area, with all the exhausting work and worry that such a project entailed, that contributed largely to her own final illness when she was 75.

But her greatest monument was her work for that not very popular social group, youthful criminals. 'Geraldine Cadbury did probably more for delinquent children than anybody in this country or in any other. She was ahead of her time, but her faith will be justified.'[3]

1. Obituary in *Guardian* (31.1.1941).
2. Obituary in *The Friend* (7.2.1941).
3. The Home Secretary, Chuter Ede (30.5.1947), quoted in Janet Whitney, *Geraldine S. Cadbury 1865–1941: A Biography* (London, George Harrap, 1948).

CANN, GLADYS
(1907–1993)

MISSIONARY NURSING SISTER IN INDIA AND EAST PAKISTAN
(NOW BANGLADESH)

Baptist

'My! Isn't she a worker!' was the comment of one of her colleagues in north India where Gladys Cann had worked in Baptist Missionary Society hospitals in Bhiwani, Palwal and Dholpur from 1934 until 1942.[1] She arrived at the jungle hospital of Chandraghona on the frontier with Burma at a critical time, just before the Japanese captured Rangoon. All European wives and families were soon evacuated, as were all the women nurses, except Gladys Cann, who insisted on staying at her post despite orders from the Royal Navy and representations from her Baptist Missionary Society superiors. She continued with her work in a hospital without electricity or X-ray equipment and threatened not only by rumours of the advancing Japanese army but by actual bandits and jackals. At one time she kept the 90-bed hospital, leprosy colony, school and dispensary going almost on her own, taking operation cases to an RAF surgeon in Chittagong for whom she had to be the interpreter from Bengali. In 1946 she added a reorganized nurses' training school for the hill tribes to her long list of responsibilities.

After Gladys Cann's return to Britain in 1959 she nursed in Surrey, Cornwall, Devon and later in Malawi. At the time of the bloody founding of Bangladesh in 1971 she returned to Chandraghona for eight months in order to help set up a children's clinic there.

Gladys Cann may serve as an example of all those nurses who are not well known outside their immediate professional circle, or the hospitals where they have worked, precisely because of their total, consuming dedication to the needs of their patients.

1. *The Baptist Times* (February 1960).

See also obituary by Walter Bottoms, *The Baptist Times* (25.2.1993).

CARTER, MAYNARD LINDEN
(1886–1962)

PIONEER OF PUBLIC HEALTH; INTERNATIONAL RED CROSS NURSE AND
RELIEF WORKER

Father: engineer in Buenos Aires

After training at St Bartholomew's (1907–11), Maynard Carter joined the Ranyard
nurses working in Stoke Newington to bring nursing and preventive medicine into
the homes of the poor. After working throughout the First World War as a Sister
at the Camberwell Hospital, she was widowed in 1921. Post-war Europe was
stricken by epidemics and famine. Typical of the pleas that went out then was that
from President Masaryk's daughter Dr Alicia Masarykova in the new republic of
Czechoslovakia:

> Our children are dying, conditions are desperate, starvation, nakedness, disease
> and poverty stalk . . . the land . . . Half a million are dying of hunger; there is
> little medicine, no serum, drugs or bandages; typhus and smallpox are
> epidemic . . . Come and help us.

Maynard Carter responded to that call and was an enthusiastic recruit to Lady
MURIEL PAGET's relief mission. She was made responsible for establishing the first
infant welfare centres in rural Slovakia, which had abnormally high rates of infant
mortality. She and a donkey laden with pots and pans, brooms and scrubbing
brushes, had to trudge up steep mountain paths to reach outlying villages. She also
helped to organize an epidemic hospital for typhus patients, a children's hospital,
food kitchens and sixteen public health stations.

Appalled by the conditions of extreme poverty that she found in Slovakia, and
by the disastrous vulnerability to epidemics in such conditions, Maynard Carter
decided that one of the first priorities in post-war Europe must be the training of
hundreds of public health nurses throughout the continent. She joined the League
of Red Cross Societies and was asked to set up an international course in public
health nursing at Bedford College, London. She herself took the course and the
examination (1922–23) in order to experience at first hand the difficulties facing
international students sponsored by the League.

Always forward-looking, Maynard Carter was one of the first to realize the new
potential for nursing service, given the recent introduction of air ambulances. She
herself took her pilot's licence and supported the training of nurses for aerial relief.
In January 1937 she organized an important international conference of experts
from 60 different national Red Cross Societies on 'Disaster relief and the role of
the nurse in war and disaster'. They would be needed all too soon. It was also in
1937 that she was awarded the Florence Nightingale medal by the International
Red Cross Committee for her outstanding contribution to raising the professional
standards of Red Cross nurses throughout the world. In the Second World War
she worked both for the National Society for Children's Nurseries and for the Czech
Red Cross in exile from Nazi occupation, training Czech women refugees in Britain
as auxiliary nurses.

Maynard Carter was a very attractive and gifted polymath; not only was she an outstanding organizer and leader, she was also a linguist able to make friends across national and racial boundaries, a skilled wood carver and furniture maker, and a quite exceptional potter. Beauty mattered to her, and her humanitarian relief efforts and public health initiatives were all part of her creative struggle against the sheer ugliness, destructiveness and unnecessary waste of sickness and avoidable death, whether caused by war or by natural disaster.[1]

1. Irene Charley, 'Maynard Linden Carter . . . a memoir', *International Journal of Nursing Studies*, **3** (July 1966), pp. 161–7. See also League of Red Cross Societies, *Monthly Bulletin* (November 1938) for anonymous article 'A loss to the nursing world'.

CASHMORE, HILDA
(22.8.1876–15.11.1943)

ADULT EDUCATIONIST;
WELFARE WORKER IN BRITAIN,
EUROPE AND INDIA

Father: Samuel Cashmore, businessman
  and country squire
Mother: Mary, née Edmunds

Quaker

Hilda Cashmore, 1934

Brought up the fifth of six privileged daughters in idyllic Somerset, educated at the Ladies' College, Cheltenham, and Somerville College, Oxford, Hilda Cashmore never forgot the revelation, when she was 7, that there were millions upon millions of unprivileged children in the world, forced to live in ugliness and poverty, often exploited as factory slaves. She kept her inner resolution to do something to change such lives for the better until she herself collapsed from cancer, malaria, pneumonia and exhaustion, a still young-in-spirit 67-year-old.

From 1911 to 1926 Hilda Cashmore was the pioneering Warden of the Bristol University Settlement, Barton Hill. There, in addition to adult education classes and mother and infant welfare clinics, she set up a country camp site as a place of escape for poor urban children. On 6 November 1914 she crossed to France as Secretary of the Quaker medical mission under Dr HILDA CLARK and later EDITH PYE to help civilian refugees from the war zone in Châlons-sur-Marne. She left in May 1915 and returned to Barton Hill. In May 1920 she volunteered to join the Quaker War Victims' Relief work among returning refugees in Galicia (now in Ukraine, at that time in Poland). She found herself in a region in the midst of the new war between Poland and Russia that had succeeded the devastation and scorched-earth policy of the fighting there between Austria and Russia in the First World War. She worked under FLORENCE BARROW near Lwow (Lviv), helping to organize soup-kitchens and the distribution of agricultural implements and seeds as well as the de-lousing of typhus carriers and cholera victims.

Hilda Cashmore's next challenge was to revitalize the decayed Manchester University Settlement in Ancoats. This she did (1924–31), bringing flowers, drama groups and political discussion, as well as education and the chance to escape for a much-needed holiday in the country, to the people of that depressed inner city.

At the age of nearly 60 Hilda Cashmore went to work in central India, setting up an adult school, a conference centre and a dispensary in the jungle near Nagpur. Her secret ambition was to lessen the exploitation and improve the living conditions of the Gond people there, and her persuasive powers and energy were such that she largely succeeded, despite struggles with human vested interests and nature's worst – hornets' nests, hyenas, wild pigs and even cobras. Often she herself would nurse the sick and dying who had been abandoned in the jungle.

On her return to Britain, Hilda Cashmore immediately worked for Czech and Jewish victims of Nazism, helping to organize individual guarantors, accommodation and, if possible, employment. After the fall of France, 200 women refugees – Jewish 'enemy aliens' – were ordered to leave Bristol within three days, and it was Hilda Cashmore who successfully organized appropriate hospitality for each one, as well as for their men when they too were released from internment. Her final work was the organization of Bristol Women's Voluntary Service to help evacuees and bombed-out families and to provide rest-centres for victims of air raids – all this while she herself was dying.

She was one of those whose altruism was always irradiated by a zest for life and beauty. '[Hilda Cashmore] knew how to foster the tiniest spark of intellectual life in others.'[1] '[Anyone] more unlike the typical organizer it is hard to imagine. Her driving force came from a rich and ardent personality and from a great love for others. Never did she allow individuals to be sacrificed to organizations or institutions.'[2]

1. Cf. Hilda Cashmore's comment on a student essay: '*Masterly*'; and on a student's teaching practice: 'There is *no* criticism. I am lost in wonder and admiration at the way in which you dealt with the subject!'
2. Marian Pease, obituary, *The Friend* (December 1943).

For further information see Anon., *Hilda Cashmore* (privately printed, c. 1945), held in Friends' House Library; *Manchester Guardian* (6.4.1933; 17.11.1943; 25.2.1944).

CAVELL, EDITH
(4.12.1865–12.10.1915)

NURSE

Father: Frederick Cavell, Anglican vicar, Norfolk
Mother: Louisa née Walming

Anglican

Edith Cavell was 30 years old before she began to study nursing at the London Hospital, but only two years later she was put in charge of an emergency typhoid hospital in Maidstone. She then served as a Poor Law staff nurse to the destitute and dying in Highgate and Shoreditch infirmaries.

In 1906 Edith Cavell went to Brussels to help set up a nurses' training school on the secular British 'Nightingale' model. In August 1914, after the German occupation of Belgium, the hospital became a Red Cross hospital and she and her staff cared for the war-wounded, both German and Allied. After the battle of Mons, she allowed her hospital to be a 'safe house' for Allied soldiers, some of them wounded, who had lost contact with their regiments and were refugees fearing execution for not having surrendered as prisoners to the German army. She sheltered several hundred men and helped them reach the neutral Dutch border. Betrayed by a French informer, in the pay of the Germans, who pretended to be a wounded Allied officer, she was arrested on 5 August 1915 and charged, with 34 others, with sheltering refugees with the intent of conducting soldiers to the enemy. She stated under interrogation: 'My preoccupation was not to help the enemy, but to help the men who applied to me reach the frontier; once across, they were free.'[1] She was tried by military court and sentenced to death. The night before she was shot she told the chaplain: 'This I would say, standing as I do in view of God and Eternity, I realize that patriotism is not enough. I must have no hatred or bitterness towards anyone.'

Statue of Edith Cavell, St Martin's Place, London (author's photograph)

SUE RYDER has commented:

Edith Cavell is to me a symbol of superb courage and faith, irrespective of race or creed, and therefore the precursor of thousands of men and women who, in the Second World War, suffered for the help they gave to those fighting in the cause of right, and who finally – without bitterness in their hearts, faced a shameful death unafraid.[2]

1. Rowland Ryder, *Edith Cavell* (London, Hamish Hamilton, 1975), p. 238. See also A. A. Hoehling, *Edith Cavell* (London, Cassell, 1958); and entry in the *Dictionary of National Biography, 1912–1921*.
2. Rowland Ryder, *op. cit.*, p. 240.

CHAPMAN, SYLVIA GYTHA DE LANCEY, MD

(27.11.1896–1.9.1995)

DOCTOR; RESEARCHER
IN MATERNAL HEALTH;
INTERNATIONAL RELIEF
ORGANIZER

Father: Frederick Chapman, New Zealand
Supreme Court Judge
Mother: Clara Jane, née Cook

Christian

Dr Sylvia Chapman (Courtesy of her niece Ann Rosenberg)

Personally unassuming, Sylvia Chapman led an extraordinarily full life dedicated to the relief of the suffering of others. Her work began in her native New Zealand, where she not only served the Lepers' Trust and the South Pacific Health Service but also concentrated on problems of women in pregnancy and childbirth. Her doctoral thesis (1934) on perinatal toxaemia led to the later discovery of the Rh factor. She was a strong supporter of pain relief by anaesthesia in childbirth, and already in the 1930s advocated the provision of free contraception. She herself had to withstand much old-fashioned, ill-informed prejudice in New Zealand then, both against spinsters and against women doctors.

It was in Sylvia Chapman's sitting room on 16 August 1944 that New Zealand's counterpart to Oxfam and the Save the Children Fund, CORSO (the New Zealand Council of Organisations for Relief Service Overseas) was founded. She herself led the medical team sent by CORSO in conjunction with UNRRA (United Nations Relief and Rehabilitation Administration) to desperate post-war Greece in 1945. There she set up mobile blood transfusion units in remote mountainous areas and supervised a medical training school in Salonika. CORSO is still New Zealand's primary non-governmental international relief agency.

Dr Chapman spent the rest of her working life in Britain, first as an anaesthetist and obstetrician and then as Hon. Assistant Secretary and Registrar of the new College of General Practitioners that was founded to raise both the standing and the standards of family doctors in Britain. Her life-companion in Britain was Daisy Dobson, the former secretary of MAUDE ROYDEN whom Sylvia Chapman had heard preach on her tour of New Zealand.

Despite the significance and diversity of her contribution to applied social medicine, Dr Sylvia Chapman's work has been left unrecorded in Britain.[1] She was too successful in being self-effacing.

1. She is remembered, however, in New Zealand. See obituary for her in *The Evening Post* (2.11.1995); and Esther Irving, 'Chapman, Sylvia' in Claudia Orange (ed.), *The New Zealand Dictionary of Biography*, vol. 2 (Wellington, Bridget Williams, 1989).

CLARK, HILDA, MB, BS
(1881–24.2.1955)

RELIEF ORGANIZER FOR THE SICK
AND STARVING DURING AND AFTER
WARTIME

*Father: William Stephens Clark, shoe
manufacturer and retailer*
*Mother: Helen Priestman, née Bright, feminist
pacifist*

Quaker

An ardent suffragist who had known what
it was to be pelted by a hostile male mob
early in the twentieth century, Dr Hilda
Clark was an experienced obstetrician, with
a specialist interest in fighting tuberculosis
and in social medicine for the working
class, when war broke out in August 1914.
Her immediate concern was for the French
mothers and children stranded behind the
fighting lines without medical help, now
that every doctor was mobilized for the
French army. Together with Edmund
Harvey MP, she persuaded the Society of

*Dr Hilda Clark in the Marne, c. 1916
(From Edith M. Pye (ed.),* War and Its
Aftermath, *privately printed, 1956)*

Friends' Meeting for Sufferings to establish a Friends' War Victims' Relief
Committee, which sent her out to northern France in November 1914 with a team
of doctors, nurses (including midwives) and several young, pacifist Englishmen to
be pharmacists, sanitary inspectors, drivers and orderlies. Greatly helped by her
lifelong companion, the distinguished midwife EDITH PYE, Hilda Clark first
established an emergency maternity hospital for women refugees in the epileptics'
wing of a workhouse in Châlons-sur-Marne. She next established a small hospital
in the devastated area of the Meuse, then organized shelter and medical care for
refugees from Rheims, and finally directed a convalescent home for sick women
and children in Haute Savoie. 'She had a clear vision of what Friends and those
who thought as they did could offer to a country at war. Her vision and organizing
power outreached the ideas of other workers – she saw what needed to be done
and held people to it.'[1] She and her fellow-workers had to endure the spiritual
contradiction of 'standing up for peace in the midst of the machinery of war, while
owing our lives and our scope for work to those who are fighting'.[2] By 1917 she
was feeling the strain from overwork and in the summer of 1918 she collapsed and
had to leave France for recuperation.

Learning from General Smuts about the desperate hunger in defeated Vienna,
Hilda Clark went to see for herself in July 1919. She immediately realized the acute
crisis affecting the babies and children of a whole generation and reported to British
Friends, asking for their backing to establish a relief team.

> Vienna in the autumn of 1919 . . . was a city of the dead . . . The streets were deserted except for queues waiting for rations of wood or sour bread, all of them, women and children as well as men, huddled in old patched army coats . . . everybody pale, everybody hungry, everybody silent and waiting . . . Dr. Hilda Clark . . . was too busy spinning plans for salvaging at least something . . . to notice that she was freezing or that there were maggots in [our] ship biscuits.[3]

No country in its former empire would supply coal to Austria, for its currency was now valueless and it could not produce goods because it had no coal. The conservative countryside would not sell food for knockdown prices to the 'Red' city of Vienna − they would rather feed it to their pigs − and in any case their cows were too feeble to produce sufficient milk. First Hilda Clark organized English currency funding to buy Czech coal for Austria. Next she started a massive agricultural and relief distribution project. Nearly 1,500 top-quality Swiss and Dutch cows bought by relief funds were handed over to farmers outside Vienna who fed them on fodder from Croatia and paid for them in milk which was sent daily to the infant welfare centres around the starving city. 'Hens and ducks, Yorkshire pigs, Swiss goats, Italian rams were imported and given to small hospitals, children's homes and land settlers, as well as large quantities of seed and fertilisers.'[4] Thus Hilda Clark pioneered a new mode of relief consisting not of short-term charity handouts, but of investment in the people themselves getting on their own feet again and reconstructing their society. She worked from 6:30 in the morning until 9:30 at night, under continually worsening conditions: the currency ever falling, the food stocks ever more depleted, unemployment rising and winter on the way.

> It is dreadful to be so close to catastrophe and never quite understand what form it is likely to take. I must say I prefer shells. In the war at any rate we shared the dangers with the people around us. Here we have to eat − it is horrible − and one can't run away from it.[5]

Eventually, by setting up a ration card system for food parcels packed by local schoolchildren, together with the welfare centres' milk distribution, tens of thousands of babies and infants suffering from hunger, rickets and tuberculosis were saved in Vienna in 1921−22. FRANCESCA WILSON is an eloquent eye witness to the authenticity and creativity of Hilda Clark's humanitarianism:

> Dr. Hilda Clark . . . could grasp a problem as a whole, and had the kind of constructive imagination that saw a way of tackling it, as well as the faith that overcomes all obstacles . . . These three women [Hilda Clark, EDITH PYE and KATHLEEN COURTNEY] had the right attitude to the people they were helping − respect, sympathy and unsentimental affection, and they were − as far as is possible in human beings − quite selfless in their attitude to their work . . . all thought of personal publicity was anathema to them. They were pure in motive and quite uncorruptible. This seems unnecessary to stress, but unfortunately I have seen relief workers (usually not among Friends) developing a *manie de grandeur*, when vested with unaccustomed authority and prestige.[6]

Despite her near exhaustion, Hilda Clark then went on to investigate and report on the terrible conditions in Poland in 1922, where she found displaced homeless families in the woods dying from dysentery on a diet of mushrooms and berries. She went on to Greece in 1923 and to Serbia, Bulgaria and Turkey in 1924. In the aftermath of the Greek–Turkish war (1919–23), there was another 'great human disaster'.[7] A million Greek refugee women and children were 'ethnically cleansed' from Turkey, arriving destitute and in despair in impoverished Greece. Hilda Clark reported that it was too much for any non-governmental organization such as the Society of Friends to tackle. The 'Exchange of Populations' under the Treaty of Lausanne 'done in cold blood makes us just sick with the cruelty of it'.[8] She would have been deeply saddened but not surprised by the continuing suffering at the start of the twenty-first century of all the inhabitants of former Yugoslavia, including the Croatian Serbs, the Bosnian Muslims and the Kosovars, not to mention the Cypriot Greeks and Turks and the still stateless Kurds.

Dr Hilda Clark (seated) and Edith Pye administering their food relief programme for the children of Vienna, 1922

Thereafter Hilda Clark put her remaining energy into support for the League of Nations in the hope that it might achieve international agreement on disarmament and the prevention of war through collective security. Once the fascist 1930s arrived, she helped Edith Pye on the International Commission for the Assistance of Child Refugees, first helping child refugees from Spain. In September 1938 she was in Vienna again, but this time helping to organize the flight *out* of Vienna of persecuted non-Aryans. 'Clearly no Jew is safe.'[9]

Hilda Clark died after ten years' suffering from Parkinson's disease. 'Love gave her strength, and love went out to all who surrounded her . . . The source of [her] power of attracting others into work she thought essential for humanity, seemed to derive from . . . her love of all living things.'[10]

'The secret of [her] work's extent lies in the fact that her eager mind, moved by a passionate desire to help, lit up sparks in others, and released in them powers they did not know they possessed. Under her leadership ordinary men and women accomplished things they would never have dreamed of without it.'[11]

She lies in the Quaker burial ground in Street, under the same headstone as Edith Pye.

1. Edith Pye (ed.), *War and Its Aftermath: Letters from Hilda Clark, M.B., B.S. from France, Austria and the Near East 1914–1924* (privately printed, 1956), p. 16.
2. Hilda Clark, letter, in Pye, *op. cit.*, p. 29.
3. Francesca Wilson, *In the Margins of Chaos* (London, John Murray, 1944), p. 106.
4. *Ibid.*, p. 109.
5. Hilda Clark, letter, in Pye, *op. cit.*, p. 48.
6. Wilson, *op. cit.*, p. 138.
7. Pye, *op. cit.*, p. 87.
8. Hilda Clark, letter, in Pye, *op. cit.*, p. 107.
9. *Ibid.*, p. 115.
10. Pye, *op. cit.*, p. 125. See also Roger Clark *et al.*, obituary for Hilda Clark, *The Friend* (11.3.1955), pp. 256–7. 'She lived her Quaker faith': Edith Pye, obituary for Hilda Clark, *Journal of the Medical Women's Federation* (July 1955), pp. 206–7.
11. Edith Pye, 'Hilda Clark', postscript to obituary, *The Friend* (11.3.1955), p. 257.

COATE, WINIFRED A.,
MBE, OBE

(25.4.1893–23.11.1977)

MISSIONARY TEACHER,
WORKER FOR PALESTINIAN
REFUGEES

*Father: Rev. Harry Coate, Anglican
rector*
Mother: Henrietta Mercy, née Nihill

Anglican

Winifred Coate, a graduate in English from Westfield College, University of London (1913), first went to work as a teacher in the Middle East under the Church Missionary Society's Jerusalem and the Middle East Mission in 1920. After four years in Palestine she taught for

Winifred Coate, c. 1956 (From CMS Outlook, *April 1957, p. 9, with kind permission of the Church Mission Society)*

another four years in Egypt. She spoke and read Arabic. For fifteen years during the turbulent period 1928–43 she was Principal of the CMS Girls' College in Jerusalem, working to maintain a 'normalcy' of civilized tolerance among the multi-ethnic, multi-faith girls and staff – Muslim, Jewish and Christian – within the school, no matter what hatred and righteous sectarian murder prevailed outside. From 1943 to 1947 she worked on child and adult literacy projects in rural Lebanon and Jordan.

At the time of the founding of Israel in the summer of 1948, Winifred Coate was sheltering from gunfire in the garden of St George's Cathedral, Jerusalem, together with the Bishop and a few others, when she declared she would join the now destitute Palestinian Arab refugees and start work at a CMS refugee relief centre at Zerka, Jordan. Two years later she reported:

> [The] vast majority of the [Palestinian Arab] refugees are still homeless and unemployed, waiting sick with hope deferred for some political settlement to solve their problems and bring an end to their exile . . . recently there has been a large influx of newcomers . . . They come sometimes in companies, fleeing by night and hiding by day as they creep through Jewish occupied territory and many arrive in a state of hysteria and exhaustion from the terrors of their journey . . . .many own property in Israel, but are receiving no rent for houses now occupied by Jews. Also many who have funds frozen in banks in Israel are forced to beg for relief here . . . many of the children are anaemic and listless . . . [Life] on the dole is inevitably demoralising and we wage constant and exhausting warfare against apathy and despair . . . One often hears a criticism of Arab refugees as lacking initiative. It is difficult to show initiative when one has no money whatever.[1]

Winifred Coate worked, with money from the Church World Service, the British

Red Cross, UNRRA and private donations, to organize a milk centre, supplementary feeding for destitute mothers and babies, an undernourished children's feeding centre, a girls' school, a young men's club, a sewing centre, a craft shop, a housing scheme, various cottage industries and a social work training centre. She was still there in 1956 when the Suez crisis caused all British missionaries to be expelled. She was one of the first two to be invited back to Zerka, Jordan, in April 1957.

Winifred Coate retired from the CMS at the age of 67 in 1960. She then began her own extraordinary refugee relief 'experiment'. With very little money she started Abdelliyeh, a pioneer farming co-operative for landless Palestinian *felaheen* families in the desert that was to prove a model for later Oxfam and Christian Aid projects. But first she had to prove that there was a submerged water source in a region known as 'eleven-year harvest' because it had at best only four inches of rainfall a year. Using the evidence from archaeology that desert castles, hunting lodges and elaborate bath-houses had existed there nearly a thousand years earlier, she urged an Arab water diviner to explore the rocky desert area as she drove him and his twigs around in her little car. 'We drilled where he indicated and there it was! It was such a good joke, finding water where the technical experts said there wasn't any!'[2] The co-operative community she founded eventually boasted tree-lined roads, productive fruit and vegetable farms, brick houses instead of tents, a mechanical repair workshop, shops, a clinic and a school. Refugees need land and work, not just 'relief'.

Shot in the thigh in cross-fire during the Jordanian civil war of 1970, Winifred Coate survived to become a legend among the Arabs among whom she lived and worked until her final illness at 84 in 1977.

1. Winifred Coate, 'Among Arab refugees in Jordan: a second year at Zerka. Report of the CMS Refugee Relief Centre for the year ended September 1950', held in the CMS archives, University of Birmingham. See also archives of the Middle East Centre, St Antony's College, Oxford, for Winifred Coate's correspondence and for the periodical *Bible Lands* (1943–77), containing several articles by her on her work.
2. Winifred Carr, 'Unassuming woman with a double mission', obituary in *Daily Telegraph* (26.11.1977).

COOPER, PHYLLIS
(31.7.1909–24.1.1994)

RED CROSS RESCUER OF WOUNDED; WORKER FOR THE RELIEF OF DISPLACED PERSONS

Father: Henry Cooper, Smithfield porter
Mother: Olive, née Flower

Christian

'Entering a minefield' was no mere metaphor for Phyllis Cooper. On 25 June 1944 she saw an Italian civilian seriously injured in a minefield near Borgo, Flora, and realized that his brother had also been injured when trying to save him. Phyllis Cooper immediately went for help to a US army captain, whom she then assisted in 'prodding' a four-foot pass through the minefield to the wounded men. They had to cross two trip wires and she then furnished her own hairpins to use as safety plugs in two anti-personnel landmines before de-capping them. Finally she led a party of stretcher-bearers to the victims and back, pointing out the trip wires. She was later awarded the King's Commendation for 'exceptional bravery and devotion to humanity in entering a minefield'.

Bravery had been Phyllis Cooper's forte much earlier, both as a champion cross-country motor cyclist and as a volunteer ambulance driver in the Runciman First Aid Nursing Yeomanry (FANY) Unit to the Finnish Red Cross after Finland had been invaded by the Soviet Union. In 1943 she had joined the British Red Cross and Order of St John as an ambulance driver. She was posted to Italy, where she worked as Liaison Officer in the Civilian Relief Service in refugee camps for Yugoslav women and children – many of them 'wounded, half-starved, naked and lousy'[1] at Bari – and where she also performed the act of heroism described above. She did further relief work, this time with homeless Italian refugees in devastated Littoria, and later in Rome.

Phyllis Cooper as a FANY, c. 1940
(By kind permission of her great-nephew Stuart Robinson)

In July 1945 Phyllis Cooper was transferred to Styria in Austria, doing relief work among undernourished Austrians (recently enemies) and displaced persons of many nationalities. The Prince Bishop of Graz was profoundly touched by her

> generous self-sacrifice: Again and again I received . . . reports painting you, Dear Miss, indefatigably fetching the [relief] goods over the whole of Styria; even dragging the chests and the parcels, loading and unloading them yourself, and struggling . . . to the [point of] exhaustion.[2]

She was again awarded the King's Commendation for gallantry in the cause of humanity and distinguished service during the Second World War.

After the war Phyllis Cooper obtained her diploma in social work from the University of London and then became children's officer for Pembrokeshire. In 1956 she married Glyndwr Devonald, an Inspector with the NSPCC in London who later became a lecturer in child welfare. He had known nothing of her wartime heroism before their wedding day.[3]

1. Phyllis Cooper, private letter (1943).
2. Cooper family papers. See also British Red Cross Reports in the Red Cross Archive, National Headquarters, Grosvenor Crescent, London.
3. *Evening News* (27.3.1956).

COOPER, SELINA, JP
(1864–1946)

WORKING-CLASS INTERNATIONALIST
SUFFRAGIST; ANTI-WAR AND
ANTI-FASCIST CAMPAIGNER

Father: Charles Coombe, railway navvy
Mother: Jane, née Uren, dressmaker

Labour Church

Selina Cooper (From Nelson
Workers' Guide, *March 1903)*

Selina Cooper is representative of many early twentieth-century socialist feminist pacifists of northern England.[1] She was outstanding, however, for her exceptional gifts as a speaker and for the sheer perseverance of her commitment to her causes, all of which were fired by her indignant humanity. After a childhood and girlhood of continuous privation and very hard work as a young carder in the mills, a washer-woman and a neighbourhood nurse, Selina Cooper had her first glimpse of education and wider horizons via the Women's Co-operative Guild.[2] She lost her only son as a baby of four months in 1897 but she and her weaver husband managed to rear their daughter, despite poor housing and economic insecurity in their Lancashire town of Nelson on Colne.

In 1900 Selina Cooper was converted to the cause of women's suffrage, believing that women needed to be full citizens if women workers, mothers and children were to begin to have their needs recognized and met in Britain at last. Although a non-violent suffragist, not a militant suffragette,[3] she had to face violent heckling as a prominent campaigner for the NUWSS (1907–14). Her clothes were torn, she was pelted with rotten eggs and roughly jostled; once, in Hull, she was placed on top of a barrel containing live bass: 'the lid started coming up. And she put her legs astride to sort of hold it . . . anyhow, she stood it.'[4]

With the outbreak of the First World War, the Coopers found themselves even more isolated, this time not as socialists or feminists but as pacifists. In August 1917 Selina Cooper headed a procession of women – Nelson Women's Peace Crusade – holding up banners saying: 'Peace our hope', 'We demand a people's peace' and 'Hail the Russian Revolution'. No band was willing to play for them. They found themselves facing a crowd of 15,000 hostile onlookers who jeered and pelted them and would not let them be heard. Yet just a fortnight later Selina Cooper organized another open meeting in Nelson.[5] As an internationalist, an outspoken opponent of conscription and advocate of a negotiated peace, she was considered a security risk and her house was searched under the Defence of the Realm Act.

At the age of 70, in October 1934, Selina Cooper accompanied MONICA WHATELY to Nazi Germany, to try to intercede for, or at least to visit, several women whom the Nazis were holding in prison as hostages for their Communist husbands. Under constant surveillance, they were refused permission to see the women, let alone to visit the women's concentration camps. On her return, Selina Cooper addressed meeting after meeting in the north of England, alerting her hearers to the terrifying nature of fascist dictatorship. She had to live through a second world war but died before she could cheer the implementation of a welfare state in Britain. Early in 1940, at the age of 76, she was expelled from the Labour Party that she had helped to establish, on account of her excessive sympathy with Soviet Russia.[6] Throughout her lifetime of uphill struggle for social justice and international peace, Selina Cooper would say that her motto was KBO: 'Keep Buggering On'.[7]

1. See Jill Liddington and Jill Norris, *One Hand Tied behind Us: The Rise of the Women's Suffrage Movement* (London, Virago, 1978).
2. See entry for MARGARET LLEWELYN DAVIES.
3. See Ray Strachey, *The Cause* (reprinted London, Virago, 1978).
4. Interview with Selina Cooper's daughter in Liddington and Norris, *One Hand Tied behind Us*, p. 220.
5. Jill Liddington, *The Life and Times of a Respectable Rebel: Selina Cooper 1864–1946* (London, Virago, 1984), ch. 16; and Jill Liddington, *The Long Road to Greenham: Feminism and Anti-militarism in Britain since 1820* (London, Virago, 1989), ch. 6.
6. Liddington, *Life and Times*, pp. 434–41.
7. *Ibid.*, p. 425.

COURTNEY, KATHLEEN D'OLIER, DBE
(11.3.1878–7.12.1974)

ANTI-WAR CAMPAIGNER; REFUGEE RELIEF WORKER; ADVOCATE OF SUPRANATIONAL GOVERNMENT

Father: Major David Courtney
Mother: Alice, née Mann.

Both parents from Anglo-Irish Ascendancy background

Anglican

Kathleen Courtney, c. 1920 (Source: the late Daisy Dobson)

Of all the leading British women suffragists who had to choose whether their feminism came before their pacifism or vice versa after the outbreak of the First World War, Kathleen Courtney's decision was perhaps the most surprising. Not only did she herself come from a military family, but she was also the closest possible colleague and friend of Mrs Fawcett, the President of the National Union of Women's Suffrage Societies, of which Kathleen Courtney was the dedicated and effective Hon. Secretary. Nevertheless, she prioritized her internationalism and anti-militarism, taking a stance that Mrs Fawcett believed to be both unpatriotic and politically suicidal from the perspective of women's suffrage prospects in Britain. Thus Kathleen Courtney was one of the organizers and supporters of the Women's International Congress at The Hague in 1915[1] and resigned from the Executive of the NUWSS, offering herself for re-election on a 'peace platform', only to be defeated. It is possible that she was won over at this crucial moment of moral choice by her committed pacifist friends MAUDE ROYDEN and HELENA SWANWICK.

At the end of 1915, impatient with committee work and organizations, Kathleen Courtney volunteered to work with the Serbian Relief Fund and was sent in 1916 first to Salonika and then to Corsica to care for Serbian refugees. Between 1920 and 1922 she supported the work of Dr HILDA CLARK and EDITH PYE in Vienna and she also visited Quaker relief centres in Poland and Greece. 'Exchange of population sounds a fine idea. But in practice it means things like moving Greek fishing families from the Black Sea to inland villages where life is totally different.'[2]

Throughout the 1920s and 1930s Kathleen Courtney gave her energy to working, first for the Women's International League for Peace and Freedom and then for the League of Nations Union, in particular on the issues of arbitration and Geneva's abortive attempts at disarmament.[3] During the Second World War:

> she, more than anyone else helped [the LNU] to keep going . . . She, with Lord Cecil, Lord Lytton, Professor Arthur Newell and a few others carried on [the] London International Assembly . . . She was at San Francisco when the Charter was drawn up, and after the war she helped to build UNA out of LNU. In 1946 at Luxembourg she helped to launch the World Federation of UNAs, and at Geneva in 1948 she was elected . . . President of the Federation [succeeding Jan Masaryk].[4]

1. See Introduction and Appendix I; Sybil Oldfield, *Spinsters of This Parish* (London, Virago, 1984), ch. 9; and Anne Wiltsher, *Most Dangerous Women: Feminist Peace Campaigners of the Great War* (London, Pandora, 1985), *passim*.
2. Mary Stott, 'Happy at ninety', interview with Dame Kathleen Courtney, *Manchester Guardian* (11.3.1968); see also Johanna Alberti, *Beyond Suffrage: Feminists in War and Peace, 1914–28* (London, Macmillan, 1989), p. 58.
3. Alberti, *op. cit.*, pp. 210–11.
4. W. Arnold Forster in *U.N. News* (September–October 1951), p. 12.

See also Kathleen Courtney papers held at Lady Margaret Hall, Oxford, and the Women's Library, London.

COURTNEY OF PENWITH, KATE, LADY
(4.4.1847–26.2.1929)

CAMPAIGNER AGAINST BOER WAR CONCENTRATION CAMPS; PACIFIST INTERNATIONALIST

Father: Richard Potter, railway magnate
Mother: Lawrencina, née Heyworth, daughter of railway entrepreneur

Attender at Quaker meetings

After insisting upon leaving her privileged Victorian home at the age of 27 in order to become an unpaid social worker, Kate Potter trained with the Charity Organization Society in Whitechapel and as an organizer of East End boys' clubs. She then joined Canon and Henrietta Barnett, the founders of Toynbee Hall and London 'settlement' work, and concentrated on improving housing conditions for the poorest in Whitechapel. In 1883 she married the Liberal Cabinet Minister Leonard Courtney, later Lord Courtney of Penwith.

Both the Courtneys were committed to the struggle against war, and on the outbreak of the Boer War in October 1899 they both became notorious as alleged 'pro-Boers' and received scores of anonymous threatening letters. Kate Courtney joined EMILY HOBHOUSE in April 1900 in founding the British Women's Committee for the South Africa Conciliation Movement that urged a negotiated settlement of the war. In June she chaired, with much trepidation, a large and remarkable women's protest meeting in Queen's Hall, London. In November, unable to keep silent about the British scorched-earth and concentration camp policies, she wrote:

> I suppose we are all grieving at the way in which the war in South Africa is dragging on and the conditions under which and methods by which it is being fought . . . Why, why, does it go on? . . .
> We have substituted uncivilised for civilised methods of warfare.[1]

Kate, Lady Courtney of Penwith (Courtesy of the National Portrait Gallery, London)

In December 1900 Kate Courtney supported EMILY HOBHOUSE's fact-finding mission to the British concentration camps, and throughout 1901 she helped her to organize relief in South Africa and to inform the British public about the suffering inflicted on Afrikaner and African women and children.

When the First World War broke out, Kate Courtney refused to wage it. She insisted, instead, on championing 'innocent enemies'.[2] To that end, she helped found the Emergency Committee to relieve destitute German civilians stranded in Britain; she visited German prisoners of war in prison ships; and she publicized the work of her German counterparts in Berlin who were seeing to the welfare of British civilians and prisoners in Germany. Between March and April 1915, now aged 68, she worked indefatigably for the first collective peace initiative organized internationally by women: the Women's International Congress at The Hague.[3] When the British government cancelled all travel permits for the British women wishing to attend, she went and persuaded the Home Secretary to allow 25 to go, before Winston Churchill at the Admiralty then 'closed' the North Sea to all shipping. After the Congress she worked to publicize its resolutions (many of which were later incorporated by Woodrow Wilson into his Fourteen Points) and arranged for the famous social reformer Jane Addams to report to Lord Robert Cecil at the Foreign Office and to Lloyd George at the War Office on her post-Congress interview with the German Foreign Ministry about the possibility of ending the war via mediation by neutral powers.[4] Kate Courtney herself spoke in Britain in April 1915 at the National ILP conference, already warning against imposing a peace of conquest or humiliation on Germany.[5]

When the war at last ended and imposed a peace of conquest and humiliation, Kate Courtney, by then recently widowed, helped organize the first Quaker food relief in starving, blockaded Germany. It was in her home in Cheyne Walk that the first meeting was held of the Fight the Famine Committee out of which came the Save the Children Fund.[6] When she gave hospitality to German and Austrian delegates to the Fight the Famine Conference in 1919, the popular press was enraged: 'Hun "Delegates" dinner party' – 'Lady Courtney of Penwith and her spiritual comrades'.[7] Also in 1919 she wrote in *The Westminster Gazette* pleading for the new anti-militarist spirit in Germany to be acknowledged and supported by a conciliatory Britain; and in 1920 she wrote to *The Daily News*:

> Let us renounce our share in the indemnity [reparations payments] in favour of those of our allies who have suffered invasion and in return get them to exact no more than Germany can pay . . . I would go further, and return to her some of the merchant shipping which is sorely needed for [her] restoration . . .
>
> Somebody must begin to be good if the better world we were promised is ever to come.

Kate Courtney, the little-known pacifist sister of Beatrice Webb, was someone beginning to be good.[8]

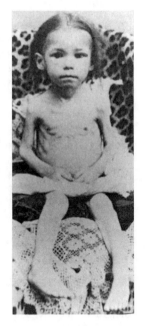

Child victim, Bloemfontein Concentration Camp (Courtesy of the War Museum of the Boer Republics, Bloemfontein)

1. Kate Courtney, letter to *The Westminster Review* (November 1900). See also Sybil Oldfield, *Women against the Iron Fist: Alternatives to Militarism 1900–1989* (Oxford, Basil Blackwell, 1989), chapter on 'The enemy's friend: Kate Courtney'.
2. Kate Courtney, *Extracts from a Diary during the War* (printed for private circulation, December 1927), held in the Women's Library, London, entry for 30.3.1915. See also Oldfield, *op. cit.*, pp. 32–4.
3. See Introduction and Appendix I.
4. See Anne Wiltsher, *Most Dangerous Women: Feminist Peace Campaigners of the Great War* (London, Pandora, 1985).
5. *Labour Leader* (22.4.1915). See also Oldfield, *op. cit.*, pp. 37–8.
6. See entries for DOROTHY BUXTON and EGLANTYNE JEBB.
7. *Daily Sketch* (July 1919).
8. For tributes to Kate, Lady Courtney of Penwith, see Beatrice Webb, *Diaries* (6.3.1929); obituary, *Manchester Guardian* (27.2.1929); Elizabeth Fox Howard, 'My Lady of Chelsea', *Friends' Quarterly Examiner* (1929); G. P. Gooch, *Life of Leonard Courtney* (London, Macmillan, 1920); and Stephen Hobhouse, *Margaret Hobhouse and her Family* (Rochester, Stanhope Press, 1934).

COUSINS, E. CONSTANCE
(22.9.1882–May 1944)

MISSIONARY DOCTOR IN INDIA AND BHUTAN

Father: missionary in Madagascar

Christian

After graduating with first-class honours in physiology in 1904 and later qualifying as a doctor, Constance Cousins was sent as a medical missionary to work at the Almora sanatorium for tuberculosis in India in 1911. In 1913 she was sent to the Presbyterian Church's Medical Mission in Kalimpong, north India.

In July 1918 she received the single most dramatic challenge of her life. A call for help came to Kalimpong from the kingdom of Bhutan, reporting a cholera epidemic; the medicines they had been sent were useless without trained medical people to administer them. No male doctor would agree to go, but Dr Constance Cousins together with Nurse Brodie volunteered to be the first European woman ever admitted into that mediaeval Himalayan kingdom. It took them a fortnight to cross the main range of the Himalayas by mule via the Tibetan border, crossing six mountain passes, the highest, Tremu La, being 16,500 feet. Having climbed 6,000 feet in four hours at one stage, they suffered, not surprisingly, from altitude sickness. When they arrived in Paro, Bhutan, they treated 240 cases of cholera, performed five operations and distributed medicine to 2,377 people living in indescribable squalor, with no sanitation and the closest proximity to pig excrement. Constance Cousins contracted typhus from the lice that flourished in those conditions; she became delirious with fever on the way home – a journey that involved riding through three feet of water and confrontations with bears. But she survived, to work for over twenty years after 1923 at Almora sanatorium, where she died in 1944, exhausted and single-handed. It was said of her that she was always more concerned with her mission as a doctor to relieve suffering than in actual conversion of those who were her patients.[1]

1. Letter from Osyth Leicester of John Murray, publishers, rejecting manuscript of 'Constance in India: the life and times of the late Dr E. C. Cousins' (mostly her letters home), typescript held, together with maps of the trek to Bhutan, in the archive of the School of African and Oriental Studies, University of London.

Cf. 'Humanitarian assistance became increasingly important in mission work': Rosemary Seaton, Introduction to *Guide to Archives and Manuscript Collections* (London, SOAS Library, 1994), p. 4.

COUSINS, MARGARET (GRETTA)
(1878–1954)

WORKER FOR THE LIBERATION OF INDIAN GIRLS AND WOMEN

Father: — *Gillespie*
Mother: —, *née Longheed*

Originally Irish Protestant, then Theosophist

'Gretta' Cousins (From J. H. Cousins and M. E. Cousins, We Two Together, *Ganesh & Co., 1950)*

In November 1908, Margaret Cousins, a Dublin music graduate and teacher, decided with Hanna Sheehy Skeffington to form a militant but democratic suffrage society, the Irish Women's Franchise League. That decision led to her solitary confinement in Holloway in 1910 and to hunger-striking in Tullimore prison, Ireland, in 1913. In 1915 she and her husband left Ireland for India, attracted by the ideas of the Theosophist leader Annie Besant. However, instead of focusing exclusively on the path to her own enlightenment as so many Western pilgrims to India have done, Margaret Cousins almost immediately tried to serve the needs of Indian girls and women, both through education as a teacher, and by supporting their own efforts at self-emancipation.[1] She differed from Mrs Besant, who at that time regarded the emancipation of women and their equal citizenship as a hindering distraction from the Indian national liberation movement.[2]

In December 1917 Margaret Cousins drafted the Address on the necessity of women's suffrage in India presented by Mrs Sarojini Naidu to the Viceroy and the Secretary of State for India.[3] As a teacher of Indian girls Margaret Cousins had been forced to witness the tragic waste of female potential and the unnecessary agony of young girls married prematurely and dying in their first childbirth.

> [Witnessing] the forcing of motherhood on little girls, with its . . . frustration of the mental development of its victims, I was revolted by the slavery and indignity put on womanhood by the inconsiderate domination of men, and there grew within me a determination to do all I could to forward all circumstances calculated to bring women into public and particularly legislative life, so that this evil and others might be rectified.[4]

Margaret Cousins refused to choose between the struggle for Indian self-government on the one hand and for the political rights of Indian women on the other, but campaigned continuously for both – and was attacked for doing so. The Indian Nationalists thought she should concentrate exclusively on political liberation, the British government thought she should stay out of Indian politics altogether. The Women's Indian Association, which she co-founded, made frequent appeals to the (British) government of India for more and better schools for girls, for more health centres, for legislation to protect children, to close up brothels, to reform the marriage laws, to enforce the Sarda Act on minimal marriage age for girls, to give women inheritance rights, and to allow entrance to temples for *harijans*. But Margaret Cousins also worked politically as a follower of Mahatma Gandhi. Her non-violent protest against the curb on Indian civil liberties in the Ordinance Bills of 1931 brought her a year's imprisonment. 'I was escorted to the Madras Penitentiary for two sleepless nights feeling anything but penitent.'[5] She was then a political prisoner in Vellore prison. On her release on 21 October 1933, 'The last words of the matron were: "Mrs Cousins, for God's sake try and get a stop put to the hanging of women"'.[6] The following month she made a public protest against the hanging of women at the Women's India Association conference in Madras.

Margaret Cousins published two books on Indian women: *The Awakening of Asian Womanhood* and *Indian Womanhood Today*. She also initiated the first degree in Indian music at Madnapalle College. It was said of her a few years before her death:

> The Indian people in general and Women in particular owe a profound debt of gratitude to Mrs M. E. Cousins who, though born and brought up in Ireland, is herself completely one with the Indian men and women and has served them as no other woman in the present time.[7]

1. James H. and Margaret E. Cousins, *We Two Together* (Madras, Ganesh & Co., 1950), pp. 299 and 310.
2. *Ibid.*, p. 331.
3. See Appendix II and Anon., *Mrs Margaret Cousins and Her Work in India* (Adyar, Madras, Women's Indian Association, 1950), held in the Women's Library, London. See also entry for ELEANOR RATHBONE.
4. Cousins, *op. cit.*, p. 331.
5. *Ibid.*, p. 583.
6. *Ibid.*, p. 590.
7. Anon., *Mrs Margaret Cousins*.

CROWDY, RACHEL, DBE
(3.3.1884–10.10.1964)

NURSING ADMINISTRATOR;
INTERNATIONALIST SOCIAL
REFORMER

Father: James Crowdy, solicitor
Mother: Mary, née Fuidge

Anglican

Rachel Crowdy (From Time and Tide, *9.9.1927)*

In 1911, at the age of 27, Rachel Crowdy, a trained nurse who had grown up the delicate youngest of four sisters, joined the newly formed Voluntary Aid Detachments (VAD) and studied for her dispenser's certificate. The VAD were originally inspired by the example of the voluntary village helpers in Russia in the Russo-Japanese War. Rachel Crowdy had wanted to encourage VAD women to do practical social work in the poorest parts of London, but the War Office ordered them to learn how to turn milk trains into ambulance trains and schools into hospitals. In September 1914 she and her friend Katharine Furse[1] saw a rest station at a railway station in Paris and recommended the 'manning' of all such rest stations by VADs for the duration of the war. In Boulogne they set up the first such casualty clearing station for the wounded in a railway siding and there, during the first battle of Ypres, about twenty nurses had to try to minister to 20,000 men. At the end of 1914, aged 30, Rachel Crowdy was deputed by Katharine Furse, who was directing the London headquarters, to be in charge of the thousands of VADs on the continent for the rest of the First World War. Rachel Crowdy set up and staffed casualty clearing stations for the wounded along all the communication lines in France and Belgium; she established ambulance depots, nurses' hostels and sick bays, as well as actual base hospitals. She was mentioned in dispatches, awarded the Mons Star and the Royal Red Cross, and created a Dame of the British Empire in 1919.[2]

After only ten days' leave in 1919, Rachel Crowdy, having proved herself an extraordinarily able administrator under almost impossible conditions, was appointed a member of the Health Section of the Secretariat of the brand-new League of Nations. As soon as the Social Section was created out of the Health Section, she became the only woman Head of Section in the League. She had moved from 'conditions of violent war to conditions of violent peace'.[3] Her first assignment was to organize the League's anti-typhus campaign in Poland and Russia (1920–21), and she herself made a fact-finding tour of many of the stricken villages. Once she became Head of the Social Section, she was responsible for the League's international campaign 'against destitution, disease and moral evils'.[4] Her particular focus was on the sex trade in women and children and on the criminal drug trade, especially opium.

Thence sprang her great classic, *The Report of the Special Body of Experts on Traffic in Women and Children*, 1927 . . . based on reports from twenty-eight countries, factually irreproachable yet full of extraordinarily vivid pictures of methods of procuration and transport for gain to a foreign country of women and girls for the sexual gratification of one or more persons.[5]

She was *persona non grata* in the underworld, receiving abusive or threatening letters by every post, hated by the drug kings and even on at least one occasion in Geneva narrowly missing an assassin's bullet. 'You cannot infuriate rich traffickers for nothing.'[6]

From 1935 to 1936 Rachel Crowdy was on a British Royal Commission investigating the private manufacture and trade in weapons; the Commission recommended far-reaching British and international regulation, but these findings were not implemented.[7] Throughout the Second World War she was Regions Adviser to the Ministry of Information, visiting and reporting on conditions in bombed cities.

Rachel Crowdy regarded herself as a social worker, and indeed she was a social worker of the world, active 'in the four corners of the world, advising on this, inquiring into that, caring for nothing but the betterment of the human race'.[8] Like Jane Addams,[9] she believed in the internationalism of the life-enabling deed as the best preventative against war. Already in 1935 she could see

that, even though war, as war, might not be at an end, understanding might yet come between nations through the levelling of social questions which concern them all. I saw that if the thinking of all countries could approach similarity in the things which concern homes and families – in social standards generally – men would be helped toward a consciousness of their 'unity' – 'unity' is a better word than 'brotherhood' – and we should have stepped forward . . . Social co-operation is easier of accomplishment than political co-operation.[10]

1. Dame Katharine Furse (aunt of Dame JANET VAUGHAN) was Commandant in Chief of the VAD Department 1914–16 and then Director of the Women's Royal Naval Service 1917–19. See *Dictionary of National Biography, 1951–1960*.
2. See Thekla Bowser, *The Story of British V.A.D. Work in the Great War* (London, Melrose, 1917 and 1918); and Katharine Furse, *Hearts and Pomegranates: The Story of Forty Five Years 1875–1920* (London, Peter Davies, 1940).
3. *Christian Science Monitor* (3.7.1935), p. 5.
4. See Articles 23, 24 and 25 of the Covenant of the League of Nations; and *Time and Tide* (9.9.1927).
5. *International Women's News* (March 1965).
6. *Evening Standard* (12.6.1931).
7. See Philip Gibbs, *Ordeal in England* (London, The Book Club, 1938), ch. 5: 'Arms and the man'.
8. Obituary, *The Times* (19.10.1964).
9. See Jane Addams, *Peace and Bread in Time of War* (first published 1920; republished Boston, G. K. Hall, 1960); and Sybil Oldfield, 'Jane Addams: the chance the world missed' in F. D'Amico and P. Beckman, *Women in World Politics* (Westport, CT and London, Bergin and Garvey, 1995), pp. 155–67.
10. *Christian Science Monitor* (3.7.1935), p. 5.

D

DAVIES, MARGARET LLEWELYN
(16.10.1861–28.5.1944)

CO-OPERATIVE SOCIALIST;
WAR-RESISTER

*Father: Reverend John Llewelyn Davies,
    Christian Socialist*
*Mother: Mary, née Crompton, suffragist daughter
    of a judge*

Humanist

*Margaret Llewelyn Davies, c. 1920
(Courtesy of her great-niece Jane Wynne
Willson)*

Margaret Llewelyn Davies had 'an intense hatred of suffering, [and a] passion to alleviate it'.[1] This was first manifest in her early decision to leave Girton College, Cambridge, the pioneer institution of women's university education in Britain founded by her aunt Emily Davies, in order to do practical social work, helping poor families to stay clear of the workhouse in Marylebone in London. Her principal lifework was to play an essential, enabling role as Hon. Secretary of the Women's Co-operative Guild (1889–1921).[2] She campaigned tirelessly and successfully on such issues as a minimum subsistence wage to be paid to women employees of the Co-operative Wholesale Society, pithead baths for miners, maternity benefit to be paid to mothers, and adult suffrage for all the women and men not yet enfranchised in Britain. She also campaigned, with less immediate success, for such far-sighted social reforms as state maternity healthcare provision, the raising of the school-leaving age, an extension of the grounds for divorce to include desertion, cruelty, serious incompatibility and mutual consent, and the introduction of a maximum 48-hour working week. Together with her lifelong companion Lilian Harris and working-class women leaders of the Guild such as Sarah Reddish, Sarah Dickenson, Margaret McCoubrey, Annie Bamford Tomlinson and Ethel Barton, Margaret Llewelyn Davies succeeded in building up the British Women's Co-operative Guild into 'perhaps the most remarkable women's organization in the world'.[3] It was an organization that enabled energetic, thoughtful working-class women in Britain, like the mother of D. H. Lawrence – portrayed as Mrs Morel in *Sons and Lovers* – to realize their potential as citizens, including citizens of the world.

Margaret Llewelyn Davies's greatest failure, in her view, was her internationalist campaign for total disarmament. As a public declaration of her rejection of the very idea of enmity between the people of the world, already in 1914 she signed the Open Christmas Letter to the Women of Germany and Austria drafted by EMILY HOBHOUSE. In 1915 she publicly supported the International Women's Congress at The Hague.[4] In 1918 her pacifist convictions backed the Women's Co-operative Guild Conference resolution asking for 'immediate peace negotiations and a non-punitive peace – no annexation of territory by conquest – and Universal Disarmament', only for it to be defeated, to her deep dismay, by 399 votes to 336 of her own members. On her retirement at the age of 60, she concentrated on the continuing struggle to abolish war by helping to found the new *International* Women's Co-operative Guild (the 'Mothers' International') with delegates from Britain, Holland, Switzerland, Austria, Czechoslovakia and Russia. She had a vision of new mutually co-operative trade relations that would make the brotherhood of nations a reality at last.[5] Her continued idealism was manifest in her support for the War Resisters International, backed by Albert Einstein. Her declaration 'Why I believe in the No More War Movement' in 1928 read:

> Because personal refusal of war service by the *people* will goad governments into arbitration, disarmament and loyalty to the League of Nations. Also, because it is impossible without *total* war resistance to cut at the roots of military propaganda and the perversion of science and to achieve the general outlook which regards war, like slavery, as an outworn barbarity. Nor, otherwise, can men's energies be directed to the all-absorbing constructive efforts which Peace demands.[6]

From 1921 to 1928, Margaret Llewelyn Davies was one of the moving spirits in the Society for Cultural Relations with Russia. Although she deplored Bolshevik violence and intolerance, she sympathized with the efforts of the Russians to create the first socialist state – perhaps in spite of their rulers. Later she became more wholeheartedly convinced by Gandhian *ahimsa*. When she was over 80 she transcribed in shaky handwriting in the last volume of her Commonplace Book Romain Rolland's 'Do not complain of not reaching the end: rejoice in taking part in a task which extends far beyond the limits of your life' and E. D. Morel's 'Death is nothing. Death will not stop us. The Cause will go on.'[7]

Margaret Llewelyn Davies was never one of those who cared about humanity in general while failing to respond to the desperate needs of individuals. On the contrary, it was she who coped with the misery in her brother Arthur's family when the five Llewelyn Davies boys (the 'lost boys' of J. M. Barrie's life[8]) were losing both their parents to cancer; it was she who took responsibility for her aged father until his death in 1916; it was she who went to grieve with her brother Maurice's family when they lost their only son, killed in October 1918, just weeks before the Armistice, and it was she who gave tremendous, and essential, moral support to Leonard Woolf during the terrible years 1913 and 1915, so that he in turn did not feel driven to abandon his mentally deranged wife to an asylum.[9] 'No one ever suffered so much for others, I believe', her great-niece Mary wrote on her death.[10]

1. Katherine Llewelyn Davies, niece of Margaret Llewelyn Davies, after 1944: family papers, c/o Jane Wynne Willson, Birmingham.
2. For Margaret Llewelyn Davies's work with the Women's Co-operative Guild see Margaret Llewelyn Davies (ed.), *Maternity: Letters from Working Women* (London, G. Bell, 1915; republished London, Virago, 1978); Margaret Llewelyn Davies (ed.), *Life as We Have Known It*, by Co-operative Working Women with an Introduction by Virginia Woolf (London, Hogarth Press, 1931;

republished London, Virago, 1977); J. Gaffin and D. Thom, *Caring and Sharing: The Centenary History of the Co-operative Women's Guild* (Manchester, Holyoake House, 1983); and Gill Scott, 'A trade-union for married women' in Sybil Oldfield (ed.), *This Working-Day World: Women's Lives and Culture(s) in Britain 1914–1945* (London and Bristol, PA, Taylor and Francis, 1994).

3. *Manchester Guardian* (24.6.1914).
4. See Appendix I; Sybil Oldfield, *Spinsters of This Parish* (London, Virago, 1984), ch. 9; and Anne Wiltsher, *Most Dangerous Women: Feminist Peace Campaigners of the Great War* (London, Pandora, 1985).
5. Margaret Llewelyn Davies, 'Farewell words to the Guild' (31.12.1921). See also Naomi Black, 'The Mothers' International: the Women's Co-operative Guild and feminist pacifism', *Women's Studies International Forum*, **7**(6) (1984), pp. 467–76.
6. W. J. Chamberlain, *Fighting for Peace: The Story of the War Resistance Movement* (London, No More War Movement, 1928), Appendix.
7. I am grateful to Margaret Llewelyn Davies's great-niece Jane Wynne Willson for allowing me access to the Commonplace Book.
8. See Andrew Birkin, *J. M. Barrie and the Lost Boys* (London, Constable, 1979).
9. See Sybil Oldfield, 'Margaret Llewelyn Davies and Leonard Woolf' in W. K. Chapman and J. M. Manson (eds), *Women in the Milieu of Leonard and Virginia Woolf: Peace, Politics, and Education* (New York, Pace University Press, 1998).
10. Letter to Dolly Ponsonby, Shulbrede papers, 1944.

See also obituaries for Margaret Llewelyn Davies in *The Labour Woman* (July 1944); and *Manchester Guardian* (2.6.1944); and articles in the *Missing Persons* volume of the *Dictionary of National Biography*; and in J. M. Bellamy, and J. Saville (eds), *Dictionary of Labour Biography*, vol. 1 (London, Macmillan, 1972).

—◆—

DEARMER, MABEL
(1872–11.7.1915)

WRITER; PACIFIST MEDICAL RELIEF WORKER

Father: Surgeon Major William White

Christian

Mabel Dearmer, a 'vital and brilliant woman',[1] had established a reputation for herself as a successful book illustrator, children's writer and producer of children's theatre when she volunteered in 1915 to accompany Mrs St Clair Stobart's Hospital Unit, for which her clergyman husband Percy Dearmer had just been appointed chaplain, to Serbia. She herself was a convinced Christian pacifist, deeply in sympathy with the vision of MAUDE ROYDEN, even though both her sons had already volunteered to fight against Germany.

What is remarkable about Mabel Dearmer is the steadfastness with which she testified to her anti-militarist internationalism even while dispensing linen for the wounded in a wartime field hospital. Throughout 1915 Mabel Dearmer wrote her 'dispatches' from the front to her literary friend Stephen Gwynn:

> Everything is so curiously mixed up. We are friends and enemies all together – half our wounded are Austrian – and strangest of all, the head doctor of the Serbian Hospital is an Austrian prisoner. He is a wonderful man, and looked after and treated 200 wounded all alone. He was taken prisoner, and never stopped his work of saving life – first as an officer of his own army, then as a doctor among the Serbs . . . We have had more than 100 patients a day at the wayside dispensary – ill with typhus, scarlet fever, intermittent fever and diptheria [*sic*] . . .
>
> The 'enemy' came to tea to-day – the Austrian doctor who is a prisoner here and has worked for the Serbian wounded so nobly that he is head of the Military

Hospital – and *a prisoner* – Oh, isn't it strange? He has in bad times dressed 500 wounds a day – besides operations – sleeping for a few hours at a time and eating when he can – and this for the *enemy*. Greater love hath no man than this, that a man lay down his life for his enemy. He only spoke German and a few words of English. Of course people are raving over the horror of the 'Lusitania' . . . If I never saw you or Geoffrey or Christopher [her sons] any more, I could no more be angry with the men or the nation that had taken you all from me than I could with an earthquake. It is all ignorance and folly, and we are working out through it to ordinary sense. The only way to see war is from a hospital . . .

War is the devil's own. When I see these wounded here I get a new obsession. I don't see you and Geoff and Chris hurt, but I see all the men that you and Geoff and Chris are going to hurt as these men are hurt and *that* is the un-bearable thing. This war will not bring peace, no war will bring peace, only terrific virtues such as loving one's enemy can bring a terrific thing like peace . . .

[The Serbs'] whole talk is of fighting. They are human beings wasted. As soon as they are well they want to go and fight again.They are like fighting dogs or cocks. That is what war has done for them – killed their souls . . . What chance would Christ have today?[2]

A few days later Mabel Dearmer was diagnosed as having typhus, and within a month she was dead.

1. David Mitchell, *Women on the Warpath* (London, Jonathan Cape, 1966), p. 160.
2. Mabel Dearmer, *Letters from a Field Hospital in Serbia*, edited by Stephen Gwynn (London, Macmillan, 1916).

See also Nan Dearmer, *The Life of Percy Dearmer* (London, Jonathan Cape, 1940).

DESPARD, CHARLOTTE
(15.6.1844–10.11.1939)

RADICAL SOCIAL INTERVENTIONIST; AGITATOR AGAINST OPPRESSION AND WAR

Father: William French, retired naval captain
Mother: Margaret, née Eccles

Catholic by conversion, later Theosophist

Charlotte Despard was a Shelleyan rebel all her life against what she believed to be *remediable* human suffering. When she was 93, in 1937, she was still saying: 'The terrible part of our social system is that it is so cruel . . . We must get away from the "I" in life, from dogmas and from creeds.'[1] She emerged from the acute depression of widowhood in 1890, and, renouncing her personal wealth and privilege, volunteered to be '*solidaire*' with the unprivileged for the rest of her life, living ascetically and suffering imprisonment, mockery and even, on occasions, stoning in the cause of that solidarity. At Nine Elms, Battersea, a notoriously wretched part of London in the 1890s, she opened its first child welfare centre with her own money and became a radical, dedicated Poor Law Guardian in Lambeth until 1903.[2] The Women's Freedom League that she founded in 1908 and led, breaking away from the despotic Pank-hurst-commanded Women's Social and Political Union, concentrated on campaigning for the vote for women as a *human* right in order to help working women to achieve a living wage and to protect women in the home from domestic violence by themselves having a part in drafting legislation and administering the judicial system.[3] In 1907 Mrs Despard led the Women's Suffrage 'Mud March' to the House of Commons that was obstructed by mounted and foot police, who arrested her. In 1908 with the Women's Freedom League at Maidstone 'she was met with a shower of broken granite and pebbles, some of which struck her in the face and caused her to bleed'.[4] She was 64. Her calm fearlessness in the van of unpopular demonstrations always lent courage to the less naturally intrepid.

Charlotte Despard, aged 91, addressing an anti-fascist rally, Trafalgar Square, 1935

The First World War found Charlotte Despard opposed politically to her beloved younger brother Sir John French, Commander in Chief of the British Expeditionary Force. For her, the 'Great War' was a crime against the people by their leaders. She was on the British Committee supporting the Women's International Congress in The Hague in 1915[5] and one of the founders of the Women's International League for Peace and Freedom; she opposed conscription and, in her mid-seventies, spoke up and down the country at huge meetings for the 'Women's Peace Crusade' to end the war (1917–18). She outfaced the hostile crowds who roared at her: 'We don't want German peace terms!'[6] At the Women's International League Congress in Zürich in 1919, she made a deep impression on the delegates from all the former belligerent nations in her passionate commitment to a new humane world order. Together with Jane Addams and CHRYSTAL MACMILLAN, she went in person to Paris to present the Women's International League's prescient criticism of the Treaty of Versailles, indicting the Allied blockade, the imposition of reparations and the one-sided disarming of the defeated.[7] On her return to Britain she worked to raise money for the new Save the Children Fund.

Throughout the 1920s Mrs Despard, a campaigner for the unification of a republican Ireland, and now living in Dublin, also championed the beleaguered Catholic ghettos in Belfast and supported the Women's Prisoners' Defence League on behalf of hunger-striking Sinn Feiners in Dublin. '[The women] were spat at, hosed upon and even shot at.'[8] Ironically, it was a Catholic anti-Communist mob which later besieged and wrecked her left-wing Irish Workers' College there. At the age of 83, in 1927 she was designated a dangerous character under Section XIII of the Public Safety Act, liable to expulsion from Ireland, and in 1931 over 30 Free State CID men battered down her door in Dublin with their gun butts and gutted her house, vainly trying to find an arms cache. Throughout the 1930s she supported the Spanish Republicans and the cause of anti-fascism, addressing a rally in Trafalgar Square at the age of 91.

Mrs Despard did not seek out underdogs or hopeless causes or martyrdom. She simply felt so addressed by injustice and cruelty that she had to speak out and act against them, trying to counter society's wrongs with her every breath, and always hoping that *this* time the fraternal, merciful and co-operative impulses in human beings would win the day. Maud Gonne, in tears at her funeral, described her as 'a white flame in defence of prisoners and the oppressed'.[9]

1. Interview in *Manchester Guardian* (16.6.1937).
2. Margaret Mulvihill, *Charlotte Despard* (London, Pandora, 1989), ch. 5.
3. See the Women's Freedom League paper *The Vote*, in the Women's Library, London, *passim*.
4. Mulvihill, *op. cit.*, p. 91.
5. See Introduction and Appendix I.
6. David Mitchell, *Women on the Warpath: The Story of the Women of the First World War* (London, Jonathan Cape, 1966), 'The lady in the black mantilla', pp. 301–12; and Jill Liddington, *The Long Road to Greenham: Feminism and Anti-Militarism in Britain since 1820* (London, Virago, 1989), ch. 9: 'The Women's Peace Crusade 1916–18'.
7. G. Timms and M. Bussey, *Pioneers for Peace: The Women's International League for Peace and Freedom 1915–1965* (London, WILPF, 1980), pp. 31–3.
8. Mulvihill, *op. cit.*, p. 144.
9. *Ibid.*, p. 194.

See also Andro Linklater's fine study *An Unhusbanded Life: Charlotte Despard: Suffragette, Socialist and Sinn Feiner* (London, Hutchinson, 1980); obituaries in *The Times* (11.11 and 14.11.1939); and entry in the *Missing Persons* volume of the *Dictionary of National Biography*.

✦✦

DOUGHTY-WYLIE, LILIAN OIMARA, OBE
(1878–1961)

MEDICAL RELIEF WORKER WORLDWIDE

Father: John Wylie, businessman, Devon and later Hampshire squire
Mother: Minnie, née Woods

Lilian Doughty-Wylie set herself to relieve the suffering of whomsoever was to hand, and in desperate need, wherever she found herself on earth. Over her 80-odd years she worked in Asia, Europe, Africa and the Middle East. While married to her first husband Dr C. H. Adams, Indian Medical Society, she established a relief centre for refugees at Bombay in 1899 when she was only 21. Widowed, she married in 1904 Charles Doughty, a former professional soldier seeking work in the consular service; they both took the name Doughty-Wylie. While stationed in Asia Minor in 1909, her husband twice beat back an infuriated Turkish mob attempting to massacre Armenian Christians at Adana. On his being seconded to Addis Ababa, Lilian Doughty-Wylie took a midwifery course and organized the training of midwives in Abyssinia.

When the Balkan War broke out in 1912 Charles Doughty-Wylie became chief director of the Red Cross units on the Turkish side while Lilian Doughty-Wylie organized the nursing staff and two emergency hospitals in Constantinople. Her husband was posthumously awarded the VC for his gallantry at Gallipoli. Thereafter his widow established hospitals in the Pas de Calais and in Salonika. In 1926 she went to Romania to set up an Anglo-Romanian dispensary for women and children in Bucharest, where she remained until Romania was about to be overrun by the Nazis. She then joined the French in Syria, first organizing a convalescent home for war wounded in Beirut and then one in Cairo until 1945, by which time she was 67. She died in Cyprus, known to British servicemen and others as 'the ministering angel of Akrotiri'.[1]

1. See entry for Charles Doughty-Wylie in *Dictionary of National Biography, 1912–1921*; and obituary for Lilian Doughty-Wylie, *The Times* (27.4.1961).

DUNBAR, ETHEL GORDON
(*c*.1885–January 1930)

NURSE; RELIEF WORKER

Father: Lt Col. Arbuthnott Dunbar of the Gordon Highlanders, Murrayshire

Quaker attender

Ethel Dunbar, a trained nurse who had specialized in mental nursing, moved away from her military family's background to identify herself with the Quaker devotion to the civilian victims of war (1914–21). First she worked with the Friends' relief efforts for French refugees in northern France, being awarded the Médaille de la Reconnaissance Française: 'elle s'est signalée entre toutes par son abnégation et son dévouement constants.' She next tended Serbian and Greek refugees in Salonika. In 1919 she volunteered for service in Poland. Discovering that the worst conditions of all prevailed in the prison camp at Bialystok, she and her friend Miss Leigh volunteered to go there. They found 3,000 prisoners with no heating or blankets and very little food, and almost without medical attention. Up to 80 per cent of the inmates were ill with dysentery, typhus or tuberculosis, 30 to 50 dying every day. Inevitably under those conditions, as they had both foreseen, Ethel Dunbar and her friend themselves went down with typhus in December 1919. 'The kind of courage it requires to go into a camp of this kind and live, working day and night, is what the American Red Cross needs more of in its work.'[1]

After recovering, as she thought, Ethel Dunbar took a course in midwifery to qualify her for more work with refugees, this time in France once again, only to collapse with pleurisy. Finally, she and Miss Leigh went out to Salonika as independent volunteer health workers among the Greek refugees expelled from Turkey. She contracted tuberculosis, an after-effect of the typhus she had nearly died from in Poland, and, though she tried to combat it and work whenever there was a period of remission, she died nine years later.

1. American Red Cross report, quoted in *The Times* obituary (7.1.1930).

See also obituary in *The Friend* (17.1.1930); and 'Index of Friends' War Victims' Relief Committee workers, 1914–1921' in the archives, Friends' House Library, London.

E

ELLIS, MARIAN, LADY PARMOOR
(1875–6.7.1952)

ANTI-WAR CAMPAIGNER;
WRITER ON DISARMAMENT

Father: John Ellis, Liberal MP, PC
Mother: Maria, née Rowntree

Quaker

Marian Ellis, Lady Parmoor, c. 1920 (By kind permission of Tony Cripps, Lord Parmoor)

Brought up in a radical Liberal family of considerable wealth, Marian Ellis was early involved in public affairs, acting as her father's secretary in 1900. At the close of the Boer War in 1901 she assisted RUTH FRY's Quaker relief projects for women victims of the war. From the very outbreak of the First World War, Marian Ellis spoke out against the chivalrous self-sacrifice of the young men volunteering to kill for a good cause. She and her twin sister Edith gave away huge sums of money in order to support the struggling families of imprisoned conscientious objectors after 1916, and it was they who largely financed the No Conscription Fellowship (NCF).[1] (Edith Ellis was actually imprisoned in Holloway in 1918 under the Defence of the Realm Act for joining with other Quakers to print a leaflet *A Challenge to Militarism* without first submitting it to the government censor.[2]) Marian Ellis herself had done much 'thinking against the current'[3] on the age-old issue of 'just war' and she had helped draft the anonymous Quaker pamphlet of 1915 expressing their absolutist pacifist stand:

> War, tyranny and revolt have produced tyranny, revolt and war throughout time . . . We maintain that the moral law is binding upon States as upon individuals . . . We hold that the fundamental interests of humanity are one . . . the reasoned worship of force [is] the real devil-worship.[4]

In her later pamphlet *The Spiritual Aspect of International Unity*, Marian Ellis pointed out:

> History is full of instances of an ideal being lost through the methods of its advocates. We are always trying to cast out Satan, if not by Satan exactly, at

least by one of the smallest of his angels . . . [The] pacifist stands for a conception of life in which the contribution of each [human being] is needed.[5]

And in 1917 she also wrote:

At the end of this war the world will have to decide which way it desires to go, towards disarmament or destruction . . . Disarmament is not merely scrapping our guns and our battleships. It is the working out of a national policy, which, being inspired by love for all men, cannot be antagonistic . . . It is the problem of India, of Ireland, of our relations with Russia and Persia, Germany and Belgium as God would have them to be.[6]

At the end of the First World War Marian Ellis, soon to become Lady Parmoor (and the stepmother of Stafford Cripps), volunteered to do 'all the grind and most of the paying too'[7] to establish the Fight the Famine Committee. Thereafter, until her death in 1952, she testified consistently to her unweaponed faith, warning as early as 1928 that 'The enormous development of the power of armaments both during and since the Great War has brought mankind within measureable distance of destruction'.[8] Throughout the 1930s she played a significant part in the India Conciliation Group that came near to resolving the issues at stake between Gandhi and the British government.[9] In her last years she advocated the admission of Communist China to the United Nations Organization and studied nuclear fission in order to discuss both the uses and the dangers of nuclear power. Two days before she died, she helped draft a Quaker message to the Prime Minister protesting against the aerial bombardment of North Korea.[10]

1. See entries for CATHERINE MARSHALL, ADA SALTER and VIOLET TILLARD.
2. See John Graham, *Conscription and Conscience* (London, George Allen & Unwin, 1922); and transcript of Edith Ellis's unsuccessful Appeal (3.7.1918) held in Friends' House Library, London.
3. Virginia Woolf, 'Thoughts on peace in an air-raid', written September 1940, first published posthumously in *The Death of the Moth and Other Essays* (London, Hogarth Press, 1942).
4. *Looking towards Peace* (issued by the Peace Committee of the Society of Friends; London, Headley Bros, 1915), pp. 4, 5, 7 and 15.
5. See Sybil Oldfield, 'England's Cassandras in World War One' in Sybil Oldfield (ed.), *This Working-Day World: Women's Lives and Culture(s) in Britain 1914–1945* (London and Bristol, PA, Taylor and Francis, 1994).
6. Marian Ellis, 'Disarmament (1)', *Friends' Quarterly Examiner* (1917), pp. 182–7.
7. Kate Courtney, *A War Diary* (privately printed, London), entry for 29.1.1919.
8. W. T. Chamberlain, *Fighting for Peace: The Story of the War Resistance Movement* (London, No More War Movement, 1928), Appendix.
9. See Chris Bryant, *Stafford Cripps* (London, Hodder and Stoughton, 1997), pp. 210–11.
10. See obituaries in *The Friend* (July and August 1952); *The Times* (7.7, 10.7 and 18.7. 1952); *Manchester Guardian* (8.7.1952).

ENGLAND, DOROTHY
(24.11.1906–   )

NURSE WITH SAVE THE CHILDREN;
EMERGENCY WORK FOR DISPLACED
PERSONS AND GERMANS

*Father: Arthur England, blind chair- and
basket-maker, Christian Socialist*
Mother: Ruth, née Little, Christian Socialist

Quaker by convincement

*Dorothy England feeding a displaced
person, Germany, 1946 (Courtesy of
Dorothy England)*

The largest enforced mass movement of people in the history of Europe after the Holocaust was the expulsion of Germans from their former eastern territories and from the Sudetenland and Poland in 1945–47, swollen by the voluntary mass flight of Germans attempting, for economic, political and/or other reasons, to escape from what they feared as 'Russian Bolshevism' in East Germany (the Soviet Zone). Eight million survivors of the trek westwards, many of them mothers, children and the elderly, arrived destitute, cold and hungry into receiving stations or barrack-like camps. They were almost totally dependent on a combination of very basic international aid and (minimal) West German funds for refugees.

Dorothy England, a German-speaking experienced general and paediatric nurse, health visitor and midwife with specialist training in infectious diseases and tuberculosis, asked to be sent to devastated Germany in 1946 as a relief worker. In part she went for personal reasons. Before the war she had lived with a German Jewish family, teaching them English before emigration, and she had made a deeply significant friendship with a German Quaker, Maria Pleissner, a schoolteacher who had been sacked and arrested by the Nazis for helping Jews and who had then suffered two years' incarceration in Ravensbrück. It was through her and her circle in Germany that Dorothy England herself had been introduced to what became a lifetime's commitment to Quakerism. Other Quakers who inspired her were MARY FRIEDRICH, JOAN FRY, Elizabeth Fox Howard, and Gwen and Corder Catchpole. Partly in the hope of a reunion with Maria Pleissner, who lived in the Soviet Zone (and whom she did manage to find again), Dorothy England volunteered for work with the Save the Children Fund in its attempt to make conditions more supportable for Germany's displaced persons and later for bombed-out German nationals.

From July 1946 to January 1947 Dorothy England was part of the Save the Children's Fund medical/nursing team in Schlutup near Lübeck, where part of a huge ammunition factory was being transformed into a hospital for non-German children from the nearby displaced persons camps. There, despite the language barriers, she trained 'displaced' girls from the Baltic States and Poland in basic, practical nursing techniques. However, she wanted to apply her social work and nursing experience more directly, and she also wanted to do something for the Germans, believing as she did that the Allies' retributive policies at Versailles, and after, had contributed to the emergence of Nazism. She believed it was high time

Teaching the linking of hands, Germany, 1947 (Courtesy of Dorothy England)

to attempt reconciliation. Organized relief work for German children was not permitted until the beginning of 1947 but, the moment that it was allowed, Dorothy England applied to be transferred to the Save the Children project in Brunswick in January 1947.

After first contacting the local Medical Officer of Health, the Mayor, and officials from Arbeiterwohlfahrt, Caritas and the German Red Cross to discover what was most desperately needed, Dorothy England started a shelter for homeless German children in a dilapidated sanatorium which they refurbished with the help of local welfare organizations. She and her team partners, Margot Rue and later Alice Glanville, also took on the visiting of hospitals, schools and children's homes, the distribution of clothes and of British Red Cross Commission supplies including medical dressings, and helped to run feeding centres. It was the terrible winter of 1946–47. They found children with pneumonia in children's wards with broken windows; they saw bands of children roaming and foraging for food; they took much-needed supplies to outlying children's homes in the Harz mountains. At one orphanage they found the children dirty, neglected and treated as imbeciles; but once given decent supplies and treatment the children were completely transformed and proved to be normal in every way. The Save the Children team worked with the German Red Cross search team looking for the families of lost, orphaned or abandoned children, sometimes achieving joyful reunions with relatives both sides of the frontier. In an attempt to reconcile Germans, Poles and other displaced persons, they liaised with the Quaker DP team to organize a 'cocoa club' with games and dancing for the children to learn to join hands – and where the parents might also begin to fraternize.

From February 1948 until August 1949 Dorothy England volunteered to work as the SCF representative at the German Transit and Screening Camp at Uelzen. More than 100,000 people passed through that camp, near Hanover in the British Zone, some of them staying for as long as three months. At first it was German refugees and expellees from Silesia and Sudetenland, some having walked or hitchhiked hundreds of miles and crossed the frontier illegally. Later thousands of expellees arrived in goods trains in the middle of the night from Denmark. All dreamed of settling in West Germany or emigrating to Canada or the USA; hundreds were sent back to the Soviet Zone because they had no papers.

Dorothy England had to start a hospital from scratch in two barracks that had only filthy straw on the bunks, with sometimes a mother and child blue with cold and without blankets sharing one bunk; only one outside lavatory for 80 patients, no crockery, just old food tins to eat out of, and one 15-watt light bulb in each barrack. 'It was a bit of a mess. I didn't know where to start.'[1] There was a general atmosphere of anxiety, fear of one another and depression, as well as physical misery. Dorothy England did not judge or speculate about the past of these refugees; she simply concentrated on responding to their acute need. She separated the infectious from the non-infectious; she put the sick babies into a separate Nissen hut with cots, food and proper nursing care; she organized the making of ammunition boxes into coal cupboards and drawers for the refugees' remaining possessions. With her two colleagues Margot and Alice from Brunswick, she collected and distributed food and clothing supplies, including tins of horse meat for the bombed-out bunker-dwellers in the town, and saw to the making of sheets and pillowcases. They took parties of undernourished children out to the woods to collect mushrooms and bilberries and have an outing in the country. Slowly the place began to approximate to a tolerable medical centre. Eventually it became one of the model camp hospitals in the Federal Republic. 'I only wish it could be conveyed to [Dorothy England and her team] somehow that they are remembered now, twelve years after they left Uelzen, with the same warm love and gratitude as when I first took over their work.'[2]

1. Interview with the author.
2. Bridget Stevenson, SCF Administrator in Germany, 'Looking back at Germany: a survey of SCF work in Germany 1949–1962', *The World's Children* (1962).

See also Douglas Botting, *In the Ruins of the Reich* (London, George Allen & Unwin, 1985); Dorothy England, 'Report of Uelzen German Refugee Transit Camp Feb. 1948–Feb. 1949', typescript sent to SCF headquarters, London.

EVANS, DOROTHY ELIZABETH
(6.5.1888–26.8.1944)

HUMANIST FEMINIST CAMPAIGNER

Father: Edward Evans, commercial clerk, London
Mother: Marian, née Smith

Freethinker

Dorothy Evans was a bonny fighter in the cause of the equal citizenship of women the world over. A qualified High School teacher of gymnastics and mathematics, she gave up her career for the suffrage struggle. Imprisoned nine times, she undertook hunger and thirst strikes and was forcibly fed. She was a pacifist supporter of the Women's International Congress at The Hague in 1915.[1] 'War she regarded as the ultimate barbarity and she addressed howling mobs begging them to insist on international arbitration rather than engage in . . . slaughter.'[2]

Once the vote had been won in Britain, Dorothy Evans focused on the League of Nations and in particular on the International Labour Organization, organizing lobbies and deputations at Geneva, year after year, to pressure the League to remember the oppressed status of women worldwide with a view to its amelioration.

She was instrumental in defeating an ILO Convention prohibiting the employment of 'indigenous' women workers outside their own villages except as domestic servants. As Honorary Secretary of the Women's Consultative Committee created by the Council of the League of Nations, she organized the deputation led by the American women's leader Dr Alice Paul in 1939, urging that the ILO should incorporate in its constitution:

(1) a provision requiring that all conventions concluded under the ILO be founded upon the principle of equal rights for men and women, and

(2) a provision requiring that there be both men and women, with equal voting rights, in all delegations to the meeting and conferences held under the auspices of the ILO.[3]

Dorothy Evans was always a battler for the civil liberties of women and for their full social, economic, political and legal equality with men. Her last book was *The Equal Citizenship Bill*. In the Second World War she worked unremittingly, and successfully, for British women civilians injured by enemy action, often as workers in the civil defence services, to be compensated equally with their male counterparts. As in the First World War, she felt compelled yet again to be an unpopular pacifist. She used to say that she felt 'the hand on the scruff of her neck', to describe an inward moral compulsion.[4] A lifelong socialist, she was praised after her death as having been indeed a tireless tribune of the people.

Dorothy Evans lived her personal life according to her commitment to responsible individual freedom and fulfilment, having a daughter (whom she called Lyndal after Olive Schreiner's heroine) by the socialist Emil Davies outside marriage. Nevertheless, despite her own personal rejection of marriage, she fought for the rights of the housewife and mother, actually founding the Married Women's Association. She died suddenly, 'in harness', having just addressed a public meeting in Glasgow. SYBIL THORNDIKE wrote of her: 'It's a wonderful thing to meet a soul of fire . . . She never sat down and accepted the wrongs of the world. She fought wrong with the right weapons – truth, honesty, . . . friendship and . . . zeal.'[5] MARGERY CORBETT ASHBY, VERA BRITTAIN, EMMELINE PETHICK-LAWRENCE, REBECCA SIEFF, Dr Edith Summerskill and MONICA WHATELY also paid tribute to Dorothy Evans's tireless moral courage and energy on behalf of the human rights of women everywhere.[6]

1. See Introduction and Appendix I.
2. Monica Whately, 'Dorothy Evans, the story of a militant' in Claire Madden (ed.), *Dorothy Evans and the Six Point Group* (London, 1946), p. 46, held in Women's Library, London.
3. Dorothy Evans, *The Six Point Group: A Brief Account of Its National and International Work* (pamphlet; London, 1946).
4. See Monica Whately, *op. cit.*, p. 57 and Anon., 'Dorothy Evans: an appreciation', *International Women's News* (August–September 1944), pp. 5, 6.
5. See Whately, *op. cit.*, p. 73.
6. Obituary appreciations in Whately, *op. cit.* See also entry for Dorothy Evans in Elizabeth Crawford, *The Women's Suffrage Movement: A Reference Guide, 1866–1928* (London, UCL Press, 1999).

F

FARRER, ELLEN MARGARET, MB, BS
(20.9.1865–14.10.1959)

PIONEER MEDICAL MISSIONARY IN INDIA, SERVING WOMEN

Father: Reverend William Farrer, Nonconformist minister, Hampstead

Baptist

On 17 October 1891 Dr Ellen Farrer, MB, BS London, left for India to work for the Baptist Zenana[1] Mission as their first woman doctor at Bhiwani in the Punjab. 'She soon won the love and trust of women patients, who were unwilling to be seen by the male doctor at the local government dispensary.'[2] During the famine years of 1896–98, helped by other women missionaries, she was responsible for dispensing relief to the many thousands of 'famine refugees' from outlying districts. Between 1903 and 1908 there were annual outbreaks of bubonic plague; Dr Farrer did a great deal of preventive inoculation work besides visiting the stricken patients abandoned by their own families, 'but the mortality was high and it was sad work'.[3] She also supervised the building of a hospital at Bhiwani and the opening of dispensaries at Dadri and Hansi, despite much distrust and discouragement. '[She] was seldom, if ever, ruffled and the only adjective she used concerning a difficult situation or person was "tiresome".'[4] Her knowledge of Punjabi enabled her to translate medical textbooks for nurses and midwives and she also served as secretary of the Women's Medical Association of India for many years. Of her meticulous work until her retirement at 68 in 1933 it was said: 'She spared no pains to arrive at a correct diagnosis and never allowed her frail body to overrule her indomitable spirit.'[5] Although it had been feared that her health would not survive another term in India in 1900 and again in 1921, in fact she lived to be 94, having continued her translation of medical textbooks long after her retirement. The government of India awarded her the Kaiser-i-Hind gold medal first class with bar.

1. See entry for MARGARET BALFOUR
2. Obituary in 'Memoirs of ministers and missionaries', *Baptist Handbook* (1961), p. 347.
3. Jean Benzie, quoting Dr Farrer in obituary, *Medical Women's Federation Review* (December 1959), p. 47; held in Contemporary Medical Archives Centre, Wellcome Institute for the History of Medicine, London.
4. *Ibid.*, p. 48.
5. *Baptist Handbook, loc. cit.*

See also Zenana Mission Reports (1892–93, 1894–95 and 1896–97), Baptist Missionary Society, Angus Library, Regent's Park College, Oxford.

FORD, ISABELLA ORMISTON

(23.5.1855–14.7.1924)

SOCIALIST FEMINIST PACIFIST

Father: Robert Ford, Quaker, reformist radical
wealthy landowner, solicitor
Mother: Hannah, née Pease, Quaker radical

Quaker

Isabella Ford (From Common Cause,
1913. Courtesy of British Library,
Newspaper Library, Colindale)

The youngest of the eight children born of radical reformist parents, Isabella Ford linked in her own person the great mid-nineteenth-century humanitarian causes – anti-slavery, the liberation of minorities, the emancipation of women – with the twentieth century's first efforts at socialist redistribution of money and effective internationalism via a League of Nations. She was nurtured on reform but grew to advocate non-violent revolution that would construct a new world.

Her first active intervention was to start a night school or adult literacy class for working girls. Next, in her late thirties, she became strike organizer for Leeds factory girls in the tailoring industry, urging them on to rebel. She could not bear that so many exploited women did not dislike 'except dumbly and helplessly, conditions which they ought to dislike, and [did not resent] treatment they ought to resent'.[1] When one of the girls on strike, near starvation, with a drunken father and an invalid sister to support, actually stole the 10 shillings she had collected for the strike fund, Isabella Ford 'was only sorry there was not more in the box. [The poor girl] had awakened to the right to possess something.'[2] She would walk through the sleet and snow with the marching girls on strike, 'often taking insults from the crowds who lined the streets'.[3]

In the early 1890s, Isabella Ford became totally committed, like KATHARINE GLASIER, to the New Life socialism of the Independent Labour Party.[4] It was the 'born again' movement of its time and Isabella Ford became one of its most effective speakers, as she publicized its commitment to creating a more just world. A humanist feminist like MARY SHEEPSHANKS, MAUDE ROYDEN, VIRGINIA WOOLF and others, feminist *because* humanist, wanting both women and men to have fulfilled lives that expressed the creative individuality of each, she soon also became a leading worker in the north of England for women's suffrage. Her socialist trade unionism fused with her feminism as, like ESTHER ROPER, she knocked on hundreds of working-class doors and stood at factory gates, helping to collect tens of thousands of signatures from female textile workers petitioning (in vain) for the vote in 1902.[5]

When put to the agonizing test of the First World War, Isabella Ford felt compelled to separate herself not only from the mass of working-class supporters of the war but also from the majority of her fellow women suffragists, including one of her closest and oldest friends, the National Union of Women's Suffrage Societies' leader Millicent Fawcett:

> Dearest Millie,
>   . . . I hate Prussianism as heartily as you do – and I long for it to go. But I do not think that war ever destroyed war – and real salvation can only come to people and nations from within.[6]

Like MARGARET ASHTON, KATHLEEN COURTNEY, CATHERINE MARSHALL, Maude Royden and HELENA SWANWICK, Isabella Ford resigned from the NUWSS Executive in April 1915, in her determination, with her sister Bessie, to support the anti-war Women's International Congress at The Hague.[7] Thereafter, although now 60, she worked indefatigably for a swift, just and lasting peace in the midst of the war. She wrote to the press; she supported the lonely anti-war voice of the ILP; she leafleted and addressed open-air meetings with VIOLET PAGET and EMILY HOBHOUSE, facing hostile abuse; she joined the Union for the Democratic Control of Foreign Policy, led by E. D. Morel; she gave consistent significant support to the Women's International League in its formative years; she was a delegate to the National Peace Congress in 1917; and she did her utmost to maintain links with women socialists and suffragists across national barriers in 'enemy' territory. Soon after the war, in May 1919, she attended the Congress of the WIL at Zürich where she joined in their unavailing attempt to 'protest against the Peace terms, to abolish conscription and armaments and to raise the [Allied] Blockade'.[8] In June 1920 she went with a delegation from the Fight the Famine Council and the Quakers to the Conservative MP Cecil Harmsworth to ask that food should be sent to Germany. She herself visited Germany and then came back to Britain to speak about the desperate necessity for better international understanding.

At what was almost her last public speech at an international gathering, the Third International Congress of the Women's International League for Peace and Freedom held in still hungry, defeated Vienna in 1921, Isabella Ford quoted her friend Olive Schreiner's consoling conviction 'that no one is alone in the Universe, and that therefore, she was not alone in her hatred of cruelty and evil, but was one amongst many who hated it and were striving to conquer it'.[9]

1. Isabella Ford, 'Industrial women and how to help them' (London, Humanitarian League, 1903), p. 11. See also Isabella Ford, 'Women's wages' (Humanitarian League, 1893), quoted in June Hannam, *Isabella Ford* (Oxford, Basil Blackwell, 1989), p. 51.
2. Quoted in Hannam, *op. cit.*, p. 48.
3. *Ibid.*
4. See S. Yeo, 'A New Life: the religion of socialism in Britain, 1883–1896', *History Workshop Journal*, **4** (1977).
5. Hannam, *op. cit.*, p. 85.
6. Correspondence files, Women's Library, London.
7. See Introduction and Appendix I; and Anne Wiltsher, *Most Dangerous Women: Feminist Peace Campaigners in the Great War* (London, Pandora, 1985).
8. Hannam, *op. cit.*, p. 190.
9. *Ibid.*, p. 197.

See also obituaries for Isabella Ford in *Yorkshire Evening Post* (15.7.1924); *Yorkshire Observer* (16.7.1924); *The Friend* (July 1924); *Daily Herald* (29.7.1924); *Daily Telegraph* (29.7.1924); and *The Times* (29.7.1924).

Isabella Ford's novels are discussed by Chris Waters, 'New women and socialist feminist fiction: the novels of Isabella Ford and Katharine Bruce Glasier' in A. Ingram and D. Patai (eds), *Rediscovering Forgotten Radicals: British Women Writers 1889–1939* (Chapel Hill and London, University of North Carolina Press, 1993).

FOSS, JOSEPHINE, MBE
(19.3.1887–23.7.1983)

PIONEER MISSIONARY TEACHER AND
WELFARE ORGANIZER IN ASIA

Father: Frederick Foss, Croydon solicitor
Mother: Anne, née Bartram

Anglican

Josephine Foss

After her initial Froebel teacher training, specializing
in science subjects, Josephine Foss taught for seven
years in London and Lancashire before training to
become a missionary at St Denys College, War-
minster. After a very strenuous decade between the
ages of 27 and 37 spent as a Society for the
Propagation of the Gospel (SPG) missionary teacher
in China and Zululand (with an interval recovering
from tuberculosis), she was sent by the SPG to St
Mary's Anglican School in Kuala Lumpur. One day in 1924 she discovered, in the
backstreets of Kuala Lumpur, a pitifully basic school for the little daughters of the
Chinese poor run by an elderly, frail English lady, Miss Gage Brown. Josephine
Foss took over when Miss Brown went back to England to die and immediately
found herself struggling for government backing for her 'Pudu English School for
Girls'. 'But money, how much I wanted and how little I got.'[1] Thanks to donations
from the local Chinese, the first kindergarten, primary and secondary classes for
girls in Malaya could begin. Josephine Foss also initiated a Girl Guide movement,
did local welfare work among lepers and battered children, and found herself the
de facto adoptive mother of several abandoned illegitimate little daughters of
prostitutes: 'before long, love and good food had their effect'.[2] Her pupils at the
Pudu Girls' School became the first women doctors, nurses, matrons, accountants,
therapists, teachers and lawyers in Malaya.

When the Japanese started bombing Singapore in 1941, 'I remember the School
Certificate examinations were on just then and I really did not take the raids very
seriously'.[3] However, the war came ever closer and she soon had to help with the
British wounded in the hospitals. Evacuated from Kuala Lumpur to Singapore, she
felt she could not leave the sinking ship but continued at the casualty centre, keeping
the sterilizer going and sorting the Chinese dead from the wounded, the seriously
from the less seriously injured. Bombed out, she dug latrine trenches in the garden
of a Rescue Home full of prostitute mothers with their babies – 'how useful my
Guiding was'.[4] When the Japanese started shelling the city,

> I [was] much more scared of shells than bombs, coward that I am and it was
> often as much as I could do to take what courage I had left in my hands to go
> up [the] outside staircase to my babies, who needed the most attention when
> the noise was greatest outside.[5]

The worst moment of Josephine Foss's life came when Singapore fell and she
and the remaining British women were marched to Changi prison camp. She was
interned for three and a half years, trying to keep up her own and her fellow

prisoners' spirits, organizing work and sewing parties as well as clandestine meetings of husbands and wives during dustbin duty; but also enduring punishment, interrrogation and the fear of interrogation on top of sickness and chronic, acute hunger.[6] After the war the Colonial Office sent her an official commendation 'for the exceptional services she had rendered to her comrades in captivity during a long period of great hardship'. On her release she was too ill and weak to walk; she had lost almost all her hair as well as five stone in weight. But former Chinese pupils from Pudu, now in India, found her and cherished her back to the beginnings of renewed health.

In July 1948, now 61, Josephine Foss returned to Singapore. No longer a headmistress, she had new work, training the first generation of Malaya's welfare officers. She went to hospitals, orphanages, leper settlements and gaols and personally demonstrated the harmlessness of being a blood donor. But once the Emergency of the Communist insurgency began in Malaya, the government used her as an interpreter of Mandarin Chinese in the courts trying young Chinese suspects. She then had to trace and reunite the families of the Communists willing to be repatriated to mainland China. (As well as Mandarin, she could speak Malay, and more than a smattering of Cantonese.)

> [The] whole thing seemed such a tragedy, the young men and women who were caught were often quite charming folk carried away by the fanatical communists . . . The most horrible part of my job was the round-up [with the Gurkhas]. The thing I hated most was when with glee they brought in a dead bandit, often so pathetically young.[7]

She herself had been told by one of the insurgents she 'was not worth a bullet'. On one occasion an elderly Communist, who knew her, showed her a track back through the jungle after her train had been blown up – 'How kind and thoughtful he was.'[8] All in all, it was a huge relief to return to welfare work.

Josephine Foss then organized programmes to tackle adult female illiteracy and health campaigns against malaria and yaws; she took salt, clothes and medicines by jeep and jungle canoe to inaccessible Malay villages, often having to cross rapids on foot. Finally, after starting up schools for boys among the Dayaks (she met only a few head-hunters as she travelled up country by river), she left Sarawak for England at the age of 70.

> After such an active and eventful life I could not settle down to doing nothing, so I started coaching foreigners in English and helping English people who had to learn Malay or Mandarin. [In particular] I was determined to teach Japanese ladies to show that I had no permanent hate against them.[9]

1. Josephine Foss, 'Unpublished memoir', typescript in SPG archive, Rhodes House, Park Road, Oxford, ch. 5, p. 30. (Hereafter all citations of 'Foss' are from this work.)
2. Foss, ch. 8, p. 42.
3. Foss, ch. 9, p. 48.
4. Foss, ch. 9, p. 51.
5. Foss, ch. 9, p. 52.
6. See entry for CICELY WILLIAMS; and Foss, ch. 10: 'The Changi rat', pp. 55–67.
7. Foss, ch. 14, p. 82; ch. 15, pp. 85 and 86.
8. Foss, ch. 15, p. 87.
9. Foss, ch. 19, p. 99.

See also obituary, *The Times* (4.8.1983).

FREEMAN, KATHLEEN, OBE

(1890–15.4.1966)

RESCUER OF REFUGEE CHILDREN;
SAVE THE CHILDREN FUND
ORGANIZER

*Father: Jack Barnato Joel, millionaire South
African gold and diamond mine-owner,
financier, racehorse breeder*
Mother: Olive, née Sopwith

*Congregationalist, member of the Church
Assembly; founder member of the Council of
Christians and Jews*

Kathleen Freeman, in The World's
Children, *June 1966 (Reproduced by
permission of Save the Children (UK))*

Kindly, intelligent and humorous, Kathleen Freeman was remembered after her death for her exceptional, practical humanism.[1] 'Her heart was as big as the causes she espoused and her sympathy and concern were expressed in direct and practical ways.'[2] Not only did she engage actively in refugee work, helping to get at least some of the victims of Nazi persecution out of central Europe in time, but she also made herself personally responsible for taking a large group of Jewish refugee children into her own home in Watford (c. 1938–45), educating and caring for them all in addition to her own family.

After the Second World War, Kathleen Freeman used her fluency in French, German and Italian, acquired as a young girl studying abroad, to travel widely on behalf of the Save the Children Fund in order to organize relief for the most desperately traumatized and needy children in devastated western Europe. For, as she later quoted EGLANTYNE JEBB: 'Every war, just or unjust, is a war against the child.'[3] In addition to working for the British National Council of Women, of which she became President in 1953, Kathleen Freeman became an outstanding officer of the Save the Children Fund and the International Union for Child Welfare. As Chairman of the UK Committee of the SCF she so energized the organization in Britain that almost 500 branches were formed throughout the country under her leadership, and she later inaugurated the series of SCF International fund-raising fêtes supported by the Diplomatic Corps in London, which, symbolically, showed the world that it was possible, even for countries officially at odds, to co-operate internationally, and very fruitfully, for such a cause.

Her extraordinary personal qualities, including her brilliant gifts as public speaker and musician, her wise statesmanship and her marvellous sense of humour, were lovingly evoked by her friends who wrote after her death: 'She stood like a rock for what in the depths of her being she knew to be right, . . .' and 'Her like will not cross our paths again'.[4]

1. See *Guardian* (20.4.1966); *The Times* (4.5.1966); *The World's Children* (June and September 1966); and *Women in Council* (Summer 1966).

2. Leonard Mayo, 'A tribute to Mrs Kathleen Freeman OBE', *The World's Children* (September 1966).
3. Kathleen Freeman, *If Any Man Build: The History of the Save the Children Fund* (London, Hodder and Stoughton, 1965), p. 39.
4. The editor, *Women in Council* (Summer 1966); and obituary in *The World's Children* (June 1966).

FRIEDRICH, MARY

(6.8.1882–9.11.1970)

CHAMPION OF PERSECUTED
VICTIMS OF NAZISM

Father: Beeston Tupholme, draughtsman
Mother: Sarah, née Watson, dressmaker,
  who bore fourteen children and kept the
  accounts for the family confectionery shop

Originally Baptist, then Quaker by
convincement

If one litmus test for compassionate integrity and moral courage is power – 'They that have power to hurt and will do none . . . / They rightly do inherit Heaven's graces'[1] – then the other test is powerlessness. A former pioneer industrial welfare worker in Britain who investigated and reported on factory conditions, Mary Tupholme decided in middle age to marry a German fellow Quaker by convincement, Leonhard Friedrich, and to live as an outsider in Germany in the darkest period of its history.

Mary Friedrich (From Brenda Bailey,
A Quaker Couple in Nazi Germany:
Leonhard Friedrich Survives
Buchenwald, *William Sessions Ltd, 1994.*
Photograph copyright Mary Friedrich's daughter,
Brenda Bailey)

From 1922 onwards Mary Friedrich experienced the grim austerity of the early 1920s, then the period of hyper-inflation, followed by the Great Depression which led to Hitler's coming to power; finally she had to endure that most inhumane of dictatorships, the Third Reich. Steadfastly through it all she defied the forces of evil then in power, refusing to obey their new, unrighteous 'laws'; she was an exemplar of *Zivilcourage*, citizens' moral courage, showing solidarity with the persecuted, offering them refuge or, wherever possible, an arduously worked-out escape from the country. Mary Friedrich lived in poverty; she was subjected to countless house searches and interrogations by the Gestapo – especially after her husband had been arrested – and she took enormous risks, among other things keeping a daily journal, even during the Second World War, using both German and English, Pitman's shorthand and sometimes codewords for her entries.

Immediately after the decree to boycott all Jewish shops, businesses and professionals (1 April 1933), for example, 'Mary decided this was the day for us both to walk through the town to visit Willi [their Jewish doctor] and all the small

Jewish shopkeepers *en route*. She ignored the warning signs, simply telling the guards she needed to speak to the shop-owner and walked through any doors that were open to talk to the frightened people inside.'[2] On 27 May 1933, she refused to give the loyalty oath to the 'great national revolution' because Quakers did not swear, and also because she disapproved of the Nazi treatment of Jews.[3] In September 1933 she was called in to be questioned by the police for the first time: a spy had reported on her husband's alleged criticism of Nazi Germany at a Quaker college in Britain.

In 1934 Mary and her husband moved to Bad Pyrmont to become wardens of the Quakerhouse there and to support and advise the nearby Quaker-funded rest home that provided a few weeks' recuperation for political and racial victims of Nazism. In the five years up to 1939 the home offered a brief asylum to 800 traumatized people. In June 1937, Mary not only scraped off an anti-Jewish poster outside the local Jewish cemetery in broad daylight, but then took the torn scraps indignantly into the Bürgermeister's office, demanding how he could bear to allow such a disgusting anti-Semitic poster to be displayed instead of the usual attractive 'Visit lovely Bad Pyrmont'. He put 'Visit lovely Bad Pyrmont' up again next morning. In September 1937 Mary was questioned by the Gestapo about Jews she was trying to help: 'a horrid visit from three Gestapo men from Hanover'.[4] Following *Kristallnacht* (9 November 1938), she both visited every local Jewish family with gifts of food and intensified her efforts to secure British guarantee affidavits for threatened Jewish Germans, including whole families with elderly parents. In May 1939 she made her last pre-war visit to Britain to organize still more sponsorships for the people she thought in most danger. She personally arranged the successful emigration of 59 Jewish Germans, ranging in age from 10 to 85.[5] She was wretched in September 1939 that emigration permits had arrived for four of 'her' families too late – a week after war began. Despite the fact that she could now be denounced simply for being seen talking to a Jew, she kept in touch with all the Jews in the Pyrmont and Hanover district, inviting them to the Quakerhouse and visiting them in their homes. It did not help that she was an Englishwoman in a Germany at war with England. She spent much of Christmas and New Year 1940–41 washing and parcelling clothing to send to the Jews deported to the east. Not knowing of the extermination policy, the Friedrichs still believed that Jews were being sent to do forced labour in Poland, and Mary helped the last local Jews to turn their duvets into padded coats, caps and leggings against the cold there.

One night in March 1942 Mary and Leonhard went to the home of the Lichtenstein family, including their 80-year-old mother, and waited up through the night with them until the Gestapo secretly collected them for transportation in the small hours. When all the last remaining Jews in their area were being rounded up and taken to the 'collection centre' near the railway station, Mary took them pans of cooked food every day and tried to do errands and shopping for the distraught, bewildered families. Again she and Leonhard stayed with them until the last moment before their deportation to Poland. Mary could not sleep for depression and anxiety over their fate.

Finally, after months of living in fear, on 29 May 1942 Leonhard was arrested 'as a Quaker for his unsuitable influence in the neighbourhood' and suffered 69 days' solitary confinement in a cell 1 metre by 3 metres. Meanwhile the Gestapo raided and sealed up the Quakerhouse. Mary went directly not only to the Gestapo headquarters in Hanover to intercede for Leonhard but also to their headquarters in Berlin. They asked threateningly: 'What have you to say about your welfare work for the Jews?' She answered: 'We helped anyone who came to us in need.' She went again in September, only to be told under the dazzling interrogation lights that her husband was to be sent to a concentration camp: 'I was devastated . . . I had to tell [Leonhard] they might be sending him to Dachau. We both wept . . . How shall we live through this?'[6] He was sent to the stone quarry at Buchenwald. Left alone in Pyrmont, sick, hungry and now aged over 60, Mary experienced over twenty house searches and cross-questionings by the Gestapo or the Chief of Police. She felt increasingly isolated and vulnerable as everyone around her, even Quakers, seemed too absorbed by their own wartime suffering to extend any sympathy to her, 'the enemy'.

At the end of May 1945, Leonhard, kept alive by Mary's food parcels – she shared her single person's rations so that he could eat – returned to Pyrmont. The joy was great, but the subsequent years often difficult: 'there were times when Leonhard would not speak to Mary for weeks on end.'[7] Concentration camp survivors did not find it easy to live with their memories or with the fact of their own survival. It seemed difficult to share experiences with their families who had not been through their hell.

Mary Friedrich may sound like a Quaker saint. She herself would not have agreed: 'Looking back, I can see it has been too important to me to be liked, instead of finding satisfaction in being the channel of love to others.'[8] But to Dr Paul Oestreicher, Senior, who only knew her after she was 79: 'Mary was one of the most personalities I ever met in my life. She had such courage, integrity and strength of spirit . . . Her open mind and hospitality for all Friends, was unique.'[9]

Perhaps it could be said of her that she, like Milton's Adam, believed in the possibility of good

> Still overcoming evil, and by small
> Accomplishing great things, by things deem'd weak
> Subverting worldly strong and worldly wise . . .[10]

More simply, in darkest times she tried to be a 'doer of the Word'.[11]

1. William Shakespeare, Sonnet 94.
2. Brenda Bailey (the daughter of the Friedrichs), *A Quaker Couple in Nazi Germany* (York, William Sessions Ltd, 1994), p. 38.
3. *Ibid.*, p. 43.
4. Mary Friedrich, manuscript journal entry, *ibid.*, p. 72.
5. Bailey, *op. cit.*, pp. 2, 97–100, 102–3.
6. Mary Friedrich, *op. cit.*, p. 153.
7. Bailey, *op. cit.*, p. 247.
8. Mary Friedrich, *op. cit.*, p. 252.
9. Paul Oestreicher, Senior, in Bailey, *op. cit.*, p. 256.
10. John Milton, *Paradise Lost*, Book 11, lines 564–8.
11. See also Hans Schmitt, *Quakers and Nazis: Inner Light in Outer Darkness* (Columbia and London, University of Missouri Press, 1997). Schmitt also mentions the defiantly humanitarian work of the Quakers Marion Fox and Elizabeth Fox Howard in Nazi Germany.

FRY, JOAN MARY
(27.7.1862–27.11.1955)

INTERNATIONAL RELIEF ORGANIZER;
SOCIAL MELIORIST; SISTER OF
MARGERY AND **RUTH FRY**

Father: (Sir) Edward Fry, Judge
Mother: Mariabella, née Hodgkin, sister of the
historian Thomas Hodgkin

Quaker

Although Joan Fry's Victorian upper-class background had prevented her from walking anywhere unaccompanied or unchaperoned until she was 30, although she did not leave home until she was middle-aged, and although her puritanical form of Quakerism forbade her to vist a theatre until she was 60, nevertheless, she managed to emerge from that restrictive background and become both an independent-minded spiritual 'Seeker' and an immensely influential social interventionist, in Britain and abroad.

Joan Fry (Frontispiece to Ruth Fawell,
Joan Mary Fry, *Friends' Home Service*
Committee, 1959)

Already in her Swarthmore Lecture 'The communion of life' (1910) Joan Fry declared: 'Quakerism is nothing unless it be . . . a practical showing that the spiritual and material spheres are not divided, . . . [that] the whole of life is sacramental and incarnational.' In *Friends and the War* (September 1914) she wrote: 'We believe there is something Divine in all men, which will respond *if* we call it out by acting on our belief.' During the First World War Joan Fry, an 'absolutist pacifist', was appointed Quaker chaplain to imprisoned conscientious objectors. She also attended many military tribunals and court-martials of conscientious objectors to check that justice was done; she was the only woman allowed to see and speak to these particular prisoners in military camps. In one case at least, she protested against a prisoner's mistreatment only just in time to save his life: Isaac Hall was a black Jamaican immigrant carpenter who took the commandment 'Thou shalt not kill' literally. His appeal to be acknowledged a conscientious objector was rejected.

> He did not report to the military and was arrested. He was taken to a training camp and, on refusing to obey an order to fall in and quick march, was dragged round the parade ground face downwards until he was unconscious. Then he was court-martialled and sentenced to two years' hard labour . . . When he refused . . . to do work on soldiers' haversacks . . . he was placed in solitary confinement on bread and water diet . . . In time this giant Negro . . . became wasted to a shadow.[1]

It was Joan Fry who reported his case to the No Conscription Fellowship, leading to his release and recuperation with ADA SALTER.

In July 1919, at the age of 57, Joan Fry, who spoke and wrote fluent German, was sent, together with three other British Friends, to defeated Germany to see how they could possibly mitigate the disastrous impact of the continued Allied Blockade through Quaker *Liebesgaben* of food and clothing.[2] Her reports testify to famine and the diseases of famine, including galloping consumption and epidemics of child rickets and pneumonia.

It is unspeakable what the tiny mites look like; the pain goes down so deep that every now and then it gives a horrid shock to one's faith in love as the key note of the world: do not ask us to tell you how we get through these sights. One tiny mite was breathing – no, trying hard to breathe – its little chest was so contracted by rickets that it can't throw off pneumonia . . .

[When] one sits beside these people and looks at their faces where one sees a hunger, physical and spiritual, not advertised, but as far as may be concealed, one feels one must go down with them into the dark places and one dare not speak words of hope which they are too sore to be able to accept as true. These people are not starving actually, but oh! they are utterly worn and sad and live in a world that seems to be going to ruin before their eyes . . . [We] told them that we were only able to come because the love of so many sent us, we told them how we have longed to come into touch.[3]

'It is impossible to record all the cases we see of children of two, three, and four and even up to seven years old who cannot walk.'[4] Despite the Germans' sullen distrust, even outright hatred, of the victorious British, Joan Fry managed to organize so massive and effective a relief distribution network, focusing on the needs of women, children and university students, that the Germans coined a new word for eating: *quäkern*. As late as 6 February 1920 Joan Fry reported to London: 'You must think of Germany as still blockaded . . . The ration of bread has been slightly reduced this week. Quaker feeding in Berlin, Cologne, Essen, the Erzgebirge, Tübingen University.' On 27 October 1921 she wrote:

The child feeding still needs to go on. Milk is still a difficulty. The Entente [Britain and France] has been creating reactionaries [in Germany] as fast as it can . . . Potato peelings are being sold in the streets again. We had a wire asking that VIOLET TILLARD be sent to Russia.[5]

During the occupation of the Ruhr in 1923 Joan Fry reported seeing French officers walking about Duisburg with whips. She intervened on behalf of Germans imprisoned by the French military. On 11 September 1923 she visited the Berlin workhouse and refuge for the homeless. Women had not even straw to lie on when giving birth, no rags, no scrap of bedding; they slept on wire bed-frames. On 21 October 1923: 'Martial law in Berlin . . . in Dresden 140,000 with no dole, in Nürnberg I saw seven men in the new "Hitler" uniform.'[6] In acknowledgement of her immense efforts for peace and reconstruction throughout defeated Germany, the University of Tübingen made Joan Fry an honorary Doctor of Political Economy in 1924.

In 1926 Joan Fry, now 64, turned her attention to social misery in Britain. She made many visits to the coalfields, helping to start feeding centres for the children of unemployed miners and to encourage small community self-help industries; she was chairman of the Friends Coalfields Distress Committee. She wanted to give new purpose of life to these stricken people, and her greatest contribution was her work for the Friends' Allotment Committee (1928–51), which enabled unemployed miners throughout Britain to grow vegetables on unused land without losing any part of their dole.[7] George V wanted to confer an honour on her in recognition of this work but she refused to profit from others' misfortune. 'Joan Mary Fry was in the best tradition of "public" Friends.'[8]

Joan Fry was short but she had a remarkable 'presence', being both 'austere and tender'[9] with her white hair, one humorous, loving eye (she had lost the other in early childhood) and her eagerness to join in the good things of life with others, especially children. She still won races against them at 90. '[To] know her and love her was to receive a life-long benediction.'[10]

1. Fenner Brockway, *Bermondsey Story: The Life of Alfred Salter* (first published London, Independent Labour Party, 1949; reprinted 1995), pp. 67–8.
2. See entry for KATE COURTNEY; and John Ormerod Greenwood, *Quaker Encounters* (3 vols; York, William Sessions, 1975–78).
3. Joan Fry, 'Journal letters from Germany, 1919' (unpublished; Friends' House Library Archives, TEMP. MSS.66), 11.7.1919.
4. *Ibid.*, 21.7.1919.
5. *Ibid.*
6. *Ibid.* See also Joan Fry, *In Downcast Germany* (London, 1944).
7. See 'Fruits of allotments', *The Friend* (13.9.1929); and Joan Fry, *Friends Lend a Hand in Alleviating Unemployment* (London, Friends' Book Centre, 1947).
8. William Hazelton, obituary for Joan Fry, *The Friend* (2.12.1955).
9. Ruth Fawell, *Joan Mary Fry* (London, Friends' Home Service Committee, 1959), p. 7.
10. *Ibid.*, p. 65.

See also obituary in *The Times* (28.11.1955); and Katharine Moore, *Cordial Relations: The Maiden Aunt in Fact and Fiction* (London, Heinemann, 1966), pp. 186–92, on Joan and Margery Fry as benign unofficial adoptive parents of Roger Fry's motherless children.

FRY, MARGERY
(11.3.1874–21.4.1958)

PENAL REFORMER; SISTER OF **JOAN** AND **RUTH FRY**

Father: (Sir) Edward Fry, Judge
Mother: Mariabella, née Hodgkin

Quaker from birth, later agnostic

Margery Fry was the sixth of the seven daughters and two sons of an extraordinarily gifted and serious Quaker family.[1] She herself, loving beauty like her artist brother Roger, vivacious and full of humorous relish for life, was reluctant initially to attach herself either to noble causes or to do-goodery. However, her fellow student at Oxford, ELEANOR RATHBONE, quickly alerted her in 1896 to the justice of women's struggle to be enfranchised in Britain and invited her to

Margery Fry (Reproduced from the front cover of Enid Huws Jones, Margery Fry: The Essential Amateur, *Sessions of York, 1990, courtesy of Pictorial Press Ltd)*

join a small women students' 'society for discussing things in general' called the Associated Prigs.[2] The Prigs discussed to good effect. A few years later, while Warden of the women students' hostel at the University of Birmingham (1904–14), Margery Fry found herself also serving on a County Education Committee and campaigning, successfully, for the appointment of the first peripatetic school nurses and, unsuccessfully, for the abolition of caning. She was a governor of a girls' remand home; she was on the committee that drafted the new bye-laws regulating child employment in Staffordshire; and she also worked to help the implementation of the first National Insurance and Mental Deficiency Bills.

When Margery Fry inherited family money in 1914, at the age of 40, she was free never to work again. A life of civilized ease was psychologically impossible for her, however; after the outbreak of the First World War, she felt she had to address the housing needs of Belgian refugees suddenly placed in Birmingham. Then she took on the much larger task of the organization of Quaker relief work for civilian war victims in the Marne and Meuse region[3] and later in all of France (1915–17). Fortunately, she spoke fluent French.

On her return to England to raise funds for the stricken areas of France, Margery Fry was deeply moved by the dying message of her aunt Susan Pease to the younger generation of Quakers: 'Let us admit our failures in our methods of reforming criminals . . . Let us be prepared to support more enlightened and humane methods.'[4] She became Secretary of the Penal Reform League, which she combined in 1921 with the Howard Association to make the Howard League. The first task was to battle for a national probation system for young offenders. Next she established educational programmes for prisoners. She visited prisons, remand homes and Borstals, and in consequence wrote sadly: 'I hate to think what man has made of man.'[5] But her overwhelming concern was the attempt to abolish capital punishment. With immense emotional courage she offered to go to Holloway to spend some hours with Edith Thompson – almost the last woman to be hanged in Britain – in her condemned cell, because she might have some last messages she would like her to deliver.

> She accepted my offer solely in order to pass a few minutes of the terrible waiting period . . . Two or three days after the execution I was greatly impressed by its effect upon all the prison staff. I think I have never seen a person look so changed in appearance by mental suffering as the Governor appeared to me to be.[6]

Margery Fry's first important publication was *Some Facts regarding Capital Punishment* (1923). She 'helped to create the National Council for the Abolition of the Death Penalty. The researches she had started were extended by Roy Calvert and these two pioneers laid the foundations on which all advocacy of abolition has been built.'[7] She worked until she died for that not generally popular cause, using all the evidence she could garner from abolitionist countries, but died ten years too soon to see the end of the death penalty in Britain.[8] She had to be satisfied with her part in instituting legal aid for the poor, the medical diagnosis and treatment of mentally ill prisoners, the attempted rehabilitation of offenders through education and work in prison, the building of 'open prisons' and the raising of the age of custodial imprisonment of the young.[9]

With the rise of fascism, Margery Fry had to renounce the absolute pacifism of Quakerism,[10] believing as she did that the world's only hope of avoiding another world war lay in collective, armed security under the auspices of the League of Nations. The League of Nations was also her hope in the field of international prison reform. 'Jointly with the League of Nations Union and the Society of Friends, the Howard League drafted a Schedule of Conditions to be observed in all Civilized Countries in the Treatment of Persons under Arrest or in Captivity on whatever Charge.'[11] It stipulated the abolition of torture, the provision of basic physical decencies and prison visiting by relatives. Penal reform, however, was very low on the international agenda in the Depression and dictatorship-stricken 1930s, with another major war imminent. But

> if today there is a Social Defence section of the United Nations, concerned with the prevention of crime and with the observing of standard minimum rules for the treatment of prisoners, credit must largely go to Margery Fry and [her colleague] Gertrude Eaton . . . when they secured a place for penal reform on the agenda of the League of Nations.[12]

Although Margery Fry visited/inspected prison regimes all over the world, including Canada, the United States, Mexico, Bulgaria and China, not to mention the women internees in Holloway, her concern was not limited to the humane treatment of prisoners. She was also exercised about the welfare of prison officers, and her final campaign, begun when she was 78, was for state compensation for the victims of violence.

> I see at the centre of Margery Fry's life her passion for justice. It was this which carried her through days of committees . . . through piles of official reports; through hours of writer's cramp producing pamphlets which she knew went into the waste-paper basket . . . 'All social reform', she once said, 'rests at bottom on the addressing of envelopes.' . . . [She] believed volunteers would always be needed to speak for voiceless, forgotten people.[13]

It might be thought that Margery Fry's life was extraordinarily productive both in its immediate, practical humanitarianism and in its contribution to humane thinking that would outlive her. But she herself was always conscious of her inadequacy and failures: 'I feel once more a useless parasite on society.'[14]

1. See entries for JOAN FRY and RUTH FRY; and *Dictionary of National Biography* entries for their Fry and Hodgkin forebears.
2. Enid Huws Jones, *Margery Fry: The Essential Amateur* (Oxford University Press, 1966, republished York, William Sessions, 1990), p. 45.
3. See entries for HILDA CLARK, EDITH PYE and FRANCESCA WILSON.
4. Jones, *op. cit.*, p. 112.
5. *Ibid.*, p. 123.
6. Margery Fry, quoted in obituary in *Daily Telegraph* (22.4.1958).
7. 'Profile – Margery Fry', *Observer* (18.4.1948).
8. Jones, *op. cit.*, p. 221.
9. '[In] an impasse, Miss Fry did not shrink on occasion from remanding a difficult small boy into her own custody in her own house': obituary in *Manchester Guardian* (22.4.1958).
10. Jones, *op. cit.*, p. 179.
11. *Ibid.*, p. 168.
12. R. Duncan Fairn, 'Margery Fry', *The Friend* (2.5.1958), pp. 539–40.
13. Enid Huws Jones, 'Margery Fry', *Social Service Quarterly* (Winter 1967–68), pp. 103 and 105.
14. Letter from Margery Fry from France in 1940, in Jones, op. cit., p. 198.

See also the publications by Margery Fry: *The Prison Population of the World* (Howard League pamphlet, 1936); with Champion B. Russell, *A Notebook for the Children's Court* (originally Oxford University Press, 1942; revised 3rd edn, Howard League, 1950); *The Future Treatment of the Adult Offender* (London,

Victor Gollancz, 1944); *Arms of the Law* (London, Victor Gollancz, 1951); chapter in J. Marchant (ed.), *What Life Has Taught Me* (London, Odhams Press, 1948); chapter in J. Marchant (ed.), *What I Believe* (London, Odhams Press, 1953).

For obituaries on Margery Fry see *The Times* (22.4, 23.4 and 24.4.1958); *Manchester Guardian* (22.4.1958); *The Monthly Record* (June, 1958).

FRY, (ANNA) RUTH

(4.9.1878–26.4.1962)

INTERNATIONAL RELIEF ORGANIZER; SISTER OF **JOAN** AND **MARGERY FRY**

Father: (Sir) Edward Fry, Judge
Mother: Mariabella, née Hodgkin

Quaker

The first public work of Ruth Fry, the youngest, frailest and least self-confident of the Fry daughters,[1] was relief for defeated and distressed Boer families, under the inspiring leadership of EMILY HOBHOUSE, after the Boer War. Next she did secretarial work for her father when he was the first British Judge on the International Court of The Hague. Her outstanding work for humanity was pioneering the Friends' War Victims' Relief operation. Their earliest project was to aid northern French refugee families by establishing a maternity hospital with Dr HILDA CLARK and EDITH PYE in the Marne, only a few kilometres from the battle zone. Ruth Fry's post started as Hon. Secretary.

> It was later to grow to the terrifying proportions of generalissimo-cum-quartermaster-general, making her responsible for a vast programme of supplies, administration, personnel management, public relations, fund-raising, leadership and inspiration, on behalf of a complex of projects the like of which had never been known in Quaker history before.[2]

Friends' War Victims' Relief, comprising about 1,070 British volunteer workers, operated in nine countries between 1914 and 1926: Belgium, France, Holland, Germany, Poland, Serbia, Austria, Hungary and famine-devastated Russia.

> The problems encountered in all nine countries [were] very similar and could be grouped [thus]:
>
> (1) Result of destruction (of houses and property) by invading armies.
> (2) Refugees exiled by invasion of their homes.
> (3) Epidemics and other damage to health through starvation, overcrowding and other war hardships.[3]

Ruth Fry herself visited every stricken country, all freezing, hungry and rife with disease. In Poland in 1919, for example, she visited typhus hospitals and promptly organized the necessary anti-epidemic measures. She also organized the setting up of clothing workshops, and food distribution for children, as well as overseeing the provision of horses, tractors, seeds and agricultural tools and timber for the homeless displaced peasants.[4] Even more extraordinary were her efforts for Quaker Relief during the Russian famine, when there was both hostility from the British government and popular political prejudice against the new dictatorial rule of the Bolsheviks. Nevertheless she found herself administering huge sums of donated money: £1,000 a day for months on end. She was asked to visit one of the very worst stricken districts, Buzuluk, in January 1922, 'an experience which burnt into one's very heart the tragedy of the situation . . . death seemed more real than life . . . death was still winning'.[5]

In 1918 and 1923 Ruth Fry travelled the length and breadth of the United States, giving nearly 100 lectures on the desperate situation in Europe, in order to raise relief funds. She then collapsed with what is now known as 'burn-out' but lived on as an invalid, for another 30 years, dedicated to the cause of eliminating war. She was Treasurer of the War Resisters International linking conscientious objectors of all lands from 1936 to 1947 – not a good period for pacifism. Her books

Naked child on threshold of hut, Buzuluk (From Friends' War Victims' Relief Committee, Russia Album, no. 39)

included *Victories without Violence* (1939) on the power of reconciliation and non-violence, and a life of EMILY HOBHOUSE (1929).

1. See entries for JOAN FRY and MARGERY FRY.
2. Bernard Canter, 'A. Ruth Fry', *The Friend* (4.5.1962), p. 525. See also *The Friend* (11.5 and 18.5.1962).
3. Ruth Fry, *A Quaker Adventure* (London, Nisbet, 1926), Preface to original edition.
4. Anne Caton, 'Ruth Fry', *Wiadomosci* (24.6.1962), Friends' House Library. See also obituaries in *Guardian* (28.4.1962); and *The Times* (28.4.1962).
5. Ruth Fry, *A Quaker Adventure* (London, Friends Service Council, 1943; abridged version of 1926 edn), pp. 49–50.

See also H. H. Fisher, *The Famine in Soviet Russia, 1919–23* (New York, Macmillan, 1927); Anna Haines, *The Russian Famine* (booklet; n.d., Friends' House Library); and John Ormerod Greenwood, *Quaker Encounters* (York, William Sessions, 1978).

See also entries for FLORENCE BARROW, MARJORIE RACKSTRAW, EVELYN SHARP and VIOLET TILLARD.

G

GLASIER, KATHARINE ST JOHN
(21.6.1867–14.6.1950)

PACIFIST SOCIALIST;
INTERNATIONALIST;
WRITER; ORATOR

Father: Samuel Conway,
 Congregationalist minister
Mother: Amy, née Curling

Christian Socialist

Katharine Glasier, c. 1930

Katharine Conway, the second of seven children, was 14 when her mother (and tutor) died in childbirth. She went on to win a scholarship to Newnham College, Cambridge, where she studied classics; in 1889 she became classics mistress at Redlands High School for Girls, Bristol, thus achieving status and security in the new women's profession of grammar school teaching. Eighteen months later she gave up the professional success to which her whole life and family background had been dedicated and crossed the class barrier to teach 70 working-class infants in a Board School in the slums of Bristol. She had been converted to social awareness by the appearance of hundreds of wet, underfed girl cotton workers, sheltering in her High Anglican church during their rain-battered strikers' march. 'I was ashamed of the privilege and elaborate refinements of which I had previously been so proud.'[1] More intellectually, Katharine Conway was converted by the idealistic socialism of Edward Carpenter's *England's Ideal* and soon came to know Shaw, William Morris and Keir Hardie. She allied herself first with the Fabians and then, in 1893, with the Independent Labour Party, which she co-founded and for which she became an inspiring orator throughout Britain, often travelling on foot with a knapsack on her back.[2]

After her marriage to her fellow socialist Bruce Glasier, both Katharine and her husband 'sacrificed comfort, leisure and security for the Cause';[3] she, in particular, was to experience the impossibility of reconciling the conflicting imperatives of work and family. Nevertheless, as a leading figure in the Women's Labour League, she campaigned vigorously for pithead baths, for widows' pensions, for cottage homes for old people, for better town and city planning, for infant welfare centres, school meals and nursery schools.[4]

Throughout the First World War Katharine Glasier upheld her pacifist international socialist principles, despite social isolation and obloquy. She was on the British Committee of the Hague Congress.[5] At the National Independent Labour Conference, the only woman on the platform, she said:

Human solidarity is not a sloppy sentiment, but a fact in nature . . . This is the darkest hour of the world's conscious life – the undoing of all the work of human parenting. We must rededicate ourselves to get children to become unselfish and to think of life as human service.[6]

Her May Day message in 1915 rang out: 'Greetings to all workers everywhere. Let us look forward to the day when patriotism means love of country but hatred of none.'[7] In 1916, Katharine Glasier took over the editorship of *The Labour Leader*, after Fenner Brockway was imprisoned as a conscientious objector, and continued to defend the unpopular values of internationalist pacifism and co-operative socialism in that paper until 1921. During the Great Depression she turned the attention of the Save the Children Fund to the children of the unemployed in the distressed areas of Tyneside and south Wales, leading a successful campaign to establish nursery schools for them.

Katharine Glasier was not 'only' an orator. She also *lived* her faith in fellowship, which to her, as to William Morris, was the heart of socialism; her last act was to bequeathe her cottage in Earby, Lancashire, to the Youth Hostel Association in perpetuity. And humanitarianism needs a few orators. For more than 60 years, her words roused thousands of people to hope and strive for a better, because a more humane, world. 'Her Socialist principles [were] based on her belief in the value of the individual human being, on her convictions that we are truly members one of another, that no one can gain by another's hurt.'[8]

1. Laurence Thompson, *The Enthusiasts: A Biography of John and Katharine Bruce Glasier* (London, Gollancz, 1971), p. 66. (Thompson's book is somewhat supercilious.)
2. See Stephen Yeo, 'New Life socialism', *History Workshop Journal*, **4** (1977); and Hannah Mitchell, *The Hard Way Up* (London, Virago, 1977), p. 86 for a first inspiring encounter with the young Katharine Conway.
3. *Daily Herald* (22.9.1947).
4. See Clare Middleton, *Women and the Labour Movement: The British Experience* (London, Croom Helm, 1977).
5. See Introduction and Appendix I.
6. *Labour Leader* (15.4.1915).
7. *Labour Leader* (22.4.1915).
8. *Daily Herald* (22.9.1947).

For other appreciations of Katharine Bruce Glasier, see *Labour Woman* (June 1950); and obituaries in *Daily Herald* (15.6.1950); *The World's Children* (July 1950); *Manchester Guardian* (15.6.1950); and *The Times* (15.6 and 1.7.1950).

GREEN, NAN
(19.11.1904–16.4.1984)

ANTI-FASCIST MEDICAL WORKER;
RESCUER OF CHILD REFUGEES;
NUCLEAR PACIFIST

Father: Edward George Farrow, company
secretary
Mother: Marie, née Kemp, housewife

Agnostic

Nan Green's ashes were scattered on a hill above Barcelona; her husband had been killed at Gandesa nearly 50 years earlier, on the last day of action by the British Battalion of the International Brigade in Spain. A musician by profession, he, like Nan, had joined the Communist Party in the early 1930s out of humane social indignation; he

Nan Green (Courtesy of her son Martin Green)

then became an ambulance driver for Medical Aid for Spain and later joined the International Brigade. Meanwhile Nan had worked in front-line International Brigade field hospitals, including one in a cave during the battle of the Ebro. After the Republicans' defeat, already a widow, she helped to rescue Spanish Republican refugee orphans, taking them to Mexico by boat.[1]

Nan Green spent the Second World War in London, working in the air-raid defence service throughout the Blitz. After 1945 she helped organize the visits of British observers to post-war Francoist Spain to monitor the political trials of anti-fascist Spaniards there. From 1953 to 1960 she worked in Beijing, first with the China Peace Council and then as an English-language editor for the Foreign Languages Press. Finally, back in Britain, she founded the Spanish Civil War section of the Marx Memorial Library, translated the works of Fidel Castro and the Spanish Communist leader Santiago Carrillo and played an important founding and supportive role both for CND and for the Greenham anti-Cruise-missile activists.

Was Nan Green's a selective humanitarianism, responding only to the victims of capitalist imperialism? Was she an example of those good kind Westerners so derided by Doris Lessing, in volume 2 of her autobiography, for having blithely and blindly continued to idealize Stalinist Communism, whether in the Soviet Union or in China? If not, how could she have borne the revelations about the *Gulag* camps? First, in the 1930s and 1940s there had been the psychological necessity to have some hope for humanity, based on faith in human goodness and social justice, in a world of fascist horrors. Hence Nan Green's long reluctance to believe the worst about the self-styled 'anti-fascist' states. In addition, there was her own first-hand knowledge of the positive, humane work carried out by countless, nameless Communists *not* in power in the Soviet Union and in China. When the massive moral betrayals by the two dictatorships became impossible for her to deny to herself, she concentrated on trying to help avert a nuclear world war between the blinkered superpowers. In 1968 she said she would tear up her Party card if the British Communist Party did not condemn the Soviet invasion of Czechoslovakia;

but they did; so she didn't. She retained her faith in the validity of a socialism that the world has not yet tried: one not subverted by authoritarianism.

Nan Green's life of inner and outer moral political struggle may be seen as paradigmatic for humanitarians of the Left in the twentieth century. She had turned to the Left in her youth because of her passion for justice in this world; the official Left betrayed her faith bitterly, time and again, as it failed the acid test of power: while she, more and more isolated, went on testifying to an alternative, truer, reality – a vision of the better world she could still imagine.[2]

1. See Martin Green (her son), Introduction to Nan Green, *Memoirs: A Chronicle of Small Beer* (published in Spanish, 1987). An extract from *A Chronicle of Small Beer* has been published in English in Valentine Cunningham (ed.), *Spanish Front: Writers on the Civil War* (Oxford, Oxford University Press, 1986).
2. Cf. Northrop Frye, *Fearful Symmetry: A Study of William Blake* (Princeton, Princeton University Press, 1947; reprinted Boston, Beacon Press, 1962), p. 27: 'The world we imagine is more real than the world we passively accept.'

See also obituaries for Nan Green in *Morning Star* (7.4.1984); *The Times* (17.4.1984); *New Statesman* (20.4.1984).

H

HARDISTY, DOROTHY,
MBE

(4.7.1881–8.1.1973)

CHAMPION OF JEWISH
KINDERTRANSPORT CHILD REFUGEES

Father: Francis Jones, master at Manchester
*   Grammar School*
Mother: Jessie, née Ferguson

Anglican

The British Refugee Children's Movement, founded after *Kristallnacht* (the shop-smashing, synagogue-burning pogrom in Germany of 9 November 1938), had succeeded by August 1939 in rescuing 9,354 unaccompanied Jewish children from Nazi persecution in Germany and Austria via the *Kindertransport* trains to Britain. Most of them were never again to see their families, left behind to be murdered for belonging to the wrong 'race'.[1] And thousands of children were not got out in time.

Dorothy Hardisty, aged about 70 (Courtesy of Mrs Jytte Hardisty)

Dorothy Hardisty, nearly 60 years old, a graduate of Manchester University and a former senior civil servant in the Ministry of Labour, was appointed General Secretary for the Refugee Children's Movement to 'sort out' the ensuing tangle of complex issues regarding placement, finance, religious upbringing, education, employment and the individual welfare of these thousands of uprooted, traumatized young people. She arrived at the Bloomsbury House headquarters in June 1940, determined to try to enable the children, whether from Orthodox, non-Orthodox, agnostic or Christian families, to have 'what Germany denied [them], a free and normal development in an atmosphere of affection'.[2] She found herself responsible, until June 1948, in some cases for the children's re-emigration and reunion with relatives in the United States or Palestine, but for the most part for finding the thousands of parentless, refugee Jewish children appropriate homes, education, training and jobs in Britain. All this became much more difficult when the mass evacuation of children, whether British or refugee, from London and other cities, was in process. To the Jewish youngsters who had been already so brutally uprooted and resettled, this new 'evacuation [not to mention later internment in 1940] was a catastrophe'.[3] Dorothy Hardisty realized that it was essential to decentralize, and so she set up twelve Regional Committees and many more smaller Local Committees, usually consisting of local Jews, Quakers, church members and trade unionists, to take immediate responsibility for the physical and psychological welfare of these now scattered Jewish children.[4]

Although Dorothy Hardisty remained at Head Office in London, this did not mean that she did not herself take ultimate responsibility for every child. Her journal gives ample testimony to her enormous personal concern for each individual, who *was* an individual and not a 'case' to her, as she battled with the Home Office, the police, sundry billeting officers, countless foster parents, the International Student Service, and, not least, the Orthodox Rabbi Schönfeld, for whom a lapsed or, worse, a converted Jew was more lost than a dead Jew.[5] Somehow she managed to supervise satisfactory placements for almost all the children and to obtain funding for those most desperate and/or most able to benefit from academic education, while also protecting adolescent girls at risk from London pimps and defending the few teenage boys arrested for juvenile delinquency.[6] She kept a file on every child. No wonder that on matters both large and small Dorothy Hardisty's Refugee Children's Movement was relied on by the children to be their 'guide, philosopher and friend',[7] as well as to sort out problems over clothing coupons. Her commitment was to the well-being of the young people, first, last and at all times in between. She never forgot that

> The children had endured over a long period of time and increasing severity such physical and mental suffering as had stolen their childhood from them. They were often old beyond their years, sometimes dreadfully experienced, *always troubled and disturbed*. It was not only that at short notice they were torn from the people they loved and trusted, and the places they knew: it was not only that they were suddenly bereft of all sense of security – these blows had been preceded by long periods of unhappiness and fear. Young children had seen the persecution of their relatives: men and boys being taken away from their homes; they had heard of the dread concentration camps. (My emphasis)[8]

On retiring from the Refugee Children's Committee in 1948, Dorothy Hardisty, then 67, began to run the Violet Melchett Infant Welfare Clinic in Chelsea. She retired at the age of 86. At 82 she was still to be seen accompanying her grandchildren on the water chute at Battersea Fun Fair.[9]

Dorothy Hardisty's own words on the Refugee Children's Movement as a whole best serve as her epitaph:

> It is not a small thing, in these years of suffering without parallel, to have given to ten thousand children the opportunity to grow up in an atmosphere of decency and normality, to work, to play, to laugh and be happy and to assume their rightful heritage as free men and women.[10]

1. See entry for BERTHA BRACEY; Karen Gershon, *We Came as Children* (London, Macmillan, 1966; reprinted 1989); Charles Hannam, *A Boy in Your Situation* (London, André Deutsch, 1977); Barry Turner, . . . *And the Policeman Smiled* (London, Bloomsbury, 1990); Veronica Gillespie, 'Working with the *Kindertransports*' in Sybil Oldfield (ed.), *This Working-day World: Women's Lives and Culture(s) in Britain 1914–1945* (London and Bristol, PA, Taylor and Francis, 1994); Mary Ford, 'The arrival of Jewish refugee children in England 1938–1939', *Journal of Immigrants and Minorities*, **2** (July 1983), pp. 137–51; Bertha Leverton, *Reunion of Kindertransport Kinder* (Lewes, Sussex, Book Guild, 1990).
2. Dorothy Hardisty, 'The Refugee Children's Movement' (typescript of Report to the Home Office, 1948), p. 10.
3. Dorothy Hardisty, journal (current whereabouts unknown), quoted in Turner, *op. cit.*, ch. 8.
4. Hardisty, Report, *op. cit.*, pp. 12, 13. See also entry for EDITH MORLEY.
5. Turner, *op. cit.*, pp. 243–50: 'Divided loyalties'; and Gillespie, *op. cit.*, pp. 128–9.

6. See Turner, *op. cit.*, *passim.*
7. Hardisty, Report, *op. cit.*, p. 10.
8. Hardisty, journal, quoted in Gillespie, *op. cit.*, p. 130.
9. Obituary for Dorothy Hardisty, *Hampstead and Highgate Express* (19.1.1973), p. 4. There was no obituary in *The Times* or entry in the *Dictionary of National Biography*.
10. Dorothy Hardisty, Foreword to Turner, *op. cit.*

Some Home Office papers on the Refugee Children's Movement are held at the Public Record Office, Kew.

HARRIS, ALICE
(24.5.1870–12.1970)

MISSIONARY ANTI-SLAVERY CAMPAIGNER IN THE UPPER CONGO

Father: Alfred Seeley, silk works manager

Christian

Alice Seeley was a 20-year-old secretary in the civil service when she first heard the 'call' to go out to Africa, from a London preacher, Dr F. B. Meyer. Her parents objected for seven years, but finally, with many misgivings, gave their consent not only to her becoming a missionary but also to her marriage to another young missionary, John Hobbis Harris. They left with the Region Beyond Missionary Union (RBMU)[1] for Balolo in the Congo in 1898, forewarned of danger not only from disease, poisonous snakes and violent natives, but above all from the white rubber-collectors working on commission for the Belgian King Leopold II.[2]

Alice Harris making her way through the Central African rain forest (Courtesy of Anti-Slavery International)

Alice and John Harris began their teaching of skills like house-building and reading, and found the local Africans quick, eager learners. But all too soon they personally encountered the atrocities being perpetrated in that 'heart of darkness'.[3] For in King Leopold's 'Congo Free State', founded allegedly to bring Christianity, civilization and development to Central Africa and to end the Arab slave-trade to Zanzibar, African women and children were in fact being captured and kept, semi-starved and chained, in the 'hostage-house', waiting for the return of their men with the required amount of tapped rubber, now so marketable for shoes, car and bicycle tyres and many other new industrial processes in Europe. If the baskets of rubber were insufficient in number or even not quite full, baskets would be filled instead with the amputated hands and feet of the hostages; sometimes the hostages were beaten to death in front of their menfolk; sometimes the women and children would be crucified.[4] Leopold's system deliberately paid the overseers and rubber-collectors too little to live on; their survival – and escape from being flogged themselves – depended on the 'rubber bonus', the extraction of rubber by *any* means. And the survival of the Congolese Africans depended in turn on their tapping trees every fortnight which should only have been tapped every year. In their terrorized desperation, the Africans would hack and pull up the very roots of the rubber trees on which they depended. The deaths of Africans in the Congo *c.* 1890–1910, whether by starvation, the policy of deliberate destruction of towns and villages, or actual mass murder, are now estimated in millions.[5]

Alice Harris and her husband adopted two skeletal abandoned children before they had their own first baby and went back to England on furlough, where their second baby was born. Alice then had to make the most difficult decision of her life. She chose to leave her two tiny children, her daughter only six weeks old, in the care of friends, knowing it could be years before she saw them again. But the imperative to go back and serve the Congo's Africans in their desperate situation overruled her own deepest personal needs, and even what others would consider her prime responsibility. In

A child mutilated by rubber-collectors, photographed by Alice Harris (Courtesy of Anti-Slavery International)

1903 the Harrises, back in the upper Congo, co-operated with the British Consul Roger Casement to campaign for an official investigation into the European barbarities. They had already written to the British press, to the British government, especially the Foreign Office, and to Belgian officials without result. They ignored death threats from the nearest rubber station officials. Alice Harris photographed the evidence, including both the brutal armed 'sentries' and the amputated hand and foot of the little daughter of a man who had not tapped enough rubber, and they reported to Casement the beheading of Congo women in order to steal and sell the women's ornamental brass collars.

Casement reported to the British government on 12 December 1903. The British government expressed 'grave misgivings' to the Belgian government, only to be told not to interfere with the internal affairs of another state. King Leopold did, however, set up a carefully packed Commission of Inquiry in 1904, and tried every means in his power to discredit the evidence of missionaries like the Harrises. John Harris was called to open the case for the natives, which he did, using Alice's many damning photographs to testify to mutilation, torture and murder. For three days he reported, calling African after African to tell of the abominations they had personally seen. The accused rubber-collector denied none of it. He was just 'working under orders'. For months the Commission's Report remained unpublished. John and Alice Harris, their evidence at first suppressed but finally summarized by the Congo Reform Association, were then under such an unmistakeable threat to their lives in an area now under martial law, and without support from any British authorities, that they decided to return to England. Their mission was no longer to bring Christianity to Africa but to indict the 'Christian' West for its crimes against Africa. Once the Commission Report was published and the 'Belgian Congo atrocities' had begun to become common knowledge, they were invited to speak at hundreds of meetings in Britain, Europe and the United States, showing Alice's 60 lantern slides of both victims and perpetrators, as well as some of the whips and chains actually in use in the Congo. 'This probably marked the first time that photographs played a major role in a human rights movement.'[6]

In 1911 John and Alice Harris went back, this time as British representatives, to report on conditions in the Congo and in Portuguese West Africa. They travelled for over a year, covering 5,000 miles, often by foot through almost impenetrable rain forest or by canoe over dangerous rapids, among scenes of desolation – an experience that left them physically and psychologically drained. Alice's gentleness and sympathy won trust from Africans who thought they would never trust a white person again.

The Harrises returned to England to continue the struggle to rouse public opinion. Together with Roger Casement and E. D. Morel, the Harrises played their part not only in effecting the eventual abolition of *de facto* slavery in the Congo but also in preventing similar extreme abuses in the exploitation of human beings for the extraction of raw materials in British West Africa.[7] They both continued their work for the Anti-Slavery and Aborigines Protection Society for the rest of their active lives, their remit coming to cover not just Central Africa, but the whole of Africa and indeed the world. In 1912, for example, Alice Harris attacked racist lynchings in South Africa, as well as in the southern states of America, if a black man were rumoured to have had sexual relations with a white woman. She pointed out how vulnerable women of colour had always been to colonizing/slave-owning whites, saying: 'The person of the coloured, no less than the white, woman should be inviolate, and the penalty be meted out to offenders irrespective of colour or creed.'[8] She also responded strongly to the allegation that African slaves – this time on the cocoa plantations of Portugal's São Tomé islands – were incapable of family feeling like other people:

> The African woman is not, as is supposed by many . . . an irresponsible and untrained savage . . . [Africans] have had their native societies, their institutions and their schools from time immemorial, their ancient orders of women and of men, and the disintegration of those systems means the breakdown and ultimate extinction of the race.[9]

She was haunted by the sullen hopelessness in the faces of the slave mothers of São Tomé who knew that their babies would also grow up slaves.

E. D. Morel singled out the Harrises as the true successor to 'the Apostolic' Swedish missionary Sjöblom, who had, at first, been the only one who had dared to confront the evil of King Leopold and his agents: 'His pendant of later times in energy and determination is John Harris[10] (and Mrs Harris), of whose courage in Africa and self-sacrifice in Europe it would be impossible to speak too highly.'[11]

1. The RBMU had been founded in 1892 as a broad missionary movement embracing all denominations.
2. See Adam Hochschild, *King Leopold's Ghost: A Story of Greed, Terror and Heroism in Central Africa* (London, Macmillan, 1999).

3. Cf. Joseph Conrad, *Heart of Darkness* (1899); and section 11: 'The deeds' in E. D. Morel, *Red Rubber: The Story of the Rubber Slave Trade Flourishing on the Congo in the Year of Grace 1906* (London, T. Fisher Unwin, 1906); as well as his *King Leopold's Rule in Africa* (London, William Heinemann, 1904), which published Conrad's letter on his experience in the Congo.
4. Cf. Brian Inglis, *Roger Casement* (London, Hodder and Stoughton, 1973), Part One.
5. Hochschild, *op. cit.* See also Mary-Jean Hasler, 'Alice Harris', BBC radio script (broadcast October 1970) in *The Women* series, no. 2, pp. 6, 7.
6. Adam Hochschild, 'Campaigners against twentieth century slavery in the Congo', *Anti-Slavery Reporter*, **5**(3) (July 1999), p. 9; and Angus Mitchell, 'New light on the *Heart of Darkness*', *History Today*, **49** (December 1999), pp. 20–7: 'The ideals and action that gave rise to the anti-slavery movement and the efforts to protect indigenous peoples in the Congo, Amazon and elsewhere became the foundations upon which current humanitarian and human rights organizations, including Amnesty International and Survival International, were founded.'
7. Inglis, *op. cit.*, p. 392: 'In 1907 the British colonial administrations in West Africa refused to allow Lever Brothers to set up a plantation system to produce palm oil; and again in 1920.'
8. *Anti-Slavery Reporter and Aborigines' Friend* (April 1911–June 1912), pp. 196–8.
9. *Anti-Slavery Reporter and Aborigines' Friend* (October 1912), p. 230. In 1933, the *Journal of the Anti-Slavery and Aborigines Protection Society* reported: 'Lady Harris spoke at a series of meetings in Eastern Scotland, including Edinburgh, Peterhead, Aberdeen, Fraserburgh, Inverurie, Edzell, and other towns. Also at Carlisle, Preston, Blackpool, Blackburn, Darwen, Kensington, Richmond, Westcliff-on Sea, Ditchling, Steyning, Petersfield.' See also entry for KATHLEEN SIMON.
10. Sir John Hobbis Harris's writings against twentieth-century enslavement, some of them dedicated to his wife – 'his companion in hardship . . .' – include: *Coolie Labour in the British Crown Colonies and Protectorates* (1910); *The Peruvian Rubber Crime* (1910); *Domestic Slavery in Southern Nigeria* (1911); *Dawn in Darkest Africa* (1912); *Present Conditions in the Congo* (1912); *Portuguese Slavery: Britain's Dilemma* (1913); *The Greatest Land Case in British History: Native Rights in Rhodesia* (1918); *The Fight for Vegetable Oils: The Right of Natives to Sell Their Produce* (1919); *Flogging to Death: South African Test Case* (1924); *Slavery or 'Sacred Trust'? League of Nations Mandates* (1926); *The Challenge of Kenya* (1930); *Slavery in Liberia* (1930); *Slave-trading in China* (1930); *The Australian Natives* (1937); and *Slaves under British Flag: South Africa* (1938). See also entry for him in *The New Dictionary of National Biography*.
11. Morel, *op. cit.*, p. 6.

The original lantern slides and photographs taken by Alice Harris, as well as some of her reported talks, are held in the Reference Library of Anti-Slavery International, Thos. Clarkson House, The Stableyard, Broomgrove Road, London SW9 9TL.

HASLEWOOD, CLARA B. L.
(1876–June 1962)

CHAMPION OF GIRL SLAVES (*MUI TSAI*) IN HONG KONG

Anglican

'That the *mui tsai* system was eventually abolished – legally and in practice – in Hong Kong is largely due to the campaign, orchestrated over many years, by Clara Haslewood and her husband.'[1] That system, nominally of domestic service by 'adopted daughters', had in fact been one of domestic slavery in which a girl child was sold by destitute parents into unpaid, often brutally ill-treated, servitude and was then liable to be resold into concubinage or brothel slavery, often being shipped abroad to 'service' foreign ports.

Clara Haslewood, who had been active in the British National Vigilance Society working for the abolition of the white slave traffic,[2] arrived in Hong Kong in August 1919 with her husband, who had just been appointed Superintendent of the Naval Chart Depot. She was at once overwhelmed by the beauty of the islands but also shocked by the presence of child drudges.

The sight of small children toiling so incessantly, and in many instances carrying weights so far beyond their strength was a painful one. They had such aged, joyless, careworn faces. We did not know that many among them were slaves, . . . But we were soon to know.[3]

A sermon in the Cathedral attacking the system of buying and selling girl children under the specious title of 'adoption' revealed the truth to her, and she herself heard a child screaming in the night with pain and terror with the police refusing to investigate 'over the weekend'. How could child slavery be reconciled with Christ, Clara Haslewood asked herself, or with British citizenship? She wrote in shocked but reasoned remonstrance to the Hong Kong papers, announcing her determination to contact sympathetic peers and MPs in Britain. The Governor of Hong Kong, Sir Reginald Stubbs, immediately prompted the naval authorities to advise Lt Comdr Haslewood 'to restrain his wife or resign'.[4] He resigned, and the two of them returned to England in January 1920 to undertake their concerted campaign for the abolition of child slavery in Hong Kong via Parliament, the women's movement, the Anti-Slavery Society and the Church.

Ah Moy, a child slave of Hong Kong (Frontispiece to the Haslewoods' Child Slavery in Hong Kong, Sheldon Press, *1930)*

At first they seemed to be succeeding, after initial attempts in high quarters to disbelieve or deny the facts. Clara Haslewood wrote to the press, she addressed public meetings throughout England and Wales, she published pamphlets and lobbied Parliament. Helped by evidence from the Chinese Anti-Mui Tsai Society, founded in Hong Kong in 1921, the Haslewoods informed Col. Ward MP of the true situation in the Colony and he in turn so effectively challenged Churchill as Secretary of State for the Colonies that the latter brought in a new Industrial Employment of Children Ordinance apparently demanding imminent abolition of the system. However,

[in] 1923 the Duke of Devonshire succeeded Churchill and authorised the Hong Kong Government to suspend Part III of the Ordinance which contained the practical proposals for implementing the law: registration, inspection, payment of wages and provision for girls who left their employers.[5]

Six years later it was clear that the Ordinance had never been enforced and that the number of *mui tsai* had actually increased. As Clara Haslewood pointed out in 1930, it was futile merely to proclaim emancipation in a written Ordinance; an illiterate, helpless, battered child could not read and therefore could not apply to any authority for her freedom. The book that the Haslewoods published in 1930, *Child Slavery in Hong Kong*, helped to re-engage public attention, as did the persistent, well-informed protests of Sir John Harris and KATHLEEN SIMON from the Anti-

Slavery Society. But the brutal mistreatment of children still went on. 'During the year 1929, 1,851 dead bodies of children were found by police in the streets and elsewhere in the colony of Hong Kong.'[6] Finally EDITH PICTON-TURBERVILL's Minority Report of 1936 set up a new, much more effective child-protection Ordinance so that by 1954 the Colonial Office could write to the Anti-Slavery Society that the system of *mui tsai* had almost ceased to exist in Hong Kong.

1. S. Hoe, *Chinese Footprints: Exploring Women's History in China, Hong Kong and Macau* (Hong Kong, Roundhouse Publications Asia, 1996), p. 189.
2. The papers of the Society are held in the Women's Library, London.
3. Lt Cmdr H. L. and Mrs Haslewood, *Child Slavery in Hong Kong: The Mui Tsai System* (London, Sheldon Press (financed by the SPCK), 1930), p. 10. A copy with Clara Haslewood's manuscript annotations and unpublished materials is held at Anti-Slavery International, London SW9 9TL.
4. Hoe, *op. cit.*, p. 190. Clara Haslewood was dismissed in Government House circles in the Colony as 'rather hysterical'.
5. Juliet Browne, 'Campaigns of the twentieth century – mui tsai', *Anti-Slavery* (January 2000), pp. 12–13.
6. Letter from Secretary of State for the Colonies (18.2.1931), quoted in H. L. Lt Cmdr and Mrs Haslewood, *Child Slavery in Hong Kong: The Attitude of the Church of England and Its Associated Societies* (4 pp.; Bath, ABC Press, 1931),where they write 'it is most disquieting to note the negative attitude towards this question shown by the Church of England . . . No bishop, for example, has ever raised the question in the House of Lords.'

Cf. also M. M. Dymond, *Yunnan* (London and Edinburgh, Marshall Bros, 1928), Preface: 'This book is written for the purpose of helping the slave girls of Yunnan, who are among the most helpless and hopeless of humanity. According to the League of Nations there are 3 million child slaves in China . . . many of whom after cruel beatings and often tortures are left on the street to die.'

HIGGS, MARY, OBE
(2.2.1854–19.3.1937)

SOCIAL INTERVENTIONIST;
CAMPAIGNER FOR DESTITUTE AND
HOMELESS 'VAGRANTS'

Father: Rev. William Kingsland, Congregational minister

Congregationalist, then Quaker by convincement

Not many women nearing 50 with their four children grown up would decide that they must now put on grimy rags and a shawl and try to 'pass' as a common vagrant, in order to investigate the conditions for destitute women in the 'casual wards' of workhouses, shelters and common lodging houses. But that is what Mary Higgs did at the turn of the twentieth century. Her resulting reports, *Glimpses into the Abyss* (1906), *How to Deal with the Unemployed* (1904) and *My Brother the Tramp* (1913) preceded Orwell's *Down and Out in Paris and London* (1933) by more than two decades. Mary Higgs, 'on the tramp', really *was* descending into the abyss, experiencing the conditions imposed on the 'untouchable' women and men of her day.

Mary Higgs (From The Friend, *26.3.1937)*

Mary Higgs had already demonstrated her unusual grit and determination as a young girl, Mary Kingsland, when she was one of the first women Cambridge University students at Girton. As such she had to take the strain of attesting the intellectual equality of women with men, taking the Natural Science Tripos examinations in 1874. She then worked as an assistant lecturer at Girton and as a grammar school science mistress until she married the Reverend Thomas Higgs, a Congregational minister, in 1879. They eventually settled in the cheerless, grimy industrial northern town of Oldham, where, inspired by her husband's success in converting a stretch of barren moor into a garden, Mary Higgs defiantly founded the Beautiful Oldham Movement: 'This work in its various developments has been copied and has brought beauty in many aspects to the slums and dreary sections of our great cities.'[1] Mary Higgs also worked in Oldham for the YWCA, for special schools, work with cripples and schools for mothers, as well as for inner-city regeneration. It was her connection with a small Oldham 'rescue home' for women that first led to her concern to find out more about lodging-houses for women.

What Mary Higgs discovered was the punitive deterrent 'philosophy' behind the treatment of women tramps as she picked oakum (untwisting tarred knotted rope inch by inch) for hours. 'Some workhouses are to be avoided like poison. There positive cruelty and insult reign, . . . the slightest resentment might be interpreted as "insubordination" and earn prison . . . Prison treatment would be preferable.'[2] What resulted, at least in part from her publication of her experience, was the formation of a National Association for Women's Lodging Houses and of a Vagrancy Reform Society which in turn led to a Government Committee of Enquiry into casual ward reform. Mary Higgs supported the building of Fellowship Hostels for the homeless, and inaugurated paper-sorting schemes for the unemployed; on her husband's death in 1907, she gave up her own home, Bent House, to be a lodging house for women and herself moved to Bent Cottage.

Lest it be thought that Mary Higgs worked 'only' for the improvement of life for the poor in Oldham or 'on the tramp', it should be added that she was also a lifelong pacifist. When she was 61 she was one of the signatories supporting the British Women's Committee for the Women's International Congress at The Hague in 1915,[3] and her outrage that men would be *conscripted* to kill in 1916 led to her applying for membership of the Society of Friends. She became a Quaker Elder and attended the Society's Meeting for Sufferings until the last months of her life.[4]

1. Obituary, *The Times* (22.3.1937).
2. Mary Higgs, *Glimpses into the Abyss* (London, P. S. King and Son, 1906), 'A Northern Tramp Ward', pp. 154–5. It is noteworthy that she singled out the Salvation Army shelters as models for relief work: see review of *Glimpses into the Abyss* in *The Englishwoman's Review* (12.10.1906).
3. See Introduction and Appendix I.
4. For further information on Mary Higgs, see Girton archives; the British Library Catalogue; and obituary in *The Friend* (26.3.1937). Her writings include *How to Deal with the Unemployed* (London, S. C. Brown, Langham and Co., 1904); *My Brother the Tramp* (1913; revised as *Down and Out*, London, SCM, 1924); and *How to Start a Women's Lodging House* (16pp.; London, P. S. King and Son, 1912).

HILLS-YOUNG, ELAINE, MBE

(3.2.1895–29.5.1983)

PIONEER MIDWIFE IN EGYPT AND THE SUDAN; RED CROSS RELIEF
NURSING ORGANIZER; CAMPAIGNER AGAINST CLITORIDECTOMY

Father: — Greenwood
Stepfather: — Hills-Young, railway engineer
Mother: — Hills-Young, formerly Greenwood

Anglican

Originally a certificated nurse in home nursing and ambulance work, Elaine Hills-
Young began what was to be her extraordinary far-ranging and demanding life-
work in nursing as a humble VAD in Edinburgh at the outbreak of the First World
War. Having qualified as a State Registered general nurse and midwife by 1921,
she went on to train in mothercraft. Then her adventurous life began.

Elaine Hills-Young was appointed to the Kasr-al-Aini Hospital in Cairo in 1923
and immediately had to start learning basic hospital Arabic, since few of the
Egyptian nurses spoke English. Her night rounds included many patients on the
floors of wards and in the corridors, quite apart from the thousand bedridden, so
that by the end 'she was glad of a cup of tea'.[1] She started the first District
Midwifery Department in Cairo and attended emergency cases in mud huts with
nothing but a couple of sacks and whatever equipment or pieces of cloth she could
bring in herself. After having been called home to nurse her ill stepfather, she was
awarded a British Red Cross Scholarship to do advanced study at London
University together with nurses from sixteen different countries. As well as hospital
and training school administration, they studied maternity and child welfare, hygiene
and the prevention of disease. Her Bedford College Principal was Gem Jebb, cousin
of the inspirational EGLANTYNE JEBB, and Elaine Hills-Young and her fellow
students became 'the Old Internationals', later the Florence Nightingale
International Nurses' Association, formed to foster worldwide friendship and nursing
education. Their motto was 'Small in numbers, great in work and full of friendship
for the world'.[2]

Elaine Hills-Young then worked for fourteen years in the Sudan, first as Matron
of Khartoum Hospital and then as Principal of the midwifery training school,
Omdurman and supervisor of midwives and child welfare organizations for the
whole of the Sudan. She visited all her district midwives in rural areas, travelling
by jeep and, when necessary in the desert, by camel. She taught the illiterate
midwives to distinguish between ergot and antiseptic by taste, and for the literate
nurses she wrote a simple illustrated textbook in Sudanese Arabic. She started public
health training for nurse/midwives and lectured on nursing to senior medical
students in Khartoum. She also founded the Red Cross First Aid services in the
Sudan.

Returning to Europe in 1943, Elaine Hills-Young was appointed to escort
severely wounded prisoners of war from Sweden to England. Then, in February
1945, as HQ Matron, British Red Cross Relief Commission, north-west Europe,
she was among the first nurses to enter Belsen; she helped organize the six British
Red Cross mobile teams sent there to cope with the desperate situation of the
60,000 survivors, including 1,500 cases of typhus and 900 of typhoid. She never

forgot the horror of seeing the starving women who could only be given vitamin pills and anti-dehydration fluid for days on end before it was safe to feed them again. '[Nothing] that has ever been written about it can truly describe Belsen – it was too ghastly for words.'[3]

Next Elaine Hills-Young was sent to take charge of hundreds of patients in displaced persons camps in Celle, Münster and the Ruhr. She did welfare work among the hungry and homeless Germans in the aftermath of the war, and helped to rehabilitate the German Red Cross after its recent Nazification. The German nurses were touchingly grateful to her for the interest she took in them and for her faith in their dedication. From her headquarters in Vlotho, in Holland, she organized penicillin banks, set up six tuberculosis preventoria and oversaw 'Operation Shamrock', which sent 50 Berlin 'waifs and strays' a week to foster parents in Ireland.

On her return to England in 1949, Elaine Hills-Young was 65 but she worked, tireless as ever, for the international abolition of clitoridectomy, for her long experience in maternity work in Egypt and the Sudan had revealed to her the appalling medical consequences of female genital mutilation. Her vigorous campaign against female circumcision, based both on her medical research and on her own nursing experience, resulted in her sending a memorandum to all members of the House of Commons prior to a question being asked in the House, and she was invited (1949/50) to present a paper on the subject to the Status of Women's Commission of the United Nations in Geneva. She never wavered in her desire to see the abolition of female circumcision, still keeping up her correspondence about it until just days before she died.

1. Marion Donaldson, SRN, SCM, RNT, 'Miss Elaine Hills-Young, MBE D.N.', typescript memoir, held in British Red Cross Archives, London.
2. *Ibid.*
3. Elaine Hills-Young, quoted in Donaldson, *op. cit.* Note also Dame Janet Vaughan's tribute: 'You would like to know what absolutely magnificent work I found the Red Cross teams doing at Belsen. We have heard a great deal of the horrors of the Camp, we have not heard enough of the heroism of the few English men and women who were first on the spot, your Red Cross teams especially': in Dame Beryl Oliver, *The British Red Cross in Action* (London, Faber, 1966), p. 496.

See also entries for EVELYN BARK, HELEN BAMBER and STELLA REEKIE.

HOBHOUSE, EMILY
(9.4.1860–8.6.1926)

CAMPAIGNER AGAINST BRITISH CONCENTRATION CAMPS; ANTI-MILITARIST

Father: Rev. Reginald Hobhouse, Archdeacon of Bodmin
Mother: Caroline, née Trelawny

Originally Anglican, later Christian humanist

For fifteen years after she was 19, Emily Hobhouse took the place of her dead mother and worked in her father's rural Cornish parish, visiting the poor, the sick and the dying, and distributing food, clothing and religious reading matter. For the last three of those years she also had to nurse her invalid, aged father. Thus she was 35 when his death released her to begin her life in the outside world, without any formal education or professional training but armed with natural ability, strength of will and an uncompromising moral idealism. Her first astonishing enterprise was to volunteer to go as a 'missionary' among the wild emigrant Cornish miners in Minnesota. Once she arrived at Virginia, near the Canadian frontier, in 1895, she discovered very few Cornishmen but many wild miners, totally given over to gambling and drink, whose addiction supplied the city revenues via 'liquor licences'. Emily Hobhouse's first unpopular cause, therefore, had to be Temperance. She travelled round the lumber camps, holding services and Temperance meetings, and started a public subscription library. From Minnesota, two years later, she moved to Mexico but left after a disappointment of the heart, and went to live in

Emily Hobhouse, c. 1917

London, working for the Women's Industrial Council, studying Industrial Law and the Factory Acts. This then was the strong-minded woman of 40, already a convinced Liberal anti-imperialist, who was to take on the British government about its conduct of the Boer War (1899–1902).

'To Emily Hobhouse, the South Africa war was inhuman from the moment that it broke out.'[1] She became Hon. Secretary of the women's branch of the South African Conciliation Committee, founded by Quakers and by Liberals including KATE COURTNEY to bring unbiased facts about the war home to the British public. Emily Hobhouse believed 'that moral laws apply to nations as much as to individuals, that a true patriot is one who speaks out against his country when moral laws are broken, and that no government has the right to suppress criticism of its policies'.[2] Early in July 1900, after addressing large meetings up and down the country, she was howled down by a hostile mob at Liskeard, Cornwall, when trying, with Lloyd George and Leonard Courtney, to criticize the war. Chairs and benches were hurled at their heads. 'I lost the majority of the friends of my girlhood, and it was a great loss.'[3]

Emily Hobhouse learned that in June 1900 (midwinter in South Africa) the British army had started its policy of farm-burning and the internment of tens of thousands of homeless Boer women and children in the world's first 'concentration camps', consisting of tents on the veldt. So strong was her sense of the immense suffering this policy must be causing that she felt compelled to go out to South Africa herself to do whatever she could to alleviate it. She founded the South African Women and Children's Distress Fund 'to feed, clothe, shelter and rescue women and children, Boer, British or others who [have] been rendered destitute and homeless by the . . . military operations'[4] and on 7 December 1900 she sailed for Cape Town, to distribute the Fund's first moneys and see the situation for herself. She managed to persuade the High Commissioner Sir Alfred Milner, a family acquaintance, to permit her to visit refugee camps no further north than Bloem-fontein, if the military allowed. Under conditions of extreme discomfort, exhausted, alone and nervous, she accompanied her truck of supplies, the only woman in a military train, to her first sight of a concentration camp. It was midsummer; flies, ants, scorpions and snakes invaded the tents where women and children were perishing from malnutrition, scarlet fever, typhoid and tuberculosis. She immediately wrote long reports home vividly describing the terrible situation: 'Will you try somehow to make the British public understand the position and force it to ask itself what is going to be done with these people.'[5] Extraordinarily, Emily Hobhouse, an unenfranchised single woman, by publicizing these conditions, including the monthly death rates in the camps, roused the conscience of at least part of the British Establishment, splitting the Liberal Party on the issue. Her campaign saved thousands of lives by persuading the British government to force the military to take more effective humanitarian measures in administering the camps, and almost certainly shortened the war.[6] But the moral intransigence of her publicity campaign, as she spoke and wrote tirelessly throughout the country on her return in May 1901, did not endear her to the government, least of all to Mr Brodrick, the Secretary for War: when she tried to return to Cape Town to inspect the camps again in October 1901, she was not allowed to land but was arrested at sea and forcibly deported. After the war was over, she did return to South Africa to report on its aftermath; as part of the reconstruction, almost single-handed, she established home industries for Boer women and girls, especially weaving, in 27 centres in the country.[7]

Then came the First World War. To Emily Hobhouse, every war was not only wrong in itself but also a crude mistake. Therefore she had to work against this one. Her first initiative was to publish an Open Christmas Letter to the Women of Germany and Austria in December 1914.

Sisters,
. . . The Christmas message sounds like mockery to a world at war, but those of us who wished and still wish for peace may surely offer a solemn greeting to such of you who feel as we do. Do not let us forget that our very anguish unites us, that we are passing together through the same experiences of pain and grief.
. . . We pray you to believe that come what may we hold to our faith in Peace and Goodwill between nations; while technically at enmity . . . we own allegiance to that higher law which bids us live at peace with all men.
. . . We hope it may lessen your anxiety to learn that we are doing our utmost to soften the lot of your civilians and war prisoners, . . . even as we rely on your goodness of heart to do the same for ours in Germany and Austria.
. . . As we saw in South Africa and the Balkan States, the brunt of modern war falls upon non-combatants . . . women, children, tiny babies, old and sick, . . . Relief, however colossal can reach but few . . . We must urge that a truce be called . . . [8]

Emily Hobhouse gathered over 100 signatures from leading Quaker, Liberal and socialist women to this appeal, and in due course, scores of her German and Austrian counterparts did indeed reply in the same spirit.[9] Her next anti-war effort was to support the Women's International Congress at The Hague in April 1915,[10] after which she worked for its international Committee of Women for a Permanent

Peace in Amsterdam. Her peace advocacy in Holland, Switzerland and Italy was noticed by the Foreign Office with some dismay. Full of misgivings, they allowed her a visa for Italy, provided she give an undertaking not to indulge in peace propaganda. They were, therefore, not pleased to learn that she had participated in an international women's meeting on the need for peace in Berne, in May 1916. Much worse, they later learned that she had actually spent June in German-occupied Belgium and even in Berlin! She had gone, she said, 'in the interests of truth, peace and humanity'.[11] She had visited British prisoners of war at Ruhleben and had had an interview with the German Foreign Minister von Jagow, who hinted to her that Germany might be willing to negotiate a peace settlement if Britain made overtures. He himself was soon sacked, however, and the war was pursued with greater ferocity than ever. The British government was predictably outraged by this woman's quixotic and apparently unstoppable sense of personal mission to right the wrongs of the world. She was accused in Parliament of deliberately betraying her country, and forbidden to leave Britain for the duration. British law was thereupon changed, making it a criminal offence under the Defence of the Realm Act to make contact with the enemy from neutral territory.

Emily Hobhouse herself had to endure the last years of the war in near despair. But the moment the Armistice was signed, she initiated three relief projects. First, she co-founded a Swiss Relief Fund for starving children coming first from Vienna and then from Germany, Czechoslovakia and Hungary. Next, in July 1919 she started a Russian Babies' Fund to send milk, clothes and soap to desperate Russian children. Finally, in September 1919, at the age of nearly 60, she made a visit to Vienna and Leipzig on behalf of the Save the Children Fund and discovered that there was now no public feeding of children in Leipzig at all. So in January 1920 she herself started a feeding programme for the pale, emaciated youngsters, beginning with 250 children and eventually providing meals for 11,000. It was said of her then: 'She was undaunted by all opposition from the authorities on her arrival in Leipzig . . . [and her] amazing power of organization did not lessen her intense sympathy with individual cases of suffering.'[12]

Five years later Emily Hobhouse was dead, having lived long enough to criticize the South African whites' conduct to non-whites in 1924: 'Personally I believe segregation of any [kind, whether] of race or colour and class the wrong policy and one which can only lead to discontent and ultimate disaster.'[13] At her own request, her ashes were buried in South Africa. At the wish of the South African government, they were interred in the monument at Bloemfontein to the memory of the 26,000 women and children who died in the Boer War.

1. John Fisher, *That Miss Hobhouse* (London, Secker and Warburg, 1971), p. 82.
2. *Ibid.*, p. 99.
3. Ruth Fry, *Emily Hobhouse: A Memoir* (London, Jonathan Cape, 1929), p. 74.
4. *Ibid.*, p. 87. See also Sybil Oldfield, 'The enemy's friend, Kate Courtney', in Sybil Oldfield, *Women against the Iron Fist: Alternatives to Militarism 1900–1989* (Oxford, Basil Blackwell, 1989), pp. 24–9.
5. Fry, *op. cit.*, p. 109.
6. See Emily Hobhouse, *The Brunt of War and Where It Fell* (London, Methuen, 1902); Fry, *op. cit.*, chs 6 and 8; Fisher, *op. cit.*, pp. 206–7.
7. See entries for RUTH FRY and MARIAN ELLIS.
8. Published in *Ius Suffragii* (January 1915) and the *Labour Leader* (January 1915). The 100 British signatories included Margaret Ashton, Louie Bennett, Margaret Llewelyn Davies, Isabella Ford, Katharine Glasier, Violet Paget ('Vernon Lee'), Sylvia Pankhurst, Priscilla Peckover, Caroline Playne, Maude Royden, Annot Robinson, Esther Roper, Ada Salter, Sophia Sturge and Dr Ethel Williams.

9. The German signatories to the reply, published in *Ius Suffragii* (March 1915), included Lida Gustava Heymann, Dr Anita Augspurg, Dr Helene Stöcker, Konstanze Hallgarten, Minna Cauer, Ottilie Hofmann, Margarete Selenka and Ida Jens – many of them later persecuted by the Nazis.
10. See Introduction and Appendix I.
11. Emily Hobhouse, letter to *The Times* (12.11.1916).
12. Lady Clare Annesley in Fry, *op. cit.*, p. 281.
13. Fisher, *op. cit.*, p. 266; see also Fry, *op. cit.*, pp. 278–83.

There was a hostile obituary in *The Times* (10.6.1926). There is no entry for Emily Hobhouse in the *Dictionary of National Biography*.

HODGKIN, DOROTHY CROWFOOT, OM, FRS, NOBEL LAUREATE

(12.5.1910–29.7.1994)

SCIENTIST

Father: J. W. Crowfoot, education officer and archaeologist
Mother: Mary, née Hood, archaeologist, textile historian

Agnostic

Dorothy Hodgkin receiving an honorary DSc from the University of Sussex, June 1965 (Courtesy of University of Sussex Photographic Unit)

Not every scientist is necessarily a humanitarian, but a strong case can be made for Dorothy Hodgkin. She herself acknowledged the great influence upon her of J. D. Bernal's *Social Function of Science*.[1] Bernal was a Marxist who believed, during the collapse of world capitalism in the Depression years, that there should be a rational i.e. a 'scientific' planned economy in which scientific research would be devoted to the eradication of poverty, hunger and disease. Bernal was her research supervisor in 1932, her friend, and, briefly, her lover. She had already been a socialist and pacifist as a student at Oxford – influenced in her idealism by her mother[2] – but between 1932 and 1934 in Cambridge with Bernal her convictions strengthened and she regularly attended the Cambridge Scientists' Anti-War Group that he had formed. Like him she believed in the application of science for humane, not military, ends and in science as a co-operative, open venture to that end.

Dorothy Hodgkin consistently chose to do research with a clear medical application. Among all the other molecules she might have elected to try to analyse, she concentrated on insulin: essential to control diabetes; on vitamin B12: essential to treat pernicious anaemia; and on penicillin. 'Her work has been about people dying or not dying.'[3] As evidence that this emphasis was not a triple coincidence, quite incidental to her 'pure' fascination with X-ray crystallography, there are her own reflections on the application of her work:

If we knew in all fundamental detail how insulin acts to control our metabolism we might be able to devise far better methods for treating the different disorders associated with diabetes, blindness for example, which insulin injections only very imperfectly control.[4]

And:

I like best to see the effects [of research] in the general improvement of life expectation; for example the yearly average of deaths in early childhood from infectious diseases in 1931–5 was 3000 in this country; in 1966 it was 500. No doubt other factors than antibiotics contributed to this effect, but still the change is staggering.[5]

In 1964 Dorothy Hodgkin was awarded the Nobel Prize for chemistry for her work in determining the structure of biochemical compounds of primary importance.[6]

Both Dorothy Hodgkin and her husband were champions of access to education in the exploited and impoverished post-colonial Third World. It was she, for example, who was instrumental in encouraging Bristol University students to fund scholarships for black students from apartheid South Africa, and she herself was always the first to acknowledge the valuable scientific discoveries of colleagues in Africa, India and China. Politically, her most important co-operative venture was to be co-founder in 1955 of Pugwash, the international organization of scientists from East and West who wanted to keep lines of communication open, despite the Iron Curtain and the Cold War, in the hope of helping to prevent a thermonuclear catastrophe.[7]

No account of Dorothy Hodgkin, however brief and inadequate, could omit some testimony to her as a person of a singularly sweet and beneficent character. Informal and egalitarian in all her dealings with her research students and laboratory teams, she amazed newcomers by her approachability and personal diffidence. Not the least of her achievements was her steady following of her own inner light as a scientist while enabling her husband to follow his, and her children and grandchildren to grow up feeling personally cherished, as well as proud of her. Her own mother, she said, had been her heroine.[8]

1. Gill Hudson, 'Unfathering the thinkable: gender, science and pacifism in the 1930s' in Marina Benjamin (ed.), *Science and Sensibility: Gender and Scientific Enquiry 1780–1945* (Oxford, Basil Blackwell, 1991), p. 275. See also Maureen Julian, 'Women in crystallography', in G. Kass-Simon and P. Farnes (eds), *Women of Science: Righting the Record* (Bloomington, Indiana University Press, 1990), pp. 71–5.
2. Lisa Tuttle, *Heroines: Women Inspired by Women* (London, Harrap, 1988), pp. 41–2.
3. Hudson, *op. cit.*, p. 279.
4. Dorothy Hodgkin, 'Discoveries and their uses', Presidential Address (British Association for the Advancement of Science, 1978), p. 10, in Hudson, *op. cit.*
5. *Ibid.*, p. 7.
6. See obituaries: by the Nobel Prize winner Max Perutz, *Independent* (1.8.1994), and by Professor Louise Johnson, *Independent* (3.8.1994); *The Times* (30.7.1994); and by her scientific colleague Guy Dodson, *Guardian* (1.8.1994).
7. See Georgina Ferry, *Dorothy Hodgkin: A Life* (London, Granta, 1998).
8. See Tuttle, *op. cit.*

For other personal reminiscences see *Observer* (13.11.1964); and 'Recollections of Dorothy Hodgkin as student, researcher and academic at Somerville College, Oxford', *Somerville College Report and Supplement* (1994).

HOLTBY, WINIFRED
(1898–1935)

WRITER; CHAMPION OF WOMEN'S
HUMAN RIGHTS AND OF AFRICAN
LIBERATION

Father: David Holtby, farmer
Mother: Alice, née Winn, governess, farmer and
County Councillor

Humanist

Winifred Holtby had barely fifteen years
(1920–35), after graduating from Somerville
College, Oxford, in which to leave her
imprint on the English-reading world. During
those years, she evolved from uncritical
Conservatism to membership of the Independent Labour Party; from equality feminism in the 1920s to a social feminism in the
1930s that also took account of biological
and socialized gender difference; from volunteering to join the Queen Mary Army's

Winifred Holtby, c. 1930

Auxiliary Corps in 1918 to pacifist internationalism; and from indifference on racial
issues to a whole-hearted commitment to the struggle for the human (and political)
liberation of Africans, especially in South Africa.

Winifred Holtby is notable for her outspoken moral courage on two issues in
particular. First, she insisted on women's right not only to birth control[1] but also
to therapeutic abortion on medical and social grounds, long before the general
British public was prepared to countenance it. She wrote about abortion in *Women
and a Changing Civilization* (1934), in her letter to *Time and Tide* (18.1.1933) headed
'Population control', and very eloquently through her depiction of a sick, poverty-
stricken mother of too many children, Mrs Holly, dying of her last childbirth in
the novel *South Riding* (1936).

Secondly, Winifred Holtby was one of the first British journalists to try to awaken
awareness of the cruelty, injustice and sheer wrongheadedness of racial segregation
in British Africa. She was alerted to the iniquitous 'colour bar' in her first visit to
South Africa in 1926. Thereafter she campaigned consistently on behalf of Africans.
Of General Hertzog's Native Policy, she wrote that 'it has been framed without
regard to black opinion, black interests or black liberties'.[2] She spelt out the National
Party's blatant plan to deprive Africans even further of their land, and of all their
civil liberties, including the franchise where they had once had it, in the Cape.
Moreover she saw that the South African racist precedent could soon be extended
northwards to Kenya, Northern Rhodesia and elsewhere. 'There is a real danger
lest the South African native policy, born of prejudice, race interest and [economic]
opportunism, may become the model for the rest of the world to follow.'[3] 'No
privileged minority can be trusted to treat with decency a subject class, sex, or
race.'[4] However likeable she found Jan Smuts, she abhorred his righteous
inhumanity to non-whites:

he does not see . . . black and brown men and women as his countrymen; he does not see them as human beings at all. Nice natives, good dogs, merry, obedient, rather stupid servants, gay singers and players, swift runners, impossible economists, tribal humorists, inheritors of folk-law priceless to anthropologists . . . yes. But human beings, no.[5]

Winifred Holtby's humanist feminist critique of fascist anti-feminism is to be found in her 'Black words for women only',[6] and in *Women and a Changing Civilization*. For her writing and speaking for the League of Nations Union, her ironic 'Apology for armourers',[7] and her increasingly urgent advocacy of disarmament, see Marion Shaw's 'Winifred Holtby and the peace movement'.[8]

But it is her posthumously published novel *South Riding* that is the most accessible and lasting testament to Winifred Holtby's profound humanism: unpretentious, down-to-earth and never out of print since 1936. She says in the novel's Prefatory Letter to her mother, Alderman Alice Holtby, that she concentrated on the implications for individual lives of the Local Government Act of 1933 in order to share the recognition that

we are not only single individuals, each face to face with eternity and our separate spirits; we are members one of another, [and have] a common battle against our common enemies – poverty, sickness, ignorance, isolation, mental derangement and social maladjustment.

The novel is imprinted with Winifred Holtby's own experience of pain and with her immense sympathy for the pain of others, as well as with her vital and energetic determination to abolish remediable suffering. Hence her four heroines: the slum-enduring mother, her gifted young daughter, the spinster headmistress and the 72-year-old woman County Councillor.

No account of Winifred Holtby, however short, should leave out the heroic humaneness of her personal life. Acutely aware of the short time she had left to live, she not only remained continually interruptible and responsive to others' needs, she even remained full of humour and zest, thus sparing everyone dear to her the pain of her suffering, but increasing thereby her own ultimate isolation.[9] Her memorial service was conducted by Canon 'Dick' Sheppard at St Martin-in-the-Fields. The first tangible memorial to her was set up in South Africa, 'a library for coloured people in Johannesburg, so successful that two more are to be opened'.[10]

1. See 'A conspiracy of silence', *Time and Tide* (28.10.1933); and *Women in a Changing Civilization* (London, John Lane at the Bodley Head, 1934).
2. *Women's International League for Peace and Freedom News Sheet* (November 1927), reprinted in Paul Berry and Alan Bishop (eds), *Testament of a Generation: The Journalism of Vera Brittain and Winifred Holtby* (London, Virago, 1985), pp. 177–81.
3. *Ibid.*
4. Berry and Bishop, *op. cit.*, p. 188. Winifred Holtby, like MABEL SHAW, acknowledged the revelations of Norman Leys concerning the racial injustice in British colonial education policy.
5. Berry and Bishop, *op. cit.*, p. 198. See also Winifred Holtby's chapter in William Ballinger (ed.), *Race and Economics in South Africa* (London, L. and V. Woolf (Hogarth Press), 1934); and Marion Shaw, *The Clear Stream: A Life of Winifred Holtby* (London, Virago, 1999), ch. 6: '"The goal of all men's longing": South Africa and William Ballinger'.
6. *The Clarion* (24.3.1934), reprinted in Berry and Bishop, *op. cit.*, pp. 84–6. See also Winifred Holtby in *News Chronicle* (May 1934).
7. In Storm Jameson (ed.), *The Challenge to Death* (New York, E. P. Dutton, 1935).
8. See W. Chapman and J. Manson (eds), *Women in the Milieu of Leonard and Virginia Woolf: Peace, Politics and Education* (New York, Pace University Press, 1998), pp. 115–16, 119 and 121–2.

9. See Vera Brittain, *Testament of Friendship* (London, Macmillan, 1940; reprinted Virago, 1980), *passim*; P. Kennard, *Vera Brittain and Winifred Holtby: A Working Partnership* (Hanover, University of New Hampshire, 1989); and obituaries in *Daily Telegraph* (30.9.1935) and *The Times* (30.9.1935).
10. See *The Times* (3.4.1936) and *Daily Herald* (3.2.1948).

Winifred Holtby's papers are held in Bridlington Public Library and Hull Public Library.

HOWARD, LOUISE, LADY
(26.12.1880–11.3.1969)

INTERNATIONALIST WRITER;
ECOLOGICAL PIONEER

Father: Carl Matthaei, commission merchant
Mother: Louise, née Sueur, musician

Christian humanist

Louise Howard, c. 1950 (Frontispiece to Mother Earth, the journal of the Soil Association, October 1953)

Louise Howard had no fewer than three separate distinguished careers. After obtaining Firsts in both parts of the classical Tripos at Cambridge (1903–04), where she had been inspired by the teaching of the socialist pacifist feminist Janet Case,[1] she obtained a research fellowship and then in 1909 became lecturer and director of studies in classics at Newnham College. In 1918 she published *Studies in Greek Tragedy*, focusing on the role of tragic accident. By then, however, anti-German feeling at Cambridge had caused Louise Matthaei, who was half German, to resign her university post. She had been incautious enough to publish two internationalist essays, pleading for an end to the collective paranoia that was demonizing all Germans during the First World War.[2] She believed that no nation was fit to judge another without a sense of the forgiveness that it was in need of itself – as indeed the whole of Europe would be in need of forgiveness when it stood before the tribunal of the coloured races. She then joined Leonard Woolf as assistant editor on his new *International Review*, being responsible, among other things, for translation and analysis of political reports from Germany and Italy. In 1920 she published her pro-Spartacist *Germany in Revolution*.

Then Louise Matthaei began her second career. She joined the League of Nations Agricultural Section of the International Labour Organization (ILO), after succeeding in the competitive entrance examination. In 1924 she was promoted to Chief of the Agricultural Section and in 1935 her huge, global overview, *Labour in Agriculture: An International Survey*, was published by Oxford University Press.

In 1931 Louise Matthaei had married her sister's widower (Sir) Albert Howard, economic botanist to the government of India and a passionate advocate of organic farming. He advocated respect for the traditional wisdom, gained from years of trial and error, of generations of peasants the world over. In 1947 Louise Howard published *The Earth's Green Carpet*, in which she anticipated the later ecological movement's central concerns with soil fertility and the depletion of forests. In that work she looked forward to a world without frontiers and to free exchange between the nations of the direct and indirect products of sunlight and of an organically fertile soil, which she held to be the birthright of all humanity. After her husband's death in 1947 she co-founded the Albert Howard Foundation, which merged with the Soil Association in 1953. She was also a leading member of the Associated Countrywomen of the World.[3] During the 1930s and 1940s she had done much to help German refugees from Nazism on their arrival in Britain.

1. Janet Case was the lifelong friend and political ally of Margaret Llewelyn Davies; see S. Oldfield, 'Virginia Woolf and Antigone', *South Carolina Review*, **29** (1) (Fall 1996), pp. 49–50. See also Virginia Woolf, *Diary*, vol. 1 (9.4.1918) and *Letters*, vol. 2 (4.11.1920).
2. See Louise Matthaei, *The Lover of the Nations: An Essay on the Present War* (Cambridge, Heffer, 1915); and her essays in *Ius Suffragii* (edited by Mary Sheepshanks) (1.9. 1915 and 1.10.1915). Louise Matthaei was on the British Committee supporting the Women's International Congress at The Hague: see Introduction and Appendix I.
3. See entry for MARGARET ROSE WATT; and biographical note on Lady Howard in *Mother Earth*, the journal of the Soil Association (October 1953).

HUGHES, MARY
('COMRADE')
(29.2.1860–2.4.1941)

RESCUER OF LONDON'S DESTITUTE AND HOMELESS

Father: Thomas Hughes, Christian Socialist,
  Judge, author of Tom Brown's
  Schooldays, *and brother of pioneer*
  philanthropist Mrs Nassau Senior
Mother: Annie Frances, daughter of Prebendary
  James Ford

Anglican, later Quaker by convincement

From the age of 23, Mary Hughes kept house for her uncle John Hughes, vicar of Longcot, Berkshire, where she was introduced to rural poverty and became both a Poor Law Guardian and a District Councillor. In 1896, when she was 36, she moved to the East End of London as an unofficial voluntary parish worker at St Jude's, Commercial Road, Whitechapel, where her sister Lilian was the wife of the vicar, the Rev.

Mary Hughes, c. 1930 (From Hugh Pyper, Mary Hughes: A Friend to All in Need, *Quaker Home Service, 1985)*

Henry Carter. There she began her real life-work of sharing, and trying to shoulder, the troubles of the most afflicted, despairing people in London. She went into the slum dwellings, the workhouses, the doss houses, the lock wards, the Poor Law Infirmary, growing more and more shabby in solidarity with the outcast. To the respectable world it seemed that she had become woefully careless of herself and her surroundings – especially after she lost her sister Lilian and her brother-in-law in the sinking of the *Titanic*.

In 1915 Mary Hughes moved into Kingsley Hall, in Bow, the community settlement of the sisters Doris and MURIEL LESTER. She lived on bread and margarine and vegetables with a very little cheese, and always refused a fire, declaring "'Indignation keeps me warm!'" . . . For thirty years she had no new clothes, no holiday and no proper bed.'[1] In 1917 Mary Hughes was made a (highly unorthodox) JP for the Tower Division, Shoreditch, sitting on 'rates' and 'educational' cases, sometimes so moved to tears by the tragedy behind the 'cases' that she herself paid the fines the law demanded. She also became a Labour councillor for Stepney, always topping the poll, though most 'of her time was spent on those with no votes, the homeless, the children or the mentally ill'.[2]

From 1918 on Mary Hughes had been accepted into the Society of Friends because she could not see how a Christian could justify war as she felt the Church of England had tried to do. She moved back to Whitechapel, becoming a Poor Law Guardian and regular visitor at the children's home and Poor Law infirmary. Every day the unemployed would knock on the door of her two-room flat in Blackwall Buildings asking if she knew of any work going. She called unemployment 'The Devil's unemployment', writing it in red ink and underlined. In 1928 she moved to a converted pub at 71 Vallance Road which she re-named The Dew Drop Inn and offered as a social centre and night refuge for the homeless of the neighbourhood. The poorest were also, understandably, verminous, and it was said of Mary Hughes: 'Her lice were her glory.'[3] She called herself a Communist (hence 'Comrade') and took part in the marches of London's unemployed, no matter how threatening, or threatened by mounted police. 'She was always there' wrote Father Groser.[4] When Gandhi visited Kingsley Hall in 1931 he asked to see her. She died in the East End on 2 April 1941, appalled by those Christians in Britain calling for retaliation on German cities for the Blitz. George Lansbury wrote: 'Our frail humanity only produces a Mary Hughes once in a century.'[5]

1. Hugh Pyper, *Mary Hughes: A Friend to All in Need* (London, Quaker Home Service, 1985), pp. 13 and 26.
2. *Ibid.*, p. 15.
3. See articles on Mary Hughes' work in Whitechapel in *Manchester Guardian* (26.8.1936); and *News Chronicle* (9.9.1936).
4. Rosa Hobhouse, *Mary Hughes: Her Life for the Dispossessed*, with a Foreword by Howard Spring (London, Rockliff, 1949), p. 114.
5. *Ibid.*, p. 92. See also obituaries in *The Friend* (11.4.1941); *Manchester Guardian* (4.4.1941); *Daily Herald* (4.4.1941); and *The Times* (5.4.1941).

I

INGRAMS, DOREEN CONSTANCE
(24.1.1906–25.7.1997)

FAMINE RELIEF WORKER;
CHAMPION OF ARAB GIRLS
AND WOMEN

*Father: Edward Shortt, barrister
and Liberal MP, Home Secretary
Mother: Isabella Stuart, née Scott,
from Valparaiso, Chile*

Freethinker

A convalescent home in Mukalla set up during the time of the 1943–44 famine. Left to right in the middle of the children: Dr Barrington, Doreen Ingrams, Harold Ingrams, helper, RAF man, helper (Courtesy of Leila Ingrams)

A political idealist and radical all her long life, young Doreen Shortt was a Home Ruler, a supporter, and a critic, of the Russian Revolution, and a vigorous opponent of racial prejudice. In 1930 she left her work as a travelling actress and married an unusually progressive-minded colonial officer, Harold Ingrams.

In 1934, after an intensive course in Arabic, they went to southern Arabia and explored the British (Eastern Aden) Protectorate of the Hadhramaut, now part of Yemen, by donkey and camel. They were the first Europeans ever to live so far east of Aden. Through her acquisition of Arabic and her ability to mix without condescension, warmly and sympathetically, with the secluded women there, Doreen Ingrams learned much about their lives, and at their request started an informal discussion group with reading lessons. 'I never wanted to thrust advice down their throats as it has always seemed to me a gross impertinence to go into someone else's house and tell them how to run it.'[1] In 1937 she adopted a little Hadhrami girl called Zahra. After peace had come to the blood-feud-riven region, in large part because of the good offices of the Ingrams,[2] Doreen was able to found the first Bedouin girls' school and a school for blind children and orphans in Mukalla.

> [Among the] thin scantily clothed boys and girls I noticed a little skeleton hanging on to the hand of another boy . . . I saw the skeleton was a blind child . . . I asked for his father and arranged that the child should be taken to Mukalla, where I promised he should be cared for . . . Subsequently Effendi, as we called him, became the first pupil in the blind school which was started [in our house] because we felt there must be so many children like him.[3]

In the drought and famine of 1943–44, the Ingrams ensured that women and children left behind in the stricken villages could come in by lorry to Mukalla to be fed and housed. The only existing hospital was for men; so Doreen and her Arab friend Rahima turned part of an empty house into a makeshift emergency hospital for

> emaciated women of all ages, some holding babies in their arms, while other children with enormous stomachs walked feebly on thin sticks of legs . . . No women in purdah would have been allowed to help there so [I] sought help amongst the able-bodied bedouin women.[4]

At first the Bedouin women were unwilling to do the dirty work of nursing but when they saw Doreen and Rahima wiping bottoms and changing the excreta-filled cotton cloths of the patients, they began to help with a will.

> I had never imagined that such frail bodies could house so many worms, some a foot long, and often vomited from the mouth, . . . It was the children who were most pathetic, their enormous eyes gazed round in pitiful bewilderment, and they died so quietly, one moment I would be cradling a child in my arms, helping him to sip water, the next his little head drooped and he was dead . . . It was a wonderful satisfaction and relief to see a child able at last to stand on his own feet when only a few days before he had been at the point of death, or to see the despairing eyes of the little girl whose mother had died . . . become normal as she found security in the newly opened beduin girls' school . . . Anyone who has seen a famine-stricken country can never forget it.[5]

After the famine, the Ingrams organized a children's village for the orphaned or homeless children of Bedouin agricultural labourers.

On her return to Britain, after further service with her husband in the Gold Coast and Hong Kong, Doreen Ingrams lectured on the Hadhramaut and the lives of Arab women and joined the BBC Arabic Service in 1956, often revisiting the Arab world, including institutions she had founded decades earlier. She was an active supporter of self-determination ('We should have left South Arabia ten years earlier than we did'[6]), an opponent of apartheid, and a champion of Palestinian rights. Her book *Palestine Papers 1917–1922: Seeds of Conflict* (1970) is a devastating, scholarly indictment of British triple-facedness:

> There were . . . by 1917 two contradictory promises made by the British Government regarding the disposal of Turkish-held territory after the war: first, the promise of independence to the Arabs given in the letter from Sir Henry McMahon to Sherif Hussein, and, second, the promise to the French given in the Sykes–Picot Agreement. In 1917 the British Government made a third promise, this time to the Zionists.[7]

In 1967 Doreen Ingrams became a founder member of the Council for the Advancement of Arab–British Understanding and after her retirement she became an active supporter of the United Nations Association and of Amnesty International. She published her book on women in Iraq, *The Awakened*, in 1983; her last work, *Records of the Yemen, 1798–1960*, co-edited with her younger daughter Leila, was published when she was 87.[8] In 1993 she was unanimously awarded the Royal Asiatic Society's Sir Richard Burton Memorial medal for her work in south Arabia (she had been overlooked in 1945 when her husband had been awarded that medal).

At the age of 91 she was made the first Patron of the newly formed Friends of the Hadhramaut, a charitable trust to help the people who live in one of the poorest corners of the Arabian peninsula. Thus she continued to work in service to others till her death. In his obituary note in *Asian Affairs* (October 1997), John Shipman quoted Doreen Ingrams' own words in *A Time in Arabia* as her epitaph: 'When you break bread with people and share their troubles and joys, the barriers of language, of politics and of religion soon vanish.'

1. Doreen Ingrams, *A Time in Arabia* (London, John Murray, 1970), p. 130.
2. In 1939 they were jointly awarded the Royal Society for Asian Affairs Lawrence of Arabia Memorial Medal for their outstanding role in bringing peace to the Hadhramaut: see obituary for Doreen Ingrams, *The British–Yemeni Society Journal*, **5** (December 1997).
3. Ingrams, *op. cit.*, ch. 15: 'A patrol with the Hadhrami Bedouin Legion, April, 1943'.
4. *Ibid.*, p. 144.
5. *Ibid.*, pp. 144–7.
6. *Ibid.*, Postscript, pp. 150–1.
7. Doreen Ingrams (ed.), *Palestine Papers 1917–1922* (London, John Murray, 1972), p. 3.
8. Obituaries for Doreen Ingrams were published in *The Times* (11.8.1997); *Guardian* (5.8.1997); *Independent* (31.7.1997); *Daily Telegraph* (13.8.1997); *Middle East International* (29.8.1997); *British–Yemeni Society Journal* (December 1997); *Asian Affairs* (October 1997); *Bulletin of The Society for Arabian Studies* (Spring 1998); and various Arab papers.

See also Doreen Ingrams, *Survey of Social and Economic Conditions in the Aden Protectorate* (London, Asmara, 1950).

I am most grateful to Leila Ingrams for her information and assistance in compiling this entry on her mother's work.

J

JAMESON, STORM
(8.1.1891–30.9.1986)

ANTI-FASCIST WRITER; REFUGEE RESCUER

Father: William Storm, sea-captain
Mother: Hannah Margaret, née Jameson

Atheist

Storm Jameson may stand as an exemplar of all those British liberal humanists in the 1930s genuinely tormented by the incompatibility of their two ethical principles in politics: their anti-fascism and their pacifism. In addition she was acutely sensitive to that other intolerable antinomy, the fact that the same capitalist liberal democracy that allowed her her writer's freedom of expression also allowed/demanded the existence of a huge exploited, and wretched, working class – many of them without work.

> In the thirties, millions of half-fed hopeless men, eating their hearts out, gave off a moral stench which became suffocating.
> There really was a stench. On one side Dachau, on the other the 'distressed areas' with their ashamed workless men and despairing women.[1]

Like so many other writers, Storm Jameson was drawn into the Common Front of the Left, feeling in bad faith because of her scepticism about Stalinist Russia, but also feeling forced to join in 'protest writing' that she suspected was futile:

> The amount of time and energy I spent on reading and writing pamphlets, and attending committees and political meetings, was prodigious. And they bored me! I felt asphyxiated by the jargon that was beginning to take the place of criticism.[2]

Even her absolute loathing of war was compromised in the early 1930s by the necessity to promote the necessity for collective, armed security under the League of Nations. By the late 1930s, the abominations of Nazism were already so vivid and repellent to her that she had to renounce her pacifism altogether, losing a close friend like VERA BRITTAIN in consequence.

> If I believe that concentration camps, the torture of the Jews and political opponents, is less vile than war, I must say so plainly . . . With physical nausea, I thought: I can't say it . . . For pacifist and non-pacifist alike, there is a choice between two guilts, two prices. The price for surrendering to the Nazi barbarians is Auschwitz, . . . [the] price of war is a million, ten million, broken tortured bodies, broken minds, and the destruction of long-living cities and villages.
> No answer, no answer.[3]

A passionate European, Storm Jameson travelled back and forth to Vienna, Prague, Paris, trying to shore up solidarity among intellectuals of the Left. The handing over of the Czechs to Hitler in 1938 struck her with a sick shame, as well as with terror for her fellow-spirits and friends now at the mercy of Hitler. For six years (1938–44) she became the first British President of International PEN. She took on the position because so many writers in Europe were desperate for help, as they sought to flee Nazi Europe:

> Letters – from Vienna, Prague, Brno – poured into our shabby office . . . [we] were in the situation of a man with a piece of frayed rope trying to save hundreds sinking into a quicksand.
> There were too many of them.
> We answered every letter, we tried to get the visas needed, an effort involving us in hundreds of letters to the Home Office and visits to overworked refugee organisations. For one person we got out, ten, fifty, five hundred sank.[4]

When the internment of 'B class aliens' was under way in Britain in 1940, her efforts to champion anti-fascist writer/refugees in Britain had to be not redoubled but requadrupled:

> The third wave of exiles had broken over us when France collapsed and the intellectuals who had fled there from Czechoslovakia and Poland had to move on . . . A few, very few, Germans escaped at the same time . . . I could only think that the jailing of all these helpless refugees opened a crack into an abyss of dull meanness.[5]

Storm Jameson's own innermost life of the imagination was taken over.

> The raw nerve-ends of our time are all outside England. Problems which with us have remained embryonic come monstrously to life in countries where . . . the most commonplace, the least heroic might suddenly have to take a decision involving the life and death of wife, child, friend . . . I laid novels in France, Poland, Norway, Czechoslovakia . . . My theme was the one that has obsessed me all my life: Why are human beings so cruel?[6]

Yet all the time she knew that as a writer her real gifts and fascination were with the complexities of the 'normal' emotional life, not with the abnormalities of a monstrous time and place. Not surprisingly, her books were banned by the Nazis and her name was on their death lists.

The end of the Second World War did not bring Storm Jameson peace of mind. She saw in the atomic obliteration of Hiroshima the self-obliteration of what she meant by civilization. And when she returned to liberated central and eastern Europe in 1946–47, she came face to face not only with the imminent imposition of the Stalinist alternative dictatorships, but also with the atrocities now being perpetrated against anyone, of any age, guilty of being an ethnic German, whether in former East Prussia or Poland or the Habibor camp in Czechoslovakia, not to mention the continuous vigorous life of paranoid folk anti-Semitism in the very countries that the Nazis had so thoroughly 'purified' of Jews. Again, however isolated and unpopular, she had to testify.

Storm Jameson was constantly aware that the speed and degree of twentieth-century technological 'advance' had outstripped the capacity to feel and think sanely.[7] And she was never able, any more than King Lear had been, to answer the question: 'Is there any cause in nature that makes these hard hearts?' Because she was so committed both to *humanitas* and to intellectual clarity, she felt constrained to wage a hard, continuous mental fight for an ethical stand, both within herself and with her contemporaries, while recognizing, tragically, that there was no unproblematic, humane resolution on offer. All she could salvage finally in the matter of principle was to live and die a nuclear pacifist and an absolute opponent of torture under any circumstances.[8]

1. Storm Jameson, *Journey from the North* (London, Collins, 1969; republished Virago, 1984), vol. 1, p. 293.
2. *Ibid.*, p. 295.
3. Jameson, *op. cit.*, vol. 1, pp. 341–2; vol. 2, p. 96. See also her argued explanation of her renunciation of pacifism in *The End of This War* (1941): *op. cit.*, vol. 2, pp. 95–6.
4. Jameson, *op. cit.*, vol. 2, pp. 18–19. See also Nicola Beauman on Jameson in *A Very Great Profession* (London, Virago, 1983); and entries for Jameson in P. and J. Schlueter (eds), *An Encyclopaedia of British Women Writers* (New York, Garland, 1988); in Virginia Blain, Patricia Clements and Isobel Grundy, *The Feminist Companion to Literature in English* (London, Batsford, 1990); and in Janet Todd (ed.), *British Women Writers* (London, Routledge, 1989). For other anti-Nazi British women writers of the time, especially Phyllis Bottome, see Barbara Brothers, 'British women write the story of the Nazis: a conspiracy of silence' in A. Ingram and D. Patai (eds), *Rediscovering Forgotten Radicals: British Women Writers, 1889–1939* (Chapel Hill and London, University of North Carolina Press, 1993).
5. Jameson, *op. cit.*, vol. 2, pp. 76–7.
6. *Ibid.*, pp. 372–3 and 364.
7. *Ibid.*, p. 95.
8. *Ibid.*, p. 365.

JEBB, EGLANTYNE
(25.8.1876–17.12.1928)

FOUNDER, SAVE THE CHILDREN
FUND; SISTER **DOROTHY BUXTON**

Father: Arthur Trevor Jebb, barrister and philanthropic squire
Mother: Eglantyne, née Jebb, Co-operative arts and crafts organizer

Christian humanist

Eglantyne Jebb, c. 1914 (From Dorothy Buxton and Edward Fuller, The White Flame, *Longmans, 1931)*

After reading history at Lady Margaret Hall, Oxford, and writing the first study of urban poverty in Cambridge, Eglantyne Jebb went out to Macedonia in 1913 to do relief work with women and children behind the lines of the Second Balkan War. It was her initiation into the tragic realization that every war, however 'righteous', victimizes children, especially the refugee children who are its direct result. She then spent the First World War in Britain, working with her sister DOROTHY BUXTON on the *Cambridge Maga-*

zine's 'Notes from the foreign press' that translated news about conditions in 'enemy' countries. By 1918 the situation in ravaged, deliberately starved, central and eastern Europe was disastrous.

> Mothers killed the babies whom they could not feed. Parents sent their children to the hospitals when they could no longer give them any bread, but in the denuded hospitals they were simply placed in rows to die . . . Even children killed themselves when unable to endure any longer the pangs of hunger.[1]

Eglantyne Jebb and her sister roused leading public opinion to back a Fight the Famine Council in January 1919 to lobby for the cessation of the Allied Blockade. But political/economic argument was not in itself effective direct relief and therefore Dorothy Buxton moved that the Council create a sub-committee responsible for sending food and clothing to the child sufferers: 'I have no enemies under seven', as Bernard Shaw put it to a hostile anti-German at the time.

Eglantyne Jebb became Hon. Secretary of the Save the Children Fund in the summer of 1919 at the age of 43 and gave the rest of her life to it. She turned out to be a brilliantly effective transnational aid organizer, pioneering professional and even scientific methods in order to raise the maximum funds for the world's needy children in disaster areas. 'We have to devise a means of making known the facts in such a way as to touch the imagination of the world.' She insisted that there should be no grounds, whether of race, nationality or creed, for excluding any child from receiving relief: 'The only international language is a child's cry . . . We must write out our belief in *deeds* before we can communicate this belief to others.'[2] Her principles were:

> that aid should be given in a planned, scientific manner;
> that it should be preceded by careful research;
> that it should be directed towards families;
> that it should be given on the basis of need and not any sectarian basis;
> that it should be constructive, self-sustaining;
> that it should stimulate self-help;
> that it should be pioneering, and able to develop models for others to follow.[3]

In its first four years the Fund made vast contributions, via donations from individuals, churches and trades unions all over the world, to relieve the suffering of starving children in defeated Germany, Austria and Hungary, the million Greeks expelled from Turkey, and then the victims of the Russian famine. 'Nansen later reported that in Saratov thirty to forty children had been dying daily but, thanks to the Save the Children Fund, deaths had been reduced to two or three a week.'[4]

But by 1923 Eglantyne Jebb realized that the Save the Children Fund must not remain a merely reactive force, responding always only *after* some terrible event of war, epidemic, famine or natural disaster. It needed now to energize all the governments of the world to be proactive and to take responsibility for ensuring a basic humanly viable life for every one of its children. She therefore drafted a *Declaration of the Rights of the Child* in 1923. It was adopted by the League of Nations and led in turn to the United Nations Declaration of the Rights of the Child in 1959.[5] Eglantyne Jebb's original Declaration stated:

By the present Declaration of the Rights of the Child, commonly known as the 'Declaration of Geneva', men and women of all nations, recognising that Mankind owes to the Child the best that it has to give, declare and accept it as their duty that, beyond and above all consideration of race, nationality, or creed:

I   THE CHILD must be given the means requisite for its normal development, both materially and spiritually.

II THE CHILD that is hungry must be fed; the child that is sick must be nursed; the child that is backward must be helped; the delinquent child must be reclaimed; and the orphan and the waif must be sheltered and succoured.

III THE CHILD must be the first to receive relief in times of distress.

IV THE CHILD must be put in a position to earn a livelihood and must be protected against every form of exploitation.

V   THE CHILD must be brought up in the consciousness that its talents must be devoted to the service of its fellowmen.[6]

By 1928 Eglantyne Jebb had recognized that the children of Africa and Asia were even more deprived than those in Europe. It was time to take on a world brief for the world's children. She planned the first international conference ever held on infant mortality, education and child labour in Africa, and she was increasingly haunted by the misery and exploitation of children in Asia. Weakened by her many journeys, rucksack slung over her shoulder, to outposts of the Fund's work throughout Europe, and by the unremitting stress of her imaginative identification with the suffering of unheard children, she died prematurely in Geneva in December 1928.

'She seemed, as it were, Humanity's conscience.'[7]

1. Eglantyne Jebb, *Save the Child* (essay; London, Weardale Press, 1929).
2. *Save the Children Fund Information Sheet 15: Eglantyne Jebb, Founder of Save the Children* (London, 1994), p. 7.
3. Eglantyne Jebb, *op. cit.*, p. 8. The later debt of Oxfam and UNICEF to the Save the Children Fund's first principles is clear.
4. Kathleen Freeman, *If Any Man Build: The History of the Save the Children Fund* (London, Hodder and Stoughton, 1965), p. 31.
5. For further information on Eglantyne Jebb see Dorothy Buxton and Edward Fuller, *The White Flame* (London, Longmans, 1931); Edward Fuller, *The Right of the Child* (London, Gollancz, 1951); Francesca Wilson, *Rebel Daughter of a Country House: The Life of Eglantyne Jebb, Founder of the Save the Children Fund* (London, Allen and Unwin, 1967).
6. See Buxton and Fuller, *op. cit.*
7. Anonymous Swiss obituarist, quoted in Buxton and Fuller, *op. cit.*, p. 87.

JEWITT, DOROTHY, SRN, MBE

(3.5.1896–20.10.1985)

MEDICAL MISSIONARY NURSE AND
MIDWIFE, NIGERIA

Father: Harold Jewitt, compositor
Mother: Harriet, née Torble

Anglican

Dorothy Jewitt and Ibo patients, c. 1930
(Courtesy of Dorothy Jewitt's step-grand-
daughter Professor Anne Stevens)

A former pupil of Mary Datchelor School, Dorothy Jewitt qualified as a nurse and midwife and then offered herself in 1922, at the age of 26, for Church Missionary Society work 'anywhere there was need'.[1] She was sent first (1924–27) to Iyi Enu in Nigeria, where she found herself without electricity, sanitation or piped water and where she rapidly had to learn Ibo to help thousands of patients. There, and later at Bethel in the Isoko swampland, she testified to a loving God as the alternative to the terrifyingly cruel gods of tribal custom. Snakes in the grass, leopards stalking the night, having to cross crocodile swamps balancing on a floating palm trunk and wearing just khaki shorts and a shirt – these were a few of the 'challenges' that faced her. Dorothy Jewitt concentrated on infant and maternal welfare; 60 per cent of her converts were women, perhaps not surprisingly as she worked against the practice of clitoridectomy, trained African midwives, and admired the beauty of African babies. She worked for over 30 years in West Africa, including Onitsha, Oleh, Warri and the Oji River leprosy colony, and at the end of her service the Africans named her Nne-ora, 'Mother of many'.[2] Her own greatest respect and admiration were for her first African students of midwifery: old Christian women who risked being punished as 'witches' should one mother or baby die in their care.

1. Dorothy Ross (the later, married, name of Dorothy Jewitt), 'The pattern of a life' (70 pp.; typescript memoir), in the Church Missionary Society archive, University of Birmingham.
2. *Ibid.*

See also her letters in the CMS archive and articles in *The Mission Hospital* (1927 and 1931).

JORDEN, ELLA PRISCILLA, MBE, ARCM
(5.3.1909–September 1993)

INTERNATIONAL RED CROSS NURSE/MIDWIFE; REFUGEE RELIEF WORKER

Father: Edward Jorden, farmer, Chepstow
Mother: Elizabeth, née Thomas

Methodist

Ella Jorden's first experience of nursing abroad also led directly to her first experience of the terrible suffering of uprooted, hunted refugees. She was Matron of Irbid Hospital, near Hankow, when the Japanese invaded China. In August 1940 she was trekking westwards down a mountain, together with thousands of desperate people, only to reach sanctuary in a gutted city without water. She had to help fight the consequent outbreak of cholera under the eyes of the Japanese occupation forces, and she was so useful in this and subsequent posts, including the maternity department of the Country Hospital, Shanghai, that her internment was delayed. In 1942, however, she was interned for two and a half years.

On her release in 1945, wearing a pair of shoes donated by the Red Cross, Ella Jorden worked in China for the International Red Cross and was so admiring of their approach, answering the urgent medical needs of anyone 'irrespective of race or creed or political considerations',[1] that she left her medical missionary society to devote herself to working for the Red Cross for the rest of her life.

> Many people are apt to associate Red Cross exclusively with war-time activities, such as tending the wounded and contacting prisoners of war, and far less is known of its civilian relief work amongst the millions of homeless and sick, suffering from the *after*-effects of war. (My italics)[2]

In September 1946 Ella Jorden was sent by the British Red Cross to work in Hamm, Westphalia, among German deportees from East Prussia, mostly old people, women and children. Next she was made responsible for nursing services in ten displaced persons camps and two children's homes. Their population comprised former slaves of Nazi Germany, imported by the Reich from Poland, the Baltic, Hungary and Yugoslavia and now homeless – and unwilling to return to countries that had become part of Stalinist eastern Europe.[3] There she learned the impossibility of rehabilitating depressed people by medical intervention alone. After 'years of being shifted like goods from one corner of the continent to another [most] were sullen, resentful, and apathetic . . . [Everybody] basically needs to be made to feel necessary. To be just kept alive is not enough.'[4]

After her years in a Japanese prison camp and her experience with displaced persons in Germany, 'I thought I knew the depths of misery to which humanity can sink. But I was wrong, for I had no conception of the terrible suffering that I was to find in the months to come.'[5] What she now had to cope with was the aftermath of the foundation of the state of Israel: the consequent flight of hundreds of thousands of Palestinian refugees. In February 1949 she was sent to a refugee camp in the Jordan valley which had 17,000 people in 1,400 ragged tents in the fly-infested desert, no doctor, no transport and no communications. She found hideous malnutrition, emaciated, wizened babies and 2-year-olds 'with legs as soft as soap, for they had never walked'.[6]

Sister Ella Jorden with sick baby and boy interpreter, Shuneh camp, Jordan valley, 1949 (From Ella Jorden, Operation Mercy, *Frederick Muller, 1957)*

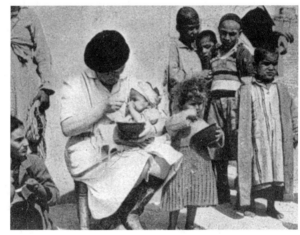

Sister Ella Jorden ensuring the feeding of girls, Palestinian refugee camp, Jordan, 1949 (From Ella Jorden, Operation Mercy, *Frederick Muller, 1957)*

Treatments had to be given in a leaking dilapidated tent and all equipment was lacking . . . [Many] seriously ill people had to be treated lying on the ground . . . In the early spring came rain and the camp was a quagmire. Sickness increased and there were cases of smallpox in addition to pneumonia, enteritis, malaria . . . and snakebite. By June the temperature reached 120 degrees F. in the shade.[7]

Clearly the situation was intolerable; eventually another, better site in the desert was negotiated and a ten-day exodus of the 17,000 people, many if not most of them in a pitiful state, was organized, largely by Ella Jorden. The refugees were resettled in parallel colonies of new tents named after their part of Palestine (to which they would never return): Jaffa, Haifa, Ramelira. One of the many problems Ella Jorden had to face was discrimination against girls: 'Unwanted girl babies were often allowed to starve because any available food would be given to sons rather than daughters, [and] often when we gave nourishment to a sick girl child it was given to her brothers.'[8]

From Transjordan, after UNRRA took over, Ella Jorden was sent in 1951 to organize British Red Cross work in Malaya after the Emergency. Here she encountered malaria but no mosquito nets or any other adequate medical supplies. 'At one time there were over three hundred tropical ulcers to be dressed, and only one set of bowls and forceps to do the work.'[9] Having started the training of the first young Malayan Red Cross detachments in First Aid and home nursing, she was then sent to her final aftermath-of-war posting: Korea. Here in 1953 once again she found stricken, destitute refugees, terrible deprivation, both in Seoul and in the surrounding countryside, and an enormous demand on emergency medical services. Patients were lying without a sheet on the bare springs of their beds. Her first job was to buy cleaning materials and disinfectant and supply basic bedlinen. She also worked for civilian relief via pioneer mobile dispensaries and re-established the war-damaged nurse training school of the South Korean Red Cross Hospital, Seoul.

For her twenty-year record of initiative and skilled devotion in next to impossible nursing situations all over the world, Sister Ella Jorden was awarded the International Red Cross's Florence Nightingale medal. She was a true internationalist, remarking at one point in her life when she was nursing 'the enemy':

There is not much place for politics in a maternity ward, and the young mothers were all my friends, whether Japanese or any other nationality . . . They were constantly reassuring me, and wishing me well, and young mothers who could not speak my language would just press my hand and smile.[10]

1. Ella Jorden, *Operation Mercy* (London, Frederick Muller, 1957), p. 70.
2. *Ibid.*
3. See entries for EVELYN BARK, DOROTHY ENGLAND, ELAINE HILLS-YOUNG, MARGARET MCNEILL and ELSIE STEPHENSON.
4. Jorden, *op. cit.*, pp. 82–3.
5. *Ibid.*, p. 93; see also entry for WINIFRED COATE.
6. Jorden, *op. cit.*, p. 104.
7. Beryl Oliver, *The British Red Cross in Action* (London, Faber and Faber, 1966), p. 509.
8. Jorden, *op. cit.*, p. 104.
9. *Ibid.*, p. 132
10. *Ibid.*, pp. 56–7.

See also material in the British Red Cross Archives, London.

JOWITT, LETTICE, MBE
(7.2.1878–15.3.1962)

EDUCATIONIST AMONG THE DEPRIVED; REFUGEE WORKER; TEACHER

Father: Reverend William Jowitt, rector of Stevenage, ex-headmaster
Mother: Louisa M.

Quaker by convincement

After a privileged education at Edgbaston High School and Somerville College, Oxford, Lettice Jowitt joined HILDA CASHMORE in her pioneering work in adult education for the deprived, founding Bristol University Settlement in 1911 and tutoring for the Workers' Educational Association (WEA). During the First World

War she worked for two years for the Friends' War Victims' Relief Committee in the Marne and Meuse.[1] After the war she moved to the grim north-east of England during its worst period of unemployment (1919–37). She set up the Bensham Grove Settlement,[2] establishing adult schools for both men and women, the first nursery school in Gateshead, WEA classes, youth groups, trade union weekend schools, and the first club for the unemployed on Tyneside; 600 people were using the centre by 1930, when she left to start a similar centre in Depression-hit Seaham. The mining communities in both places took her to their hearts, knowing she was totally on their side, determined for them to have life and to have it more abundantly.

At the age of 61, in 1939, Lettice Jowitt took a holiday. Unfortunately she chose Syria and was called on during the Second World War to take over the running of the Friends' High School in Brummana through the fighting between the Vichy French and the British in Syria; she had to lead a community that was suffering under bombardment, the incursion of refugees and requisitioning by the military from both sides. In September 1942 she left for England via South Africa, where she was urged to go on to investigate the condition of 3,000 Polish refugees who had ended up in camps in Tanganyika and Uganda after incredible suffering in Siberia. Lettice Jowitt spent the next two years living with them in their mud huts, teaching them English.

Between 1946 and 1947, now 68, Lettice Jowitt visited Quaker Relief teams working in France, Poland and Germany. In 1955 she was so incensed by the passing of the Bantu Education Act that she felt she must try to make a personal intervention in the cause of African education: she went to South Africa for a year at her own expense, visiting what educational institutions Africans still had, and herself did night-school work, teaching illiterate African men in the township of Langa, outside Cape Town, ignoring racial barriers and having no fear as she walked alone there at the age of 77. 'In her last years it was the advancement of education among Africans . . . which lay nearest to her heart.'[3]

Lettice's tenderness showed itself in a gift for listening, . . . Her sympathies were personal and particularized – never vague and generalized . . . [She] was a woman so liberated from preoccupation with her own personal problems, doubts and griefs that she was able to liberate others from *their* doubts, *their* griefs, *their* problems . . . [In] her last years . . . enquiring as to the activities of her friends, she would delightedly comment 'Well done, well done.'[4]

1. See entries for EDITH PYE and HILDA CLARK.
2. See Jessie Hetherington, 'Bensham Settlement', *One and All*, journal of the National Adult School Organisation (May 1995), pp. 11–12.
3. Obituary for Lettice Jowitt, *African Affairs* (July 1962).
4. *Friends' Yearly Meeting Proceedings* (1963), pp. 49–50. See also obituary in *The Friend* (23.3.1962), pp. 339–40.

K

KERR, ISABEL, MB, ChB
(30.5.1875–22.12.1932)

PIONEER MEDICAL MISSIONARY TREATING LEPROSY

Father: John Bain Gunn, farmer, died in Isabel Kerr's infancy
Mother: Mary, née Garden

Presbyterian

Isabel Kerr, having graduated MB, ChB, from Aberdeen in 1903, went out to Hyderabad, India, with her Wesleyan missionary husband Rev. G. M. Kerr, a former joiner, in 1907. Having studied Telugu, she set up a wayside dispensary and travelled from village to village by bullock cart. She worked all hours of the day and night and in all weathers, including the monsoon. On one occasion, during an outbreak of plague, the English were blamed for the epidemic and she and her husband were stoned.

Dr Kerr was particularly appalled by the scourge of leprosy in the city of Nizamabad, where in 1911 one person in every hundred had the disease:

> To view with equanimity the leper, clothed in rags, flaunting his indescribable sores by the roadside; to have his little children come to the dispensary, and recognize without horror to what they are doomed, requires an indifference to the interests of humanity impossible to any who follow the Christ . . .[1]

At a time when there was still no cure for leprosy, the diseased suffered social ostracism and were often driven to suicide; the only treatment was isolation and the dressing of sores. Dr Kerr opened the first home for leprosy sufferers at Dichpali, Nizamabad in 1915, funded by a wealthy Hindu, serving every religion and caste. But, as Isabel Kerr herself admitted, from the medical point of view it was heartbreaking work, since it could only be palliative treatment.[2] In 1921, however, after Leonard Rogers and John Muir discovered the curative efficacy of hyndocarpus oil, Dr Kerr was able to pioneer the *curative* treatment of leprosy by intramuscular injections. Now segregation was necessary only in the infectious secondary stage of the disease, the Leper Home could become the Wesleyan Leper Hospital, and, as Dr Kerr insistently declared: 'No leper child need ever grow up a leper.'[3] The older, incurable sufferers voluntarily left to make room for young, treatable patients who became symptom-free. The first leper boys' football team in the world started up in Nizamabad. In addition to her internationally famous teaching work at the Dichpali hospital, and at her later clinic in Hyderabad, Dr Kerr also did outreach work, travelling hundreds of miles, often starting on the 2 a.m. train. She even found and treated the Muslim women with leprosy secluded in zenanas, whether in ordinary homes or palaces. Of her 2,800 leprosy patients, over 1,000 had their disease arrested.

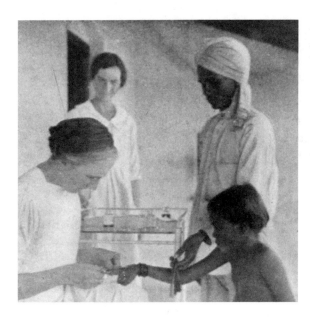

Dr Isabel Kerr treating child patient, c. 1930 (from Dermott Monahan, The Lepers of Dichpali, *Cargate Press, 1938)*

This work, constantly touching those considered untouchable, was not all that she did. 'She was always learning, never content to rest on her oars. Her subsidiary activities were endless',[4] ranging from organic soil experiments in rice cultivation to learning new handicrafts suitable as occupational/physiotherapy for her patients. In 1923 she was awarded the Kaiser-i-Hind gold medal for her work in India.

Isabel Kerr died of pneumonia, probably aggravated by exhaustion, at the age of 57.

1. Dermott Monahan, *The Lepers of Dichpali* (London, Cargate Press, 1938), pp. 23–4.
2. *Ibid.*, p. 39.
3. *Ibid.*, p. 54. Dr Kerr 'probably did more than anyone else to show that the world can be freed of the dread disease': *Aberdeen University Review*, **20** (1932–33), p. 189.
4. Monahan, *op. cit.*, p. 82.

See also Frank Oldrieve, *India's Lepers* (London, Marshall Bros, 1929); T. Carter, *Rosalie Harvey, Friend of the Leper* (London, Zenana Press, 1933); Donald Miller, *A Bridge of Compassion* (London, The Mission to Lepers, 1955/60), pp. 38–41; and obituaries for Isabel Kerr in *The Times* (24.12.1932); and *Aberdeen Press and Journal* (24.12.1932).

Dr Kerr had broadcast for the BBC from Edinburgh on her work with leprosy sufferers (17.8.1930).

———

KERRIDGE, PHYLLIS, PhD, MRCP
(*c.*1900–22.6.1940)

MEDICAL RESEARCHER; PIONEER OF HEARING AIDS FOR THE DEAF

Father: W. A. Tookey, consultant engineer

Humanist

Beginning as a young scientist graduating in chemistry, Phyllis Kerridge went on to research hydrogen ion concentration and the study of pH determination of blood and other biological fluids; she also carried out important investigations into proteinuria. Realizing that her biological research would be benefited by medical training, she qualified as MRCS, LRCP in 1933 and became an MRCP in 1937, without interrupting her other scientific work.

Dr Kerridge's most important contribution to medical science was her pioneering, patient and thorough work on hearing aids. She started clinics, first for children and then for adults, where the deaf could be accurately tested and 'where the appropriate hearing aid could be prescribed as carefully and exactly as the oculist prescribes glasses'.[1] Many other hospitals followed the immensely successful example of her clinic at University College Hospital, London, where patients valued her gentleness and understanding and mourned her early death.

1. A. Winner, obituary for Phyllis Kerridge, *Medical Women's Federation Quarterly Review* (July 1940), pp. 64–5.

See also obituaries in *The Lancet* (6.7 and 13.7.1940); and *British Medical Journal* (6.7.1940).

KEVIN, MOTHER MARY, OSF, CBE
(28.4.1875–17.10.1957)

MISSIONARY MEDICAL WORKER; TEACHER IN AFRICA

Father: Michael Kearney, Irish smallholder
Mother: Teresa, née Grennell

Roman Catholic

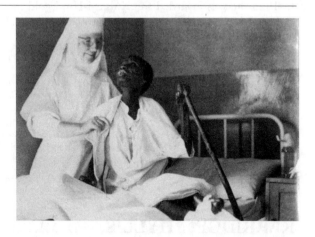

Mother Mary Kevin tending patient suffering from leprosy (From Sister M. Louis, Love Is the Answer, *Dublin, Fallons, 1964. Courtesy of Franciscan Missionary Sisters for Africa, Mount Oliver, Dundalk, Co. Louth, Ireland)*

Born in a small farmhouse in County Wicklow, Teresa Kearney lost her father before she was born and her mother before she was 10. There was no family money to train her as a teacher; so from the age of 15 she worked as a children's carer and nursery governess in various Dublin charity schools, before entering the Franciscan Order in St Mary's Abbey, London, as a novice in 1895. In 1898 she made her vows as Sister Kevin, hoping to serve the Mission to the American Negroes in Baltimore.

In the event, she was chosen to join the first contingent of missionary Sisters in 1902 to Uganda, where, twenty years earlier, some of the first African converts (later canonized) had been burnt alive by order of the Kabaka of Buganda. What she and her five fellow nuns now encountered, besides the exotic excitements of sleeping in a railway carriage besieged by hyenas and crossing the crocodile-infested Lake Victoria, was a people suffering from the famine and disease that followed every period of endemic civil war: malaria, yaws, leprosy, sleeping-sickness and even plague. Sister Kevin found her dispensary under a mango tree totally inadequate for the long lines of pitiful sufferers queuing, in heartbreaking hope, for help at last. The small band of nuns persevered, however, despite their own malnutrition and frequent bouts of disease, learning to speak Luganda and fearlessly tending the sick and dying, no matter how contagious, building the first attempts at clinics and schools where writing was taught in the sand. They introduced the cultivation of new vegetables and fruit, as well as the elementary hygiene needed to cut the appalling rate of infant mortality, so often due to gastroenteritis. Once one primitive convent settlement was established, Sister Kevin was deputed to go and start another, this time in lion country where the local witchdoctors stoned them and they were plagued not just by ants and rats but by locusts eating everything they had struggled to grow. The Africans flocked to Mother Kevin (as she became in 1910), asking for more clinics and schools, but she still had only half a dozen Sisters and her frustration was almost unbearable:

> There is nothing so hard as to have to refuse help where help is greatly needed. It was utterly heartbreaking to have to send sick people away because we could not take them in; to know that babies were dying in the villages when we might have been able to save them.[1]

On furlough in 1919, Mother Kevin took on the Church authorities to try to persuade them of the necessity for her studying gynaecology and obstetrics in order to be enabled to help the young African mothers otherwise doomed to die in childbirth, and their babies with them. But canon law forbade nuns to be midwives and her petition to study and qualify was refused. All that Mother Kevin could be permitted to do, using the influence of the Archbishop of Westminster, was to take a modified six months' course in obstetrics at a Catholic hospital run by nuns in Alsace. But she was still forbidden either to qualify or to practise. "'Believe me", she said, "that legislation will soon be changed, at least for missionary countries".'[2] And it was, in 1936, partly because of her trail-blazing and persistent urging behind the scenes.

On her return to Uganda in 1921 Mother Kevin founded the first training school for Catholic nurses in Africa, recognizing, after a terrible smallpox epidemic, that a handful of European nurses would never meet African health needs. Her seven African girls duly passed the qualification in maternity work that she herself had been denied. When other African girls came to her wanting to become nuns, although she could not pay their cattle bride-price to their families, she acted on her faith in their vocation – in the teeth of much white racist scepticism – and founded the Congregation of the Little Sisters of St Francis. By 1939 she had founded nineteen convents, each with clinics, dispensaries and schools, and always Africanizing the missions as she went. The girls were taught typing and book-keeping in addition to horticulture and domestic science; they could then go on to teacher training colleges. The first secondary school for girls founded by her in 1940 produced Africa's first Catholic woman legislator, its first woman BSc and its first woman doctor – this time in the teeth of African traditional opinion. But Mother Kevin was an irresistible force when it came to the education of girls.

Not that Mother Kevin was over-dedicated to the book-learning of which she herself had been deprived; her energy also went into stacking the brick kilns before a new building was started, working out the plumb-lines for the foundations, planting saplings for a new forest, helping with the laundry, and the baking and the hoeing in the garden, as well as serving in the dispensary and on the wards. She started the first leprosarium – a village in which leprosy sufferers could work and study and nurse one another – in Uganda and the first blind school. By 1952, after 50 years in Africa, she became the first Superior General of a new Order: the Franciscan Missionary Sisters for Africa. There were by now over 150 Sisters, from both races, working in twenty convents in Uganda and four in Kenya.

Mother Kevin's last years were spent literally begging for the mission in Africa, standing with a collecting basket in all weathers at church doors in the United States and Canada. After she died in Brighton, Massachusetts, her body was flown in state to be buried at the convent of her Order in Dundalk, Eire. But the Buganda would not accept that 'Kevina' should be buried anywhere than among them, and by public subscription, her body was flown out again, to rest, finally, in one of her very first foundations, Nkokonjeru, saluted by all races and creeds.[3]

1. Sister M. Louis, OSF (Franciscan Missionary Sisters for Africa), *Love Is the Answer: The Story of Mother Kevin* (Dublin, Fallons, 1964), p. 80.
2. *Ibid.*, p. 101.
3. There are today 700 African Sisters in missions vacated by the Franciscans; a great deal is being done for AIDS sufferers and for AIDS orphans needing adoption. The Franciscans have 22 Sisters still in Uganda working with the African Sisters. (Information from Sister Hyacintha Hudson, Mount Oliver, Dundalk, Co. Louth, Eire.)

See also Sister S. O'Hara, OSF, *Dare to Live! A Portrait of Mother Kevin* (Dublin, Veritas, 1979); Sister M. Louis, *The Unconventional Nun* (Dublin, Catholic Truth Society of Ireland, 1968); obituaries in *The Times* (19.10 and 24.10.1957); and *The Catholic Citizen* (15.11.1957).

KNIGHT, ELIZABETH, MB, DPH
(August 1869–31.10.1933)

CHAMPION OF HUMAN RIGHTS OF WOMEN WORLDWIDE

Father: John Knight, of the Knight's Castile soap family
Mother: Hannah, née Lucas

Quaker

It was said of Dr Elizabeth Knight: 'She had no idea of fear at all.'[1] After her initial study of classics at Newnham College, Cambridge, she took a long time to succeed in qualifying as a doctor at the London School of Medicine for Women but then almost immediately put her hard-won professional career at risk by her militant, though non-violent, commitment to the suffrage campaign. As an activist in the Women's Freedom League, led by CHARLOTTE DESPARD, she was arrested several times between 1908 and 1914, and imprisoned in Holloway at least three times; despite her highly privileged, sheltered background, she felt that she had to protest against the disenfranchised non-citizenship of women, if necessary by withholding her taxes. She also had to protest against war, and was on the British Committee supporting the Women's International Congress at The Hague in 1915.[2]

But above all Dr Elizabeth Knight felt she had to continue Josephine Butler's protest against the sexual reification of women in Parliamentary Acts designed to 'clean up' women for recreational use by the armed forces. Thus she 'was untiring in her opposition to the hateful 40D Regulation which involved the compulsory examination of women suspected of having transmitted venereal disease to a member of His Majesty's Forces',[3] and in her very last year she directed protests against the British government's signing of the French draft protocol at the League of Nations regarding traffic in women and children.

Dr Elizabeth Knight was active in every aspect of the social emancipation of women, and not just in Britain. She actively advocated the enfranchisement of Indian women, among whom she had close friends, and she was an enemy to every manifestation of colour prejudice. As a doctor she worked, until her premature death in a road accident, at the Evelina Hospital for Sick Children, the South London Hospital for Women, and the Mount Vernon Hospital for Consumption. She wrote for the Women's Freedom League's organ *The Vote* and published *Social and Sanitary Conditions of Prison Life*.

1. Obituary, *Daily Telegraph* (1.11.1933), quoting Miss Florence Underwood. Other obituaries in *Manchester Guardian* (1.11.1933); and *The Friend* (10.11.1933).
2. See Introduction and Appendix I.
3. Stella Newsome in *The Women's Freedom League* (1933), p. 19.

L

LACEY, JANET, CBE
(23.10.1903–11.7.1988)

INTERNATIONAL REFUGEE SERVICE AND RELIEF ORGANIZER;
CO-FOUNDER, CHRISTIAN AID AND VSO

Father: Joseph Lacey, property agent
Mother: Elizabeth, née Smurthwaite

Originally Methodist, then Anglican

Janet Lacey eventually became a world force for social intervention as Director of Christian Aid and co-founder, in 1958, of Voluntary Service Overseas (VSO), but her beginnings could hardly have been more humble or obscure. Although she had trained in drama and tried to go on the stage, in fact she failed to make a living and had to switch to train as a youth leader, working with the Young Women's Christian Association in Kendal. The misery of the pithead villages in the north, especially Durham, during the General Strike of 1926 made her join the Labour Party.[1] From 1932 to 1944 she ran a combined YMCA–YWCA community centre in Dagenham, but it was only when she went to work for the YMCA as Education Secretary serving with the British Army on the Rhine in defeated, devastated Germany in 1945 that she first felt addressed by the immeasurable suffering of refugees. She voluntarily, and unofficially, extended her youth work to reach out to young Germans as well as to British servicemen and displaced persons.

In 1947 Janet Lacey joined the British Council of Churches in London as Field Secretary of its youth department and moved from there to become temporary Secretary and then, in 1952, Director of its Aid and Refugee Service, soon to be known as Christian Aid. Under her directorship, Christian Aid grew from a staff of three to a staff of over 100 that raised more than £1,250,000 a year for relief projects in Europe, the Middle East, Africa and Asia. She travelled tirelessly, appointing agriculturalists and educationists to help promote projects in the field. 'This made the contribution of the British churches to overseas aid the largest and most influential in the world, and was due entirely to Miss Lacey's vision, imagination, remarkable energy and high efficiency.'[2] It was she who helped establish World Refugee Year and, above all, Christian Aid Week.

Janet Lacey was a committed ecumenicist who coined the phrase 'need not creed'. She was the first woman to preach in St Paul's Cathedral, where she spoke about the role of practical Christianity in tackling refugee problems and earthquake disasters, and was granted a doctorate of divinity in 1975. She wrote *By the Waters of Babylon*, about the worldwide needs of refugees, and *A Cup of Water* (1970). An exceptionally capable strategic planner and administrator, she would cultivate a blunt, no-nonsense manner in her unstoppable drive to turn pity into effective aid;

though autocratic, she had the wisdom to recognize expertise in others, to whom she would then delegate responsibility, with great results.[3]

1. See entry in the *Dictionary of National Biography, 1985–1990*.
2. Obituary, *Daily Telegraph* (16.7.1988).
3. For other obituaries see *Independent* (20.7.1988); and *The Times* (14.7.1988).

LEE, VERNON, *see* Paget, Violet

LESTER, MURIEL
(9.12.1883–11.2.1968)

SOCIAL REFORMER; EVANGELIST FOR
NON-VIOLENCE, CO-OPERATION AND
RECONCILIATION

Father: Henry Lester, wealthy London businessman
Mother: Rachel, née Goodwin

'Trying to be Christian'

It was her first meeting with the factory girls of Bow in the East End of London when she was 19 that decided the direction of Muriel Lester's life:

> They were much more mature and more independent than I. Why were some of them pale, others thin, with bent shoulders? . . . Why should they go on working, . . . bound to a machine for ten and often for eleven hours a day . . . Producing pleasure and ease for such as I?[1]

Muriel Lester (Courtesy of Jill Wallis)

She was drawn to return again and again to Bow, joining in the Girls' Club activities and eventually starting a 'Women's Meeting' there that heard talks on labour laws, industrial compensation and alcoholism, as well as on life in foreign lands. Her own life was still divided between 'apprenticeship' to the East End and months with her family wintering on the Riviera. But by 1906 she had become a socialist, influenced by George Lansbury and Beatrice Webb's Minority Report on the Poor Law Commission, and by 1910 she was entreating the preacher at the City Temple to give a Sunday address on the Belgian atrocities in the Congo; for years she was tormented by the conviction that she ought to go herself to King Leopold and confront him with the facts. In 1911 she was converted to absolute Christian pacifism by Tolstoy's 'The Kingdom of God is within you', and at last, at the age of 28 in 1912, she actually moved to live in Bow, lodging with her younger sister Doris at 60 Bruce Road. They started an adult school and, like MARY HUGHES, a teetotal pub. 'Kingsley Hall [named after their dead brother] . . . was an overdue act of justice . . . Everybody must have a decent place wherein to spend the evenings.'[2]

The known pacifism of Kingsley Hall led to anonymous threatening letters and even 'roughing up' for Muriel Lester when she protected victims of anti-German rioting in the East End during the First World War; and it was early in that war (December 1914) that she found, indeed co-founded, her other lifework: the Fellowship of Reconciliation.[3] Her own 'war work' after Conscription in 1916 was to support conscientious objectors at their tribunals, visit them in prison and see to the maintenance of some of their families. Immediately after the war she met German and Austrian pacifists through the Fellowship, her 'first contact with the enemy'.[4] In 1921 she could no longer endure the contradiction between her Christian faith in brotherhood and justice and her own privilege. Together with Mary Hughes and Rosa Hobhouse, she took on, and invited others to take on, the condition of 'voluntary poverty', as opposed to the 'compulsory want' imposed on millions of underfed, slum-housed Britons. She and the dozen or so other 'Brethren of the Common Table' met once a month to tell each other exactly how much money they had earned or received in the past month and how they had spent it. Any surplus was taken, as of right, by anyone who needed it: 'The only Christian, the only rational basis for distribution of goods is need . . . We found it the hardest thing we had ever done . . . From very shame of confessing, one lowered one's weekly expenditure on self.'[5] Muriel Lester gave up not only gloves and coats but, much harder, giving presents and subscriptions to worthy causes. As Chairman of the Maternity and Child Welfare Committee for the borough of Poplar (1921–24) she oversaw a huge reduction in infant mortality and fought, successfully, against a government order to cut the supply of free milk. She also roused public opinion about homelessness, rat-infestation and flooding by sewage in the East End: 'Telling the truth is perhaps the pacifist's only weapon.'[6] As well as writing articles and letters to the paper, and occasionally broadcasting, she would also fight her agonies of self-consciousness each weekend and speak out at open-air meetings in Hyde Park for the Fellowship of Reconciliation. 'One starts talking to a dog, a lamp-post, and one's companion who makes a valiant attempt to appear a stranger arrested in the act of passing by.'[7]

In 1926 Muriel Lester made her first visit to India, at the instigation of Tagore's son-in-law, who had been a speaker at Kingsley Hall, and there she joined Gandhi's ashram. Audaciously, she invited him back to England, not to teach those in power but to learn from the English poor. On condition that she first roused public opinion in Britain against the British countenancing of the drink and opium trades (having first collected evidence in India from Indian Civil Service officials and even Governors and the Viceroy), Gandhi agreed that he would visit England.

Back in England, Muriel Lester addressed meetings up and down the country criticizing British policy in India; she made over her inheritance from her father into a 'Restitution Fund' supplying home helps to needy women in Poplar; and she hit upon a system of communal living and working in the new Kingsley Hall in Powis Road whereby 'we would all take part in the cleaning, fire-stoking, floor polishing, door-keeping and locking up'.[8] Anyone could volunteer to give full-time service in exchange for food and shelter and two shillings (10p) pocket money. Not surprisingly, time and again, the seven volunteers were shocked by their own failure to live out their idealism; it was not easy to turn out of one's own little cell whenever someone homeless or a foreign visitor needed to be put up, and there was never, ever, any privacy. For all the shortcomings of life at Kingsley Hall, however, it was only there, in one of its seven 'roof cells', that Gandhi wished to live during weekdays on his visit to Britain for the abortive Round Table Conference after his great Salt March.

Next came China and Japan. In 1932 the Fellowship of Reconciliation asked Muriel Lester to go to both countries to witness to anti-militarism, now that Japan had begun to invade China. For decades she had felt deep shame with regard to Britain's nineteenth-century Opium Wars against China; now she would try to do something, however slight, for the Chinese. First, in Japan, she contacted the pacifists there, led by Toyohiko Kagawa (1888–1960), while she herself spoke of the Gandhian Non-Violence Movement, always knowing that her speeches on war-resistance were being reported by government agents. The Japanese public believed the propaganda that their army was in China only to help the Chinese get rid of bandits. Muriel Lester told them that the rest of the world, via the medium of broadcasting, reported 'every new bite you take out of the living body of China'.[9] She confessed to her own shame at British imperialism and appealed to Japanese women intellectuals to protest against Japanese imperialism. In China she saw the struggle against the Japanese occupation and investigated the child labour in the cotton mills; in Hong Kong she checked on liberated *mui tsai* slave girls.[10]

Then back to India to rejoin Gandhi. Muriel Lester found she could be useful as a go-between, interpreting the stance of the Congress movement to the Governor of Bengal and even the Viceroy, and vice versa. She was clearly trusted by both sides to have an inner understanding of their points of view. She decided to spend longer travelling throughout India and resigned her position of responsibility at Kingsley Hall. Next she went to lecture in the United States in order to finance a prolonged tour of China and Japan, where she found herself involved in fact-finding and reporting on the new Japanese drug-trafficking in China that was intended to weaken the Chinese not only through opium but also by addiction to heroin and cocaine. Her 'meddling' in Shanghai entailed personal danger. She had interviews with the Japanese Consul-General in Tientsin (Tianjin) and then went on to Tokyo to give her evidence to Ministries and statesmen, all of whom purported to be shocked. In 1936 her evidence was laid before the Opium Advisory Committee of the League of Nations in Geneva.

There was one other consequence of Muriel Lester's involvement with the misery of China in the 1930s: her nephew George Hogg, who later dedicated his book *I See a New China* to her, was inspired to go with her in 1938 to China, where he later worked with Rewi Alley for the Chinese Industrial Co-operative Movement, teaching refugee boys how to combine study and productive work, until his death.[11]

Very possibly because of her absorption in conditions in Asia, Muriel Lester was less acutely aware of what was being perpetrated in Europe. Unlike MAUDE ROYDEN, she was not reluctantly converted from pacifism by the imperative to resist Nazism. In September 1939 she was in the United States for the International Fellowship of Reconciliation and decided, after much thought, to stay there and campaign for non-intervention by America in the war. Not surprisingly, the British government took the opportunity during her travels to intern her in Trinidad between August and November 1941, for her ill-timed pacifist evangelism. On her return to Britain she was escorted to Glasgow police station, where she was strip-searched and, after a night in a filthy cell, was moved as an internee to Holloway. Strings were pulled and she was released to return to the Kingsley colony. For the rest of the war she was, like VERA BRITTAIN and EDITH PYE, active in the unsuccessful Food for Occupied Europe campaign that attacked the Allied food blockade of countries like Belgium, Holland and Greece. After the war she supported the Save Europe Now Movement, largely organized by Victor Gollancz and ELEANOR RATHBONE.

Muriel Lester's post-war work for the International Fellowship of Reconciliation (IFOR) started in August 1946, when she left for India, China, Hong Kong and, she hoped, Japan. It 'would be both difficult and dangerous . . . India was a veritable tinder-box; civil war was raging in China and the Cold War was just set to begin.'[12] In India, Gandhi showed his regard for her by sending her as his ambassador of reconciliation to the most intransigent, militantly Islamic trouble-spots in Afghanistan, Baluchistan, Karachi, Lahore, Assam, Bombay and Calcutta, to witness to non-violence. When intercommunal massacres broke out in Noakhali, East Bengal, Muriel Lester went straight there, before Gandhi began his 'walking tour . . . which would not end until either the killing stopped or he dropped'.[13]

In 1950 Muriel Lester confronted the racism of South Africa, seeing for herself the cruelties of apartheid as she stayed in DOROTHY MAUD RAPHAEL's Ekuteleni in Sophiatown; and at the end of 1950 she started what was perhaps her most audacious campaign of all: for clemency for convicted Japanese war criminals sentenced to death in Burma and the Philippines. She did not mince her words about the atrocity of Japanese militarism when speaking throughout Japan, but she also asked for forgiveness for the atomic bombing of Hiroshima, and she never ceased to testify to the moral courage of the anti-militarists in Japan.[14] She 'was not blind to negative, destructive, barbaric forces, but she constantly sought instead to find and cultivate the positive, the constructive and the humanitarian'.[15]

In 1955 Muriel Lester made her eighth round-the-world lecture tour, testifying to non-violence; and in 1958, at the age of 75, her ninth. As Gandhi wrote of her, years before, in *Harijan*: 'Many persons have written like Miss Lester before now . . . [But] she endeavours every moment of her life to practise what she professes.'[16]

1. Muriel Lester, *It Occurred to Me* (New York, Harper and Bros, 1937), pp. 20–1.
2. *Ibid.*, p. 59.
3. See Vera Brittain, *The Rebel Passion: A Short History of Some Pioneer Peace-Makers* (London, Allen and Unwin, 1964); and Jill Wallis, *Valiant for Peace: The History of the Fellowship of Reconciliation 1914–1989* (London, Fellowship of Reconciliation, 1991).
4. Lester, *op. cit.*, p. 80.
5. *Ibid.*, pp. 90–1.
6. *Ibid.*, p. 107.
7. *Ibid.*, p. 100.
8. *Ibid.*, p. 150.
9. *Ibid.*, p. 187.
10. See entries for CLARA HASLEWOOD and EDITH PICTON-TURBERVILL.
11. See Rewi Alley, *Sandan: An Adventure in Creative Education*, ed. H. Winston Rhodes (Christchurch, New Zealand, Caxton Press, 1959); and Jill Wallis, *Mother of World Peace: The Life of Muriel Lester* (Middlesex, Hisarlik Press, 1993), pp. 218–19 and 227–8.
12. Wallis, *Mother of World Peace*, p. 223.
13. *Ibid.*, p. 227.
14. See Muriel Lester, *The Other Japan* (London, Friends' Peace Committee, September 1945); and Wallis, *op. cit.*, pp. 247–9.
15. Wallis, *op. cit.*, p. 247.
16. Quoted in Richard Deats (ed.), *Ambassador of Reconciliation: A Muriel Lester Reader* (Philadelphia, New Society Publications, 1991), p. 3.

Muriel Lester's papers are now held in the Muriel Lester archive, Kingsley Hall, Dagenham, Essex.

LITTLE, ALICIA
(1845–26.7.1926)

CAMPAIGNER TO END FOOT-BINDING IN
CHINA

*Father: Calverley Bewicke, Leicestershire squire, resident in
Madeira*
*Mother: Mary Amelia, daughter of Rev. Nathaniel John
Hollingworth*

Christian humanist

*Alicia Little rock-climbing in
China, photographed by
Archibald Little (From* In the
Land of the Blue Gown, *Fisher and Unwin, 1902)*

Alicia Ellen Neave Bewicke spent her young
womanhood as a (minor) novelist writing on the
restricted options of young women in Victorian
society. The heroine of her most autobiographical
novel, *Miss Standish* (1883), is a passionate
humanitarian, supporting women's suffrage, married
women's right to own property and the repeal of the
Contagious Diseases Acts: 'human questions . . .
[they] don't concern only women . . . I cannot bear
the misery of the world.'[1]

In 1886 Alicia Bewicke married Archibald Little, a
merchant, traveller and Sinologist of many years'
experience in China. After dogged persistence, Alicia
Little managed to walk the streets of Chungking
(Chongqing) in the far west of China unmolested –
unheard-of for a European woman then – but both she and her husband were
sometimes pelted by foreigner-hating locals in rural areas. She admired many aspects
of Chinese culture, although she was deeply upset by the extreme poverty of the
people and the routine infliction of torture to induce false confessions 'made [her]
blood boil'.[2] But what she absolutely could not bear was the binding of the feet of
Chinese girls. She saw the countless crippled girls, hobbling with a stick, dark lines
under their sad eyes, their pale faces rouged to look healthy; she heard many gruesome
accounts of gangrenous limbs, amputations, mortification; she saw ladies having to
be helped by their (unbound) women slaves to cross a room; she saw women carried
on the backs of men like sacks because they could not walk; she knew of their being
killed or committing suicide in times of civil war or bandit attacks because they could
not run away; she learned from doctors of the lifelong injury done to their reproductive
organs from having to throw the weight of their whole bodies on to their heels; in
the west of China she noted how poor women even tracked boats

> with bound, hoof-like feet, besides carrying water, whilst in the north the
> unfortunate working women do field work, often kneeling on the heavy clay soil,
> because they are incapable of standing. It is only at Canton that bound feet are
> in any sense a mark of gentility, though in Shanghai and many other parts they
> are a sign of respectability.[3]

On one unforgettable day Alicia Little came face to face with a little girl. She gained
permission to loosen her bandages a little:

But the poor little girl, who had never had her bandages touched except to tighten them, cried out and looked at me with an expression of such hopeless agony as I had never seen on a child's face and hope never to see again . . . how many thousands, nay, millions of little girls have been, are, and will be in like case, unless this practice of torturing tender little girls that they may eventually win favour in the eyes of men . . . can be brought to an end?[4]

Alicia Little knew that a few missionaries had already campaigned against foot-binding, forbidding the practice to girls at their own schools and even finding husbands willing to have them. But she also knew that this handful of Christians could have little influence on Confucian China. Any reform movement that she started must be quite separate from Western religious evangelizing and must be supported, as soon as possible, by men of high Chinese authority, capable of influencing public opinion on this cruelly misguided female fashion. In April 1895, therefore, Alicia Little started the T'ien Ysu Hui or Natural Feet Society, first asking European ladies in Shanghai for support. They published poems on the subject by two Chinese ladies as well as medical tracts and the influential 'Suifu Appeal' by an eminent Chinese official against this custom of a thousand years: 'no pain [is] more injurious than the breaking of the bones and sinews . . . It makes the daughters cry day and night, aching with pain . . . I do not think much of such respect for ancestors . . . '[5] Other learned tracts followed in classical Chinese, including one by a descendant of Confucius himself, and were posted as placards by Alicia Little's Society all over China.

Encouraged by her husband and supported by his network of important contacts, Alicia Little then braced herself to make personal lecture tours throughout the cities of southern China, as well as Hong Kong and Macao.[6] She used X-ray slides and medical photographs to prove beyond doubt the crippling damage done to the girls' growing bones. She spoke to businessmen, high officials, women's drawing room meetings (with many hundreds of girls and women present), and assemblies of secondary schoolboys, who pledged themselves to marry only an unbound girl. For over ten years (1896–1906), Alicia Little was the acknowledged, eloquent and apparently fearless leader of the anti-foot-binding movement. She 'played a more active public role than any of her European contemporaries'.[7] '[She], more than any one person, was responsible for the abolition of foot-binding in China.'[8] She

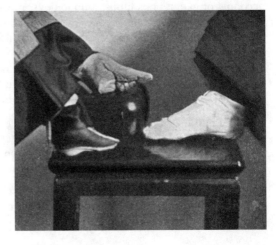

An adult Chinese woman's bound foot compared with an unbound foot (From In the Land of the Blue Gown, *Fisher and Unwin, 1902)*

was even called the second Chinese Goddess of Mercy by the Taotai of Foochow (Fuzhou). After her departure for England in 1908, Chinese men and women carried on the movement; it eventually triumphed over the whole of China.[9] Alicia Little had helped to put Chinese girls and women on their feet again, out of sheer horror at their unnecessary agony.

Alicia Little was remembered in Britain twenty years later when another human rights campaign was being waged for little Chinese girls: the *mui tsai* or domestic slaves of Hong Kong. In 1921, aged 76, she got in touch with CLARA HASLEWOOD and confessed her sense of her own remissness on that issue:

> She told me that at one time she taught a number of children in Shanghai who had all been slaves, and who almost without exception, had been tortured, . . . A young Chinese man . . . [on his death bed] had said to her, 'Why, oh why, did you not fight the slavery?' The thought still troubled her that she had chosen the lesser evil to combat, and she set herself to help our crusade in every way that she could.[10]

1. Alicia Bewicke, *Miss Standish* (London, 1883), vol. 2, pp. 17 and 10.
2. Alicia Little, *In the Land of the Blue Gown* (London, Fisher and Unwin, 1902), p. 193.
3. *Ibid.*, p. 343.
4. *Ibid.*, pp. 351–2.
5. Alicia Little, *Intimate China* (London, Hutchinson, 1899), p. 159.
6. For Archibald Little (d. 1908), see *Who Was Who*.
7. E. Croll, *Wise Daughters from Foreign Lands* (London, Pandora, 1989), p. 23.
8. S. Hoe, *Chinese Footprints: Exploring Women's History in China, Hong Kong and Macau* (Hong Kong, Roundhouse Publications Asia, 1996), p. 19.
9. See Fan Hong, *Footbinding, Feminism and Freedom: The Liberation of Women's Bodies in Modern China* (London, Frank Cass, 1997). See also obituary in *The Times* (6.8.1926); Ruth Butler, letter to *Daily Telegraph* (21.12.1954); and Pat Barr, *To China with Love: The Lives and Times of Protestant Missionaries in China 1860–1900* (London, Secker and Warburg, 1972).
10. Lt Comdr H. L. and Mrs Haslewood, *Child Slavery in Hong Kong: The Mui-Tsai System* (London, Sheldon Press, 1930), p. 50. See also note to entry above for CLARA HASLEWOOD for quotation from M. M. Dymond, *Yunnan*.

LLEWELYN DAVIES, MARGARET, *see* Davies, Margaret Llewelyn

LONSDALE, KATHLEEN, DBE, FRS
(28.1.1903–1.4.1971)

SCIENTIST; PACIFIST; PRISON REFORMER

Father: Harry Frederick Yardley, postmaster
Mother: Jessie, née Cameron

Baptist by birth, Quaker by convincement

The first woman crystallographer to gain a worldwide reputation, Kathleen Lonsdale was the youngest of the ten children (four of whom had died in infancy) of a desperately poor family. The brilliance and importance of her scientific work is summarized elsewhere;[1] here it is necessary only to point to her integrity and selflessness as a scientist. In 1936 she served the scientific community not only by working out the first simplified and practical formulae for X-ray crystal structure but also by personally writing out nearly 200 pages of them by hand so that they could be reproduced without the possibility of printer's errors. During the Second World War she also went to considerable trouble to attribute due credit for original work on X-ray diffraction phenomena to an obscure French scientist, Laval, then imprisoned by the Germans.

Kathleen Lonsdale (From The Friend, *16.4.1971)*

Kathleen Lonsdale's questioning of war had begun as a child in the First World War when she saw a Zeppelin shot down in flames: ' "Oh, the poor men, the poor men," her mother cried in tears. "But mother, . . . they are Germans." "Yes, I know", she replied, "but they are boys." '[2] Kathleen and her husband, a fellow scientist, joined the Society of Friends in the mid-1930s, convinced by Quaker social commitment in the Depression and by the Quaker testimony to peace. They took into their home families of refugees from Nazism, sent through TESSA ROWNTREE. During the Second World War Kathleen Lonsdale was imprisoned for a month in Holloway for her absolute insistence on not being *forced* to register for the civil defence duty of fire-watching – although in fact she was already doing voluntary fire-watching. That month revealed to her the unnecessarily degrading aspects of imprisonment, including the dirt and the prohibition on any personal belongings that might have strengthened self-respect or just personal identity. In 1949 she put her prison experience to use as a member of the Board of Visitors for Aylesbury Prison for Women and Borstal Institution for Girls. She quickly summed up the prisoners' ever-recurrent problems: 'broken homes, husbands or boyfriends in prison, babies in care, drugs or neurotic troubles'.[3]

Kathleen Lonsdale's public witness to peace began after the dropping of the atomic bombs. She had an overwhelming, ever-present, sense of the scientist's responsibility, both individual and collective, for the consequences of his or her research. In 1947 she wrote:

> We have to choose, as individuals, as a nation, as a world community, whether we shall go on applying scientific knowledge to the invention of still more ghastly weapons and to possible methods of defence against such weapons, in case they are used against us; or whether, acting on our Christian instincts, we shall refuse to use either the new or the old weapons of reprisal . . . even though we cannot see exactly where such a refusal may lead us.[4]

In 1950 she took part in a conference on 'The biological hazards of atomic energy' where her paper 'The scientist's responsibility as a citizen' triggered the eventual production of an International Labour Organization code of practice, controlling the exposure of industrial workers to radiation. In 1951 she was part of a détente-seeking Quaker delegation to Russia. She joined the Atomic Scientists Association, the Pugwash movement,[5] the Women's International League for Peace and Freedom, and the East–West Committee of the Society of Friends. She, like Albert Einstein, advocated not merely total nuclear disarmament but total disarmament, for 'the weapon is always ahead of the defence'.[6] Is such disarmament really possible?

> I think anything is possible if you believe in it enough – and if you can make enough people believe in it . . . I think that we are being driven in the direction of accepting that sooner or later war has to be abolished altogether; we're learning that even war without nuclear weapons is terrible enough.[7]

In addition to her scientific work and her social intervention, Kathleen Lonsdale had three children and ten grandchildren. She would have been the first to say that her husband Thomas was the 'primary carer' throughout their marriage who made her work outside the family possible.

1. See G. Kass-Simon and P. Farnes (eds), *Women of Science: Righting the Record* (Bloomington, Indiana University Press, 1990), pp. 354–9; and obituary, *Independent* (2.4.1971); also Dorothy Hodgkin, 'Kathleen Lonsdale: a biographical memoir', *Biographical Memoirs of Fellows of The Royal Society* (London, The Royal Society, 1974), pp. 446–84.
2. Hodgkin, *op. cit.*, p. 452.
3. *Ibid.*, p. 469; see also Kathleen Lonsdale, *Prisons for Women* (The Prison Medical Reform Council, 1952).
4. Kathleen Lonsdale, *Christianity in an Atomic Age* (London, Friends' Home Service Committee, 1947), pp. 9, 10.
5. See entry for DOROTHY HODGKIN.
6. Kathleen Lonsdale, 'Security', Occasional Paper delivered to Friends' World Conference, London (26.6.1952).
7. 'Dame Kathleen Lonsdale talks to Susanne Puddefoot', *The Times* (23.8.1968). See also Kathleen Lonsdale, *Quakers Visit Russia* (London, Friends' Service Council, 1952); *Removing the Causes of War*, Swarthmore Lecture (1953); *Is Peace Possible?* (London, Penguin, 1957); *I Believe*, Eddington Memorial Lecture (Cambridge University Press, 1964) (held in Friends' House Library, London).

M

MABER, LESLEY
(20.7.1906–6.1.1999)

TEACHER; REFUGEE RESCUER;
RESISTANCE HEROINE

Father: Frederick Maber (d. 1911)
Mother: Maud, née Hawkins

Christian Socialist (Anglican)

Lesley Maber, aged 50 (Courtesy of her nephew Dr Richard Maber)

It was as a schoolgirl at North London Collegiate School, where she met her friend Ishbel MacDonald, daughter of Britain's first Labour Prime Minister, that Lesley Maber acquired what was to be a lifelong commitment to Christian Socialism. Unlike most others in such a situation, on inheriting a fortune at 21, she gave it all away. After distinguished studies at Lausanne, Manchester and Lyons (she wrote a doctoral thesis on the poetry of George Herbert), she became a social worker with children in Haute Savoie and the Rhône during the 1930s.

When the Second World War broke out, Lesley Maber was taking a party of deprived children for a recuperative holiday to Le Chambon in the Cévennes. This commune was Protestant, and its pastor André Trocmé suggested she stay there and help as teacher and matron at his school, the Collège Cévenol. From 1940 on, under the Vichy regime, the school, and indeed the whole village, became a hiding place for Jewish refugees. Lesley Maber's own *pension* was often more than half full of Jewish children, while Le Chambon itself became a stage in an escape route into Switzerland. In 1943 the Gestapo raided a student hostel in the village and deported the Jews there, together with the French warden, who was killed in Majdanek. Lesley Maber herself was also arrested and deported in 1943 but by an extraordinary intervention was released from the train while it was still in France: in the nick of time the Préfet of Haute Savoie had been informed of her arrest and intervened successfully to have her released, on the grounds of her having legally adopted in 1932 two abandoned French babies, the little daughters of a child prostitute. (Both girls were successfully fostered, one in England, one in France.) After she had returned from a train from which no one else on board returned alive, Lesley Maber went back to Le Chambon to continue 'to work as a teacher, nurse, distributor of food and false papers, [and make] contact with resistance groups'.[1] Her Girl Guide troop helped organize the local escape routes; 5,000 Jews were sheltered in Le Chambon and in 1990 'it became the first community to be honoured as Righteous Gentiles by the Yad Vashem Holocaust Authority in Jerusalem'.[2]

After the war Lesley Maber continued her Christian humanitarian witness in another extraordinary way. Focusing now on the priority of reconciliation between former enemies, she acquired a list of anti-Nazi community leaders in Germany, mainly Lutheran pastors of the *Bekennende Kirche*. She then went to visit them, one after the other, asking what she could do to be of practical use, which in starving, defeated Germany was often quite a lot. They were deeply moved by her seeking them out and she in turn was moved by the depth of their gratitude.[3]

Next Lesley Maber 'sought renewal by living in poverty, working in a cotton-mill for a year before returning to teach at the Collège Cévenol'.[4] She taught until 1971. In many ways, above all in the practical testimony of her whole life, Lesley Maber was the nearest English equivalent to Simone Weil – a Simone Weil with an English sense of humour.

1. Douglas Johnson, obituary for Lesley Maber, *Independent* (6.2.1999).
2. *Ibid.*
3. Personal communication from Dr Richard Maber, nephew of Lesley Maber.
4. Richard Maber, 'Saving the lost children', obituary for Lesley Maber, *Guardian* (11.2.1999).

Lesley Maber's papers are held by Dr Richard Maber, University of Durham.

She disagreed with some aspects of Philip Hallie's account of Le Chambon, *Lest Innocent Blood Be Shed* (1979), and wrote her own, still unpublished, account of the war years; later, in 1987, she helped the film director Pierre Sauvage in making his documentary *Les Armes de l'Esprit* (Weapons of the Spirit) about the rescue of endangered Jews in the Cévennes.

MACARTHUR, MARY
(13.8.1880–1.1.1921)

SOCIALIST PACIFIST TRADE UNION LEADER

Father: John Duncan Macarthur, prosperous draper
Mother: Elizabeth, née Martin

Born Presbyterian, later humanist

Mary Macarthur, like MARGARET ASHTON, ISABELLA FORD and KATHARINE GLASIER, was one of those who felt compelled to set aside her own class background and allegiance to an affectionate family in order to dedicate all her energy to serving the needs of exploited, unorganized working women. Her parents could sympathize neither with her end nor with the very public means – often on a soapbox in dingy if not outright squalid surroundings – to that end. However, Mary Macarthur persisted and her short life has gone down in Labour history as exemplary in its principled, non-ego-aggrandizing, focused struggle. '[She] fought for the woman worker in the interest of all workers',[1] insisting that women should not undercut men and that men should, in turn, back women's right to a living wage. She probably did more than any other single person to right the wrongs of the sweated woman worker at the beginning of the twentieth century in Britain,[2] but she herself refused the offer of all honours and titles or honorific government posts.

In the First World War, like her close friend and colleague in the cause Margaret Bondfield,[3] she publicly declared herself a pacifist internationalist, supporting the Women's International Congress at The Hague.[4] This cost her dear in 1918 when she stood for election as Labour candidate at Stourbridge. '[On] the platform and the doorstep she was a Bolshevik, a pacifist, a defeatist: a woman who had held up the supply of munitions and now refused to exact the just penalties of crime from the Hun.'[5] She lost. A few months later she was devastated by a different loss: the death of her husband Will Anderson. In April 1919 she forced herself to accept a call to speak in America. She toured all the great cities, speaking to tens of thousands of people on the necessity of achieving a better, because a more just, peace than that laid down by the fatally wrong-headed Treaty of Versailles. To that end, every nation needed a better educated, i.e. a more enlightened and therefore more humane, citizenry, for 'Just as no chain is stronger than its weakest link so no nation is wiser than its most ignorant citizen'.[6] In

Mary Macarthur (Frontispiece to Mary Agnes Hamilton, Mary Macarthur: A Biographical Sketch, *Leonard Parsons, 1925)*

October 1919 she went again to America, this time as adviser to the British workers' delegation to the first conference of the International Labour Organization.[7] A year later, she was dead.

Of all the many tributes to Mary Macarthur as a person,[8] perhaps the most eloquent is the fictionalized portrait as Miss Doremus in Kathleen Woodward's *Jipping Street*:

> Her manner bore a silent apology for her privileges and advantages, and betrayed not the slightest trace of a desire to flaunt them in our faces. She came humbly to Jipping Street, not as did so many others to see how the poor lived and give them the doubtful inspiration of their presence and the even more doubtful good of their benevolence – she came humbly, and because she felt so deeply soon learned to put away any temptation she might have felt for 'doing good', preferring rather to suffer with us.[9]

1. Mary Agnes Hamilton, *Mary Macarthur: A Biographical Sketch* (London, Leonard Parsons, 1925), p. 133.
2. See David E. Martin in J. M. Bellamy and J. Saville (eds), *Dictionary of Labour Biography*, vol. 2, pp. 256–7.
3. See 'Margaret and Mary', in Mary Agnes Hamilton, *Margaret Bondfield* (London, Leonard Parsons, 1924); and Marion Miliband, 'Margaret Bondfield' in *Dictionary of Labour Biography*.
4. See Introduction and Appendix I.
5. Hamilton, *Mary Macarthur, op. cit.*, p. 175.
6. Mary Macarthur, 'Why I am a Labour candidate' (election manifesto, 1918).
7. See entry for SOPHY SANGER.

8. See obituaries in *The Times* (2.1, 3.1 and 5.1.1921); *The Nation* (8.1.1921); *Labour Woman* (February 1921); *The Woman Worker* (February 1921); and entry in the *Dictionary of National Biography, 1912–1921*.
9. Kathleen Woodward, *Jipping Street* (1928; reprinted London, Virago, 1983), pp. 222–3.

McMICHAEL-ASKINS, JOAN

(8.2.1905–6.8.1989)

PIONEER OF PUBLIC HEALTH AND CARE FOR HANDICAPPED CHILDREN; 'DOCTOR AT WAR WITH WAR'[1]

Father: — MacPherson, later Inspector-General in the Indian Police

Humanist

Dr Joan McMichael-Askins at work in a London County Council clinic, c. 1945

Born in a tent in the Punjab to a family of the Raj, Joan MacPherson was converted to socialism when she was a medical student treating injuries inflicted by police on strikers in the General Strike of 1926. She turned from the Labour Party to Communism in the 1930s and worked both for Medical Aid for Spain and for Medical Aid for the Communist Chinese attacked by Japan.

However, Dr McMichael, as she then was, was not the kind of radical fired only by idealized conflicts abroad; she also worked long and very hard for unglamorous medical goals at home. During the Second World War she worked with Dr JANET VAUGHAN for the blood transfusion service based in Slough, and as Medical Officer in the Hoover factory, West London, where she pioneered industrial workers' health measures including mass radiography for tuberculosis. After the war she worked as a Medical Officer for the London County Council (LCC), specializing in the health of children with physical or mental handicaps.[2] She also took a prominent part in the homeless families squatters' movement in London in 1947. During this period (*c.* 1927–47), she was twice married and gave birth to four children.

Dr McMichael continued to work as Assistant Medical Officer of Health specializing in children until 1978 when she was well into her seventies, despite the fact that for the previous fifteen years, since 1963, she had also been deeply involved in founding and running the Medical and Scientific Aid Organisation for the People of Vietnam, Laos and Kampuchea (MAV).[3] She was still working in the Medical

Aid office the Friday before her last illness, when she was 84.

> [People] who have seen much of the world, who are passionately committed to a political philosophy and who are actively caring about humanity as Joan McMichael-Askins was, must keep a very tough intelligence and a very soft heart, . . . [She] is one person, of all the multitudes that I have seen passing in my life, of whom I can truly say that she was splendid.[4]

1. Dorothy Hodgkin, obituary for Dr Joan McMichael-Askins, *Guardian* (16.8.1989).
2. See her book *Handicap: A Study of Physically Handicapped Children and Their Families* (London, P. Staples, 1971).
3. See Hodgkin, *op. cit.*; and Joan McMichael-Askins, *Health in the Third World* (with special reference to Vietnam) (London, Spokesman Books, 1976).
4. Mary Cowan, obituary for Joan McMichael-Askins, *Independent* (18.8.1989).

MACMILLAN, CHRYSTAL, B.Sc., MA, LLB
(13.6.1872–21.9.1937)

PACIFIST INTERNATIONALIST; PIONEER WOMAN BARRISTER

Father: John Macmillan, wealthy Edinburgh tea merchant
Mother: Jessie, née Finlayson

The only girl in a family of nine children, Chrystal Macmillan proved herself a brilliant student, graduating with first class honours in mathematics and natural philosophy before going on to study mental and moral philosophy at Edinburgh, and German in Berlin. She was a leading Scottish suffragist, working under Miss Sarah Siddons Mair (grand-daughter of Sarah Siddons). Early in the twentieth century she moved from Edinburgh to London, working under Mrs Fawcett on the executive of the (British) National Union of Women's Societies and later (1913–23), as Hon. Secretary of the (global) International Women's Suffrage Alliance.

Chrystal Macmillan was not merely an international organizer, she was a deeply committed internationalist, believing that what all people have in common is far more significant than what divides them. She helped draft the last-minute 'International Manifesto of Women' signed by representatives of twelve million women, and delivered to Sir Edward Grey and all European Ambassadors in London on 31 July 1914, entreating them to avert 'the threatened unparalleled disaster' of a general war by a last effort at conciliation and arbitration.[1] It was also she who, with MARY SHEEPSHANKS, negotiated money guarantees from the Belgian Ambassador in London and then bought and took the first food relief to homeless Belgian war refugees, across the U-boat-patrolled North Sea to Flushing.

In December 1914 Chrystal Macmillan proposed to Dr Aletta Jacobs, leader of the Dutch women's movement, that an International Women's Congress be held at The Hague (Holland being a neutral country) to discuss the principles on which peace should be made and, if so agreed, to act internationally.[2] She was one of those British suffragists who chose her pacifism over her lifelong feminism in the First World War. When The Hague Congress voted to send delegates to carry its resolutions in person to belligerent and neutral nations, petitioning them to end the war, she made the case for mediation by neutrals to that end to foreign ministers in Copenhagen, Oslo, Stockholm and Petrograd in April/May 1915 – but without success: they were all waiting on the United States to take such a lead. In May 1919 she took the Women's International League congress resolutions on disarmament and economic co-operation from Zürich to the Paris Peace Congress, only to be ignored again.

In 1924 Chrystal Macmillan became one of the first women called to the English Bar.

> She was the right kind of lawyer, one who held that Law should be synonymous with Justice . . . Her chief aim in life – one might call it her passion – was to give to women of every class and nation the essential protection of justice. She was, herself, a great and a very just human being . . . She could not budge an inch on matters of principle but she never lost her temper and never bore a grudge in defeat.[3]

1. Sybil Oldfield, *Spinsters of This Parish: The Life and Times of F. M. Mayor and Mary Sheepshanks* (London, Virago, 1984), ch. 9, pp. 178–9.
2. See Introduction; Appendix I; and Anne Wiltsher, *Most Dangerous Women: Feminist Peace Campaigners of the Great War* (London, Pandora, 1985).
3. Cicely Hamilton in *Time and Tide* (16.10.1937).

See also obituaries in *The Times* (22.9.1937); *News Chronicle* (22.9.1937); *Manchester Guardian* (23.9.1937); *Daily Telegraph* (21.2.1938); *The Scotsman* (September 1937).

➤➤

McNEILL, MARGARET
(8.6.1909–1.4.1985)

REFUGEE RELIEF WORKER IN POST-WAR GERMANY; PEACE WORKER IN ULSTER

Father: George Martin McNeill, Protestant Belfast businessman
Mother: Anne Marie, Protestant

Congregationalist, later Quaker by convincement

Margaret McNeill's fluency in German helped her not only in the 1930s and early 1940s when she befriended refugees from Nazism in Belfast, but also after the Second World War when she went with the Friends' Relief Service to Germany. She served from 1945 to 1948, mostly with displaced persons from eastern Europe, and returned to work for the Friends' Service Council in Brunswick from 1949 to 1952.

A thoughtful, reflective person and gifted writer, Margaret McNeill sent journal letters to close friends and family, and occasional articles for the *Manchester Guardian*.[1] In them she revealed her shock at the triumphalist attitudes of elements in the British army, exemplified by road-side notices near Osnabrück which read 'You are entering Germany. Behave like conquerors', and her dismay at the destruction to which German cities had been subjected. But her greatest concern was for the displaced persons in the camps where she worked, particularly at Goslar. There

Poles, Lithuanians, Ukrainians, Latvians, Ruthenians and Estonians were housed, with little to occupy their time and a future which was uncertain. Some had been Nazi slave-workers; some had collaborated, to a greater or lesser degree, with the German forces. As well as working to break down hostility between the inmates of the camps, Margaret McNeill challenged the bureaucracy associated with displaced persons work. She helped to fight the inhuman methods sometimes employed in their repatriation, which took little account of the conditions that now obtained in once-occupied regions, or the terror aroused in some, like the Ukrainians, at the prospect of being sent to areas under Russian control. Her description in an article in the *Manchester Guardian* in autumn 1945 of the conditions under which the British repatriated a group of Poles to an unknown destination makes uncomfortable comparisons with the manner in which the Nazis had transported slave-workers from occupied territories to work in Germany.

Margaret McNeill returned to Northern Ireland in 1971, after retiring from her post as Extension Secretary at the Quaker College in Birmingham, where she had worked since her return from Europe in 1952. She spent the last fourteen years of her life involved in Quaker projects associated with the Troubles. As the first Organizing Secretary of the Ulster Peace and Service Committee, she helped to establish a canteen for visitors at the Long Kesh Internment Centre (later the Maze prison) and to organize holidays for those who might not otherwise have had one.[2]

1. The experiences of this period are recounted in Margaret McNeill, *By the Rivers of Babylon: A Story of Relief Work among the Displaced Persons of Europe* (London, Bannisdale Press, 1950).
2. See McNeill papers, held in Friends' House Library, London; and Joyce Neill, obituary, *The Friend* (19.4.1985).

MACPHAIL, KATHERINE STEWART
(*c.* 1885–1974)

MEDICAL RESCUER IN WARTIME AND IN THE AFTERMATH OF WAR

Father: — *MacPhail, Lanarkshire doctor*
Mother: —, *née Stewart*

As soon as she had graduated MB, ChB from Glasgow, young Katherine MacPhail joined Dr Inglis's Scottish Women's Hospital Unit in Serbia.[1] Once there she found thousands of men dying of gangrenous wounds, paratyphoid, enteric and typhus. She herself caught typhus and was invalided out, briefly, to work in Dr HILDA CLARK's convalescent home for French refugee women and children in Savoie.[2] She insisted on rejoining the wounded, defeated Serbians, and after having been briefly interned by the temporarily victorious Austrians, she accompanied the Serb Refugee Relief Unit first to Corsica and then to Salonika. The last period of the war found her in the mountains of Macedonia, tending refugee women and children. Immediately after the Armistice she went to Belgrade to fight another terrible outbreak of typhus, and there she discovered her life-work.

What Katherine MacPhail found was a host of abandoned, uncared-for sick children. She decided to open a hospital for them herself with £25 of her own in a disused army hut. She began the project almost totally unaided, with the exception of devoted nursing colleagues like Sister Catherine O'Rorke,[3] but she was soon helped by several voluntary societies, notably the newly formed Save the Children Fund. Hers was at first the only children's hospital in the whole of the new state of Yugoslavia; it had 50 beds and a large out-patients' department, and by 1934 170,000 children had been treated there, and hundreds of Yugoslav girls trained in the basic nursing of sick children. In 1934 she handed over the hospital to the Yugoslav government, using the money she was paid for it to build a specialist home for children with tubercular diseases of the joints and bones; it had to be disbanded in April 1941 when Yugoslavia was again invaded, and she herself was taken prisoner by the Italians. In 1945 she returned with UNRRA to re-open the children's hospital but in 1947 she had to hand it over to the new, Communist, Yugoslav government.

Dr MacPhail was criticized in some quarters

Dr Katherine MacPhail, c. 1930 (From Francesca Wilson, In the Margins of Chaos, *John Murray, 1944)*

for giving her expertise to Yugoslav rather than to Scottish children,[4] but she felt herself called to be an ambassador to the ordinary people of a country she had fallen in love with ever since 1915 and about whom the British government seemed to care little or nothing.

1. See Monica Krippner, *The Quality of Mercy: Women at War, Serbia 1915–18* (London, David and Charles, 1980) for an account of the many British women doctors and nurses who served the defeated Serbians and went with them into exile.
2. Francesca Wilson, *In the Margins of Chaos* (London, John Murray, 1944), pp. 10, 11 and 13.
3. Sister Catherine O'Rorke, who had been arrested with Edith Cavell in Belgium in 1915, went on to nurse the wounded with the Scottish Women's Hospital at Royaumont and then fight a typhus epidemic at Vranja, Serbia. She joined Dr MacPhail's Anglo-Serbian Children's Hospital in Belgrade in 1921, being in charge of its out-patients' department until 1930, when she contracted her fatal illness. See obituaries in *The Times* (13.1.1932) and *Evening Standard* (13.1.1932).
4. Wilson, *op. cit.*, p. 4.

MARSHALL, CATHERINE

(1880–1961)

LEADER OF NO CONSCRIPTION FELLOWSHIP

Father: Frank Marshall, housemaster,
Harrow School
Mother: Caroline, née Colbeck, Liberal
suffragist

Agnostic

Permit Book№ 118614

Permit of Miss Lydia Smith, leading worker for No Conscription Fellowship under Catherine Marshall, to attend hearings at tribunals for conscientious objectors, 1916

Catherine Marshall had two deeply committed periods of political engagement, the first devoted to her feminist commitment to women's suffrage,[1] the second to her absolutist pacifism. For her, pacifism was the logical extension of right-not-might, 'maternalist' feminism;[2] moreover, she saw non-violence as an integral, indispensable means in the wider struggle for co-operation and justice on earth. When she had to choose, therefore, in 1914–15, between the campaign for the suffrage and the campaign to bring the First World War to a negotiated conclusion (while committing the women's suffrage movement to internationalist peace education), she chose internationalist pacifism over Mrs Fawcett's 'patriotic' feminism.[3] Having resigned as Hon. Parliamentary Secretary of the NUWSS in 1915, she took first *a* and then *the* leading role in the No Conscription Fellowship.

The NCF, originally the brainchild of Lilla Brockway, first wife of Fenner Brockway, campaigned for the right of men to be conscientious objectors: their right to refuse to kill on order and their right to humane treatment when arrested and imprisoned.[4] Once conscription had become law in 1916, the leading men in the movement were all imprisoned and Catherine Marshall had to take over its direction and administration as Hon. Secretary. '[She] contributed more to the Fellowship's success and survival than any other individual. She was truly a human dynamo.'[5] The No Conscription Fellowship head office was regularly raided by police, and Catherine Marshall saw to it that the case histories of 16,000 conscientious objectors, from their first appearance before a tribunal to their last known prison or camp, were not only kept meticulously up to date but also duplicated and dispersed to six different offices. She 'planted' questions in the House of Commons which the War Office then had to apply to her in order to be able to answer. It was also Catherine Marshall whose pressure behind the scenes via sympathetic MPs ensured that 'absolutist' prisoners were transferred from military to civil prisons; and it was she who organized an immediate and effective outcry when batches of conscientious objectors were sent to France to be shot as deserters.[6] She even risked arrest and jail herself for helping 200 objectors evade arrest, and finding them casual work. 'She once calculated that she was liable for two thousand years' imprisonment for her many offences against the regulations that forbade aiding such outlaws.'[7]

Not surprisingly after the intense strain of the war years on such a committed anti-war 'subversive', Catherine Marshall suffered a breakdown. Nevertheless, from November 1920 to March 1921 she served as the League of Nations Representative on the International Commission convened by the Red Cross in Geneva to tackle the Russian famine. She also tried to persuade the Women's International League for Peace and Freedom to work closely with the League of Nations, deeply flawed though its origin and composition were. In 1923 she went with other envoys of the Women's International League to interview statesmen from the victorious powers to try to persuade them to modify the reparations demanded of Germany. When France refused, even sending troops to the Ruhr, she published a letter supporting the German passive resisters in the Ruhr. 'You have shown to the world the great example that force can be defeated by a refusal to resort to force.'[8]

1. See Olive Banks, *Biographical Dictionary of British Feminists*, vol. 2 (New York University Press, 1990); and Jo Vellacott, *From Liberal to Labour with Women's Suffrage: Catherine Marshall, 1906–1913* (Montreal, McGill-Queen's University Press, 1993).
2. See Catherine Marshall, 'Women and war' and 'The future of women in politics', both written in 1915 and reprinted in Margaret Kamester and Jo Vellacott (eds), *Militarism versus Feminism: Writings on Women and War* (London, Virago, 1987); see also Sybil Oldfield, *Spinsters of This Parish* (London, Virago, 1984), pp. 310–11.
3. See Introduction and Appendix I. See also Jo Vellacott, 'Anti-war suffragists', *History*, **62** (October 1977), pp. 411–25; and Anne Wiltsher, *Most Dangerous Women: Feminist Peace Campaigners of the Great War* (London, Pandora, 1985).
4. Most First World War conscientious objectors in Britain suffered brutal treatment and extreme hardship in prison; some of them died. See John Graham, *Conscription and Conscience* (London, Allen and Unwin, 1922); David Mitchell, *Women on the Warpath: The Story of the Women of the First World War* (London, Lowe and Brydone, 1966), pp. 331–6; Jo Vellacott, *Bertrand Russell and the Pacifists in the First World War* (Brighton, Harvester, 1980).
5. See Thos. C. Kennedy, *The Hound of Conscience: A History of the No-Conscription Fellowship 1914–1919* (Fayetteville, University of Arkansas Press, 1981).
6. Mitchell, *op. cit.*, p. 336.
7. *Ibid.*
8. Johanna Alberti, *Beyond Suffrage: Feminists in War and Peace, 1914–1928* (London, Macmillan, 1989), p. 195.

MAUD, DOROTHY, *see* Raphael, Sister

MITCHELL, HANNAH
(1871–1956)

PACIFIST SOCIALIST FEMINIST PIONEER IN LOCAL GOVERNMENT

Father: — Webster, Derbyshire small farmer
Mother: reluctant farmer's wife

Agnostic

After a bleak start as a battered child, domestic drudge and family scapegoat, with only two weeks' schooling to her name, Hannah Webster would have been justified in concentrating on nothing but her own survival ever after she ran away from her violent mother at the age of 14. But Hannah Mitchell, as she soon became, was exceptionally intelligent and spirited, and concerned for humanity, not just for herself. Every free moment from her long hours as a seamstress she spent reading or trying out the different religious preachers or discovering politics at the street corner soapbox. It was the young KATHARINE GLASIER who actually converted her to a lifelong, independent-minded brand of socialism.[1]

Hannah Mitchell became an elected Poor Law Guardian in 1904 and she, who had known years of hunger and hardship, thenceforth battled for 'the paupers' against those who could only see them as 'a burden on the rates'. A passionate feminist, she worked for Mrs Pankhurst's Manchester-based Women's Social and Political Union even before the tactic of militancy had started. For her, as for many women from all social classes, the ensuing 'struggle of the women seemed like the quest of the Holy Grail'.[2] As a well-known speaker for 'the Cause' throughout the north of England she suffered raucous heckling and rough handling from frighteningly hostile crowds to the point where, exhausted, she collapsed with a serious nervous breakdown. On her recovery she left the WSPU to join CHARLOTTE DESPARD's democratic, secessionist Women's Freedom League.

The years 1914–18 were terrible for her. 'All my life I had hated war . . . The idea of men killing each other had always seemed so hideous to me, that my first conscious thought after my baby was born was that he should be brought up to resist war.'[3] When war came, that son was 16 and she was in terror lest, like so many other idealistic lads, he decided to volunteer for his country. 'I waited, in such agony of mind, that I look back on that time as a reprieved man might look back on the time spent in the condemned cell.'[4] Then came Conscription. 'As the time drew near for his call-up I felt I couldn't bear to live if I knew he had killed another woman's son but it was for him to decide.'[5] Her son did become a conscientious objector doing alternative service; Hannah Mitchell, who regarded soldiers as victims of war 'like the rest of us', sent parcels and wrote to the boys she knew at the Front.

From 1923 to 1935 Hannah Mitchell served as a Labour/ILP City Councillor for Manchester, together with ELLEN WILKINSON, and won libraries and bathhouses for the city. She also worked as a magistrate whose credo ran: 'Personally, I think that we shall never get rid of the juvenile offender until every child has its birthright – cleanliness, food, clothes, and room to live.'[6] She wrote her autobiography, rejected by publishers in her lifetime, during the Second World War, having to recognize that she and her fellow socialists had failed to build up the international brotherhood that would have made war impossible.

> We had failed but at least we had tried . . . I have not yet seen any reason to change my earlier beliefs . . . I still believe war to be an evil thing, and the worst possible way of settling any dispute. I still desire a more equitable distribution of the world's wealth . . . More intensely than ever I believe in woman's right to equality, whether married or single, the right to her own individuality, her own soul.[7]

1. Cf. Stephen Yeo, 'A New Life: the religion of socialism in Britain, 1883–1896', *History Workshop Journal*, **4** (1977).
2. Hannah Mitchell, *The Hard Way Up* (London, Faber and Faber, 1968; reprinted London, Virago, 1977), p. 135.
3. *Ibid.*, p. 183.
4. *Ibid.*, p. 186.
5. *Ibid.*
6. *Ibid.*, p. 230.
7. *Ibid.*, pp. 241–2.

MONTAGU, LILY, CBE

(22.12.1873–22.1.1963)

PACIFIST SOCIAL AND RELIGIOUS
REFORMER

*Father: Samuel Montagu, Lord Swaythling, financier
and philanthropist*
Mother: Ellen, née Cohen

Liberal Reform Jew

Lily Montagu, c. 1920 (From Ellen M. Umansky, Lily Montagu and the Advancement of Liberal Judaism, Edwin Mellen Press, 1983)

Lily Montagu was brought up with her elder sister Henrietta Franklin in a wealthy, strictly Orthodox Jewish family. Although devoted to her parents, Lily nevertheless felt compelled to follow her own light and initiate both social and religious changes that she knew were quite foreign to their understanding. At the age of 17 she and her sister Marian started to run evening classes for working girls. This first encounter with poor, culturally deprived girls gave her the revolutionary idea to try to provide a space where they could receive some sort of education and have their first opportunity for self-development. With her cousin Beatrice, she therefore started the West Central Jewish Girls' Club in the unsalubrious district of Soho in 1893, thus beginning her pioneering life work for the Girls' Clubs and Youth Clubs movements. She also became involved with the terrible economic situation of 'her' girls, and worked to ameliorate their miseries of unemployment, bad housing and sweatshops. In 1913 her West Central Jewish Girls' Club moved into its own premises, in Alfred Place off Tottenham Court Road, adding a Day Settlement there in 1919.[1]

Meanwhile Lily Montagu had also been a spiritual 'seeker'. Frustrated by the relegation of Jewish women to non-public participation in Jewish religious life and by the archaic irrelevance of much formal Orthodox ritual observance, she pondered a new, much more liberal interpretation of Judaism. 'Lily Montagu was in fact, the founder of the Liberal Jewish Movement in 1901 in England and the individual most responsible for its growth.'[2] Influenced by the scholar Dr Claude Montefiore, she wrote an article 'The spiritual possibilities of Judaism today' and persuaded him in 1902 to become President of the Jewish Religious Union which sponsored the first Liberal Jewish Synagogue in Britain. It then branched out with congregations in the provinces and eventually, in 1926, became part of a World Union for Progressive Judaism, of which Lily Montagu was Honorary Secretary. Meanwhile she herself had taken the extraordinary step of becoming the minister or rabbi of her own congregation at the West Central Synagogue. By 1933 she was still 'the world's only female spiritual leader of a synagogue and major religious movement'.[3]

What did Lily Montagu believe? In her hundreds of sermons and open letters as well as her anthology *Daily Readings from the Old Testament* (1922), she testified to what she believed to be the universal ethical teaching contained in Judaism.

> Peace is the culmination of the Religious Ideal. 'Depart from evil and do good; seek peace and pursue it.' We must all work for the time when the world will accept the 'way of God' and the law of love will enthral the world . . . The unity of man is dependent on the Unity of God. Fundamentally our natures are the same, and as worshippers before God there is no last or first.[4]

Although a feminist and one of the few Jewish women suffragists, when she had to choose between the immediate interests of 'patriotic' suffrage or allying herself with the dissident pacifist feminists in April 1915, Lily Montagu chose the latter and was one of the signatories supporting the Women's International Congress at The Hague.[5] Similarly, as a 'universalist' she was also opposed to nationalistic Zionism, at the same time as organizing help for refugees from Hitler. 'Many Jewish families alive in the world today owe their existence to her. She saved hundreds of lives and, indirectly, thousands.'[6] Nevertheless, when her club and settlement, the life-work of 50 years, were destroyed in the Blitz on 16 April 1941, she still refused to find any comfort in the thought of revenge on the Germans:

> As I left after our beautiful service on Saturday, April 19, a man pressed my hand in a kindly, sympathetic way, and said, 'All right, Miss Montagu, we shall have our revenge!' If he meant that a Berlin woman who had given her life to some piece of work for nearly 50 years should experience my kind of heartache when she saw the outward shell destroyed in a few minutes; if he meant that another woman should see the place shattered which had echoed night after night for 27 years with the joyous sounds of young people bent on recreation and education, and revelling in activity; if he meant this, then indeed he offered me a poor form of consolation.
>
> In memory of our dead, I would urge you to cast hatred out of your hearts as hatred is destructive, and through hatred we lose our standards and aspirations.[7]

'She was in her way a saint.'[8]

1. See Lily Montagu, *My Club and I* (London, Herbert Joseph, 1942).
2. Ellen M. Umansky, *Lily Montagu and the Advancement of Liberal Judaism: From Vision to Vocation* (New York, Edwin Mellen Press, 1983), Preface.
3. Linda Kuzmack, *Woman's Cause: The Jewish Woman's Movement in England and the United States* (Columbus, Ohio State University Press, 1990), Conclusion, pp. 186–7.
4. Lily Montagu and Henrietta Franklin (eds), *Daily Readings from the Old Testament* (London, Williams and Norgate, 1922). See also Lily Montagu, *The Faith of a Jewish Woman* (London, Allen and Unwin, 1943).
5. See Introduction and Appendix I.
6. Yehudi Menuhin, 'A woman to remember', *The Times* (24.4.1964).
7. Lily Montagu, letter to the Montagu Circle (April 1941), quoted in Menuhin, *op. cit.*
8. *Ibid.*

MORLEY, EDITH, MA, JP, OBE
(15.9.1875–18.1.1964)

REFUGEE RESCUER

Father: Alexander Morley, dental surgeon, London

Born into Orthodox Jewish family, became agnostic

An 'academic fixture' at the University College of Reading, where she taught English from 1901 to 1940 and edited the many published volumes of the manuscript *Journals* and *Correspondence* of Henry Crabb Robinson, Professor Edith Morley's early social commitment had been largely devoted to support for women in public life. She joined the Pankhursts' Women's Social and Political Union and the Fabian Society. 'The inception of the Women's Police Force and the Probation service in Reading owe much to her',[1] and in 1934 she herself became a JP. With the advent of Nazi persecution in Germany and Austria, however, her social concern had to change focus; she felt compelled to spend her sixties, between 1935 and 1945, doing all in her power to help the victims of Nazism find asylum in Britain. She became Hon. Secretary of the Reading and District Refugee Committee from its foundation in 1938.

'Committee work' – unpaid attendance at innumerable meetings, engaging in huge files of correspondence and meticulous record-keeping, volunteering for work as a liaison officer at 'tribunals for enemy aliens' to support the refugees' case – all that unglamorous, energy-draining drudgery behind the scenes is the invisible face of humanitarian effort. Edith Morley's unflagging intervention on behalf of hundreds, if not thousands, of desperate, innocent people is attested not only in her unpublished autobiography,[2] but also by the files in the archives of the British Federation of University Women (BFUW) labelled 'Old Refugee Cases', 'Refugees, from July 1941; Cases A–F, G–H, L–R, S–Z', 'Displaced Persons – Lists and Correspondence', 'correspondence with Central Committee for Refugees' or 'BFUW Relief Work'.[3] Edith Morley took a leading part in Reading's outreach committee that was directed from DOROTHY HARDISTY's Central Committee for Refugee Children at Bloomsbury House, and hence she was part of the great effort to find British homes for the 10,000 *Kindertransport* children.[4] But she also worked hard on behalf of countless adults, first asking Bloomsbury House to arrange for the escape of named individuals from Germany and Austria and then supporting them in Britain when so many were appalled to find themselves eventually summoned before tribunals, or even interned as wartime security suspects in the country that they thought had at last granted them a place of safety.

> Our Refugee Office was besieged by miserable women whose fears it was impossible to allay: in addition there were all kinds of business matters with which to cope – irate landlords, unpaid rent, . . . furniture to store, maintenance to provide. Those were weeks of nightmare to us, . . . to the refugees they must have been veritable hell.[5]

In retrospect Edith Morley, although very critical both of the British government's grudging immigration policy in the face of Nazi pogroms in 1938–39 and of its obtuse, heavy-handed, even inhumane treatment of anti-Nazi, German-speaking 'enemy aliens' in 1940–41, had nothing but praise for the huge humanitarian effort of Bloomsbury House and for the refugees' own resilience. '[Eight] years work in their cause has left me with an added respect for human nature and the heights to which, on occasion, it can rise, despite indescribable sufferings, – spiritual, physical and material.'[6] In every instance Edith Morley and her Committee did their best to think of the refugees not as 'cases' but as individuals and friends. It was at the instigation of 'her' refugees that she was given the OBE.[7]

1. *University Women's Review* (May 1955), p. 5. See also Edith Morley (ed.), *Women Working in Seven Professions: A Survey of Their Economic Conditions and Prospects* (London, Fabian Society, 1914). Edith Morley's own professional struggle for academic status and recognition is chronicled by Carol Dyhouse, *No Distinction of Sex? Women in British Universities 1870–1939* (London, UCL Press, 1995).
2. 'Looking before and after: reminiscences of a working life', typescript held in Reading University Archives.
3. See British Federation of University Women archives, Women's Library, London.
4. See Morley, 'Looking before and after', *op. cit.*, pp. 177–80.
5. *Ibid.*, pp. 181–2.
6. *Ibid.*
7. *University Women's Review, loc. cit.* See also obituary, *The Times* (21.1.1964).

N

NEWTON, FRANCES, DAME OF JUSTICE OF THE ORDER OF ST JOHN OF JERUSALEM

(1872–1955)

WELFARE WORKER; CHAMPION OF PALESTINIAN ARABS

Father: Charles Edward Newton, Derbyshire banker/squire, related to Isaac Newton
Mother: Mary Henrietta, née Moore, Evangelical

Anglican

Frances Newton was only 17 in 1889 when she first accompanied her elder stepsister, a worker for the Church Missionary Society, to Jaffa, where another of her sisters, Constance, was nursing at the hospital built by their father. She herself trained to be a missionary, though she never 'succeeded in being one in the accepted sense of the word, for [she] was too inclined to kick against the pricks!'[1] She trained in district nursing and social work in Birmingham in 1894, followed by a course in mission work in London before returning to Palestine in 1895. She later came to regard her early missionary efforts as having been quite fruitless, but at least she learnt to speak and read and write fluent Arabic, which was to be the grounding of all her later, secular work with Arabs. First she superintended ten village schools for boys and girls and their eighteen teachers. On being moved to Haifa, she then built and helped to fund two large girls' schools, one for Christian Arabs and one for Muslim girls; in addition she had charge of another school at Acre, which she visited each week despite dangerous quicksands in the estuary crossing that frightened her horses, not to mention herself. In 1914 she was no longer able to tolerate all the restrictions imposed on her by the Church Missionary Society entirely because of her gender, and she resigned from missionary work.

During the First World War Frances Newton was back in Britain 'but the claims of my adopted country and of my beloved Arabs could not be disregarded'.[2] She became Travelling Secretary of the Syrian-Palestine Relief Fund for the Arabs then suffering from famine and disease, for whom she raised nearly £150,000. When she returned to Palestine in 1919 it was to begin what was for her two decades of heart-breaking witness to the alienation of the Arabs from what they regarded as their land, now under a British Mandate influenced by the Balfour Declaration that promised a homeland to the Zionist Jews. 'It was impossible to hold aloof from the struggle to establish the justice of [the Palestinian Arabs'] cause.'[3] And in recognition of her long and intimate connection with the land and the people, going back 40 years, she herself was called as a witness to give evidence to the Palestine Commission in Jerusalem in November 1929.[4] At first she rejoiced that the British governance was progressive for everyone. In particular

[it] was a source of real joy to me to feel that an awakening to a sense of the part women could take in social activities and responsibilities was due in great measure to the work of mission schools in the past.

Girls [who] . . . had had to fetch water from the village spring or sweep the dung for fuel from under the cattle in their homes, had blossomed out into well-dressed young women employed in Government service as postal clerks, nurses and teachers.[5]

She herself started a social centre for Arab girls in Haifa, Newton House, run by the girls, which eventually became the administrative centre for medical and social service in the area. By 1945, however, she had to mourn the loss of employment prospects, especially in the professions, for educated, intelligent young Arabs of either sex in a country that no longer promoted their life-chances.

Frances Newton's memoir *Fifty Years in Palestine*, written in 1946–47 when she was in her mid-seventies, chronicled her unsuccessful attempts to present the case for the evicted Arab peasants to high officials on the spot and her setting up, with her sister Mrs Fox-Strangeways, of a Palestine Information Centre in London in 1936 which was taken over by an Arab committee a year later. In 1937, after personally investigating the situation, she published a pamphlet, *Searchlight on Palestine*, attacking the British administration for 'using methods of terrorism and intimidation in Palestine in order to coerce the Arabs into submission to the policy of the creation of a Jewish State in Arab territory'.[6] In London, an Inspector of Police arrived at her house in October 1938 with an emergency regulation from the Colonial Office forbidding her to re-enter Palestine. She had indeed become a black sheep.[7]

Frances Newton acknowledged after 1945 that the plight of persecuted, stateless Jewry rightly concerned all Christians. What she argued was that the self-obligating powers, especially Great Britain and America, rather than the Palestinian Arabs alone, should be asked to make sacrifices to answer the needs of the Jews. She supported the British solution of 1939 that envisaged a Palestinian state in which there would be power-sharing by Arabs and Jews, rather than the Zionist claim to the whole of Palestine as Eretz Israel. The alternative, denying Arab claims to Palestine altogether, she predicted would cause war in the Middle East.

In 1948 Frances Newton, one can only imagine with what soreness of heart, set up a fund to try to relieve some of the distress of the now displaced/expelled Palestinian Arab refugees.[8] She left a considerable portion of her estate after her death to medical services for Palestinian Arabs in Jordan.

1. Frances Newton, *Fifty Years in Palestine* (London, Coldharbour Press, 1948), p. 23.
2. *Ibid.*, p. 108.
3. *Ibid.*, p. 128.
4. See *Evening Standard* (26.11 and 27.11.1929); *Daily News* (29.11 and 30.11.1929).
5. Newton, *op. cit.*, p. 161.
6. *Ibid.*, p. 283.
7. *Ibid.*, p. 289. The Expulsion (or Exclusion) Order was rescinded in 1943.
8. See obituary, *The Times* (15.6.1955).

P

PAGET, LEILA, DBE
(1881–24.9.1958)

NURSE OF ALLY AND ENEMY IN BALKANS

Father: General Sir Arthur Paget
Mother: Minnie, née Stevens, New York socialite

Leila Paget astonished her family and friends, who had only known her as a delicate, well-bred young daughter accompanying her mother around Europe's fashionable spas, when she joined her diplomat husband in Belgrade in 1910 and began to run a hospital for the wounded in Belgrade during the First and Second Balkan Wars. Her actions after the First World War began were even more extraordinary.

In mid-November 1914 she arrived with her First Serbian Relief Fund Unit at Skoplje to establish a 600-bed hospital there, a project demanding all her capacities as leader, tireless worker and brilliant organizer. She found streams of neglected wounded men, many suffering from sepsis, frostbite and even gangrene. In the subsequent bitter winter she and her nursing team had also to treat typhoid, dysentery, tetanus and typhus among the men, as well as treating the local civilians as out-patients. To fight the epidemic of typhus, to which she herself and many of her staff were to succumb, Leila Paget finally managed to set up two isolation blocks a mile away from the city, the 'typhus colony'. Simultaneously she discovered the appallingly neglected state of the wounded Austrian prisoners of the Serbians, including unburied dead. She then treated the Austrians alongside the Serbians in her hospital wards and relied on the fitter Austrians, who had already survived typhus, to be orderlies in her 'typhus colony', acknowledging that she could not have managed without them.

Skoplje lay directly in the path of the 'enemy' Bulgarian advance, virtually undefended. In mid-October 1915 Leila Paget's Relief Unit was ordered to evacuate. With the unanimous agreement of her staff, she refused to join the chaos on the roads and elected that the hospital staff stay at their post with their patients and wait to be taken prisoner by the Bulgarians (some of whom she had also nursed). The piquant element in this decision was that it was her husband Sir Ralph Paget, as Allied emissary in Belgrade, who had had to pass on the order from military headquarters to evacuate the hospital, and it was his wife who insisted on disobeying, assuring him that their reserves of food and clothing would be distributed to retreating Allied Serbian troops and civilian refugees as they passed through Skoplje before the city fell.

Within a week of the Bulgarian capture of Skoplje, the city faced total famine and chaos, the retreating Serbian army having destroyed the road and rail links to the countryside, taken all livestock and burnt all crops. A month later Leila Paget persuaded the Bulgarian authorities that she should be allowed to administer relief to the starving refugees, who included Turks, Albanians and Bulgarians as well as Serbian civilians, but she was soon accused of favouring Serbians and her relief operation was ordered to be suspended. She then made her declaration of principle. She gave 'to all who were absolutely destitute and without resources, *regardless of nationality*' (my italics).[1] Gradually she regained the trust of the victors and could administer relief again. The hospital had no form of heating that winter and the nurses had to dress wounds by candlelight. Hundreds of refugees, including women and orphaned children, froze to death in their terrible trek through the snow to Skoplje; some went mad with hunger, some only had rags to cover them and no shoes on their frostbitten feet. The hospital had also had to become a distribution centre for clothing and flour. In December the German army arrived and tried to wrest authority from the Bulgarians, commandeering the hospital. Leila Paget sought Bulgarian aid in regaining control of the hospital and seeking repatriation of the British medical and nursing staff via the International Red Cross. The unit left for Sofia in February 1916 and thence by Bulgarian hospital train through Romania and Russia, finally arriving in England in April.

On her return to wartime Britain, Leila Paget was subjected to criticism and cold-shouldered for her alleged excess of friendly, co-operative relations with 'enemy' Bulgarians – who themselves had earlier accused her of excessive friendship with 'enemy' Serbians, while the Serbians had had to tolerate her nursing of their wounded 'enemies' from Austria and Hungary. She had proved herself a pioneer of true internationalist humanitarianism.

Leila Paget lived for 40 more years after the First World War, and it was said of her that 'she never lost her two loves, the care of the sick, and the Serbian people'.[2]

1. Lady Paget's First and Second Serbian Relief Fund Reports, 'With our Serbian allies', held in the Imperial War Museum, London; quoted in Monica Krippner, *The Quality of Mercy: Women at War, Serbia 1915–18* (London, David and Charles, 1980), p. 155. Monica Krippner's book is invaluable for its account of the many other British women doctors, nurses, administrators and orderlies, who, like Mabel Dearmer and Leila Paget, struggled to alleviate suffering in an atrocious war zone in 1914–18. See especially her appreciation of Dr Frances Wakefield, Sister Rankin and Nurse Flora Scott, all notable for their selfless service.
2. *The Times* (26.9.1958). See also obituary, 'Dame Leila Paget', *The Times* (25.9.1958).

PAGET, LADY MURIEL, CBE
(19.8.1876–16.6.1938)

HUMANITARIAN RELIEF ORGANIZER

Father: Murray Finch-Hatton, 12th Earl of Winchilsea
Mother: Edith, née Harcourt, Countess of Winchilsea

Anglican

Muriel Paget was nearly 30 before she discovered her vocation to organize relief for the desperately needy. Before 1905, as the wife of the inventor Richard Paget, later Sir Richard Paget, Bart, she had led a totally conventional life as an upper-class Society lady, wife and mother, interspersed with frequent 'cures' for her ill health. But in 1905 she discovered the wretched-ness, including sheer hunger, that was endemic in Southwark when her aunt Lady Templetown suggested she become Honorary Secretary of the charity that organized soup kitchens there. What Muriel Paget discovered was that the task needed much more application than a token one day a week from a Society lady, and that *all* the poor districts of London needed soup kitchens. From that moment she put all her hitherto unused mental and physical energy into con-necting her own Society network with the desperate struggle for survival of London's poor. She founded a new association, the Invalid Kitchens of London, persuaded her friend the Duchess of Somerset to chair it, and together they raised the money. 'Muriel was a pioneer of charity balls, and she soon discovered that she had a flair for organizing them and for collecting money for good causes.'[1] By 1913 there were soup kitchens for mothers, children and old people not only in Southwark but also in Stepney, Victoria Docks and St Pancras. One possible explanation for just why it should have been Muriel Paget, rather than any of her

Lady Muriel Paget, c. 1921 (From Wilfred Blunt, Lady Muriel, *Methuen, 1962)*

hundreds of aristocratic friends and acquaintances, who thereafter gave herself totally to the relief of the suffering of others – and on an enormous, heroic scale – was perhaps that, like Josephine Butler before her, she had experienced unassuage-able loss at first hand, her only brother having died when he was 9 and her first son when he was less than a year old.

When the First World War broke out, Muriel Paget was pregnant again; in November 1914 she gave birth to her fifth child, another son after three daughters. But in 1915 she was already organizing the funding and staffing of an Anglo-Russian base hospital in Petrograd (St Petersburg), influenced by her friend Bernard Pares' reports of the appalling suffering of the Russian armies; and in 1916 she left her daughters at boarding school and her son with his nurse and began a life of almost non-stop humanitarian intervention abroad that would end only with her death, from cancer and exhaustion, at 62. Her family saw her at Christmas and Easter and birthdays. Face to face with the agony of millions, she had absolutely no doubt as to where her first duty lay.

At Lutsk in the Galician Ukraine in 1916, for instance, she saw hundreds of untended Russian casualties lying bleeding, unbandaged, undrugged, among many more hundreds of flyblown corpses. Field hospitals had to be the answer. She sent cable after cable from Petrograd pleading for British funds for *100* ambulances for her dressing stations. In 1917 the Russian Revolution engulfed Petrograd. Lady Muriel found herself 'looking into the mouth of a revolver with a fierce Russian behind it. I pushed the revolver away and laughed at the soldier, who let me pass.'[2] She was then asked by the British and French authorities to organize civil relief in

Odessa in the south, which had not yet fallen to the Bolsheviks. The situation in Kiev was even worse than in Odessa, so, having briefed her relief committee, she left Odessa for Kiev, only to find her food kitchens for 6,000 people there under direct bombardment. The Bolshevik siege of Kiev was victorious; she and 40 other British subjects, plus the Czech nationalist Thomas Masaryk, were evacuated from Russia in February, crossing Siberia by train, reaching Kyoto by sea from Korea and then on to America and Canada, finallly arriving in England at the end of May 1918.

Lady Muriel Paget was politically colour-blind. She was immune, therefore, to the twentieth century's terrible selective indignation and pity that always demanded to know whether victims were on the politically desirable side or not. 'She never distinguished . . . between Imperial and Socialist Russia.'[3] In December 1919 she founded her Women and Children of Russia Relief Fund that supported a hospital in the Crimea run by Dr Isobel Emslie, a veteran of the Scottish Women's Hospitals, until Wrangel's last-ditch White Russian stand was defeated in November 1920. During the Russian famine, Lady Muriel was permitted to return to the Soviet Union in September 1922, to try to set up child welfare centres and a training school for Russian nurses, funded by Britain, but without success. However, she was hugely successful elsewhere: by 1920 she was organizing relief work in Slovakia, the Baltic states and Romania as well as Poland, often in conjunction with the Save the Children Fund.

'Her energy is terrifying. She sends Prime Ministers scuttling at her behests' wrote Harold Nicolson during a spare moment at Versailles in 1919. 'She telephoned incessantly to London and Prague [about the desperate social situation in Czechoslovakia]; she ruthlessly waylaid ministers, deputies, – "I go straight to heads which seems a good plan".'[4] Her capacity for non-stop personal intervention in several places at once was almost unbelievable. In one ten-day period at the end of 1919, for example, she was to be found in London, Paris (twice), Geneva, Berne, Prague (twice) and Vienna. Whenever she was in London she would raise funds like one possessed and interview idealistic volunteer social workers, nurses and other medical staff for the most recent project to intervene in Europe where there was starvation, smallpox or typhus. The result was millions of pounds' worth of aid from President Hoover, the American Red Cross, the Foreign Office and a 'famous train-load of clothes, fats, rice, condensed milk, and medical stores steaming out of the Gare de L'Est for Prague. The Paget Mission to save Slovakia was under way.'[5] One of the most important aspects of that mission was the training of local paediatric nurses and social workers under the leadership of Miss Grace Vulliamy, so that the clinics, food distribution and vaccination centres, schools for disabled children, tuberculosis hospital, etc., could continue under Czechoslovak auspices – though with periodic inspection visits from British medical professionals to ensure that the new sanitation, isolation and inoculation prodecures were still carried out.

The new Baltic states, Latvia, Lithuania and Estonia, were still enduring the chaos of civil war, revolution and counter-revolution in 1919–20, and when Lady Muriel found herself in one of their battlefields, she unpacked a white jersey, tied it to a stick and gave it to her escort to wave them through. The people of Riga, Taunus, Vilna and Dvinsk all owed to her nurses some of their earliest food kitchens and feeding centres, infant welfare clinics and travelling First Aid units. 'Am buying two hundred cows @ five pounds each cheap' she reported from Lithuania in response to the devastation in Latvia following the drowning of thousands of people and animals by melting ice floes in April 1922.

Not everyone was impressed. *John Bull* characteristically preferred a Britain First policy after the First World War, ignoring her continuing commitment to the Invalid Kitchens of London. And she also received letters like this:

Dear Lady Muriel,

Is it rude of me to suggest that there are many people in this country who badly need relief? . . .

Exactly why we should help the Viennese, who were very hostile and cruel to the Italians, and neglect our friends, I am unable to divine.

I am quite sure that my newspapers would not be at all inclined to support these enterprizes [*sic*].

Yours sincerely
Northcliffe.[6]

Muriel Paget's final cause was to support the destitute and friendless last surviving British subjects stranded in Stalin's Russia: elderly governesses, nurses, former employees of British firms married to Russians and their Russian-speaking children. At first she only sent money and food parcels, but by 1930 she decided to go to their rescue in person. On being told they were mere riff-raff, 'she said, "I know. That's why I want to save them. No one else will."'[7] And save them she did, eventually getting them all evacuated to Estonia in 1938.

1. Wilfred Blunt, *Lady Muriel* (London, Methuen, 1962), p. 43.
2. *Ibid.*, p. 109.
3. Robert Byron, in *The Times* (21.6.1938).
4. Blunt, *op. cit.*, p. 137.
5. See entry for Maynard Carter above; and Blunt, *op. cit.*, pp. 138–9.
6. Blunt, *op. cit.*, p. 147.
7. *Ibid.*, p. 243.

Lady Muriel Paget's unjudgemental, life-loving, infectiously hope-filled personality is appreciated in several obituary notices in *The Times* (17.6, 18.6, 21.6, 22.6 and 23.6.1938).

PAGET, VIOLET
(pseudonym **VERNON LEE**)
(14.10.1856–12.2.1935)

WRITER; PACIFIST THINKER

Father: Henry Ferguson Paget, political refugee from Poland in 1848, private tutor
Mother: Matilda, née Lee-Hamilton

Humanist

Whereas most humanitarians are interventionists after a catastrophe, Vernon Lee's humanitarianism was enlisted in trying to prevent the catastrophes she foresaw; and whereas most humanitarians engage in practical attempts to alleviate suffering, Vernon Lee's medium was William Blake's 'mental fight'. She was a cosmopolitan intellectual who, precisely because she had no one exclusive tribal geographical/linguistic/religious affiliation, could see just where the warring European nationalistic imperialisms were heading, long before the actual outbreak of the First World War.

As early as 1907 Vernon Lee wrote to the *Westminster Gazette* to counter a French writer's call to England to keep Germany in '*un rôle subalterne*' in the world. She then translated for the *Westminster Gazette* an article by the anti-Prussian Lujo Brentano regretting the naval arms-race between Britain and Germany but warning of Germany's real fear of the possibility of a British naval blockade. After the Agadir incident (July 1911), she was appalled when in France to hear her French friends openly expect Britain's support in a war against Germany; she thereupon wrote to *The Nation* asking for clarification of Britain's precise commitments under the Entente Cordiale. She also wrote to a French periodical seeking French radical

Violet Paget ('Vernon Lee'), c. 1912

intellectuals' support for a Franco-German *rapprochement*.[1] Throughout 1913 she wrote in English, French, German and Italian papers to express the fears of liberals in each of these countries of the rôle performed by 'the international ring of armament manufacturers in playing on national suspicions . . . with the encouragement it gave to the . . . Navy League in England and the *Flottenverein* in Germany to increase war-preparedness'.[2] Perhaps no other woman, except Bertha von Suttner on the Continent and KATE COURTNEY, CAROLINE PLAYNE and SOPHIA STURGE in Britain, was as far-seeing or as full of foreboding then.

Almost immediately after August 1914, Vernon Lee made herself very unpopular by denouncing H. G. Wells's appeal to neutral America to cut off supplies from Germany in his article subtitled 'Victualling our enemies'. 'This . . . is what Mr Wells is imploring America to desist from. Let . . . America use and show her neutrality by starving Germany.'[3] On 3 October 1914 she wrote an Open Letter to Rosika Schwimmer[4] in the *New York Post*, supporting the latter's call for continuous mediation between neutrals in order to stop the competition in massacre. She was no longer able to be published anywhere in Britain except for the pacifist *Labour Leader*, as she persisted in warning that an enduring peace must be an 'endurable peace . . . It is not the diplomatists and soldiers who can end . . . this butchery and destruction . . . otherwise than in some new sowing of dragon's teeth.'[5]

The climax of Vernon Lee's Cassandra-like percipience was her pamphlet *Peace with Honour: Controversial Notes on the Settlement*, published, with a disclaimer of responsibility for its opinions, by the Union for the Democratic Control of Foreign Policy in 1915. In it she foresaw a punitive Allied victory and foretold that a *revanchiste* 'peace settlement' would assuredly lead to a second world war:

A huge war-indemnity imposed upon a defeated Germany would be both self-defeating in its damage to her trading partners and, far from 'crushing' German militarism, England and her Allies [would have] hit upon an infallible recipe for giving it a new lease of life. A humiliated, insecure, or hemmed in Germany would . . . mean a Germany arming once more for a Leipzig after a Jena.

How could Vernon Lee be so sure? Her lifetime spent investigating, analysing and interpreting the cultures of the four major European cultures had taught her something about human psychology, both individual and collective. The so-called enemy 'is a creature as like ourself as our own image in the glass . . . We have therefore [only] to ask ourselves "How should we feel and behave if a victor . . . tried to crush us?"'[6]

All the rest of Vernon Lee's writing, which was devoted to a desperate attempt to prevent her prophecy of a second world war from coming true, focused on this predicate of universalist human psychology. Her *Ballet of the Nations* (1915; developed into the much longer *Satan the Waster*, 1920) was a profound and still relevant – though still unheeded – diagnosis of our all too human 'war mentality'. In this work she shows how the devil of war always enlists the tender humane responses of pity and indignation at injustice in order to get the fighting started; it is these, the most noble human feelings, that are called on when war – prepared for by long years of rather less noble territorial annexation and economic competition for raw materials, markets, arms and 'spheres of influence' – at last erupts. And once the killing has started, then, again, the terrible self-sacrifice of the young on each side demands validation by only the noblest feelings of pity and indignation at injustice. Our hatred is always righteous. Every belligerent sincerely believes that it did not want war, that the war was entirely the fault of the enemy; each sincerely fears that it is being threatened and has to defend itself; each can only see itself as wholly in the right and the enemy as wholly in the wrong. We can always only perceive the atrocities perpetrated by the other side, never our own:

> Thus . . . the drowning of those few poor children on the *Lusitania* has stamped itself on the pitying and indignant Anglo-Saxon soul; while our blockade's slow, steady killing of scores of Central European children, born and unborn, has barely caught the tail of our eye: . . . Moreover, as we cannot compare the seen with the unseen, still less weigh what is felt against what is not felt, there comes to be . . . a loss of all scale and proportion.[7]

And contrariwise, our 'enemy' cannot see the atrocities perpetrated by his side or feel any suffering but his own.

Not surprisingly, Vernon Lee not only made countless enemies through her pacifist witness in wartime but also lost countless friends.[8] Before she died she had to experience the advent both of Mussolini and of Hitler, who would, as she had foretold, make lethal capital out of the Treaty of Versailles. Her analysis of our war-making psychology is still pertinent at the beginning of the twenty-first century, alas.

1. Peter Gunn, *Vernon Lee* (Oxford University Press, 1964), pp. 200–1.
2. *Ibid.*, p. 202.
3. *Ibid.*, p. 204; and Sybil Oldfield, 'England's Cassandras in World War One' in Sybil Oldfield (ed.), *This Working-day World: Women's Lives and Culture(s) in Britain 1914–1945* (London and Bristol, PA, Taylor and Francis, 1994), p. 93.
4. Rosika Schwimmer was the Hungarian-born pacifist feminist who initiated the project of the Women's International Congress at The Hague in April 1915 and the ensuing dispatch of women

envoys to the world's war-capitals as well as neutrals to try to prepare the ground for ending the First World War: see Anne Wiltsher, *Most Dangerous Women: Feminist Peace Campaigners of the Great War* (London, Pandora, 1985). Vernon Lee was a signatory both to the British Committee supporting the Congress (see Appendix I) and to Emily Hobhouse's Open Letter to German women. In December 1914 she wrote about her memory of hearing Bach's *Christmas Oratorio* in Leipzig for Mary Sheepshanks' *Ius Suffragii*.

5. Quoted in Oldfield, *op. cit.*, pp. 93–4.

6. Vernon Lee in *Labour Leader* (1.4.1915) and *Peace with Honour*, quoted in Oldfield, *op. cit.*, pp. 94–5.

7. Vernon Lee, *Satan the Waster: A Philosophical War Trilogy* (London, John Lane, Bodley Head, 1920), Introduction, p. xxxvi.

8. See also obituary, *The Times* (14.2.1935); and entry for Violet Paget in the *Dictionary of National Biography*.

PANKHURST, (E.) SYLVIA
(1882–1960)

SOCIALIST FEMINIST CAMPAIGNER
FOR THE EXPLOITED AND OPPRESSED

Father: Richard Pankhurst, barrister, radical
political campaigner
Mother: Emmeline, Suffragette leader

Humanist

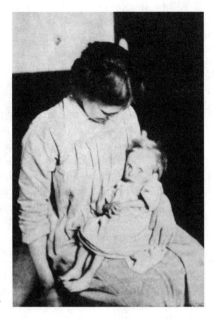

'As they came to us' – Nurse Hebbes and one of the war sufferers brought to The Mothers' Arms (From Sylvia Pankhurst, The Home Front, *first published 1932. Photograph by Norah Smyth, courtesy of E. S. Pankhurst archives, IISG, Amsterdam)*

Sylvia Pankhurst's commitment to the militant campaign for women's suffrage and her founding of the East London Federation of Suffragettes are well known.[1] She was not free from the Pankhurst need to dramatize her own rôle and martyrdom and achieve a cult following,[2] but aided by devoted friends, she, unlike her mother and elder sister, did practise the humanitarian imperative of attempting to answer the needs of desperate strangers – and on a massive scale.

The outbreak of the First World War brought Sylvia Pankhurst, in Old Ford Road, Bow, face to face with the insupportable hardship of women and children left destitute after their breadwinner had enlisted. A sharp rise in unemployment meant there was no work, or only sweated work, and the government was slow to pay out the minimal separation allowance to the dependants of its armed forces.[3] Sylvia Pankhurst not only protested time and again to the government via letters, petitions and deputations from the East End – fruitlessly – but also thought up one practical scheme after another to tackle the huge deterioration in living standards in what was already one of the poorest parts, if not the poorest part, of England.[4] Backed by the indispensable support of wealthy friends such as Lady Sybil Smith and Norah Smyth and the personal labour of dedicated women like Nurse Hebbes, Dr Barbara Tchaikowsky and Muriel Matters, she realized her dreams of a milk distribution centre, a communal cost-price restaurant, a mothers' clinic, a Montessori nursery and a small toy factory to provide creative employment at a decent wage. She and her friends lived on bread and margarine and tea as, with inspired pacifist-feminist symbolism, they transformed a former pub, The Gunmakers' Arms in Old Ford Road, into The Mothers' Arms to provide adequate space for their mother and baby clinic and their day nursery for the children of working women. Her social intervention was far from unique in the East End in the First World War,[5] but her passionate energy ignited many followers to spread and implement her ideas. Moreover, she herself also worked day and night to intervene personally to help individual women at the end of their tether. 'Her [greatest] contribution was her direct service to the widows, the orphans, the hungry and the disabled. Often she herself accommodated homeless women until she could find adequate quarters for them',[6] and she often crusaded, this time successfully, on behalf of particular hard cases: whole families who were starving because of inflexibly oppressive wartime bureaucracy.

A characteristic later example of Sylvia Pankhurst's indignant humanitarianism was her unsuccessful, but passionate and disinterested, attempt to rouse the world to intervene effectively with Mussolini's government in 1932 on behalf of the victimized wife and children of the murdered Italian anti-Fascist Matteotti.[7] Her final humanitarian achievement was the building of the Princess Tsahay Hospital in Addis Ababa, though here again her role was that of ideas-woman and polemicist/publicist while others, including Lord Amulree and the Emperor Haile Selassie, supplied the funding.

There can be no doubt that Sylvia Pankhurst was a female Don Quixote, always in thrall to her latest, outraged cause and needing to realize her own idealized idea of herself as crusader for the social good of the world. Nor can it be denied that her very vehemence and absolutist idealism[8] were more often than not counter-productive in gaining her point with the men in power who alone could implement what she wanted done – not excluding Lenin. Nevertheless she was also capable of inspiring the devotion of a great many people, mostly women, who *were* capable of implementing her vision, at least in part; her vision was a steadfastly humane one in all its different, even contradictory, political manifestations; and she gave of herself totally in her attempt to answer others' needs. She did not just care about abstract 'others' but addressed the needs of the penniless, pregnant orphan girl or the homeless, unemployed boy on her doorstep.

1. See, e.g., Sylvia Pankhurst, *The Suffragette Movement* (London, Longmans Green, 1931); Olive Banks, *The Biographical Dictionary of British Feminists*, vol. 1: *1880–1930* (New York, New York University Press, 1985); Les Garner, *Stepping Stones to Women's Liberty* (London, Heinemann, 1984); Barbara Winslow, *Sylvia Pankhurst, Sexual Politics and Political Activism* (London, UCL Press, 1996).
2. See many articles on and photographs of 'Our Sylvia' in *The Women's Dreadnought*, later *The Workers' Dreadnought*, which Sylvia Pankhurst edited and largely wrote; and Patricia Romero, *E. Sylvia Pankhurst: Portrait of a Radical* (New Haven and London, Yale University Press, 1987).
3. Sylvia Pankhurst, *The Home Front* (London, Hutchinson, 1932; reprinted London, Cresset Library, 1987).
4. *Ibid.*; Romero, *op. cit.*, ch. 5; Winslow, *op. cit.*, ch. 4.
5. See entries for CHARLOTTE DESPARD, MARY HUGHES, MURIEL LESTER, MURIEL PAGET and ADA SALTER.
6. Romero, *op. cit.*, pp. 103–4.
7. *Ibid.*, pp. 205–6.
8. See Kathryn Dodd, *A Sylvia Pankhurst Reader* (Manchester, Manchester University Press, 1993).

PEARCE, JOYCE, OBE
(23.11.1915–1985)

TEACHER; PIONEER OF VOLUNTEER
YOUTH WORK WITH REFUGEES;
FOUNDER OF THE OCKENDEN
VENTURE

Father: Vic Pearce, shopkeeper
Mother: Mary, née Quartermaine, Red Cross
nurse

Christian

*Joyce Pearce and young refugees (From
Pamela Watkin,* Joyce's Ockenden, *Broadmead Press, 1993)*

After graduating in history in the mid-1930s from Oxford, where she had heard Albert Schweitzer speak movingly about the world's ever-growing population of refugees, Joyce Pearce became not only a teacher but a committed pacifist. Promoted very young to senior history mistress during the Second World War, she was deeply concerned after 1945 how best to help her pupils engage with the new, unbearable facts of the atom bomb and Auschwitz, without becoming either desensitized or clinically depressed. She decided to take her pupils out of the classroom and into the local Law Courts and Council offices as a first lesson in educated citizenship. She also brought her sixth-formers home to her flat for open-ended weekend discussions on international affairs and the struggle for peace and justice. In 1947 she turned a family home, 'Ockenden', in Woking, Surrey, into a residential sixth-form centre to run weekends with the help of sympathetic teachers and challenging guest speakers. The first-ever such weekend was on 'The colour bar', led by two Jamaican students from London University. A year later, 60 schools were sending their sixth-formers to 'Ockenden' from as far away as Liverpool, Lincolnshire and Sheffield. In 1948 Joyce Pearce made her own venture of faith and gave up her teaching career altogether in order to organize such courses full-time.

The first 'outreach' from Ockenden into the world of the refugees was in 1951 when the sixth-formers, learning of the thousands of workless, homeless, schoolless 'displaced' young people still in West Germany, asked whether some of them might not be brought across to Ockenden for a holiday. The project became Woking's contribution to the Festival of Britain. Out of that first brief stay of a handful of Estonian, Latvian and Polish youngsters, escorted to Britain by SUE RYDER, there grew a second project for the education of refugee children in Britain, using Ockenden, and later a second 'Pearce' house, Donington, as their base.[1] Over the next 30 years the Ockenden Venture grew to extend volunteer aid to refugee children from Tibet, South Africa, Biafra, the Sudan and Vietnam, bringing many of them to Britain for education. In the desert of southern Algeria, which the girl children could not leave but where they had no chance of education, Joyce Pearce, in conjunction with UNICEF, founded their first school. But she failed to fulfil her dream of founding a school where poor Lebanese and poor Palestinian refugee children might grow up together.

At the beginning of her 'venture' Joyce Pearce had hoped merely to teach a few young British people about the terrible human fall-out of war. By the end of her life she wanted a revolutionary change: an educational curriculum that would put global humanitarian issues at its centre and so create a network of young people alerted to the remediable suffering of others and determined to reach out wherever human rights were being violated.[2]

1. Pamela Watkin, *Joyce's Ockenden: The Story of a Vision That Became a Venture for Refugees* (Woking, Broadmead Press, 1993), p. 47.
2. *Ibid.*, pp. 179–80.

See also obituaries in *The Times* (18.7.1985); and *Daily Telegraph* (19.7.1985).

PECKOVER, PRISCILLA HANNAH
(27.10.1833–8.9.1931)

PIONEER CAMPAIGNER FOR PEACE AND DISARMAMENT

Father: Algernon Peckover, Quaker banker
Mother: Priscilla, née Alexander

Quaker

Priscilla Peckover was 45 years old when she first felt addressed by the Quaker injunction to bear Christian testimony against all war. Quaker women, like men, were now to be asked to make public witness. She decided to initiate a Peace Pledge campaign, on analogy with the Temperance Pledge, among women in Britain, and composed the Declaration:

I believe all war to be contrary to the mind of Christ, who says: 'Love your enemies, do good to them that hate you, etc.,' – and am desirous to do what I can to further the cause of Peace.

Priscilla Peckover (from The Friend, *18.9.1931)*

She not only asked local Quaker women to sign but went from door to cottage door, saying that this was her view and asking her poor neighbours to consider their own. She felt too timid to ask local tradesmen's wives and too aware that they might only sign because of her family's local importance – 'and I wanted real conviction'.[1] Therefore she was overjoyed when a convinced shopkeeper's wife volunteered to collect dozens of signatures herself. Amazingly, through her commitment and organizational energy, Priscilla Peckover's Wisbech Local Peace Association eventually grew to have 30 branches with 15,000 members in Britain as well as affiliated groups in 31 countries on all continents, her Declaration being translated into French, German, Polish and Russian. During the fighting in the Sudan in the 1880s, she issued thousands of copies of her 'Earnest appeal to all women everywhere' and her own example encouraged both British and foreign women to speak in public on the issue of peace or war.

Priscilla Peckover's call for the elimination of war was not mere abstract emotional rhetoric. Every three months for the next 50 years she brought out her journal *Peace and Goodwill*, in which she advocated the settlement of all international disputes through the arbitration of an internationally sanctioned International Court; she educated public opinion regarding the risks, immorality and expense of military 'preparedness'; and she urged Members of Parliament that Britain should take the lead in proposing 'a mutual and simultaneous reduction of armaments as the first step to their eventual abolition'.[2] She also regularly translated the anti-militarist news from other countries and campaigned against attempts to introduce compulsory military service in Britain, including by way of youth movements such as the Boys' Brigade.

At the beginning of the First World War, Priscilla Peckover signed Emily Hobhouse's 'Open Letter to German Women', and her beloved younger sister Algerina was on the British Committee supporting the Women's International Congress at The Hague.[3] At the age of 83 she was visited in 1917 by the local Superintendent of Police, who confiscated all her copies of a leaflet *May a Christian Be a Soldier?* that had been found objectionable by the military authorities. *Peace and Goodwill* had to be submitted to the censor: 'I felt very clear that I would rather go to prison than lower our standard. But neither alternative was required.'[4] She was still writing for it on her deathbed at 97.

Priscilla Peckover, as well as being exceptionally intelligent, had an extraordinary gift for languages, essential to her success in setting up a world movement; as one contribution to internationalism of the spirit, she translated the Bible into Esperanto. Her one-woman contribution to the abolition of war was no more successful in the twentieth century than that of Bertha von Suttner; her only satisfaction was to have lived to see the founding of both the International Court at The Hague and the League of Nations; she was spared the Second World War and the atomic bomb.[5]

1. Priscilla Peckover, *Incidents in the Rise and Progress of the Wisbech Local Peace Association* (London, The Peace Society, 1st edn 1906; 2nd edn 1925), pp. 2–3.
2. Thomas Kennedy, entry for Priscilla Peckover in Harold Josephson (ed.), *Biographical Dictionary of Modern Peace Leaders* (Westport, CT, Greenwood Press, 1985), p. 737.
3. See Introduction and Appendix I.
4. Peckover, *op. cit.*, pp. 28–9, 'War Time . . . that retrograde period'.
5. For further reading on Priscilla Peckover see obituary and appreciations in *The Friend* (18.9.1931); and Jill Liddington, *The Long Road to Greenham: Feminism and Anti-Militarism in Britain since 1820* (London, Virago, 1989).

Priscilla Peckover's Wisbech family home is now part of the National Trust. Both the records of the Wisbech Local Peace Association and the entire run of *Peace and Goodwill* are held in the Swarthmore College Peace Collection, Swarthmore, PA, USA.

PENMAN, MARY BAKER

(30.8.1883–26.2.1951)

NURSE, RESCUER AND ADOPTIVE MOTHER OF
CHILD REFUGEES

Father: Joseph Allen Baker, MP, Quaker
Mother: Elizabeth Balmer Moscrip, Quaker

Quaker

Mary Baker, later
Penman, as VAD in
Ireland, 1916 (Courtesy
of her daughter,
Clare Campion)

Mary Penman was that rare species of humanitarian, a
woman who not only went out into the world to alleviate
remediable suffering there but also took many victims from
abroad into her own home, simply adding them to her
family. As a young woman in the First World War she
testified to her Quaker principles both by signing her
support for the anti-war Women's International Congress
at The Hague[1] and by training as a VAD nurse. She served
first at Dunkirk in a hospital established by the Friends'
Ambulance Unit led by her brother Philip Noel Baker (who
was much later to be awarded the Nobel Peace prize for
his work on disarmament). Next she joined a Quaker unit
in Corsica caring for Serbian refugees. She then went to
Ireland in the tense year 1916 and nursed wounded officers,
followed by a period in London where she had discovered a hospital that cared for
wounded German prisoners. After the war she went out to Belgrade to help Dr
KATHERINE MACPHAIL to establish a hospital for children with tuberculosis.

In 1922 Mary Baker married her sister's widower, the Quaker Frank Penman,
and mothered her sister's children as well as the daughter born to her. Their home
became an unofficial international meeting place and stay-over for literally hundreds
of foreign visitors. In 1929, for example, the British Yugoslavia Society asked for
her help in looking after a 13-year-old boy who had been stranded in Britain. He
came to her for a fortnight and stayed as an adopted son for three years.

In 1938, appalled and ashamed by the Munich agreement that bought time for
the West by sacrificing Czechoslovakia, Mary Penman flew to Prague with her
eldest daughter to start a small Quaker relief centre and emigration office for socialist
Sudetenländer in danger from the Nazis because of their socialism and unwanted
by the Czechs because of their Germanness.[2] She visited the camps in which they
were interned and distributed relief supplies. Once back in Britain, and throughout
the war, her home became a refuge to 'Ma's adopted Czechs'. She was someone
who felt immediately addressed by others' pain and who succeeded, by her practical
intervention and warmth of personality, in convincing those others that they had
not been abandoned. 'She championed the cause of the oppressed, the lonely and
those she felt were in any kind of distress or need . . . Her determined pluck and
courage combined with her gift for universal fellowship formed the radiance which
she has shed into the world.'[3]

1. See Introduction and Appendix I.
2. See entries for TESSA ROWNTREE and DOREEN WARRINER.
3. *The Friend* (23.3.1951); see also obituary, *The Friend* (16.3.1951).

PETHICK-LAWRENCE, EMMELINE
(1867–1954)

PACIFIST FEMINIST ACTIVIST

Father: Henry Pethick, wealthy Liberal JP

Emmeline Pethick-Lawrence (Frontispiece to her memoir My Part in a Changing World, *Victor Gollancz, 1938)*

Emmeline Pethick-Lawrence, together with her staunchly idealistic husband Fred, was someone who stood up to be counted for her humane politics. She left her affectionate, privileged family home in 1890 to live and work in the West London Mission for women and girls, leaving it five years later to found a girls' club and social settlement and a dress-making co-operative that provided decent working conditions, a living wage and the first paid annual holiday for its workers in Britain. Her feminism was rooted in her socialism: she wanted the vote in order for the mass of poor women to gain some measure of control over their lives. In her commitment to the Women's Social and Political Union (1906–12) she was imprisoned five times, despite her initial dread of Holloway, and finally joined in a sympathetic hunger strike to secure better treatment for her suffragette fellow prisoners. She was forcibly fed.

Emmeline Pethick-Lawrence's immediate reaction to the outbreak of the First World War was that it must be brought to the swiftest possible end. In October 1914, therefore, she travelled to the United States, ostensibly to be a key speaker for the suffrage campaign there, but really to enlist the support of the huge women's movement in neutral America in initiating moves to end the war by means of negotiation, brokered initially by mediating neutral powers, led by the USA. She joined forces, first with Madeleine Doty and Chrystal Eastman of the Women's Peace Party, and then with Rosika Schwimmer, Jane Addams, Dr Aletta Jacobs, KATHLEEN COURTNEY and CHRYSTAL MACMILLAN, in their concerted project to organize a Women's International Congress at The Hague, which she attended in April 1915.[1]

In autumn 1915 Emmeline Pethick-Lawrence became Honorary Treasurer of the British Section of the Women's International League. 'From this time forward the main purpose of my life was to spread as far as possible, the conviction that peace and negotiation alone could promote a stable condition in Europe.'[2] She wrote to *The Nation* criticizing the Prime Minister, Lloyd George, for refusing to negotiate in 1916, when he declared his determination to give the enemy 'the knock-out blow' and to carry on fighting to 'the last man and the last shilling'.[3] In March 1917 she supported her husband when he was a Peace-by-Negotiation Parliamentary candidate at a by-election in Aberdeen: '[It] was the longest election contest that I ever experienced and the most difficult and unpleasant.'[4] Missiles were thrown at them and the windows broken where they spoke. In November 1918 she herself stood for election as Labour candidate in a Manchester constituency. Again she found war fever still at its height with the public mood all out to 'make Germany pay'. Working-class women voted against her in loyalty to their men; it was the demobbed soldiers who saved her deposit. But '[what] really mattered was that the electors on that day voted, although they did not know it, for another world war . . . [adding] the sanction of the people of the whole country to the many other inducements afforded to the victors to make the Treaty of Versailles an instrument of vengeance.'[5]

In April 1919 Emmeline Pethick-Lawrence led the protest march of thousands, with the banner 'Lift the Hunger Blockade!', from Trafalgar Square to 10 Downing Street. In May 1919, at the Second Women's International Congress, this time in Zürich, she had 'what was perhaps the most moving experience of [her] life'.[6] She met again her pacifist counterparts from the 'enemy' nations, now gaunt with deprivation and suffering. Together they vowed to dedicate the rest of their lives to reconciliation and the promotion of peace, in the teeth of the punitive Treaty of Versailles. In June 1926 she addressed tens of thousands of women in Hyde Park at the culmination of their Arbitration and Disarmament Pilgrimage. But the government remained deaf.[7]

In his funeral address for her, her husband said:

> At all stages of her life she was a champion of the weak against the strong . . . she stood out against class injustice and racial prejudice . . . She risked her life to call a halt to oppression in Ireland. She loathed war and pleaded for justice to beaten foes. She espoused many lost causes and turned them into winning ones . . .
>
> But of the many victories she won the greatest of all was the victory over herself – over her fears, her limitations and her frailties.[8]

1. See Introduction and Appendix I; and Anne Wiltsher, *Most Dangerous Women: Feminist Peace Campaigners of the Great War* (London, Pandora, 1985).
2. Emmeline Pethick-Lawrence, *My Part in a Changing World* (London, Victor Gollancz, 1938), p. 316.
3. *Ibid.*
4. *Ibid.*, p. 317.
5. *Ibid.*, p. 323.
6. *Ibid.*, p. 326.
7. Jill Liddington, *The Long Road to Greenham: Feminism and Anti-Militarism in Britain since 1820* (London, Virago, 1989), pp. 144–6.
8. Address by Lord Pethick-Lawrence (16.3.1954), held in Women's Library, London. See also obituaries in *The Times* (12.3.1954); and *Manchester Guardian* (12.3.1954).

PICTON-TURBERVILL, EDITH, MP, OBE
(1872–31.8.1960)

CAMPAIGNER AGAINST GIRL SLAVERY

Father: Col. John Picton Turbervill, JP, ex-Indian Army, mine-owner, landowner
Mother: Eleanor, daughter of Sir Grenville Temple, Bart

Anglican

An immensely tall, athletic aristocrat, Edith Picton-Turbervill had many strengths but her most important quality as a humanitarian was her stubborn adherence to her own conscience. This led her in youth, like a latter-day Dorothea Brooke,[1] to kneel in the mud of navvies' hovels, passionately praying for their conversion to

Christ and teetotalism, her ardent, total sincerity alone protecting her from their abuse. A little later she was to be found in the slums of Shoreditch, appalled by the misery of the sweated women matchbox makers, but again feeling impelled to speak to them only of their souls. Nevertheless those insights into British destitution in the late 1890s would later convert her, the daughter of a Conservative MP, into a Labour Party activist and candidate during the 1920s. Arthur Henderson's *The Aims of Labour* (1918) finally convinced her that fundamental socialist measures were both necessary and 'in harmony with Christian thought and ethics'.[2]

Edith Picton-Turbervill

During the First World War Edith Picton-Turbervill might again seem to have accomplished nothing but conventional, patriotic war work as she organized hostels and canteens for girl munitions workers, the Women's Army Corps in France and the Women's Land Army under the auspices of the YWCA, of which she was national Vice-President. But again her uncomfortable conscience led her to think 'against the current'.[3] She wrote in her diary at the time: 'Intercessions in the churches for peace. I am in a fog. We pray for peace but everyone is very angry if we talk of peace.'[4] Therefore she became one of the few, and very unpopular, women who in April 1915 'had tried to go to The Hague to discuss peace with women of other nations'.[5] Throughout the 1920s she supported both the Women's International League for Peace and Freedom and the League of Nations Union, and at the end of her life she wrote *Christ and International Life*.

Another unpopular cause to which Edith Picton-Turbervill stubbornly (and unsuccessfully) adhered was the ordination of women as priests in the Church of England.[6] However, during her short career as a Labour MP, she did succeed in carrying through one Bill: to prohibit the passing of the sentence of death upon expectant mothers. In fact, over the past 70 years, expectant mothers had been reprieved from hanging and their sentences commuted to penal servitude for life; nevertheless the Judge had still been constrained to pass sentence of death by hanging, since a woman could only claim she was pregnant *after* sentence. Edith Picton-Turbervill's Bill ensured that a woman could declare herself pregnant before being sentenced so that the death sentence could not be passed in court.

But Edith Picton-Turbervill's greatest contribution to humanitarian reform was her championing of the girl slaves or *mui-tsai* of Hong Kong and Malaya. Sir John Simon[7] had reminded the House of Commons in 1931 that small girls, disguised under the name of 'adopted daughters', were sold into domestic servitude or prostitution and almost always cruelly treated thereafter, in several parts of the British Empire. Edith Picton-Turbervill was the only woman appointed to the three-person commission of investigation in 1936. ELEANOR RATHBONE had suggested that there should be two women as well as two men on the commission but the Colonial Secretary told the House: "'I think Miss Picton-Turbervill will be able to hold her own." (Laughter)[8] And hold her own she did. She wrote a Minority Report that disagreed with the two men who thought existing safeguards sufficed. Instead, she advocated the official notification and consequent protection of every girl living in a family not her own, and that became the basis of laws which led to the final abolition of the age-old *mui tsai* system. Her new Ordinance was popularly called 'the Children's Charter' in Malaya.

Edith Picton-Turbervill lost her seat at the parliamentary elections of 1931, having decided to stand by the Labour Party rather than follow her old friend Ramsay MacDonald in his formation of a 'National Government'. Thereafter she devoted herself to extra-Parliamentary lobbying for social reform via the Children's Minimum Committee and the National Council of Women. She was a lifelong 'woman-identified woman' whose path to humanitarianism was her chivalric instinct to protect and rescue the most vulnerable and friendless girls and women, whether in Britain or the Empire. At the age of 70, during the Second World War, she gave what the *Manchester Guardian* called 'a memorable radio talk' in the BBC series 'Calling the Home Front'.[9]

1. George Eliot, *Middlemarch*.
2. Edith Picton-Turbervill, *Life Is Good: An Autobiography* (London, Frederick Muller, 1939), p. 155.
3. 'Mental fight means thinking against the current, not with it': Virginia Woolf, 'Notes on peace in an air-raid' (1940) in *The Death of the Moth* (London, Hogarth Press, 1942), p. 155.
4. Picton-Turbervill, *op. cit.*, p. 131.
5. *Ibid.* See also Appendix I.
6. See Picton-Turbervill, *op. cit.*, ch. 7.
7. Sir John Simon was briefed by his wife KATHLEEN SIMON of the Anti-Slavery Society (see entry below); see also entry for CLARA HASLEWOOD.
8. *Manchester Guardian* (9.3.1936).
9. For further information on Edith Picton-Turbervill, see Olive Banks, *The Biographical Dictionary of British Feminists*, vol. 2 (New York, New York University Press, 1990); and obituaries in *The Times* (3.10.1960); *Daily Telegraph* (3.9.1960); *Guardian* (3.9.1960); and *The Catholic Citizen* (15.10.1960).

PLAYNE, CAROLINE E.
(2.5.1857–27.1.1948)

CULTURAL HISTORIAN; SOCIAL PSYCHOLOGIST

Father: George Frederick Playne, Fellow of the Geographical Society, Nailsworth, Gloucestershire
Mother: Margarrettia, née van den Bosch, Dutchwoman

Anglican

Caroline Playne was a lifelong internationalist whose tragic self-imposed task it was to document the hostile cultural nationalisms that had helped kindle the First World War. She could not prevent the horror she saw coming and then lived through; all she could do was analyse its causation in retrospect, anticipating the much later UNESCO declaration: 'Wars begin in the minds of men.'

Caroline Playne's commitment to international peace, like that of her friend Vernon Lee (VIOLET PAGET), her distant relative KATE COURTNEY and the Quaker SOPHIA STURGE, was, unusually among her contemporaries, already manifest before 1914. She was a founder member of the National Peace Council that was constituted as a permanent body in 1908 at the International Peace

Congress in London attended by Bertha von Suttner.[1] It was also in 1908 that she wrote and published a paper on 'The evolution of international peace'.[2] Shining through that pamphlet, based on the words of Kropotkin, L. T. Hobhouse, Grotius, Kant and Tolstoy, is her determination to counter the vulgar social Darwinism of her day that was translating the catchphrases 'the struggle for existence' and 'the survival of the fittest' into a 'mad competition between the principal *civilized* nations of the world in armies and navies'.[3] In place of that accelerating arms race she appealed to the characteristic social capacities of the human animal for mutual aid and co-operation, and to the evolution of an International Court at The Hague to regulate relations between nations on a basis of peace, equity and justice. She also looked to Britain to be the first to stop the arms race by unilateral disarmament.

It may be imagined, therefore, just how emotionally and morally devastating the outbreak of the First World War was for Caroline Playne. She immediately joined the Emergency Committee for the Relief of Distressed 'Enemy Aliens'; she joined the Union for the Democratic Control of Foreign Policy; she suppported the Women's International Congress at The Hague;[4] she worked for the Nailsworth Peace Association Society and the National Peace Council, which arranged a postal service for personal correspondence between the belligerent countries and traced missing persons; a fluent linguist, she translated and published articles from the *Berliner Tageblatt* responding to Quaker relief efforts for German civilian internees and prisoners of war; she collected suppressed pacifist pamphlets;[5] she gave a paper at the Conference on the Pacifist Philosophy of Life in London (July 1915);[6] she kept notes of the dismal pro-war propaganda in the daily press; and she also kept a private diary of the war years, chronicling her depression as she addressed vindictively patriotic women at a branch of the Women's Co-operative Guild, or attended a sad Christmas service with a whole congregation wearing mourning in 1916, or felt depressed and disgusted with herself that she could now see ambulances of the war-wounded or read of the latest battle losses as just 'part of the day's routine'.[7]

> The first time I chanced to read that a man, a family connection I had known from boyhood, had been killed, I screamed, I was upset all day, I could not contain myself as I thought of slaughtered youth and the slaughtering of young men [was] brought home to one. Now one's emotions are dried up. There is no more sorrow – or indignation, or shame – or pity. You begin to doubt the reality of existence . . . 28 Dec. 1917.[8]

After the war, and for the rest of her life, Caroline Playne dedicated herself to studying just how such a mad competition in mutual massacre could have come about. In other words, she deliberately lived in spirit in the cultural preconditions for man-made hell, hoping that her reminder of those culturally determining preconditions might effectively prevent Germans, French and British from being quite so vulnerable again to the mass media's hate propaganda. Her first study, *The Neuroses of the Nations* (1925), focused on the militarism, megalomania and self-glorification of the extremist pan-Germans from 1880 onwards (which, as she points out, were much criticized by rational Germans at the time); and on the militarism, megalomania and self-glorification of the 'pan-French' Action Française and other such groups in France. Her subsequent study, *The Pre-War Mind in Britain* (1928), focused on British jingoism and British imperialism that fused crass materialism and exaggerated sentimentalism. She showed how the French and German militarist polemicists were mirror images of each other, as were the historians Spencer Wilkinson, Professor of Military History in Oxford, and Heinrich von Treitschke, Professor of History in Berlin, while Cecil Chatterton was a mirror image of the hysterical pan-Germans. Caroline Playne's deepest loathing, however, was for the millionaires of the popular press who found that nothing sold as well as righteous hate.[9] Northcliffe and Harmsworth were her villains, guilty of deliberately infecting the British collective mind with an irrational conviction of mass danger (hence the drive for more and more Dreadnoughts) and an equally irrational sense of British total decency and German total beastliness. Particularly telling and ironic, therefore, was her demonstration in *The Neuroses of the Nations* of how the Germans had been convinced by the evidence of British atrocities towards civilians during the Boer War that the Germans alone still had a sense of decency and that the British were beasts. As for self-proclaimed democratic, civilized France, how could its alliance with the brutal Tsarist despotism of Russia look in German eyes like anything except a plot to encircle Germany on the Continent, while Britain made sure that its mastery of the seas would prevent German expansion abroad for ever? Caroline Playne did not deny the significance of materialist, economic motives or the concomitant political factors in international rivalry; what she highlighted was the accompanying, underlying role of nationalistic popular culture in so debasing, and indeed unhinging, the collective psyche that August 1914 was greeted with joy. 'Everywhere among the nations which we have been considering, it was applauding shouts which drowned sane considerations.'[10]

Her only obituarist remembered her in her seventies:

You would meet her shopping with her string bag, and she would tell you that she was leaving tomorrow for Prague . . . to attend a Peace Congress, . . . adding that she might be called upon to act as interpreter in French, German or Dutch . . . Then came the death of her sister to whom she was devoted, and the outbreak of Hitler's war; her indomitable spirit was broken.[11]

Given the still lethal potency of nationalism and religious communalism on every continent at the beginning of the twenty-first century, and the still uncontrolled arms race in weapons of mass extermination, it might be helpful to reprint Caroline Playne.[12]

1. Caroline Playne's last work was *Bertha von Suttner and the Struggle to Avert the World War* (London, George Allen and Unwin, 1936), a book she had been thinking of writing since 1910.
2. Paper read for the Anglo-Russian Literary Society, Imperial Institute, London (6.10.1908).
3. Caroline Playne, 'The evolution of international peace', p. 1.
4. See Introduction and Appendix I.
5. Now held in the Playne papers, Special Collections, University of London Library, Senate House, which include her diary and cuttings from the First World War.
6. 'Bergson and free will', now held in the C. E. Playne collection, Swarthmore College Peace Collection, Swarthmore, PA.
7. Manuscript journal, Playne papers, University of London Library.
8. *Ibid.*
9. Cf. Dubravka Ugrešić on the responsibility of the media for the recent ethnic wars in the Balkans in *The Culture of Lies* (London, Phoenix House, 1998), pp. 71–3: 'Is it possible for the media to provoke war? . . . Justifying themselves by . . . the national myths served up by the media, Serbian nationalists collectively supported the Serbian repression of the Albanians in Kosovo . . . And when the Croatian media also filled with tales of [atrocity] – the preparations were laid for war. [The] media have succeeded in legalizing lies.'

10. Caroline Playne, *The Neuroses of the Nations* (London, George Allen & Unwin, 1933), 'Summary', p. 463.
11. B. C. Boulter in *Hampstead and Highgate Express* (6.2.1948).
12. Caroline Playne's writings on peace and war, not already mentioned, include: *The Disarming of Hatred*, translation of article in *Berliner Tageblatt* (pamphlet; Friends' Peace Committee, 1915), held in Friends' House Library; *German Pacifism During the War* (London, National Peace Council, n.d. [1918/19]); *Society at War: 1914–1916* (London, George Allen and Unwin, 1931); *Britain Holds On: 1917, 1918* (London, George Allen and Unwin, 1933).

PYE, EDITH, SRN, SCM, CHEVALIER DE LA LÉGION D'HONNEUR

(20.10.1876–16.12.1965)

MIDWIFE; INTERNATIONAL CHILD RELIEF ORGANIZER

Father: William Arthur Pye, JP, wine merchant
Mother: Margaret, née Kidston, daughter of James Kidston, Writer to the Signet

Quaker by convincement

Edith Pye, aged about 60 (From War and Its Aftermath, *privately printed, n.d.)*

By 1907 Edith Pye was superintendent of all District Nurses in London. In 1908 she joined the Society of Friends, having been introduced to the Society by her lifelong friend and companion Dr HILDA CLARK. As early as 26 September 1914, she flew to Paris to check with the French authorities whether Friends' War Victims' Relief could aid the civilians now trapped behind the French lines in the area of the Battle of the Marne. All French doctors had been called up for the army and refugees were fleeing Rheims and the surrounding countryside; there was desperate need for an emergency maternity hospital. Edith Pye assembled her team, including Hilda Clark, and in December 1914 arrived at Châlons-sur-Marne, fifteen kilometres away from the trenches, to set up her hospital in an abandoned epileptics' wing of a grim old people's institution without running hot water or electricity. 'We fell upon it with scrubbing brushes and disinfectants.'[1]

Almost a thousand babies later, after having survived shelling, Zeppelin attacks, the failure of fuel supplies in the coldest winter on record, food and milk shortages, the day and night rescuing of patients from Rheims under heavy fire, bombing, and enforced evacuation into underground champagne cellars in July 1918, Edith Pye re-emerged. She had lost only two mothers, one of whom had arrived 'chez les anglaises' too late to save and the other who had had chronic and then acute heart disease. She was made a Chevalier de la Légion d'Honneur.

From March 1921 until October 1922 Edith Pye, with her 'drive, energy, genius for detailed organisation and experience in infant welfare',[2] was assisting Hilda

Clark's immense, and successful, project to save the starving children of Vienna. In May 1923 she was sent by the Quakers to report on conditions in the Ruhr, then occupied by the French army. Although deeply sympathetic to France as well as fluent in French, she could only recoil at France's oppression of 'a disarmed and absolutely helpless people'[3] that she knew could only produce inevitable future enmity. '[Nothing] she saw in France [in the First World War] came near the sadness, misery and wretched condition of things she saw in the Ruhr . . . There was a complete absence of civil justice, which had driven despair into the hearts of the people.'[4]

In May 1928 Edith Pye was sent by the Women's International League for Peace and Freedom on a mission of friendship to Indo-China, China and Japan. She reported back on the women's movement there and on child labour, concubinage and girl slavery, as well as on the recent advances in women's education and status in China. In 1929 she became President of the British Midwives Institute, later called the Royal College of Midwives, a post she occupied for twenty years. During her period of office, and with her strong encouragement, the chloroform capsule was developed that first enabled midwives to administer effective pain relief to women in childbirth in their own homes.[5]

With the triumph of fascism in the 1930s Edith Pye had to campaign again. In 1934 she helped to found the Friends' German Emergency Committee to succour Jewish and other German refugees from Hitler. During the Spanish Civil War she instigated in Geneva the international commission for the assistance of child refugees in and from Spain, which fed 40,000 children in 1938. From January 1939 until June 1940 she was working on the French–Spanish border to aid the tens, if not hundreds, of thousands of desperate fleeing Spanish Republicans:

> a tragedy so immense that one hardly sees how to tackle it. I understand they spent the nights standing, as one stands in the Tube in rush-hours . . . Shall not be here long . . . am telegraphing Pollock [of the Foreign Office] that we must have more money for France . . . Children unable to cross frontier where they are without shelter, because of lack of accommodation.
>
> Can't possibly come away because it needs someone to deal with over-worked officials in their own tongue, . . . I seem to have slipped back to 1914–15–16.[6]

Having sailed on the last British boat to leave Bordeaux, Edith Pye worked for the rest of the war as Honorary Secretary to the Famine Relief committee, chaired by Bishop Bell of Chichester, which tried, in vain, to persuade the British Ministry of Economic Warfare to allow the Red Cross to send food, vitamins and medical aid to children, and pregnant and nursing mothers in German-occupied Europe.[7] 'She is always hurrying. She hurried out of France a few hours before Hitler's tanks reached the Channel in 1940; hurried back again just behind British tanks in 1944.'[8] She toured liberated France immediately after the Normandy landings of 1944 to arrange bulk food supplies for the children she found suffering from malnutrition, and then went on to help freezing, hungry but liberated Paris. A little later she organized relief operations in Greece. She was nearly 70. '[Her] activities for refugees and humanitarian causes have in their own way been as assiduous as those of the late ELEANOR RATHBONE.'[9] She herself said she belonged to the secular arm of the Society of Friends. She is buried under the same headstone as Hilda Clark in Street, Somerset.[10]

1. Edith Pye (ed.), *War and Its Aftermath: Dr. Hilda Clark's [annotated] Letters from France, Austria and the Near East, 1914–1924* (privately printed, n.d., *c.* 1956), letter (December 1914). See also Edith Pye, 'For the babies of the Marne', *Maternity and Child Welfare* (March 1919), reprinted Friends' War Victims' Relief Committee, held in Friends' House Library, London.
2. Francesca Wilson, *In the Margins of Chaos* (London, John Murray, 1944), p. 138.
3. Edith Pye, letters and report (1923), in Friends' House Library, London.
4. Society of Friends Council for International Service report; and Women's International League meeting report (November 1923), in Friends' House Library.
5. See Edith Pye, 'Anaesthetics in labour from the midwife's point of view', *Newsletter of the Medical Women's Federation* (July 1932). See also entry for JULIET RHYS WILLIAMS below.
6. Pye, *War and Its Aftermath*, letters (late January and 2.2.1939).
7. See entry for VERA BRITTAIN.
8. *Daily Herald* (18.10.1946).
9. *Manchester Guardian* (10.10.1946).
10. See also obituaries in *The Friend* (31.12.1965); *The Times* (21.12.1965); *Guardian* (20.12.1965).

PYM, DIANA

(18.10.1908–9.9.1993)

CAMPAIGNER FOR GREEK POLITICAL PRISONERS

Father: Brigadier-General K. Gough, VC, KCB, killed 1915
Mother: Dorothea Agnes, née Keyes, secretary to Vicereine of Ireland

Atheist

Diana Pym came on both sides from high-ranking army families. After reading history at Newnham College, Cambridge, she married an architect in 1930, had three children and became a Labour Party borough councillor for St Pancras, London, where she worked for improvements in housing and social welfare (1936–46). She was also a member of Shoreditch Public Assistance Committee. In 1940 she went still further against her background by joining the Communist Party. From 1941 to 1946 she was Secretary of the St Pancras Anglo-Soviet Committee.

In 1945 Diana Pym became secretary of the Greek Maritime Unions through her contacts with the Greek Cypriot community in north London. On learning of the conditions in the prison camps in Eritrea and the Sudan where members of the Greek National Liberation Army (ELAS) were held by the British, she helped form the League for Democracy in Greece pressure group, of which she became the Honorary Secretary and driving force. The League's aims included the provision of relief to those Greeks and their families who were suffering hardship on political grounds and for a general amnesty for all Greek political prisoners. 'One early success was an emergency campaign in 1948 which roused the British and American governments to intervene to prevent the mass executions of nearly three thousand members of the resistance jailed *before* the outbreak of the civil war' (my emphasis).[1] She continued to campaign, successfully, for the release of all Greek political prisoners and then, after the Greek Colonels' coup in 1967, for the restoration of democratic government in Greece. Her fluency in both written and spoken demotic Greek was essential to her life-work.

It may be asked whether Diana Pym's humane commitment was exercised only on behalf of Communists whose political ideology she approved and who, she claimed, were 'democrats'. Atrocities perpetrated by Greek Communists during the

Diana Pym during a peace march in Greece in 1966 (From The Times, *15.9.1993)*

civil war in Greece (1946–49) have been much publicized and documented in the West. However, it is also incontrovertible that Churchill and the British Foreign Office had great responsibility in 1944/45 for the original descent of Greece into civil war through their insistence on the restoration of the Greek monarchy despite its collusion with the Metaxas dictatorship.[2] Diana Pym felt morally impelled to try to right the wrongs she saw inflicted by the British government on the Greek partisans, many of them tortured before being sentenced to death. Though she was obviously a partisan herself in her own way, her intervention via tireless political lobbying was not that of a soldier or guerrilla fighter but rather that of a non-violent life-saver.[3]

1. Obituary for Diana Pym, *The Times* (15.9.1993).
2. See Diana Pym and Marion Sarafis, 'The League for Democracy in Greece and its archives', *Journal of the Hellenic Diaspora* (Summer 1984), pp. 73–5.
3. *Ibid.*, pp. 73–83.

R

RACKSTRAW, MARJORIE
(24.6.1888–28.4.1981)

REFUGEE AND FAMINE RELIEF WORKER

Father: Matthew Rackstraw, wealthy owner of London department store
Mother: Fanny, née Blofeld

Anglican

It was her encounter with MARGERY FRY at Birmingham University, where she studied history *c.* 1910, that led Marjorie Rackstraw to tackle refugee relief work during and after war throughout much of the first half of the twentieth century. In the First World War she joined Margery Fry on the Marne front, where she carried out Quaker relief work for the Emergency and War Victims' Relief Committee, first at Sermaize-les-Bains and then at the Châlons-sur-Marne maternity hospital under EDITH PYE.

In 1920 Marjorie Rackstraw volunteered for the truly grim post of district organizer for Quaker famine relief in Russia at Alexievky. Before 'Nansen' food relief[1] began to arrive from Odessa, it had been possible to feed only a certain percentage of the starving:

> The mothers went down on their knees begging us to allow their children to take it in turns to have the meal provided, but we knew that the ration was so small that the children could not live on less, and to divide it would mean that all would die. To refuse was heart-breaking but there was no alternative.[2]

The time of the thaw ending each winter was paradoxically a particularly frightening time, since the grain trains might be cut off by flooding rivers.

> March 10, 1922 . . . It is just possible we might be able to do something with rafts . . . March 22nd. Well, the miracle has happened. Winter has returned with great fierceness. At any other time we should be groaning, but now everybody is rejoicing: the trains are in, and all the sleighs hurrying to Buzuluk and Pavolovka! . . . our feeding came just in time; a fortnight later and all the people would have been dead. Now, . . . they are beginning to look like human beings once more.[3]

There were at one time 900 feeding points in 280 villages in the English relief area. Marjorie Rackstraw served two years in Russia.

On her return to Britain she worked at Edinburgh University as Warden of a women's hostel and general adviser to women students. She moved to London in 1937 and worked for refugees from Nazism, to some of whom she opened her own home. Again she worked for the Quakers on the Continent, helping to get Jewish and Basque refugees out from France immediately before Hitler invaded. In 1944

A group in one of the children's homes, Buzuluk area, 1921 (Friends' War Victims' Relief Committee, Russia Album, *no. 28)*

she joined UNRRA and was in one of the first teams to enter defeated Germany, where she became Chief Welfare Officer for Displaced Persons for No. 1 Corps area of the British Zone; she was by then in her late fifties.

Already in 1940 Marjorie Rackstraw had been a founder member of the National Old People's Welfare Council in Britain, and on her return from Germany early in 1946 she devoted herself to public work for the elderly. As well as being a Labour member of Hampstead Borough Council and its representative on the Local Fuel Advisory Committee in the freezing post-war winters, she was also the moving spirit in developing the all-party Hampstead Old People's Housing Trust, founded in 1947. The Trust eventually housed over 200 people.

When Marjorie Rackstraw died at the age of 92 it was revealed that she was, in fact, a very rich woman; she had never let that prevent her from living a whole 'lifetime of unbounded compassion and service'.[4]

1. Fridtjof Nansen (1861–1930), the Norwegian Arctic explorer, was awarded the Nobel Peace Prize in 1922 for his organization of relief work in the Russian famine.
2. Francesca Wilson, *In the Margins of Chaos: Recollections of Relief Work in and between Three Wars* (London, John Murray, 1944), p. 141.
3. Ruth Fry, *A Quaker Adventure: The Story of Nine Years' Relief and Reconstruction in Europe* (Friends' Service Council, abridged edition, 1943), pp. 52–3. Evelyn Sharp testified to Marjorie Rackstraw's work in Russia: 'she spoke Russian fluently and her efficiency was . . . great . . . She had, too, the sympathetic temperament of a leader, and was very popular with the members of the village Soviet': *Unfinished Adventure* (London, John Lane, 1933), p. 260.
4. Anthony Greenwood, obituary, *The Times* (11.5.1981), quoted in entry by Joyce Bellamy and Marjorie Bucke in J. M. Bellamy and J. Saville (eds), *Dictionary of Labour Biography*, vol. 8, p. 210.

Marjorie Rackstraw's papers and glass slides from the Russian famine relief operation are held in the Special Collections of Edinburgh University Library. Friends' House Library holds articles by her published in *The Friend* and *International Service* (1921–22), as well as Friends' Emergency and War Victims' Relief Committee Reports for 1915–18 and 1921–23.

RAPHAEL, SISTER DOROTHY, CSMV

(1893–14.2.1977)

ANTI-RACIST MISSIONARY SOCIAL
WORKER IN SOUTH AFRICA

Father: Bishop John Primatt Maud
Mother: —, née Furse, sister of Bishop of Pretoria

Anglican

Sister Dorothy Raphael, c. 1957, as assistant to the Mother Superior at Irene, South Africa (From Audrey Ashley, Peace-Making in South Africa: The Life and Work of Dorothy Maud, *New Horizon, 1980)*

After leaving her undemanding girls' secondary school in 1911, Dorothy Maud spent most of the next decade working at home as secretary to her father, the suffragan Bishop of Kensington, and participating in such bodies as the Girls' Diocesan Association and the Society for the Propagation of the Gospel (SPG). Nothing could have been less like life in the native shanty township or 'location' of Sophiatown, without roads, drainage, lighting or even adequate water, where Dorothy Maud went in 1927 as a 34-year-old missionary worker at St Cyprian's Church, Johannesburg. (She had been trained 1924–25 at the SPG Missionary College of the Ascension, Selly Oak, Birmingham, and spent 1926 becoming acclimatized to South Africa at a mission in Zululand.) It was on her arrival in Johannesburg that she made her radical, pioneering decision that the only way for any white Christian to have the slightest chance of helping the Africans, who were so callously forced to live in brutalizing conditions, was to go and join them. She therefore started a settlement in the centre of the 'location', to offer social and spiritual service to the people of Sophiatown and Orlando, where she had to struggle to overcome not just the obstructiveness of the white municipal authorities but also the all too understandable suspicion, indifference and active resentment of whites among the Africans themselves.

Starting single-handed, Dorothy Maud insisted on educating the white Christians in Johannesburg about the dehumanizing living conditions in the squalid township and trying to raise money for her settlement. By 1930 there was a tiny corrugated iron church, always overcrowded; a clinic/dispensary run by Dr Mary Tugman; two classroom blocks for 1,200 schoolchildren to pack into; a club hall for women's meetings, a baby clinic, cookery, First Aid and dressmaking classes, meetings of Guides and Brownies (called Wayfarers and Sunbeams) and games; finally there was the European women's living quarters and social work centre called Ekuteleni, 'House of peace-making'. More than half a century before Archbishop Tutu preached interracial reconciliation in South Africa, Dorothy Maud saw the necessity for whites first to acknowledge and then to begin to end the intolerable oppression of which they were guilty, if blacks were ever to forgive them and renounce their otherwise inevitable enmity. The foundation stone for Ekuteleni had been laid on

9 September 1928 by three little girls, one African, one Coloured and one white – something the Africans never forgot.

Having gradually won the confidence of local people, who called her 'Seester', Dorothy Maud initiated a Woman's Council of Sophiatown to meet every month to discuss the need for such basic amenities as water, roads and light. Then the battle with Johannesburg Council would begin. After intense periods of prayer, Dorothy Maud would write hundreds of letters and personally interview every possible influential individual or group concerned until the appropriate committee finally voted the necessary money for half a dozen standpipes or electric light in nearly every narrow street. 'I *hate* being an importunate spinster',[1] but there was no alternative to her importunacy and, finally, no resisting it. Dorothy Maud wrung out of the white authorities the salaries for a dozen teachers for the 1,200 black schoolchildren and a safe playground on waste land. From benefactors in Britain and South Africa she got money for a soup kitchen for the hungry pupils, and for a much-needed day nursery school in Orlando for the infants of mothers out at work: Thabong, 'Place of joy' in Sesuto, was the first African nursery school ever built.

But it was not to be a simple heartwarming story of progress in achieving minimal social provision. The counter-pressures of the whites' superiority complex and their material exploitation of the black majority also grew in strength in South Africa year by year. In the mid-1930s, for example, Dorothy Maud and her co-workers actually had to resign in protest when their African girl Wayfarers, the veterans of many a Guide camp with Dorothy, were not allowed to be an integral part of the Girl Guide Movement, but this particular wrong was put right by May 1937. Then during the huge expansion of the native township of Orlando in 1937, the municipality suggested that the European women would now want to 'clear out of this place as it would be surrounded by native houses. I asked if they thought we were here for a rest cure and told them nothing short of an Act of Parliament would get us out.'[2] The years 1942–43 were particularly energetic as Dorothy Maud continued to struggle against what she called the barbarous injustice that could only produce barren bitterness in its turn. She fought for reduced rents in the townships, for the provision of spectacles for children with visual impairment, for municipal schooling for the children wandering the streets, for education and workshops for the disabled, and finally for the promised free meals for undernourished black children. She lobbied and lobbied until at last 'the money [materialized] into soup'.[3]

By 1944 when Dorothy Maud retired from Sophiatown and Orlando in order to test her religious vocation as a Benedictine in Britain, there were two large churches, four nursery schools and a nursery training college, seven primary schools with 4,800 boys and girls, and a hospital, as well as all the social and sports groups she had encouraged. But when she returned to Sophiatown in 1957, as Sister Dorothy Raphael of the active Wantage Community,[4] she had to witness just what the 'forcible removal' policy of apartheid had succeeded in destroying.

> Here and there along every street are piles of rubble or gaping walls where the people have been turned out of their homes and carted off . . . It is so heart-rending and so blind and disastrous for the future, but we must just pray with tremendous faith. It is so glorious to go into the Church of Christ the King in Sophiatown . . . The Sunday I was there a terrific thunderstorm broke . . . but

though floods of rain came, over two hundred people were there, and there is nothing like the joy of being with them . . .[5]

But by 1961 Thabong nursery school had had to close and Ekuteleni too was empty, the area around it declared 'white'. Not surprisingly, the destruction of her life-work had its effect on her health; nevertheless Sister Raphael continued to work in South Africa until she was 71, serving the needs of unmarried teenage mothers and their babies, of mentally handicapped girls and of destitute old women in a traumatized black area. After her death in England in 1977, a memorial service was held for her in Johannesburg, ending with every race there joining in to sing the ANC anthem 'Nkosi Sikheleli Afrika'.

Father Trevor Huddleston, who had worked with Dorothy Raphael in Sophiatown and then succeeded her there, writing *Naught for Your Comfort* about apartheid in action, later testified that the uniqueness of her mission settlement, which had rejected bogus 'parallel, separate development' and insisted instead on being one interracial Christian body, had owed its existence to the uniqueness of Dorothy Raphael herself.[6]

1. Letter from Dorothy Maud, quoted in Audrey Ashley, *Peace-Making in South Africa: The Life and Work of Dorothy Maud* (Bognor Regis, Sussex, New Horizon, 1980), p. 35.
2. Dorothy Maud's co-worker Margaret Leeke, later Sister Margaret Johanna, CSMV (Community of St Mary the Virgin) of Wantage, quoted in Ashley, *op. cit.*, p. 57.
3. Ashley, *op. cit.*, p. 69.
4. Dorothy Maud had been rejected as unsuitable for the contemplative life in July 1947.
5. Ashley, *op. cit.*, p. 99.
6. See obituary for Sister Dorothy Raphael, *The Times* (28.1.1977); and H. P. Thompson, *Into All Lands: The History of the Society for the Propagation of the Gospel in Foreign Parts 1701–1950* (London, SPCK, 1951), pp. 539–41 and 563.

RATHBONE, ELEANOR, MP

(12.5.1872–2.1.1946)

CHAMPION OF THE WORLDWIDE EMANCIPATION OF WOMEN AND GIRLS; RESCUER OF REFUGEES

Father: William Rathbone, Liberal MP for Liverpool
Mother: Evelyn, née Lyle, nursing reformer

Christian humanist – 'I do not think I am un-Christian' (Eleanor Rathbone's notes for her funeral)

'Benign and yet menacing, she would stalk through the [Parliamentary] lobby, one arm weighed with the heavy satchel which contained the papers on family allowances, another arm dragging an even heavier satchel in which were stored the more recent papers about refugees . . . ; recalcitrant Ministers would quail before the fire of her magnificent eyes.'[1] No eyewitness has evoked Eleanor Rathbone better than did her fellow MP Harold Nicolson.

Five generations of Rathbones had been social reformers in Liverpool and later in Britain, their motto being 'Whatever ought to be done can be done'.[2] Eleanor Rathbone was to take on the world. She was born into a wealthy family, but her education was unsystematic until she was privately tutored by Lucy Silcox,

Headmistress of Liverpool High School for Girls, in preparation for reading philosophy at Somerville College, Oxford (1892–96). There she gained a reputation as a brilliant philosophical thinker, and made friends with MARGERY FRY and Barbara Hammond, the future Labour historian. She met her lifelong companion, the social work practitioner and theorist Elizabeth Macadam, in 1902 when the latter was Warden of the Liverpool Victoria Women's [University] Settlement on Merseyside.

So extensive and so various were Eleanor Rathbone's efforts to make the world a more humane place that the clearest account of her life-work is simply an annotated, chronological listing of her socio-political activism, including not only her committee work, her writings, and her record as an Independent MP, but also her many extra-parliamentary campaigns after she came down from Oxford:

Eleanor Rathbone, c. 1945 (From Mary Stocks, Eleanor Rathbone, *Victor Gollancz, 1949)*

1897 Visitor for Liverpool Central Relief Society and Hon. Secretary of Liverpool Women's Industrial Council.

1898 Parliamentary Secretary to Liverpool Women's Suffrage Society.

1902 *The Problem of Women's Wages.*[3]

1903 *Report on the Results of a Special Inquiry into the Conditions of Labour at the Liverpool Docks.*[4]

1909 *How the Casual Labourer Lives* (Liverpool, Liverpool Women's Industrial Council).[5]

1909 Elected first woman member of Liverpool City Council as an Independent. She consistently championed every 'woman's issue' in the city.

1913 *Report on the Liverpool Women's Industrial Council Survey of Widows Under the Poor Law.*[6]

1913 Elected to the National Executive of the National Union of Women's Suffrage Societies.

1914–18 Noted the beneficial impact on the standard of living and general health of working-class families when administering the Separation Allowances paid directly to the wives of men in the armed forces. Ironically, the absence of the 'breadwinner' actually meant more bread. This revelation led to her subsequent 30-year campaign for a weekly 'family allowance' to be paid directly to the mother.[7]

1915 Not one of the British women anti-militarists who broke with

Mrs Fawcett over whether or not British women suffragists should support and attend the Women's International Congress at The Hague.[8] At that time she gave what she saw as the interests of the British women's movement priority over a negotiated cessation of the First World War and the prevention of a probable second world war. (Her staunch internationalist anti-militarism developed after 1919.)

1917 'The remuneration of women's services' in Victor Gollancz (ed.), *The Making of Women: Oxford Essays in Feminism* (London, Allen and Unwin).[9]

1917–45 Set up and chaired the Family Endowment Committee, claiming that British mothers did not merely need a wage, they earned it.

1918 *Equal Pay and the Family* (London, Headley Bros), written together with KATHLEEN COURTNEY, MAUDE ROYDEN, Mary Stocks, H. N. Brailsford and Emile and Elinor Burns.[10]

1919 Elected President of the National Union of Women's Suffrage Societies (later National Union of Societies for Equal Citizenship).

1920–28 Campaigned and lobbied outside Parliament for the Guardianship of Infants Act, giving women equal rights to their children, for the Summary Jurisdiction Act (regarding Maintenance Orders), the Matrimonial Causes Divorce Reform Act, and the Contributory Pensions Act (for Widows and Orphans). Throughout this decade she articulated her belief in a new 'social feminism', grounded in equality not defined as identity with men but based on women's experience and needs and expressed in women-respecting legislation and in the economic independence of every woman, whether single or married. Family allowances paid to the mother, birth control, better housing and international peace: these, she declared, were the priorities for most women.[11]

1924 *The Disinherited Family: A Plea for the [State] Endowment of the Family* (London, Edward Arnold). Eleanor Rathbone's case was rooted in her sense of the human right of women and children not to be powerless 'dependants', all too often overworked and ill. Even a 'good husband' is no solution to the vulnerability of the powerless. 'A man has no right to want to keep half the world in purgatory, because he enjoys playing redeemer to his own wife and children.'[12] Her book had enormous influence on the thinking of Beveridge.

1929 Called for free milk and free school meals for the children of the unemployed in conjunction with the Children's Minimum Council. Throughout the Depression she also spoke against any cut in unemployment benefit.

1929 Elected MP as an Independent to represent the Combined English Northern Universities. Her uppermost motive in seeking election was her hope of being able to do something effective for the health, education and status of the girls and women of India, still under British imperial rule. Ever since she had read Katherine Mayo's *Mother India* (1924), Eleanor Rathbone had been unable to forget the plight of India's girl children, liable to suffer premature, arranged marriage, premature child-bearing and/or premature, lifelong, childless widowhood. At first she alienated some educated Indian women nationalists who were offended by any criticism of Indian society emanating from a British oppressor; however, on learning of Indian women's own efforts to abolish child marriage, she succeeded in making common cause with them, and with the Indian men working for the social and political emancipation of Indian women.[13]

From 1930 on   Eleanor Rathbone challenged the Under-Secretary for the Colonies with many questions on behalf of women of colour under British rule, concerning, among other topics, 'the training of [African] women medical officers in Tanganyika, educational and medical services in Kenya, education of native girls in Nigeria, the education of Moslems in Northern Nigeria, and marriage rites of native women [including clitoridectomy of girls]'.[14]

1931   Deplored the failure of the League of Nations to apply sanctions when Japan invaded Manchuria.

1932   *On Slavery within the Family: Memorandum to the [Parliamentary] Committee for the Protection of Coloured Women* (with the Duchess of Atholl [KATHERINE STEWART-MURRAY] and Josiah Wedgwood). Here she suggested, with regard to the status of African women throughout British Africa, the legal limitation of 'bride price', a minimum age for marriage, the spread of education for girls, and the establishment of the legal right to divorce a cruel husband.

1932   Fact-finding visit to India.

1933   Responded to Hitler's rise to power as an evil boding 'very ill for the peace and freedom of the world', a comment that might seem banal but was far from generally shared in Britain at that time.[15]

1933   Asked her first Parliamentary question on the subject of Palestine, then under the British Mandate, concerned about both the voting rights of Jewish women and the practice of child marriage among the Arabs.

1934   *Child Marriage: The Indian Minotaur* (London, George Allen and Unwin), dedicated 'To all Indian women who have suffered from or are struggling to remedy the evils described in this book'. Eleanor Rathbone did not single out child marriage as the sole evil suffered by Indian girls; she also spelt out in her Preface the 'utter insufficiency of medical, nursing and midwifery services; illiteracy and a preposterously small share of educational opportunities; unfair marriage laws; . . . the Hindu widow's lot and purdah'. She accused herself as well as her fellow British of having struggled too weakly to right these wrongs. Above all, she indicted the male institution of the British Raj for having 'kept off' the woman question out of fear of alienating Indian men. Her evidence for the cost in ill health and mortality to Indian girls of premature marriage was taken from exclusively Indian sources. A supporter of Indian independence, she insisted that any really worthwhile freedom movement must have the welfare of girls and women high on its agenda.

1935–45   Eleanor Rathbone 'had long been busy with the victims of German political and racial persecution'.[16]

1937   Became an active member of the National Joint Committee for Spanish Relief and for the Basque Children's Committee which she co-founded with the Duchess of Atholl during the Spanish Civil War. (She had visited Spanish Republican-held Spain on a fact-finding tour in 1937, and she had tried in vain to persuade the British government to intervene against the Franco forces.)

1938   *War Can Be Averted: The Achievability of Collective Security* (London, Victor Gollancz). In a passionately committed argument for preventing German, Italian and Japanese fascism from overrunning the world, Eleanor Rathbone here made a last, humane plea for Britain to honour its League of Nations Covenant obligations and join in collective resistance to Hitler's aggression. Like Lady VIOLET BONHAM CARTER, she was absolutely opposed to defeatism and the appeasement of fascism.

1938   Joined in the unsuccessful attempt to intercede with Hitler for clemency for Liselotte Herrmann, sentenced to death for sending evidence abroad of German rearmament for war.[17]

1938   After *Kristallnacht* (9 November), backed the German-Jewish Aid Fund.

1938–39   Pressed the government time and again to assist the evacuation of political refugees from Spain, Austria, the Sudetenland and Czechoslovakia: 'More and more . . . of her insistent Parliamentary questions concerned their finances, their passports, their immigration conditions, their visas.'[18]

1939   Made a lightning visit to Prague to investigate the situation of those desperate to get out just before Hitler invaded: 'never have I dwelt in such a Heartbreak House as the refugee problem.'[19] All the time, the stream of refugees into Britain 'was a trickle where in Eleanor's view it should and could have been a spate'.[20] Then, and again in 1943, she felt deeply ashamed of Britain, and of her own failure to effect an adequate government change of heart and wring enough immigration visas for Jews out of the Home Secretary.

1940   Visited the British internment camp at Huyton for 'enemy aliens', i.e., German Jewish refugees now rounded up as Germans, promising them 'You have not been forgotten', and secured their release along with hundreds of other political and Jewish internees on the Isle of Man, for many of whom she had intervened individually.

1941–45   The Holocaust. Eleanor Rathbone knew of the horror but was literally forbidden to broadcast it. She 'thought of this terrible question day and night. It is on our consciences all the time . . . [But] if we say publicly all we know . . . we are told that we are informing the enemy and hampering efforts that might otherwise be planned. So we have kept silent for months . . . Then nothing happens.'[21] She asked to speak on the BBC in

December 1943, but the Director General said 'she must be refused'.[22]

1944   *Falsehoods and Facts about the Jews* (London, Victor Gollancz): 'in these days, everything which expresses or encourages Anti-Semitism may do incalculable harm.'

1945   The end of the war. Worked on behalf of the Poles against Stalin, and for the Greek Communists against the monarchists. She saw the Family Endowment Bill passed that, after her 30-year campaign, at last gave mothers of infants and schoolchildren a weekly payment from the state, however inadequate.

Joined Victor Gollancz in founding the Save Europe Now Movement that worked to increase food allocation to starving Germany, if necessary by cutting rations in Britain: 'We are not a nation of grown-up greedy babies.' She was so moved by the revelation of a martyred German Resistance, especially by the young brother and sister Scholl of the Munich White Rose Group, that she challenged the British public: 'Ask yourself what you would have done, were you a German.'[23]

2 January 1946   Having worked day and night to 'Save Europe now', Eleanor Rathbone, aged 73, collapsed and died from exhaustion. It was world news.

Eleanor Rathbone was, unquestionably, the most tireless and wide-ranging of all the British women humanitarians of the twentieth century. She was the outstanding example of someone whose exceptionally sensitive conscience compelled her to intervene almost with her every waking breath, for those who were in remediable pain and who had no other advocate. She herself was never at any risk of suffering what these strangers were enduring: she would never be an unemployed Liverpool docker, or an Indian 11-year-old dying in the struggle to give birth, or a working-class mother in Tyneside worn out before she was 40, or a defeated Spanish Republican or a persecuted Jew or a starving German. But she was not interested in herself, she merely spent herself, knowing that she roused much hostility and even mockery by her hammering at men in power both in Parliament and outside. Many a time she would rise to speak in the House, only to have the Speaker deliberately not notice her; when she *was* called to speak, she spoke at hundreds of words a minute in her anxiety to get the essential facts of the current injustice or abomination across, and despite constant interruptions and heckling from the hostile Conservative majority.

What lay behind Eleanor Rathbone's continual need to intervene? Not only did she have an exceptionally acute imaginative sense of others' pain – 'suffering and injustice anywhere roused in her a depth of emotion which very few feel except for those whom they know personally'[24] – but she also had a convinced intellectual/philosophical conception of our collective personal responsibility towards all our fellow humans, especially those who are powerless and inarticulate. '[Everyone] in the world is responsible for every calamity that happens in the world if he or she has left undone anything he could have done without neglecting greater responsibilities, to prevent or mitigate the calamity even one iota.'[25] Thus she was a self-imposed Atlas with the whole world on her shoulders: 'Die ganze Welt der Schmerzen, muss ich tragen' (Heine: 'the whole world of suffering must I bear'). And she challenges the rest of us to help carry the load.

Among the countless tributes and expressions of grief at her loss was that in the *Daily Herald* (4.1.1946), 'Our Garibaldi':

A list of all the causes she championed with . . . lion-hearted courage would run to several pages.

However . . . the people whose plight moved her most passionately were the refugees. The last battle in her life was for them. She believed that perhaps the proudest of all the treasures of this country was the principle of the right of asylum traditionally granted to the hunted of every race.

A monument to Eleanor Rathbone should be set up in the Home Office. Every politician in future who holds that place would work with her watching eye upon him.[26]

1. Obituary for Eleanor Rathbone, *The Spectator* (11.1.1946), quoted in Mary Stocks, *Eleanor Rathbone: A Biography* (London, Victor Gollancz, 1949), pp. 142–3. Mary Stocks' biography, written from close personal knowledge, is still the most vivid.
2. Eleanor Rathbone, *William Rathbone: A Memoir* (London, Macmillan, 1905), p. 452.
3. Johanna Alberti, *Eleanor Rathbone* (London, Sage, 'Women of Ideas' series, 1996), p. 158. Johanna Alberti's annotated bibliography of Eleanor Rathbone's speeches and writings is the most complete and helpful to date.
4. *Ibid.*, p. 155.
5. *Ibid.*, p. 156.
6. *Ibid.*, p. 159.
7. See Suzie Fleming, Introductory Essay to Eleanor Rathbone, *The Disinherited Family* (reprinted Bristol, Falling Wall Press, 1986).
8. See Anne Wiltsher, *Most Dangerous Women: Feminist Peace Campaigners of the Great War* (London, Pandora, 1985), ch. 4.
9. Alberti, *op. cit.*, p. 161.
10. *Ibid.*
11. See Eleanor Rathbone, *Milestones: Presidential Addresses* (Liverpool, National Union of Societies for Equal Citizenship, 1928), *passim*; and Stocks, op. cit., ch. 9: 'The new feminism'.
12. Eleanor Rathbone, *The Disinherited Family* (London, Edward Arnold, 1924), p. 273. See also Stocks, *op. cit.*, ch. 8: 'The campaign for Family Allowances'; Fleming, *op. cit.*; and Alberti, *op. cit.*, pp. 163–7.
13. See Stocks, *op. cit.*, pp. 124–6 and ch. 11: 'Voyage to India'; Alberti, *op. cit.*, pp. 171–2. In Sybil Oldfield, 'Eleanor Rathbone and India; cultural imperialist or friend to women?', *Asian Journal of Women's Studies*, **3**(3) (1997), pp. 157–68, I argue that Eleanor Rathbone anticipated by 60 years the current United Nations view expressed by UNICEF and UNIFEM that there is a category of 'gender-crime' to include bride-burning, dowry-related crime and domestic battering, etc., as constituting fundamental human rights abuses.
14. Pamela Brookes, *Women at Westminster: An Account of Women in the British Parliament 1918–1966* (London, Peter Davies, 1967), p. 88.
15. *Ibid.*, p. 106.
16. Stocks, *op. cit.*, p. 244.
17. See entries for SYBIL THORNDIKE and LADY VIOLET BONHAM CARTER. See also S. Oldfield, 'German women in the resistance to Hitler' in S. Reynolds (ed.), *Women, State and Revolution* (Oxford, Basil Blackwell, 1986), pp. 90–1.
18. Stocks, *op. cit.*, p. 257 and the whole of ch. 15: 'Munich and after'.
19. E. F. Rathbone, 'A personal view of the refugee problem', *New Statesman and Nation* (15.4.1939), quoted in Stocks, *op. cit.*, p. 258.
20. Stocks, *op. cit.*, p. 263; see also pp. 300–1.
21. E. Rathbone, speech in the House of Commons (14.12.1943), quoted in Alberti, *op. cit.*, p. 176.
22. See Stephen Ward, 'Why the BBC ignored the Holocaust', *Independent on Sunday* (23.8.1993).
23. See W. Bayles (ed.), *Seven Were Hanged* (London, Gollancz, 1945).
24. Arthur Salter, letter to *The Times* (4.1.1946).
25. Eleanor Rathbone, speech in the House of Commons (26.10.1945), one of her last speeches, quoted in Alberti, *op. cit.*, p. 153.
26. The Women's Library, London, holds a very large, if not comprehensive, collection of obituaries on Eleanor Rathbone. For a more recent tribute see Frank Field, MP, 'Portrait of a great MP', *Financial Times* (21.9.1996).

REEKIE, STELLA JANE
(29.7.1922–28.9.1982)

RED CROSS NURSE IN POST-WAR GERMANY, 1945–49

Father: Arthur Reekie
Mother: Jane

Presbyterian

Stella Reekie giving out milk to child survivors of Belsen, 1945. Note the flowers. (Courtesy of British Red Cross)

The youngest of eight children, Stella Reekie trained as a nursery nurse at Wellgarth Nursery Training College in 1939. One evening in 1943 she saw a Red Cross film at the Greek Embassy in London showing the hunger and poverty in Europe and calling for relief workers. She decided to train with the Red Cross after work at night, in preparation for working with refugees overseas.

On her arrival in Belgium in 1945 she was suddenly called with her team to go to the just discovered concentration camp at Belsen. 'I saw in the horrors of Belsen what man could do if Christ was not in the centre of men's lives and at the centre of the world.'[1] Separating the dead from the living, she found a sack of bones; it whimpered; it was a living child. Stella Reekie's great task as British Red Cross Child Welfare Officer was to rehabilitate both the surviving Jewish child prisoners and the children of Polish slave labourers. She started the Polish School of Bergen-Belsen at the Hohne displaced persons' camp.

> [She] worked day and night, trying to seek out those capable of providing necessary tuition, to find sources of desks and paper, to search for Polish books, and to cater for all the physical needs of the children . . . providing . . . the semblance of a normal life.[2]

Under her care the children became children again with amazing speed.

After the Hohne camp was at last emptied, Stella Reekie went to work in hospitals in Bad Pyrmont and Bad Rehburg where malnourished children were dying of tuberculosis. It was said of her that her example must have persuaded many people to survive: 'it was her own personality and devotion . . . on which she . . . built up the tremendous love and affection from all those who came into contact with her.'[3]

Stella Reekie left Germany with the British Red Cross Commission in 1949 and trained as a missionary at St Colm's College, Edinburgh (1949–51). Sent to Sialkot in Pakistan, she worked at the mother and infant welfare clinic. She was the only foreign missionary left in Gujrat after Partition, and distributed relief food and clothing. She was known everywhere for working at all hours:

> 'The Miss-Sahiba of Gujrat
> who baked her cakes adhi rat' (at midnight).
> . . . She would take everyone under her wing – the homesick stranded foreigner, the destitute widow, the seeking student, the blustering landlord, the sick, the sad, the unemployed – and they all responded to her knack of bringing out the best in them.[4]

But she was never satisfied with herself. After her death the following anonymous meditation was found in her desk:

> Lord, when I am hungry,
> give me someone to feed.
> When I am thirsty,
> Give water for their thirst.
> When I am sad,
> Someone to lift from sorrow.
> When burdens weigh upon me,
> Lay upon my shoulders
> The burden of my fellows.
> Lord, when I stand
> greatly in need of tenderness,
> Give me someone who yearns for love . . .[5]

1. J. Adamson *et al.*, *Stella: The Story of Stella Jane Reekie 1922–1982* (privately printed, 1984), p. 2.
2. *Ibid.*, p. 3.
3. Stella Jane Reekie papers, British Red Cross Archives, London.
4. Adamson, *op. cit.*, p. 10.
5. *Ibid.*, p. x.

RHYS WILLIAMS, JULIET EVANGELINE, LADY, DBE

(17.12.1898–18.9.1964)

CRUSADER FOR SAFE, PAIN-FREE CHILDBIRTH

Father: Clayton Glyn
Mother: Elinor Glyn, romantic novelist

Christian

Juliet Glyn left school in 1914 before she was 16 to become a VAD. Four years later she was private secretary to the Director of Training and Staff Duties at the Admiralty and, in 1919, Assistant Secretary to the War Cabinet Demobilization Committee. Clearly someone had realized that she was exceptionally intelligent and alert. After her marriage to the Liberal MP Lt Col. Brandon Rhys Williams in 1921, Juliet Rhys Williams had four children, an experience that helped determine her extraordinary contribution to maternal and perinatal welfare in the twentieth century. In 1928 she co-founded the National Birthday Trust Fund to discover the causes of the high rate of maternal mortality in Britain. She also became London Treasurer of the Queen Charlotte's Hospital appeal to appoint an anaesthetic resident – the first post of its kind – to alleviate the pain of childbirth.

Juliet Rhys Williams (Courtesy of Wellcome Institute Library, London)

Few women at that time received any form of pain relief during childbirth . . . With Mrs Stanley Baldwin, [Juliet Rhys Williams] persuaded the [Royal] College of Obstetricians and Gynaecologists to . . . [investigate] obstetric analgesia and anaesthesia . . . the public and professional conscience was aroused and maternity hospitals began to provide obstetric analgesia.[1]

Lady Rhys Williams, as she had become, next tackled the high rates of maternal mortality and post-puerperal infection in the most deprived regions of Britain, beginning with the Rhondda valley. In 1933–34 she organized a 'New Deal' for pregnant women: better antenatal care, midwives, improved care in labour and modern antisepsis; still dissatisfied, she went on to ensure the provision of extra milk and vitamins via the National Birthday Trust Fund. She set up what she called a 'Samaritan fund' in the Rhondda, providing not only decent nutrition for mothers and infants but also baby clothes and blankets (1934–42). The success of this experiment in reducing maternal mortality and ill health led to the extension of similar improved maternal care, first to the depressed areas of north-east England, and then as standard practice throughout Britain. In 1958 she initiated the Perinatal Mortality Survey, published in 1963, 'unique in the world in scope, execution and analysis, . . . and probably her greatest memorial, the apogee of her achievement'.[2]

Juliet Rhys Williams had two other large-scale projects. First was her economic scheme for national social security as an alternative to the Beveridge plan, ensuring every citizen a basic subsistence allowance plus liberal family allowances and giving every housewife an income of her own, funded by income tax.[3] Secondly, she was a passionate advocate of European unity after the Second World War. She became Secretary of the European League for Economic Cooperation and influenced policy to help the economic rehabilitation of the Continent. Shortly before her death, she was helping to prepare a memorandum urging 'a more generous policy of aid from the industrial countries to the recently emerging states'.[4] 'She was indefatigable as a worker to redress injustice and relieve distress and suffering wherever she could find it . . . Always dominant, she was never domineering; always dignified, she was always modest and very polite. That is why she was so great.'[5] She had 'a most loveable, warm-hearted and cheerful disposition'.[6] 'She was a tremendous dynamo.'[7]

1. Professor W. C. W. Nixon in *The Times* (22.9.1964).
2. *Ibid.*
3. See Juliet Rhys Williams, *Something to Look Forward to: A Suggestion for a New Social Contract* (London, Macdonald, 1943); and obituary, *The Times* (20.9.1964).
4. Edward Beddington-Behrens, additional note, *The Times* (29.9.1964).
5. *British Medical Journal* (September 1964).
6. Beddington-Behrens, *op. cit.*
7. Obituary, *The Times* (20.9.1964).

The Contemporary Medical Archives Centre, Wellcome Institute for the History of Medicine, London, holds very full Juliet Rhys Williams papers in the National Birthday Trust Fund archive, including her speeches and several obituaries. See also obituaries in *The Midwives' Chronicle and Nursing Notes*, **77** (November 1964); *Western Mail* (Cardiff) (19.12.1964); and *The Medical Officer* (2.10.1964).

~ ~

ROBINSON, ANNOT ERSKINE
(8.6.1874–30.8.1925)

SOCIALIST FEMINIST TEACHER; PEACE ACTIVIST

Father: John Wilkie, poor shopkeeper
Mother: Catherine, née Erskine, schoolmistress

Presbyterian, later agnostic

Until her premature death at 51, Annot Robinson was an intrepid left-wing socialist,[1] a staunch feminist[2] and a pacifist internationalist. She suffered for all her causes, facing 'gibing and mockery'[3] as well as prison for the sake of women's suffrage, poverty for her socialism and even violence for her anti-militarist witness in the First World War. She had been converted to socialism and feminism by Agnes Husband and her sisters in Dundee *c.* 1900, when Annot Wilkie, as she then was, struggled to teach classes of 100 children and was confronted with the terrible poverty of Scottish mining families. In the evenings she worked successfully to gain the Ladies' Licentiate in Arts (LLA) external degree from St Andrews University, which did not permit attendance by women students.

Annot Robinson testified to the primacy of her humanitarian values when she broke with colleagues in both the Labour Party and the National Union of Women's Suffrage Societies in trying to bring the First World War to a rapid, negotiated end. She was one of those who applied in vain to go to the Women's International Congress at The Hague in April 1915,[4] and signed EMILY HOBHOUSE's Open Letter to German Women. Like MARGARET ASHTON, SELINA COOPER, CHARLOTTE DESPARD, ETHEL SNOWDEN and HELENA SWANWICK, and others, Annot Robinson addressed huge women's meetings up and down the country, but particularly in the north, in support of the Women's Peace Crusade of 1917–18.[5] She worked tirelessly during the war for the relief of poverty-stricken women in Manchester, and also served on the Profiteering Committee (exposing a scandal about milk supplies) and on the Women's Housing Advisory Committee.

After the war Annot Robinson worked as lecturer and organizer for the Women's International League for Peace and Freedom, British Section, until there was no more money to employ her. She visited starving Vienna in 1921 for the WILPF Conference there, and also investigated conditions in Ireland during the occupation by the 'Black and Tans', reporting in America to the American Commission on Ireland, also in 1921.[6] She was eventually obliged to return to teaching in Scotland in order to support herself. The sudden death of this 'big woman and . . . powerful personality [with her] tradition of freedom and passion for justice'[7] came as a shocking loss to her former WILPF colleagues who subscribed to a fund for the education of her two young daughters.

1. See J. M. Bellamy and J. Saville (eds), *Dictionary of Labour Biography*, vol. 8, pp. 215–19.
2. See Olive Banks, *The Biographical Dictionary of British Feminists*, vol. 2: *1900–1945* (New York, New York University Press, 1990).
3. W. R., obituary, *The Northern Voice* (11.12.1925), p. 5.
4. See Appendix I.
5. See Jill Liddington, *The Long Road to Greenham: Feminism and Anti-Militarism in Britain since 1820* (London, Virago, 1989), Part Two, ch. 6: 'The women's peace crusade'.
6. See *The Nation* (New York), **112** (2907), section ii (23.3.1921), pp. 457–60 for Annot Robinson's report to the American Commission on Conditions in Ireland.
7. Ellen Wilkinson, MP, obituary for Annot Robinson, *The Woman's Leader* (6.11.1925), p. 324.

Unfortunately K. A. Rigby's MA thesis for Manchester Polytechnic, 'Annot Robinson, socialist, suffragist, peaceworker: a biographical study' (1986), has been lost.

ROPER, ESTHER, BA
(4.8.1868–28.4.1938)

SOCIALIST FEMINIST AND PACIFIST

Father: Edward Roper, pioneer missionary in Nigeria
Mother: Annie, née Craig, Irish

Labour Church

Esther Roper, 1892 (From Gifford Lewis, Eva Gore-Booth and Esther Roper, Pandora, 1988)

Esther Roper, a lifelong champion of the human rights of women, had a most unusual background. Her father, whom she accompanied to his sermons and lectures and even nursed on his deathbed when she was only 8, had been an early Church Missionary Society catechist among the Yoruba in Nigeria, and recounted stories of his captivity as a hostage in intertribal war and his confrontations with the domestic enslavement of women in West Africa, who risked death if they converted to Christianity. Esther Roper's early sense of the intolerable injustice of a mother and child being literally owned by the father of the family and liable to be sold, clearly fed into her later feminist activism. One 1890s pamphlet from her political work for the women in the Lancashire and Cheshire textile industries cried out:

> First – why are working women paid five shillings a week and working men twenty five shillings? Secondly – why do working women live on bread and margarine while working men eat beefsteak and butter? – Because women have no votes.[1]

Esther Roper not only worked for the civil rights of hundreds of thousands of women textile workers but also, together with her lifelong companion Eva Gore-Booth, for the right to work of such stigmatized and not altogether 'acceptable' women as barmaids, pitbrow women, women gymnasts, circus performers and flower-sellers.[2] She contributed, as did ISABELLA FORD, MARY MACARTHUR, KATHARINE GLASIER, SYLVIA PANKHURST and CHARLOTTE DESPARD, a lively awareness of *class* injustice to the gender cause of women's suffrage in the early twentieth century, and was herself a respected influence on younger socialist women in the suffrage movement.

In her concern for Eva Gore-Booth's sister Constance Markievicz, sentenced to death for her part in the Irish Nationalist rising of Easter 1916, Esther Roper visited her in Dublin's Mountjoy prison and was overwhelmed by the extreme misery of the Irish poor.

> [The] terror of the people in the slums, who by now saw a spy in everyone, the squalor and starvation only too plain there – these things made an impression never to be wiped out. Rebellion and revolution are the natural outcome of conditions of life as terrible as those I saw in the slums of Dublin.[3]

Despite this understanding of the roots of violent resistance in a colonial context, Esther Roper was herself committed to non-violence. It was said of her 'she would not shoot a pursuing tiger!'[4] She and Eva Gore-Booth were signatories to EMILY HOBHOUSE's Open Christmas Letter to German Women (December 1914); they were also both on the British Committee supporting the Women's International Congress at The Hague in April 1915.[5] After the Conscription Act of 1916, she and Eva Gore-Booth travelled all over Britain to give evidence to tribunals of the genuineness of men arrested as conscientious objectors.

After Eva's death Esther Roper supported herself as a history teacher and served the campaigns to abolish the death penalty and to promote internationalism. She had to witness the advance of fascism but was spared the Second World War.[6]

---

1. Gifford Lewis, *Eva Gore-Booth and Esther Roper: A Biography* (London, Pandora, 1988), p. 85.
2. *Ibid.*, p. 3.
3. Esther Roper, Foreword to her edition of *Prison Letters of Countess Markievicz* (London, Longmans, 1934), quoted in Lewis, *op. cit.*, p. 139.
4. Lewis, *op. cit.*, p. 163.
5. See Introduction and Appendix I.
6. The only obituary was in *The Woman Teacher* (20.5.1938), the journal of the National Union of Women Teachers, which Esther Roper had co-founded in 1919; it is quoted in Lewis, *op. cit.*, pp. 180–1. See also Olive Banks, *The Biographical Dictionary of British Feminists*, vol. 1 (New York University Press, 1985).

ROUGHTON, ALICE, MB
(21.1.1905–16.6.1995)

MEDICAL CAMPAIGNER;
ANTI-NUCLEAR ACTIVIST; ECOLOGIST

Father: — Hopkinson, Professor of engineering
Mother: —, née Siemens, philanthropist

Freethinker

Alice Roughton, aged about 55

Not only was Dr Alice Roughton a GP, she was also an innovative, anti-Freudian psychiatrist, a constant provider of asylum for foreign refugees in her own home, a farmer, a pioneer ecologist, a defender of ancient buildings and the co-founder, with the Quakers Margaret and Lionel Penrose, of the Medical Association for the Prevention of [nuclear] War.[1] The obituaries written about her after she died at the age of 90 resonate with delight in the existence of such a human being.

Alice Roughton's open house in Cambridge was very open. 'Former psychiatric and other patients were welcome and the state of world politics could be charted by the influx of refugees passing through [her] doors.'[2] Central European Jews were followed by the entire Danish Ballet Jooss, then by those fleeing Stalinism, or oppressive regimes in West Africa, South Africa and Latin America, not to mention a continuous flow of foreign students in trouble, while German prisoners of war after 1945 had been invited to tea each week. Many visitors who came to eat found themselves staying for 'a spot of healthy digging' on her small organic farm.

> None was turned away; Arabs lived alongside Jews, anti-Communists from the former Soviet Union beside Latin American revolutionary militants. It was Roughton's earnest intention to see, even to prove, that of course peace is possible within humanity.[3]

Alice Roughton's personal commitment to her patients was quite extraordinary, and certainly never ended with surgery or clinic hours.

> If, in assessing prospective Borstal boys or dangerous psychotics, she found they didn't quite warrant incarceration, she brought them into her home . . . Long before R. D. Laing, she was literally living with her patients. Her motives were not theoretical, but humanistic; one woman she brought out of a locked ward had not seen grass for seventeen years.[4]

After she had retired as a GP at 65 and as a psychiatrist at 75, Alice Roughton continued to teach people with dyslexia to read and to counsel women about to have abortions, as well as to run the drug containment unit at Addenbrooke's Hospital and to campaign for nuclear disarmament. She was hugely loved by her much-tried family and countless friends.[5]

1. See Frances Partridge, obituary for Dr Margaret Penrose Newman, *Independent* (29.7.1989).
2. Amanda Hopkinson, obituary, *Guardian* (28.6.1995).
3. Teresa Deutsch, obituary, *Independent* (29.6.1995); see also *Independent* (8.7.1995).
4. Deutsch, *op. cit.*
5. See also obituary, *The Times* (30.6.1995).

ROWNTREE, ELISABETH HARVEY ('TESSA') (later CADBURY)
(28.5.1909–30.9.1999)

REFUGEE RESCUER

Father: Arnold Rowntree, Liberal MP for York, businessman, educationist
Mother: Mary Katherine, née Harvey, BA

Quaker

'[Tessa Rowntree] looks a tough girl,' said the Labour MP David Grenfell in Prague on 1 November 1938; so it was she who was detailed to take the third party of Sudetenland Social Democrat leaders on Hitler's death list across Slovakia and into Poland as far as the port of Gdynia, from where they could reach asylum in Britain.[1] Before taking on that risky courier assignment in Nazi-threatened Europe, Tessa Rowntree had had an upper middle-class professional education at the Mount School, York, and the London School of Economics. She qualified in social work and sociology and for the previous four years had been a social worker in London, organizing social and educational clubs for unemployed women.

In March 1938 she and a friend were on holiday in Europe. As soon as Hitler's next plans became clear, they went from Germany to Vienna where they volunteered to help with Quaker work there with the refugee exodus. But the Vienna Quakers had recently received a request for help from the tiny Quaker group in Prague, and since Tessa had already spent a few weeks in Czechoslovakia it was decided that she should go and help Prague Friends. At that time the largest immediate refugee problem for Czechoslovakia were the numbers of *Reichsdeutsche* Germans who had sought a haven in Prague from what was now Nazi-controlled Germany in the Sudetenland. She therefore joined MARY BAKER PENMAN and, later, DOREEN WARRINER for a tragic autumn and winter in Prague, where they struggled to prevent or at least to diminish the tragedy for some of the most vulnerable stranded there. As well as feverishly trying to locate the most threatened socialist men in the temporary camps around Prague, procuring visas and transport for them, Tessa Rowntree managed to take out two large groups via Poland before Hitler controlled that region also. In March 1939, after the German invasion of Prague, it was clear that many of the women and children whose menfolk had been earlier helped to get to England (some on their way to resettlement in Canada at Peace River, Alberta) now needed to leave Czechoslovakia as soon as possible, since everyone felt that war might start any day. As these women and children, unlike their husbands, were not politically endangered, it was decided to risk taking them via Germany to the Dutch border, although some of them were without proper exit permits or even passports. A few others, including Jewish children, were added who did have sponsors in England and proper exit permits and passports.[2] Grim-faced Nazi officials on the train took away their invalid papers, but Tessa Rowntree urged that they all had to travel together and talked sufficiently persuasively for the papers to be returned and the transport, mercifully, was allowed to proceed. At least one of the rescued Jewish children, Henry Berman, 'almost worshipped Tessa for the way she managed'.[3]

During the war Tessa Rowntree, now Cadbury, helped to train Polish, Czech and French women exiles in London for work after the war; she also organized a training programme for British women who were to become the women's arm of the Friends' Ambulance Unit.[4]

1. The first two parties had been led by Doreen Warriner. See Doreen Warriner, 'Winter in Prague', *Slavonic and East European Review*, **62** (2) (April 1984), p. 213.
2. 'Tessa Rowntree risked her life to rescue artists and musicians': Lilly Gill, née Spielmann, who had been one of the rescued Jewish youngsters, reminiscing in *The Times* (4.3.1996). Tessa Rowntree Cadbury has told the author that in fact there was no policy to single out artists and musicians for rescue.
3. Personal communication from Clare Campion, daughter of Mary Baker Penman, to the author.
4. For further information on the Quaker refugee work in Vienna and Prague in 1938–39 see Hans Schmitt, *Quakers and Nazis: Inner Light in Outer Darkness* (Columbia and London, University of Missouri Press, 1997).

There was an obituary for Tessa Rowntree Cadbury in *The Burlington County Times* (New Lisbon, NJ) (October 1999).

ROYDEN, A. MAUDE,
CH, Hon. DD

(23.11.1876–30.7.1956)

CHRISTIAN SOCIALIST, FEMINIST, PACIFIST

Father: Sir Thomas Royden, Bart, shipowner,
*   Mayor of Liverpool*
Mother: Alice Elizabeth, née Dowdall,
*   daughter of a stockbroker*

Anglican, later non-denominational Christian

Maude Royden, c. 1925

Maude Royden was probably Britain's most powerful woman speaker of the twentieth century. Hundreds, even thousands, of people would drop everything to hear her, either at great suffrage rallies in the Albert Hall, at peace and disarmament meetings, at the City Temple and Guildhouse in London, on her world preaching tours, or listening to her on the BBC. What was it she had to say? Her kind of Christianity was her lifelong attempt to apply the humaneness of Christ to an inhumane world.

Although born rich and hugely privileged, educated at Cheltenham Ladies' College and Lady Margaret Hall, Oxford, Maude Royden felt compelled, as a young woman, to join in the life of the poorest. She therefore worked herself almost to death as a rather unsuccessful University Settlement social worker in the slums of Liverpool and later in Poplar. She was better suited to University Extension lecturing on literature to working-class students. Her realization of the brutalizing poverty suffered by the mass of the British working class at the beginning of the twentieth century made her both a socialist and a suffragist, and she first achieved national fame as the most charismatic and beloved of all the public speakers for women's suffrage. The struggle for the vote 'gave me a sympathy – and I believe an understanding – which linked me to all disfranchised persons and nations'.[1] For her, the enfranchisement of women was a necessary means to constructing a more civilized world, one that would put the needs of the world's children first. 'Whomsoever harms one of these little ones . . .' A member of the National Executive of the constitutional National Union of Women's Suffrage Societies, and Editor of its weekly *The Common Cause*, Maude Royden was prevented by her abhorrence of violence, and by her belief in democracy and in the rational justice of the women's cause from succumbing to the temptation to martyrdom as a militant suffragette.

When the First World War erupted, Maude Royden wanted to be convinced of the justice of Britain's participation, but she could not be convinced. To the horror of some of her closest colleagues in the women's movement, especially its leader Millicent Fawcett, she, together with MARGARET ASHTON, her great friend KATHLEEN COURTNEY, CATHERINE MARSHALL and others, actually tried to win the whole movement over to an internationalist, anti-militarist stance. In January 1915 she published her incandescent pacifist pamphlet *The Great Adventure*, the first call to non-violent direct action against the war-machine to be published in Britain. In it she declared what Britain *should* have done in August 1914: disarmed itself. And if Germany had still attacked a totally non-resisting nation:

> We could have called for the peace-lovers in the world to fling themselves – if need be – in front of the troop trains. If millions of men will go out to offer their lives up in war, surely there are those who would die for peace! and if not men, we could have called out women![2]

Not surprisingly, Maude Royden was one of those who felt conscience-bound to resign from their beloved National Suffrage Union in their prioritizing of the cause of world peace over the popularity of a 'patriotic' British feminism in 1915.[3] Maude Royden went on to preach pacifism to hostile audiences throughout Britain, until the hate climaxed in a mobbing outside Hinckley. She was hit on the head, her 'peace caravan' smashed and burned to the ground before the police intervened; she was driven to the conclusion that her pacifist preaching was counter-productive.

After the war Maude Royden devoted her gift as a preacher to thinking out how to apply the Sermon on the Mount to the world. Rejected for ordination as an Anglican priest and forbidden to preach in an Anglican church,[4] she was offered a pulpit at the Congregationalists' City Temple Church in London; soon afterwards she founded, with Percy Dearmer, not a new Church, but a new kind of inter-denominational church service at the Guildhouse, Eccleston Square. Her services were always packed out, with hundreds of people queueing early in their anxiety to hear what she had to say. She preached against punitive peace terms for Germany; she petitioned for the cessation of the Allied Blockade of the defeated. (She herself had taken in and fostered a small victim from starving Vienna.[5]) She preached and collected money for the famine-stricken in Bolshevik Russia; she preached in favour of international disarmament. Foreign policy 'is a human question too. It means the lives of suffering, tormented children.'[6] She publicized and collected money for the cause of the Welsh miners and Labour; and she and her congregation gave lavishly to Albert Schweitzer's hospital at Lambaréné, enabling him to open a ward for the mentally ill. She preached and wrote in favour of prison reform and against the death penalty.[7] She preached in favour of family allowances and birth control and against any cut in unemployment benefit. 'What courage she had! How she would blaze at injustice and cruelty!'[8] During the 1926 General Strike the press kept ringing her for her standpoint until nearly midnight. She was always being asked for her views on current issues.

After the Sunday service, Maude Royden would have an 'After-Meeting' of questions, including personal troubles, which could last till the middle of the night.

> Appeals to her poured in on all sides and she had a gigantic correspondence, not only from individuals who wanted her counsel . . . but from whole groups or nationalities which thought themselves oppressed. On one occasion she looked up from a long letter in a pile of correspondence and said wearily: 'Must I save the Dodecanese?' 'Well I wouldn't if I were you,' said her secretary, and that particular appeal was not taken up, but she was exhausted by the constant demands upon her sympathy . . .[9]

After the Japanese invasion of Manchuria in 1931 Maude Royden developed her project of an International Peace Army of unarmed, middle-aged and older volunteers (she would not accept the young as volunteers) to interpose their bodies between the combatants. Nothing came of this in the event, though there were hundreds of recruits and she did go down to Tilbury Docks to protest against Britain exporting arms to Japan. She spent the years 1932–37 in the struggle, together with Rev. Dick Sheppard, to prevent another world war. But then the unbelievable happened: it became clear that there was something even worse than war. 'She could not bear what Hitler was doing to the Jews.'[10] In October 1939 Maude Royden not only publicly renounced her now world-famous pacifism but then, in 1941, went on a tour of the United States to use her influence to bring the Americans on to the Allied side. Back in Britain in 1942, aged over 60, and despite increasing disability from her lifelong lameness resulting from her dislocated hip, she volunteered to drive a car to take messages on ambulance duty during air raids.

At the end of her life in the 1950s Maude Royden was haunted by the same sense of failure that so many humanitarians suffered as they reflected on the triumph of brutal totalitarianism and world war in their time. It was all too easy to feel disappointed in her youthful hopes for socialism, feminism and pacifism, as well as in herself. 'Others have succeeded a thousand times better than I in living up to Christian ideals.' The true monument to her quite exceptional gift of sympathy was the difference she made to countless people, who, through hearing her, found their personal lives made more bearable.

1. Maude Royden, chapter in Margot Asquith (ed.), *Myself When Young* (London, Muller, 1938).
2. M. Royden, *The Great Adventure: The Way to Peace* (pamphlet: London, 1915), held in the Women's Library, London.
3. See J. Vellacott, 'Anti-war suffragists', *History*, **62** (October 1977); Sybil Oldfield, *Spinsters of This Parish* (London, Virago, 1984), ch. 9; Anne Wiltsher, *Most Dangerous Women: Feminist Peace Campaigners of the Great War* (London, Pandora, 1985); and Appendix I below.
4. For Maude Royden's struggle with the Anglican Church over the ordination of women see Sheila Fletcher, *Maude Royden: A Life* (Oxford, Basil Blackwell, 1989).

5. See M. Royden, *Political Christianity* (London, G. P. Putnam's Sons, 1922).

6. *Ibid.*

7. See Maude Royden, *Christ Triumphant* (London, G. P. Putnam's Sons, 1924).

8. Martin Shaw, 'In Memoriam Maude Royden' (The Guildhouse Fellowship, September 1956), in Royden papers, the Women's Library, London.

9. Kathleen Courtney papers on Maude Royden in the Women's Library, London. See also Maude Royden, 'Bid me discourse', unpublished autobiographical typescript, also in the Women's Library, London.

10. The late Daisy Dobson, Maude Royden's secretary, personal communication to the author. See also Sybil Oldfield, 'The political preacher, Maude Royden' in S. Oldfield, *Women against the Iron Fist: Alternatives to Militarism 1900–1989* (Oxford, Basil Blackwell, 1989; reprinted New York, Edwin Mellen Press, 2000).

RUSSELL, DORA

(1894–1986)

BIRTH CONTROL CAMPAIGNER; NUCLEAR PACIFIST

Father: Sir Frederick Black, civil servant in the Admiralty
Mother: Sarah, née Davissons, civil servant

Humanist

Dora Russell's two significant humanitarian projects were her attempts to gain access to contraception for all working-class women who wanted it and her consistent opposition both to the Cold War and to the threat of global nuclear war after 1945. When Dora Black first agreed to live with Bertrand Russell in 1919 she was already a young socialist idealist, fired by the coming of the Bolshevik Revolution and impressed by Bertrand Russell's moral courage in having gone to prison for his pacifist principles in the First World War. Dora Russell's campaign to 'normalize' contraception for the poor, on the humanitarian grounds of the health of the mother and the right of every child to be a wanted child, was waged within the Labour Party from the moment that Labour formed its first government in 1924. She and a fellow campaigner coined the slogan: 'It is four times as dangerous to bear a child as to work in a mine, and mining is men's most dangerous trade.'[1] Her deputation to the Ministry of Health asked (a) that in institutions under Ministry control, birth control information should be given to mothers who desired it, and (b) that doctors at medical centres should be able to give such information whenever medically advisable. These requests were rejected by Labour's Roman Catholic Minister of Health, who told them it was a matter for Parliament. Dora Russell and her allies, including KATHARINE GLASIER, then went to the Labour Party Conference (14 May 1924), where their motion was passed by 1,000 votes to eight. She next toured the country on what she, like MARIE STOPES, ELEANOR RATHBONE and MAUDE ROYDEN among others, now realized was '*the* central issue of women's emancipation'.[2] In 1926 she was in the Welsh mining areas, as well as campaigning successfully among some of the poorest local authorities in Britain, eighteen of which by now supported the legalization of birth control information; but 1926 was also the year of the defeated General Strike and demoralization within the Labour Party. Fear of losing the Roman Catholic vote prevented the party leaders from acting on that year's Conference resolution on birth control advice as an integral part of maternity care. Disillusioned with the Labour Party, but still a

Women's Caravan of Peace, Edinburgh–Moscow–London; part of the Aldermaston march, Easter 1959 (From Dora Russell, The Tamarisk Tree vol. 3: Challenge to the Cold War, Virago, 1985)

dynamo of energy and conviction, she switched from struggling for social reform via political means to focusing on social change via alternative, libertarian education.[3]

After her years of child-rearing and education, and after her work in the Second World War for the Soviet Relations Department of the Ministry of Information, helping to edit *British Ally*, the second of Dora Russell's lifelong preoccupations began: she sought nothing less than to mitigate and to challenge the Cold War. 'We peoples had come so near to a longed-for reconciliation and peace [after the victory over Nazism] if only our statesmen would implement our desires.'[4] She endured several years of witnessing the tragedy of the hardening of Cold War positions on a planet now, after Hiroshima, forever threatened by nuclear extinction. 'Why [did] we the mass of the people allow half the world to be shut out of our lives?'[5] From 1949 on she defined her anti-separatist feminism, like that of VERA BRITTAIN: 'While in no way departing from the human rights which feminism demanded, for me the struggle of the women's movement *for peace* was first on the agenda' (my italics).[6] From 6 February 1957, Dora Russell supported the birth of the Campaign for Nuclear Disarmament in Britain.[7]

To Dora Russell her first struggle for birth control for all who want it and her later struggle against a third, final world war were one struggle. At all times she was impelled by her heartfelt wish that every child on earth should have a life worth living. 'If we are to survive, surely it is the care, nurture and quality of our children that will determine our future? . . . Only by learning to love one another can our world be saved.'[8] Dora Russell's own care for her children was of the heroic mould; she took responsibility for her schizophrenic son John until his death when she was 90.

1. Dora Russell, *The Tamarisk Tree*, vol. 1: *My Quest for Liberty and Love* (London, Elek/Pemberton, 1975), p. 171.
2. *Ibid.*, p. 175.
3. See Dora Russell, *The Tamarisk Tree*, vols 1 and 2, on her experimental Beacon Hill School.
4. Dora Russell, *The Tamarisk Tree*, vol. 3: *Challenge to the Cold War* (London, Virago, 1985), p. 60.
5. *Ibid.*, p. 109.
6. *Ibid.*, p. 118.
7. *Ibid.*, pp. 217–18. Dora Russell deplored the fact that CND focused on banning the H-bomb rather than on the more positive, broader brief of peace and disarmament.
8. *Ibid.*, pp. 325 and 328.

See also her *Religion of the Machine Age* (London, Routledge, 1983), which demonstrated the interrelation of the continued domination of women by men in every society, the uncontrolled exploitation of the earth by industrial and post-industrial technology, and the threat of nuclear extinction. Her humanist-feminist, child-centred, military-bloc-renouncing remedies for our predicament are found in *The Dora Russell Reader: 57 Years of Writing and Journalism 1925–1982* (London, Pandora Press, 1983). See also articles on Dora Russell in *The Times* (2.10.1974); *Guardian* (2.6.1986); and *The Times Educational Supplement* (13.6.1986); and Olive Banks, *The Biographical Dictionary of British Feminists*, vol. 2 (New York University Press, 1990).

RYDER, SUE, BARONESS RYDER OF WARSAW,
CMG, OBE
(3.7.1923–2.11.2000)

CHAMPION OF CONCENTRATION
CAMP SURVIVORS, AND OF VICTIMS
OF WAR AND DISEASE WORLDWIDE

*Father: Charles Foster Ryder, gentleman
farmer*
*Mother: Mabel Elizabeth, née Sims, daughter
of Anglican vicar, social interventionist*

*Anglican by birth, converted to Roman
Catholicism*

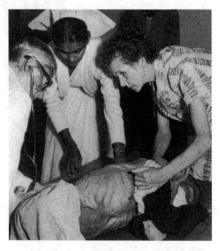

Sue Ryder visiting a tuberculosis patient in the Ryder–Cheshire Centre, Raphael, Dehra-dun, India (Courtesy of Ryder–Cheshire Foundation)

Although Sue Ryder was to achieve the foundation of many diverse humanitarian initiatives throughout the world still active today,[1] this entry will focus on her earliest work (1945–*c.* 1950).

Sue Ryder's comfortable rural childhood was spent in close awareness of two kinds of great suffering. The first was the endurance of dehumanizing squalor in some of Britain's poorest slums in nearby Leeds:

> The dreariness of their surroundings, with no lavatory, often no water tap, little to eat and frequently no change of clothes or shoes horrified me . . . I was moved, at [a] very early age, to think how human beings could live in better conditions and with dignity.[2]

The second shadow on her childhood insouciance was the aftermath of the mass bereavement of the First World War: 'Written and verbal descriptions of the battles and the terrible drawings and photographs of disfigured men and buildings haunted me as a child.'[3] What helped her to cope with this early awareness of the suffering of others was her mother's positive example of tireless intervention to try to remedy what was remediable; Mabel Ryder did continuous fund-raising for housing regeneration and holidays for inner-city children; she headed subscription lists for hospitals and district nursing provision; and later she helped the escape of Jewish refugees fleeing Hitler. 'It was my mother . . . who had the greatest influence on my childhood, and, indeed, on my entire life.'[4] In the mid-1930s their German

Jewish friends told the Ryder family what was being perpetrated on anti-Nazis in Dachau, Esterwegen and Oranienburg-Sachsenhausen. The 12-year-old Sue Ryder, like her contemporary HELEN BAMBER, 'began to feel that every day we lived brought us closer to the Second [World War]'.[5]

Sue Ryder was only 17 in 1940, when, after having done some emergency nursing training which was later to prove invaluable, she volunteered, like PHYLLIS COOPER, to join the First Aid Nursing Yeomanry (FANY). She was trained in advanced First Aid, night map-reading, driving (including seven-ton lorries) and vehicle maintenance and was selected for the Special Operations Executive (SOE). From that time on, as she truly said, 'The familiar, ordinary world was left behind, and I never returned to it.'[6] Sue Ryder lived out the whole Second World War at the extreme of human emotional and physical endurance. Each day and night she spent assisting Resistance fighters from occupied Europe, and in particular Czechoslovakia and Poland, as they prepared for parachute sorties back into their homelands, knowing that they faced every probability of torture and execution. Time after time, Sue Ryder drove such young men and women by night to a secret airfield, having learned to esteem their huge courage, only to learn later that they had been captured, tortured and shot.

> To live and share, however briefly, in the lives of great, yet unknown, people, made a profound impression on me and I felt it was a privilege never to be forgotten . . . I began then to think of ways in which the qualities they possessed – tolerance, faith, courage, humour and gaiety – might be perpetuated. I thought that instead of trying to remember all those who died fighting . . . or in prison camps by means of a plaque or monument, one should go out and provide assistance and comfort to those who are sick and in need, wherever they might be, regardless of nationality or religion, creating in this way a 'Living Memorial' to the dead.[7]

Sue Ryder was only 22 in 1945; she could never in later years feel equal to the task of saying what she had witnessed when the Allied forces liberated the concentration camps, only 'I had seen what happened to people when everything, even their hair, was taken from them, and their minds and bodies subjugated until some could only crawl on all fours or lie in silence'.[8] At one point she found herself having to dodge the British Military Police as she hid Russian prisoners of war whose papers she had helped forge, driving them in her ambulance to hospitals and camps where they might escape forced repatriation to Stalin and Siberia.[9] She was then sent to do relief work in Rouen and Caen, where she learned to navigate her medical truck through the unlit streets by 'the different smells of open sewers, choked drains, [and] decomposing bodies not yet recovered from the ruins'.[10] Despite hunger, cold, rats and damp, morale was high as the FANYs struggled to serve the needs of French civilians even hungrier and colder than they were in the ruins of Normandy.

It was Sue Ryder's outraged sense of justice, as well as her total commitment to help those who had no one else to help them, that impelled her next to tackle what was possibly the most extraordinary of all her extraordinary humanitarian projects. In 1945 she became a prison visitor for all the non-German youths on remand or serving sentences in German prisons. These were the young stateless 'displaced persons' who, after seeing the destruction of their families in occupied Europe, or being taken as slave labourers for the Reich, or surviving Nazi concentration camps, had, in the chaotic aftermath of the war, committed 'crimes' in order to survive in the ruins of Germany. Sometimes their offences had been as venial as being found without identity papers or stealing food; in other cases they had been found carrying an illegal weapon or had even wounded or killed a former camp guard or SS man. They became Sue Ryder's 'Boys'. She kept a file on every case, travelling again and again to every prison in West Germany, distributing parcels, seeking legal aid, applying for the remission of their draconian sentences and in many cases for the eventual deletion of their 'criminal' records, thus enabling them to emigrate and start life again. She fought for compensation for camp survivors, for residence and immigration permits for them, often in the teeth of official Allied indifference and all too often having to win the assent of prison directors who themselves had had appalling records as executors of 'Nazi justice'.[11]

It was the sheer unwantedness on earth of the 'Boys' that contributed to Sue Ryder's determination to do even more than try to remedy years of injustice or to alleviate, through holiday schemes,[12] the unbearably depressing monotony of life in displaced persons camps. She decided she must found permanent homes for the most desperately homeless. Helped by her mother, who was her wholehearted supporter, she started her first Sue Ryder Foundation Home in her mother's home at Cavendish, Suffolk, in 1953.

I wanted to commemorate the millions lost in both World Wars by providing relief from suffering and insecurity of all kinds through personal contact and service, restoring dignity to the humiliated, irrespective of age, sex, race or religion. By these means I hoped to contribute towards the building of a better world.[13]

1. At the time of writing (2000), the 22 Sue Ryder Foundation Homes in Britain care not only for some of the last concentration camp survivors but also for terminal cancer patients, homeless and physically disabled old people, and sufferers from Huntington's disease, motor neurone disease, Alzheimer's disease, Parkinson's disease, AIDS and other diseases. There are also Sue Ryder Foundation Homes overseas for, among others, cancer sufferers in Albania, Serbia, Macedonia and Italy; Huntington's disease sufferers in the Czech Republic; tuberculosis and leprosy patients in India; the elderly disabled in Eire; deficiency disease and eye disease sufferers in Malawi; and young rheumatoid arthritis sufferers in Poland.
2. Sue Ryder, *Child of My Love* (London, The Harvill Press, 1997), p. 3.
3. *Ibid.*, p. 23.
4. *Ibid.*, p. 8; see also pp. 226 and 258–9.
5. *Ibid.*, p. 29.
6. *Ibid.*, p. 64.
7. *Ibid.*, pp. 78 and 107.
8. *Ibid.*, p. 159.
9. *Ibid.*, p. 155.
10. *Ibid.*, p. 169.
11. See *ibid.*, ch. 8: 'The Boys', pp. 176–222.
12. See entry for JOYCE PEARCE and the Ockenden Venture.
13. Ryder, *op. cit.*, p. 226.

See obituary, *Guardian*, 3.11.2000.

See also Sue Ryder, *And the Morrow Is Theirs* (Bristol, The Burleigh Press, 1975). Articles on the work of the Sue Ryder Foundation can be found in Strahan Soames, 'Servant of humanity', *Guardian* (7.6.1961); Alex Coleman, 'Back to life', *Sunday Times* (7.11.1965); and *Guardian* (27.6.1979); as well as in the Sue Ryder Foundation's magazine *Remembrance*. The Foundation's Museum is in Cavendish, Suffolk, and the movement are funded largely by the 500 Sue Ryder charity shops run by volunteers. The Ryder–Cheshire Foundation's headquarters is Albert House, 82 Queens Road, Brighton BN1 3XE. (The Cheshire Foundation had been established for the incurably sick in many countries by the former bomber pilot Leonard Cheshire, VC, before he and Sue Ryder married in 1959.)

S

SALTER, ADA
(20.7.1867–5.12.1942)

SOCIALIST; PACIFIST; LONDON
COUNCILLOR; ENVIRONMENTALIST

*Father: Samuel Brown, Methodist farmer,
Raunds, Northamptonshire*

Quaker by convincement

Ada Salter (From Fenner Brockway,
Bermondsey Story, *1949; republished
1995. Courtesy of Independent Labour
Party Publications)*

In her late twenties Ada Brown left her comfortable home to join the West London Mission, initially out of a spirit of religious evangelism, but she rapidly developed a sense of serious social mission. At the age of 30 in 1897 she moved to the Bermondsey Settlement, recently founded by Dr Scott Lidgett, becoming the worker in charge of girls' clubs. The girls were 'rough and tough'[1] rag-pickers, wood-choppers, tinsmiths in the local factories, who sometimes arrived drunk at the club. Ada Brown's gentleness and affectionate concern for them won many of them over to her own values of kindness and a responsiveness to beauty, even in their grim world. In 1899 she startled her friends and family by becoming engaged to a 'revolutionist' five years younger than herself: the Settlement's militant socialist, pacifist, agnostic teetotaller Dr Alfred Salter. Very soon she was as radical as he about the need for political, social and economic change in Britain.

As the wife of a poor people's doctor who only charged 6 (old) pence – or even nothing – for a consultation, Ada Salter willingly led a life of altruistic self-denial herself. They first lived in two rooms above the surgery in Jamaica Road and later moved to 5 Storks Road, Bermondsey, whose unlovely situation and aspect Ada so startlingly transformed that 30 years later she was invited to write in *The Lady* in 1940 about her 'garden in Bermondsey'. Dr Alfred Salter worked from early morning until late at night, seeing up to 60 patients in an evening; meanwhile Ada did unpaid social work among the poorest families he discovered in his practice, as well as continuing her work with the Settlement girls and beginning her political life with the then reformist Liberal Party, becoming President of its Rotherhithe Women's Association. They had one child, Joyce, born in June 1902. Very soon they were faced by the supreme challenge to their social conscience: should they protect their only child from the dirty, verminous, sick children of Bermondsey and eventually send her away to a Quaker boarding school? They felt they could not give her the chances denied to the unprivileged slum children around them, and Joyce attended the local Keeton's Road School. Twice she caught scarlet fever: in 1910 she was attacked by the disease for a third time and on 10 June she died. 'Ada's sadness never quite left her.'[2] Thereafter both parents dedicated themselves with even more commitment to the needs of the poorest parents and their children in London.

In May 1908 the Salters had given up their promising political career prospects with the Liberal Party in order to found the first branch of the young Independent Labour Party (ILP) in Bermondsey, and in November 1910 Ada Salter was the first woman borough councillor to be elected in London. Her dream was to introduce gardens and beautiful parks, as well as maternity and child welfare centres, into Bermondsey. In August 1911, when the whole working population of Bermondsey went on strike for decent employment conditions, it was Ada Salter who organized free meals for the women and children, as she did again in the 1926 dockers' strike.

The First World War was a second tragic challenge to the Salters. As declared pacifists they had to witness the destruction not only of their idealistic faith in the international working class but also of much of their own welfare work for the London poor, now poorer than ever. Their own house was attacked by enraged patriotic stone-throwing mobs, and Ada had to work long hours as the trusted Treasurer of the Maintenance Department of the No Conscription Fellowship, which supported impoverished families of imprisoned conscientious objectors. The Salters purchased and used Fairby Grange in Kent as a convalescent home for released, weakened conscientious objectors. The Salters themselves nursed and housed for nine months in their own home one such ex-prisoner, the Jamaican carpenter Isaac Hall, reduced by mistreatment to a skeleton.[3] In 1915 Ada Salter was accepted into the Religious Society of Friends, remaining a Quaker to the end of her life. At the end of the war she represented the British section of the Women's International League for Peace and Freedom in Zürich and Vienna, bringing back hungry Austrian women and children to recuperate at Fairby Grange.

In the borough council elections of 1922 Ada Salter was again successful for the ILP, and she was chosen to be the first woman Labour Mayor in London, and indeed, in the British Isles. She refused to wear the mayoral robes or chain of office or to impose chaplain-led prayers on the council. She initiated a hugely successful Beautification Committee that planted 9,000 trees and 60,000 plants in the hitherto dreary borough. She struggled to convert churchyards into the only open spaces for children's recreation and to substitute a cottage rehousing plan for the demolition of the worst slums, but the exigencies of the Depression defeated her on the latter: new tenements were built instead. Together with her husband and other Labour colleagues she introduced a solarium to fight tuberculosis and several health clinics, resulting in a 30 per cent fall in infant mortality and an even greater fall in maternal mortality in the borough. In 1924 she was elected to the London County Council and became Vice-Chair of its Parks Committee. In 1934 she secured the highest Labour vote and majority yet recorded, and between 1934 and 1938 she worked successfully for the Green Belt policy that she had so long advocated.

The Second World War was tragic for both the Salters. Once again they were isolated as pacifists even within the Labour Party; they lost many of their

Bermondsey friends in the Blitz, as well as their own lifelong home. But still worse was the descent of the world into competitive barbarism once more. Ada struggled to hold to her faith – and to convince her despairing husband – that the ultimate victory must, one day, be that of the forces of creativity and kindness. Dr Alfred Salter was overwhelmed in December 1942 by the hundreds of written tributes to his wife after her death coming from all over Britain. The Quaker James Hudson wrote:

> by her faith in the people for whom she laboured [she brought] ennoblement of spirit . . . They revered her . . . They often saw her frail figure threading its way on cycle through their streets . . . They knew of her investigations, her encouragements, her committees without end . . . Socialism in action; that is what she was.[4]

Over 40 years earlier Alfred Salter had written to his wife: 'You and I . . . are living and working for the same goal – to make the world, and in particular this corner of the world, happier and holier for our joint lives.'[5] The Old English Garden in Southwark Park was named, in gratitude, the Ada Salter Garden. Does it still exist?

1. Fenner Brockway, *Bermondsey Story: The Life of Alfred Salter* (Bermondsey Independent Labour Party Ltd, 1949), p. 15.
2. *Ibid.*, p. 43.
3. See entry for JOAN FRY.
4. *Friends' Quarterly Examiner* (1.3.1943), p. 12.
5. Brockway, *op. cit.*, p. 16.

SANGER, SOPHY
(3.1.1881–7.12.1950)

PIONEER OF INTERNATIONAL LABOUR LAW REFORM; CO-FOUNDER OF INTERNATIONAL LABOUR ORGANIZATION

Father: Charles Sanger, wealthy London businessman
Mother: Jessie, née Pulford

Humanist

While she was a student at Newnham College, Cambridge, reading mathematics and moral sciences, Sophy Sanger heard Dr HILDA CLARK give a visiting lecture on the misery caused by the Boer War at that time, and was converted to pacifism. On leaving university she did voluntary work for MARY MACARTHUR, who was building up the Women's Trade Union League. There she learned of the incidence of industrial injury, 'sweating' and occupational disease. She mastered insurance regulations for workers' compensation and studied labour law. Already at the age of 23 she was called to give evidence on Workmen's Compensation before a Parliamentary Commission in the Lords, and she also helped Labour MPs prepare their case for the Shops Bill. She soon realized that many industrial evils could only be effectively combated via international intervention. 'Sweating' and child labour were the result of attempts to undercut competitors in the world market; lead and phosphorus poisoning and anthrax infection were caused by handling noxious materials at both the production and the distribution end of manufacture and trade. In 1905, therefore, she decided to set up a British Section of the International Association for Labour Legislation and to bring out an English edition of its French and German *Bulletin*. Between 1909 and 1919 she edited and largely wrote the quarterly *The World's Labour Laws*. Her immediate aim was to cut the injury and death rate of the world's most exploited workers, including children, by setting an international minimum of well-being; but her ultimate hope was that 'by working together to banish industrial evils, the nations would by degrees form the habit of co-operation and lose the habit of war'.[1]

The First World War came as a blow to Sophy Sanger's tireless internationalist endeavour.[2] Nevertheless, she kept the British Section alive until, in the *Contemporary Review* (October 1918), she wrote her seminal article 'Labour questions in the Peace Settlement', in which she advocated 'the establishment of a permanent organisation to deal with labour problems which should include a Council representative of employers, employees and governments'.[3] In February 1919 she attended the Second Socialist International, in Berne, as interpreter for the British Labour and TUC delegation.

Sophy Sanger, c. 1919 (Frontispiece to Maud Allen, Sophy Sanger: A Pioneer in Internationalism, Glasgow University Press 1958)

> [She] was possibly the most practically useful woman of the party. She speaks four languages with equal fluency. What Miss Sanger does not know about the world's laws regulating labour and labour conditions, especially those affecting women, is said not to be worth knowing.[4]

She was the author of the Draft on Labour Affairs that the Second International then presented to the Paris Peace Treaty Commission and which then became the basis of the International Labour Organization or ILO.

When the ILO was actually set up in Geneva, Sophy Sanger was appointed Chief of the Legislative Section and met not only international lawyers but also delegates from trades unions, and factory inspectors, both men and women, from many parts of the world, including those recently at war with each other. In 1921 she lectured international jurists at The Hague on 'The Permanent Court of International Justice and Labour Cases', and she wrote the article on the ILO for the *Encyclopædia Britannica*. Unfortunately internal political intrigue at Geneva led to her being edged out of the organization she had done so much to found by ambitious male colleagues.[5]

Sophy Sanger returned to England and studied successfully for the Bar in order to be equipped to write a definitive work on labour legislation and the international community. However, by the early 1930s it was all too clear that there was no real international community any longer: nationalisms, militarisms and dictatorships were triumphantly poised to destroy parliamentary government and the rule of law throughout Europe. She who had believed in Goethe's apparent paradox 'Only law can give us freedom' had to see new 'laws' that legalized the *Gulag* and Dachau. Finally, she had to renounce her lifelong pacifism and back armed resistance to Hitler. But the ILO is still in existence.

1. A. M. Allen, obituary for Sophy Sanger, *Newnham Roll* (1951), p. 34. (Sophy Sanger's brother, the brilliant lawyer C. P. Sanger, friend of Bertrand Russell, first encouraged his sister to investigate labour laws.) See also S. Sanger, 'The new spirit in international industrial relations' in Lucy Gardner (ed.), *Some Christian Essentials of Reconstruction* (London, G. Bell and Sons, 1920).
2. Sophy Sanger was one of the British Committee supporting the Women's International Congress at The Hague: see Introduction and Appendix I.
3. Allen, *op. cit.*, p. 36.
4. Ethel Snowden, *A Political Pilgrim in Europe* (London, Cassell and Co., 1921), p. 3.
5. See A. M. Allen, *Sophy Sanger: A Pioneer in Internationalism* (Glasgow University Press, 1958).

SHARP, EVELYN
(1869–1955)

FEMINIST ANTI-MILITARIST; INVESTIGATIVE FOREIGN REPORTER

Father: James Sharp, slate merchant
Mother: Jane, musician

Humanist freethinker

At the age of 26 Evelyn Sharp felt she had to escape from her life as a dutiful daughter at home and become a self-supporting writer in London. Her personal struggle for emancipation led to her commitment to the struggle of all British women for economic independence and self-fulfilment. To her, the women's suffrage campaign was a bloodless 'fight for human freedom'.[1] She suffered imprisonment, went on hunger strike and experienced the forcible distraint of her possessions in the cause. The First World War made her a pacifist and she was one of those suffragists who split from Mrs Fawcett on the issue of whether or not the British women's suffrage movement should support the Women's International Congress at The Hague in 1915.[2] When, in 1918, Evelyn Sharp's first great cause, the suffrage, was won, at least in principle, she gave her energetic commitment to other public-spirited projects.

First, from May to August 1920, she joined JOAN FRY's Quaker endeavour to feed students in starving Germany and sent back reports to the *Daily Herald* about the continuing wretchedness there. She was most struck by the contrast between the children's clean, neat clothes and their shocking thinness as they each secretly tried to smuggle home a part of their Quaker bread ration for a hungry 'Mutti'. In January 1921 she went to collect facts, sift evidence and be an eye witness to what was then happening in Ireland. She evaded suspicion by carrying a shopping bag in the streets of Dublin, Cork and Limerick; what she saw and heard there was

inexpressibly painful. Worst of all kinds of shame is the shame one feels on being unable honestly to defend one's own country; and I think that, spiritually, the credit of England can scarcely ever have sunk lower than . . . when the Auxiliaries and Black-and-Tans were let loose upon the population of Ireland.[3]

Witnessing the British military occupation of Ireland, she had to engage with the most terrible mystery of the twentieth century: the transformation of 'ordinary men' into tormentors and executioners of '[enemy] civilians, including women, children and old men'.[4]

When she was nearly 52, in January 1922, Evelyn Sharp joined RUTH FRY on her investigative visit to the famine regions of Russia for the Friends' Relief Committee. Her journal entries, after she joined that 'brave and gallant woman' VIOLET TILLARD at Buzuluk, anticipate the trauma experienced by all later aid workers as she encountered the impossibility of saving everyone, even as she herself survived:

Jan 17th . . . we went out in the car to the warehouse. Left a woman wailing on the doorstep. We cannot help one or we should be besieged by hundreds and end in helping no one effectually . . . Jan 19th. The woman who cried outside was found dead in the snow fifty yards away this morning – I know we could not have saved her, that she would have died on her way to the hospital, that it would have made things worse a hundredfold for the poor wretches crowded there, that if we had brought her in here she would have died all the same and it would have brought hundreds to our door at once and paralysed our real work here. And yet – ! This is the kind of incident that I find almost intolerable . . . It is that fatal propensity to 'get used' to things no one should see unmoved that causes most of the cruelty in the world to go on.[5]

In 1923 Evelyn Sharp reported twice from Germany, first on the chaos in the Rhineland and then on the French occupation of the Ruhr and the desperation caused by hyperinflation, which had in turn been caused by Hjalmar Schacht's 'solution' to Germany's unpayable reparations debt. From her hotel window in Essen she saw women dropping dead from starvation in the long queue for potatoes. When she returned one last time to Germany, in the middle of the Great Depression in 1931, she heard the young Stormtroopers shouting for *Judenblut*, Jewish blood. The relentless sequence of extreme social deprivation and oppression in post-war Germany had produced extreme alternatives: the righteous cruelty either of Communism or of Nazism. Evelyn Sharp ended her unfinished autobiography, early in 1933, brooding on the universal potential for cruelty: 'Nothing in life seems to me to matter so much as cruelty'[6] and struggling to believe that we are all also capable of transcending it.

1. Evelyn Sharp, *Unfinished Adventure: Selected Reminiscences from an Englishwoman's Life* (London, John Lane Bodley Head, 1933), p. 1170. See also ch. 8: 'My journey to Holloway'; ch. 9: 'The four years'; and her biography of Hertha Ayrton (London, Edward Arnold, 1926).
2. See Anne Wiltsher, *Most Dangerous Women: Feminist Peace Campaigners of the Great War* (London, Pandora, 1985); and Appendix I below. Note Evelyn Sharp's witty, engagé article on 'The Congress and the press' in *Towards Permanent Peace: A Record of the Women's International Congress held at The Hague, April 28th–May 1st, 1915* (24 pp.; 1915), pp. 20–1, held in the Women's Library, London.
3. Sharp, *Unfinished Adventure*, p. 214.
4. *Ibid.*, p. 221.
5. Evelyn Sharp papers, MS ENG.Misc.e 632, the Bodleian Library, Oxford. See MARJORIE RACKSTRAW.
6. Sharp, *Unfinished Adventure*, p. 305.

For Evelyn Sharp's writing on deprived children in the Depression see her *The London Child* (London, John Lane, 1927) and *The Child Grows Up* (London, John Lane, 1929), as well as her report on *The*

African Child: An Account of the International Conference of African Children (organized by Save the Children International) (London, Longmans, 1931). For an assessment of her from a feminist perspective see Johanna Alberti, *Beyond Suffrage: Feminists in War and Peace, 1914–1928* (London, Macmillan, 1989). For obituaries of Evelyn Sharp (then Mrs H. W. Nevinson) see *The Times* (21.6.1955); *Manchester Guardian* (20.6.1955).

SHAW, MABEL, OBE
(3.12.1888–25.4.1973)

PIONEER MISSIONARY; EDUCATOR
OF GIRLS IN CENTRAL AFRICA

Father: Walter Shaw, manager of teashop
Mother: Elizabeth Ann, née Purchase

Ecumenical Christian

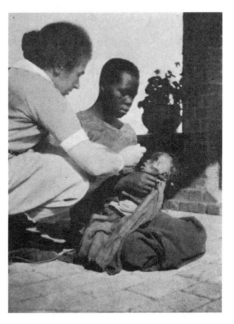

Mabel Shaw with young mother and sick baby
(From Mabel Shaw, Dawn in Africa, *Edinburgh House Press, 1927)*

Mabel Shaw was 26 in 1915 when, after four years' study at St Colm's Church of Scotland Women's Missionary Training College, Edinburgh, she sailed to Cape Town. St Colm's, under the inspirational ecumenical Principalship of Ann Hunter Small, had educated her in an informed respect for non-Christian religious traditions and beliefs, in non-dogmatic pedagogy and in a willingness to 'understand and sympathise with the inner character and thought of the people of Asia and Africa'.[1] After nineteen days by sea and a week's journey by rail to Broken Hill, Mabel Shaw continued for a month's trek overland, carried by bearers across plains, forests and rivers and camping in the open, until she reached Mbereshi in what is now Zambia, to start the Christian education of girls. Her first year there she spent learning the Cibemba language and beginning to understand the traditional upbringing of girls. She decided to build her own school on African foundations, the school being a 'village' with Christ as Chief.

Mabel Shaw had a genuine, deep respect for Africans and in particular for the potential of her fearless girls. She was sorely concerned by the social destabilization and degradation of girls resulting from the West's exploitation of the Copper Belt with its shanty towns, drink, gambling and prostitution. She was also appalled by the racial superiority complex and concomitant injustice of white colonial settlers, she herself being a good example of Kenneth Kaunda's ideal of 'colour-blindness' (one of her pupils later became Kaunda's wife).

After 25 years' service in what was then Northern Rhodesia, having laid the foundations for girls' primary education, teacher training and nursing education, Mabel Shaw retired to publicize the cause of African women and girls in Britain. On 8 June 1941 she gave a talk on the BBC Home Service, describing the appalling attitude of white male settlers to three of her tall, intelligent, barefoot pupils about

215

to start their teacher training course in Bulawayo, 1,000 miles from home: '"What are you damned nigger women doing on our platform?" they said as they shoved and trod the girls aside.'[2]

Mabel Shaw made common cause with Norman Leys, the anti-colonial doctor/writer, author of *The Colour Bar in East Africa* (1941), who warned her on her return to Britain 'You won't have an easy time in trying to shake them open. I haven't had.'[3] Like him, she was passionately opposed to the colonial education policy that restricted most African children's educational aspirations to what white children were expected to know by the age of 10. She died almost destitute and unknown in Britain, grieving that she could do nothing more for 'her' girls, but her ashes were flown back for burial at a massively attended funeral celebrating 'Mama' Shaw at Mbereshi.

1. A. H. Small, Preface to *Missionary College Hymns* (Edinburgh, 1914), quoted in Olive Wyon, *The Three Windows: The Story of Ann Hunter Small* (London, James Clarke and Co., 1953), p. 76.
2. Mabel Shaw, 'In the tracks of Livingstone', BBC Home Service programme (8.6.1941).
3. Letter from Norman Leys to Mabel Shaw (24.7.1941), held in Shaw papers, SOAS Archive, University of London.

See also Mabel Shaw, 'A school village in Northern Rhodesia', *International Review of Missions* (October 1925), pp. 523–36; and *Dawn in Africa* (London, Edinburgh House Press, 1927).

SHEEPSHANKS, MARY RYOTT

(25.10.1872–21.1.1960)

PACIFIST FEMINIST; INTERNATIONALIST; RESCUER OF REFUGEES

Father: John Sheepshanks, Bishop of Norwich
Mother: Mary, née Ryott, descendant of Oliver Cromwell

Atheist

Mary Sheepshanks, c. 1940 (Courtesy of the late Christina Bewley)

Mary Sheepshanks was a redoubtable, strong minded woman. The eldest, least cherished girl in a huge clerical family, she had grown up in Liverpool seeing some of the worst poverty in Britain, and her lifelong solution for her own personal unhappiness was to tackle the world's remediable ills. Her first chance came while a student at Newnham College, Cambridge: she took adult literacy classes and distributed weekly old age pensions for the Charity Organization Society. After coming down from university she had to earn her own living, because her father had cut her off from contaminating the rest of the family with her aggressively atheistic views.[1] Mary Sheepshanks became one of the first trained social workers (1895–97) in some of London's worst black spots: the Nelson Square Settlement, Lambeth, and later in Stepney.[2] Then for fourteen years she was Vice-Principal (*de facto* Principal) of Morley College for Working Men and Women, situated, amazingly, in the bowels of the Old Vic theatre.[3] Predictably, she became a leading speaker for the National Union of Women's Suffrage Societies (1908–13),[4] and soon she worked for the International Women's Suffrage Alliance (IWSA). In 1913 she went on a gruelling international suffrage lecture tour that included Brussels, Paris, Vienna, Munich, Berlin, Prague, Cracow, Warsaw and Budapest, speaking in French or German on women and local government, women and Temperance, women in industry and in education.[5]

It was in Mary Sheepshanks' London office of the IWSA that the unheeded, last-minute entreaty to every European Ambassador in London from the world's women's movement was drafted on 31 July 1914:

> Powerless though we are politically, we call upon the governments . . . of our several countries to avert the threatened unparalleled disaster . . . Whatever its result the conflict will leave mankind the poorer, will set back civilization . . . We women of twenty-six countries . . . appeal to you to leave untried no method of conciliation or arbitration . . .[6]

Soon after the First World War actually began, Mary Sheepshanks did three things. After the fall of Antwerp, together with CHRYSTAL MACMILLAN, she crossed to Flushing in the Netherlands with relief supplies for some of the almost half a million Belgians now stranded there:

> Hundreds of women and children were on barges, many without warm clothing and often clutching some useless thing such as a bird-cage. That was the first wave of the tragic flood of refugees that has swept across large tracts of the world ever since, involving broken homes and broken lives.[7]

Meanwhile she was also doing everything in her power to succour the German women and children stranded in what was now enemy Britain.[8] And finally she was continuing to edit and bring out her monthly journal, *Ius Suffragii*, the organ of the IWSA, in a humanist feminist, neutral and internationalist mode.[9] In October 1914 she wrote her incisive and prescient editorial 'Patriotism or internationalism':

> Each nation is convinced that it is fighting in self-defence, and each in self-defence hastens to self-destruction . . . The men are fighting; what are the women doing? They are, as is the lot of women, binding up the wounds that men have made . . . [The] world is relapsing into a worse, because a more scientific, barbarism than that from which it sprang. [Therefore] women must use not only their hands to bind up, they must use their brains to understand the causes of the European frenzy.

Mary Sheepshanks did not cease to use her brains thereafter. Immediately the war was over, she became Secretary to the Fight the Famine Council out of which grew the Save the Children Fund.[10] In 1920, on behalf of the Council, she lobbied the League of Nations, unsuccessfully, for the immediate admission of Germany and for revision of the punitive reparations clauses of the Treaty of Versailles. In 1923, when she spoke in Berlin on international conciliation and disarmament, Albert Einstein called her address 'masterly'. In 1927 she became International Secretary of the Women's International League, based in Geneva, where she edited its monthly paper *Pax International*. In 1928 she headed another unsuccessful deputation to the League of Nations, this time calling for an urgent world disarmament conference before the momentum of post-war rearmament became irreversible. In 1929 she organized the first international conference of scientists on the impact of aerial bombardment on civilians in future warfare, and in 1930 she organized the first international conference on statelessness in Europe.

Never an easy person to work with, and, as she admitted, never a good subordinate, Mary Sheepshanks resigned from the WIL International Executive at the end of 1930, feeling out of sympathy with what she believed to be the counter-productive, uncritical Communism or 'Left-extremism' of her French and German colleagues. Pacifists can also wage war.[11] By then nearly 60, and very arthritic, Mary Sheepshanks went on a secret fact-finding mission to East Galicia and to Pilsudski's Poland in order to investigate reports of recent Polish atrocities in the Ukraine. 'The bullied had become the bullies.'[12] She had clandestine interviews with the traumatized survivors of Polish attacks on at least 500 villages. She then did everything she could to arouse world opinion. She contacted sympathetic socialists in the German Reichstag in Berlin. She urged the International Transport Workers' Union President in Amsterdam to 'black' Polish iron until the oppresssion ceased. Then she lobbied British MPs, the TUC and the Labour Party and wrote to the *Manchester Guardian* and *The Times*. In her old age Mary was told by a Ukrainian emigrant that there were 300,000 Ukrainians in Canada who loved her. 'The very thought keeps me warm.'[13]

During the late 1930s Mary Sheepshanks opened her London home to a succession of exiles: first the Trotskyists from the Soviet Union, then the Sudetenland socialists, and finally, increasingly, German and Austrian and Czech Jews. She had hostile slogans painted on her wall – asylum-seekers were less than welcome, then as now. Hitler forced her to renounce her lifelong pacifism, but she could not accept the necessity for dropping the atomic bomb. At first, after 1945, she was near despair over the human species, but finally, when she looked back over her long life, she wrote: 'When I have felt tempted to take a dim view of human nature I think of the hundreds of decent people I knew at Morley College.'[14] And even of her French and German opponents within the Women's International League she finally said:

> They were a body of high-minded women . . . I often crossed swords with [them] but I always respected and admired them, and I count it as one of the blessings of my life that . . . I had [always] such fine people to work with.[15]

1. See Sybil Oldfield, *Spinsters of This Parish: The Life and Times of F. M. Mayor and Mary Sheepshanks* (London, Virago, 1984), pp. 37 and 50.
2. *Ibid.*, p. 51.
3. *Ibid.*, ch. 4.
4. *Ibid.*, ch. 7.
5. For Mary Sheepshanks' account to Bertrand Russell of the rival nationalisms, imperialisms, militarism, authoritarianism and anti-Semitism, not to mention the secret police, that she encountered in Europe in 1913, see Oldfield, *op. cit.*, pp. 153–9.
6. *Ibid.*, pp. 177–9.
7. Mary Sheepshanks, unpublished autobiography, 'The long day ended', typescript in archives, Women's Library, London, quoted in Oldfield, *op. cit.*, p. 182.
8. Mary Sheepshanks not only published Emily Hobhouse's Open Christmas Letter to German Women in *Ius Suffragii* (January 1915), and their reply (March 1915), but she also sided with the

pacifist feminists in their support of the Women's International Congress: see Introduction and Appendix I.

9. Oldfield, *op. cit.*, pp. 185–8.
10. See entries for EGLANTYNE JEBB and DOROTHY BUXTON.
11. Oldfield, *op. cit.*, pp. 247–57.
12. Sheepshanks, *op. cit.*, ch. 20, quoted in Oldfield, *op. cit.*, pp. 263–7.
13. *Ibid.*
14. *Ibid.*, p. 288.
15. *Ibid.*

SIEFF, REBECCA, OBE
(23.2.1890–8.1.1966)

CO-FOUNDER OF ZIONISM; RESCUER OF JEWISH WOMEN AND CHILDREN

Father: Michael Marks, Russian Jewish refugee, licensed hawker, later successful entrepreneur, the co-founder of Marks and Spencer
Mother: Hannah, née Cohen

Liberal Jew

Rebecca ('Becky') Marks attended Manchester High School for Girls and, briefly, Manchester University, where she read English, but her 'real school was *The Manchester Guardian*, Hallé concerts and that grand group of people, men and women, who made up the circle of C. P. Scott. *The Manchester Guardian* was [her] second bible.'[1] She had been brought up at home in a spirit of committed, energetic altruism and solidarity with persecuted Jews; her father 'would go to the Docks to meet the ships bringing Jewish immigrants from Russia or Poland. Often he would come home without his overcoat having given it away.'[2] It was not, therefore, surprising that she and her young husband Israel Sieff should have been among the first converts before the First World War to their friend Chaim Weizmann's vision of 'Zion', the establishment of a permanent national home in Palestine for persecuted Jews. During the First World War Becky Sieff became one of the Manchester Daughters of Zion and raised funds both for Polish Jewish Relief and for the Restoration and Preparation Fund which preceded Keren Hayesod, the Jewish National Fund.

After the Balfour Declaration of 1917, Becky Sieff created in early 1919 the Federation of Women Zionists of the UK, which eventually led to the establishment of an international organization 'with the special objects of safeguarding the interests of women and children in Palestine', the Women's International Zionist Organization (WIZO).[3] She was not yet 30 but she both recognized and realized a rôle for women to support women in what was otherwise an exclusively masculine project. In 1920 she went with Israel Sieff and Chaim Weizmann on her first visit to Palestine, where she was appalled by the desperate poverty of the Jewish settlers: she found women driven into prostitution to support their starving families; others were mending roads and breaking stones.[4] Throughout the 1920s, by now a dynamic, wealthy society hostess in London, she raised funds to found in Palestine a major agricultural and domestic science school for Jewish girls, infant welfare centres, and facilities for the education of Jewish women, especially in Hebrew. The original – and continuing – policy of WIZO was 'to include all people, whether

Young and old traumatized Jewish survivors arriving from Europe at a WIZO reception camp in Israel, 1948 (from Rosalie Gassman-Sherr, The Story of the Federation of Women Zionists of Great Britain and Ireland, *Federation of Women Zionists, 1968. Courtesy of WIZO)*

Arab, Christian, Circassian or Jewish in their welfare work', giving help to anyone who asked.[5]

Then came 1933. 'Rebecca Sieff's concern, starting with the persecution of the Jews, broadened to include all Hitler's victims – liberals, socialists, trade unionists and Christian dissenters.'[6] She abhorred all racial oppression. She set up a Women's Appeal Committee to work in conjunction with the Central British Fund for German Jewry in the special interests of women and children. Through her personal efforts for Youth Aliyah, 1,000 Jewish children from Germany, including many older girls, and 500 Jewish families from Czechoslovakia were rescued. At the last pre-war WIZO Conference in Geneva in 1939 she said:

> Come what may, a remnant of the Jewish people will survive and will, as they have done throughout the ages, help to keep alight, together with those other standard-bearers of civilisations who belong to the Christian faith or to any other religious or national group, the torch of civilisation. The torch may grow dim – we know not – but it will not be extinguished.[7]

In November 1943, faced by revelations of the deliberate hunting down and extermination of Jewish children as if they were not children at all but merely a kind of vermin, she cried out:

> We meet . . . in the knowledge that our people have suffered a calamity which transcends in magnitude all those tragic events in the centuries of [the] long drawn-out agony of our people . . . And if it is true, as we have been told by one who escaped from the Ghetto of Warsaw, that not one single Jewish child remains alive in Poland, then indeed evil has reached its apotheosis and the darkest depths of man's mind [have been] plumbed.[8]

In September 1946 Becky Sieff went to Germany to spend the Jewish New Year with survivors, now displaced persons, at Bergen-Belsen. Not surprisingly, she was

220

more than ever committed to the establishment of a Jewish national state in Palestine 'so that never again shall our people be hopeless victims . . . forced to wander upon the face of the earth'.[9] From the time that Israel was founded in 1948 Becky Sieff moved there and made it her permanent home, working for women to be allowed to help politically in the construction of the new state. She continued to see that WIZO welfare activities included day care centres, youth clubs, women's clubs and vocational and cultural courses for non-Jewish women and children. Her funeral cortège in 1966 was over a mile long and included not only world leaders of Jewry but also delegations from nearby Arab and Druze villages.[10]

1. Becky Sieff, interviewed in *International Women's News* (October–November 1940).
2. Marie Nahum, 'The early years', *Jewish Woman's Review* (February 1966), p. 4.
3. P. Bookbinder and L. Marder, catalogue of exhibition 'Speaking for women: Rebecca Sieff and the WIZO movement' (Beth Hatefutsoth, The Nahum Goldmann Museum of the Jewish Diaspora, Tel Aviv, Winter 1990).
4. *Ibid.*
5. Andrea Epstein, Publications Co-ordinator, British WIZO, letter to author (2.3.1998).
6. Jennie Lee, MP, 'An appreciation of Rebecca Sieff', *Jewish Woman's Review* (February 1966), p. 2.
7. *Jewish Woman's Review* (February 1966), p. 5.
8. Bookbinder and Marder, *op. cit.*
9. *Ibid.*
10. See obituary, *The Times* (10.1.1966); *Jewish Woman's Review* (February 1966), p. 5; as well as Rosalie Gassman-Sherr, *The Story of the Federation of Women Zionists of Great Britain and Ireland 1918–1968* (London, Federation of Women Zionists, 1968).

SIMON, KATHLEEN ROCHARD, LADY, DBE
(1864(?)–27.3.1955)

CHAMPION OF SLAVES AND OTHER OPPRESSED PEOPLE

Father: Francis Eugene Harvey, of Kyle, Co. Wexford, Ireland
Mother: Frances Elizabeth, née Pollock

Born into Church of Ireland, later humanist

'For Lady Simon slavery was a flaming injustice. She could not live in peace in the same world with a single man who claimed another as his property.'[1] It was said of her that it was from her parents in Ireland that she originally inherited 'that love of liberty and hatred of servitude which inspired her every activity'.[2]

After first training as a nurse, Kathleen Harvey deliberately sought work in some of the grimmest areas of London in order to learn at first hand the conditions faced by the poorest mothers, both in childbirth and in struggling to rear their babies. Her first marriage, to Dr T. Manning, led to her living in Tennessee, 'where the racial discrimination that remained as the aftermath of slavery . . . made a deep impression on her'.[3] Her book *Slavery* (1929), written after she had been widowed and then become the second wife of Sir John, later Viscount, Simon, and dedicated to Amanda, a black girl she had met in Tennessee, 'caused a sensation by its exposure of slavery existing under the Union Jack'.[4] It included chapters on the slaves of Abyssinia, the Sudan, Arabia, Sierra Leone, China, Burma, and Nepal. A supplemental chapter in the second edition published the most recent evidence of the abuse of forced labour and suggested that she had originally underestimated the number of slaves in the world when she had put it at four million.

Dame Kathleen Simon, c. 1930
(Courtesy of Anti-Slavery
International)

As the ever-growing mass of material has passed before me, the impression of the immensity and urgency of the problem became deeper. I felt that it should be brought home to civilised humanity everywhere, what it means for a human being to be a mere property – a property to be raided, to be tortured, to be sold in the market to the highest bidder.[5]

The only solution she saw was effective international pressure and policing by the League of Nations.

Kathleen Simon did not only write; she also spoke tirelessly at meetings throughout Britain on behalf of the Anti-Slavery and Aborigines Protection Society, alerting the British public to what was still being perpetrated within the British Empire and explaining what Britain could do as a member of the League of Nations in order to intervene outside the Empire as well.[6] She was, perhaps, particularly incensed about the fate of the millions of girls in China, Malaysia, Hong Kong and Ceylon sold as *mui tsai*, 'adopted daughters', by impoverished parents into domestic servitude and thereafter effectively defenceless against the most extreme exploitation and cruelty, including in some cases brothel slavery (cf. CLARA HASLEWOOD and EDITH PICTON-TURBERVILL). In 1933 she was appointed DBE for her public work. But 1933 was also a terrible year for human rights in Europe, given the triumph of Nazism in Germany. In subsequent years Kathleen Simon also battled against the forces of anti-Semitism.

The dominant note of her life was a passion for liberty. This caused her to work on behalf of persecuted Jews, the Irish during the period of the Black-and-Tan [*sic*] in Ireland and for the abolition of slavery . . . She carried her [emancipatory] mission to Brazil, India, Egypt, Italy, France and Switzerland.[7]

1. Obituary, *The Annual Report of the Anti-Slavery Society* (31.3.1955).
2. Obituary, *The Times* (21.4.1955).
3. C. W. W. Greenidge, *Slavery* (London, Allen & Unwin 1958), p. 167.
4. Obituary, *The Times, op. cit.*
5. Kathleen Simon, *Slavery* (London, Hodder and Stoughton, 1929), Author's Foreword. See also her articles 'Britain's lead against slavery', *The Empire Review* (1930); and 'Slave cargoes – past and present', *The Trident* (July 1939). For her unpopular revelations about slavery under Haile Selassie in Abyssinia, see Suzanne Miers, 'Britain and the suppression of slavery in Ethiopia', *Slavery and Abolition: Journal of Slave and Post-Slave Studies*, **18** (3) (December 1997).
6. See *Anti-Slavery Reporter and Aborigines' Friend* (December 1933) for reports of Kathleen Simon's public lectures in the preceding October and November in Hull, Sale, Letchworth, Oxford, London

and Wisbech. See also entry for ALICE HARRIS above. Material on Kathleen Simon is held at the headquarters of Anti-Slavery International, Thomas Clarkson House, London SW9 9TL.
7. Extract from obituary, *Manchester Guardian* (28.3.1955), quoted in *Anti-Slavery Reporter* (May 1955), p. 23.

SIMPSON, ESTHER
('TESS'), OBE, Hon. LLD
(31.7.1903–19.11.1996)

RESCUER OF REFUGEES

Father: Ellis Simpson, originally Ilya
*   *Sinonovitch, textile worker from Lithuania*
Mother: Sara Liba, née Perevosnik

Quaker by convincement

Tess Simpson, c. 1940

A schoolgirl in the First World War, Tess Simpson had an elder brother who was a conscientious objector; through him she first met Quakers, who were to inspire her way of relating to people ever after. A gifted musician and linguist, after having graduated brilliantly in modern languages at Leeds, she taught herself the Gregg system of trilingual shorthand for English, French and German and became a sought-after secretary/translator/interpreter, first for the International Fellowship of Reconciliation in Vienna and then, briefly, for the World YMCA in Geneva.

Immediately on Hitler's accession to power Tess Simpson was alerted to the dismissal of German academics on the crassest racist grounds and asked one of the exiled, Leo Szilard, if there were any useful work she could do for the newly established Academic Assistance Council just founded in London to help such persecuted scholars. She started work there on 17 July 1933 and did not stop for the next 60 years.[1] 'What was happening [in Germany] . . . was anti-human and I wanted to do something to mitigate against that . . . Each [refugee organization] could only do so much but of course I felt terrible about the plight of others.'[2] The Academic Assistance Council (in 1936 renamed the Society for the Protection of Science and Learning) was run, not exclusively by British Jews for German Jews, but by British scholars to rescue other scholars regardless of their race, nationality or political or religious creed. Tess Simpson became a one-woman reception centre, accommodation bureau and specialized academic re-employment exchange for something like 2,600 refugee intellectuals between 1933 and 1940. Some of them were to become the most eminent people in their field in the world, but all were Tess Simpson's 'children'. They arrived in Britain rejected, nearly destitute, traumatized by humiliation and hatred, with apparently no prospects. She greeted them with warmth, sympathy, a highly cultured intelligence, and immense practical help, and set them 'on the stairway to survival and success'.[3] For many she found sanctuary and employment in Britain; for others she found a new life, first of all in small colleges in the United States or in universities in the British Commonwealth. For almost all of them, their broken lives were mended. 'I really look upon her as one of the great therapists of our society.'[4]

In 1940, after the fall of Norway, the British War Administration, headed by Churchill, panicked about the 'enemy aliens' in their midst and decided to 'collar the lot'.[5] Tess Simpson was appalled to learn that over 500 of 'her' refugee scholars, many of them now doing work of national importance and anti-Nazis to a man, were about to be arrested and interned in camps behind barbed wire, and that they even risked deportation. Her protests to the Home Office were futile; it was to take a year of non-stop day-and-night lobbying, letter-writing and interviews, all backed by the most meticulous documentation attesting the integrity of each individual 'case', before Tess Simpson, aided by Professor A. V. Hill, Vice-President of the Executive Committee of the Society and MP for Cambridge University, and ELEANOR RATHBONE, succeeded in having all the interned intellectuals released. 'Do you know the story of Bruce and the spider? I am that spider.'[6]

From 1944 until 1966 Tess Simpson worked as secretary of the Society for Visiting Scientists. She continued to aid refugee scholars, whether they were forced to flee Czechoslovakia in 1948, Hungary in 1956, apartheid South Africa after 1960, Czechoslovakia again in 1968, or Poland, Chile, Greece, Brazil, Argentina, Bangladesh, Zambia, Rhodesia, Iraq, Iran or China – in fact, wherever a brutal regime targeted independent-minded, critical intellectuals.[7] It was said of her that all her refugees and their families were living inside her head and that she used her quite phenomenal memory to work out which contacts could best enable them all to fulfil their potential. 'She always thought the best of everyone.'[8]

Tess Simpson retired as a voluntary Secretary of the Society for the Protection of Science and Learning when she was 75. 'Calm, lively and forthcoming to the end',[9] she was still working unofficially for 'the cause' at 93. 'I cannot think of anyone else with the same combination of warm affection for the individual scholars and iron toughness in the face of officialdom'[10] – *un esprit dur, un coeur tendre*.[11]

1. Ray M. Cooper (ed.), *Refugee Scholars: Conversations with Tess Simpson* (London, Moorland Books, 1992), pp. 29–39.
2. Interview with Tess Simpson, *The Times* (1.7.1992).
3. Obituary, *Hampstead and Highgate Express* (November/December 1996).
4. Sir Gordon Wolstenholme, speaking at a reception for Tess Simpson at the Ciba Foundation (2.7.1992) (Ciba is a scientific and educational charity established in 1949 in London as part of the Novartis Foundation to promote the general knowledge of science and to encourage international co-operation in scientific research).
5. See Peter and Leni Gillman, *'Collar the Lot!' How Britain Interned and Expelled Its Wartime Refugees* (London, Quartet Books, 1980); and Cooper, *op. cit.*, pp. 134–92.
6. Letter from Tess Simpson (9.7.1940), in Cooper, *op. cit.*, p. 134.
7. Interview with Tess Simpson, in Cooper, *op. cit.*, pp. 46–7.
8. Personal communication to the author from Andrée Hastings.
9. Obituary, *Independent* (24.12.1996).
10. Dr Max Perutz, OM, speaking at a reception for Tess Simpson at the Ciba Foundation (2.7.1992).
11. 'A tough spirit, a tender heart': the motto of the German Resistance martyr Sophie Scholl.

See also obituaries for Tess Simpson in *Guardian* (30.11.1996); *The Times* (30.11.1996); *Daily Telegraph* (3.12.1996); and *Jewish Chronicle* (13.12.1996).

SLADEN, MOTEE BOOTH-TUCKER, COMMISSIONER

(SALVATION ARMY)
(14.8.1891–6.4.1975)

ORGANIZER OF RELIEF FOR
REFUGEES AND DISPLACED PERSONS,
FINLAND AND WESTERN EUROPE

Father: General Frederick Booth-Tucker,
Salvation Army
Mother: Consul Emma Booth-Tucker, Salvation
Army, née Booth, youngest daughter of
William and Catherine Booth

Commissioner Motee Booth-Tucker
Sladen, Salvation Army, c. 1945

After the Soviet Union had invaded and defeated Finland in 1940, the Salvation Army co-ordinated relief efforts for the people then fleeing their burnt farms and destroyed villages to find asylum in the far north. Motee ('pearl') Sladen, cousin of MARY and OLIVE BOOTH, reported back on the Calvary road she witnessed in northern Finland:

> One felt the chill darkness of tragedy and heartbreak . . . we met hundreds of thousands of people . . . Convoys of lorries, . . . piled high with furniture [and] mattresses. Mothers and children sat on top in the bitterly cold wind . . . The wayside was lined with furniture dumped in the snow, and with cows and calves that had died from exhaustion and cold.[1]

She oversaw the Salvation Army distribution of emergency food and clothing in Lappeenranta, Mikkeli, Savonlinna, Joensuu and Varkaus before returning to Helsingfors. In December 1945 she returned to Finland, travelling from Helsinki to Rovaniemi, again seeing the devastated towns and villages and people sheltering in cellars and cardboard tents, and she promised increased aid for the Finnish people in their Arctic climate.[2]

Meanwhile, from 1942 to 1944, she and her husband Commissioner Hugh Sladen had been given responsibility for Salvation Army relief work in Europe. In co-operation with the Red Cross, the Friends' Ambulance Unit, the Save the Children Fund and other organizations, they formed a Council for British Societies for Relief Abroad that trained specialized relief teams to go into each west European country once it had been liberated from Nazi occupation. They began in Holland with soup canteens for the starving and house-to-house visits to mothers, children and old people too weak to walk to the canteens. In July 1945 Motee Sladen visited the 'work of mercy' in Holland, Belgium and France, and also oversaw the Salvation Army's first relief efforts for starving German mothers and children, including 700 destitute orphans, in the British Zone.

A mother with a Salvation Army officer,
Germany, c. 1945

Mother and child reunited through Salvation
Army tracing agency, Prague, 1945

Our first concern is for those whose sufferings have been almost beyond human endurance . . . Unknown millions are far from their homes − of these a great many have been prisoners of war, inmates of concentration camps, forced labourers in alien lands, refugees from battle, from cruelty, from starvation . . . In many countries confusion and chaos have followed the cessation of hostilities. In such circumstances those who go to help must be prepared to experience hardship and discomfort, conditions which may be at first very similar to or worse than those endured after heavy air raids . . .

The [Salvation] Army will help mainly with Mass Feeding, Distribution of Clothing . . . Child Welfare, Investigation, Information and Case Work, tracing and reuniting missing relatives, etc.[3]

'We are soldiers of the love that overcomes hatred', as Evangeline Booth had said in 1939.

Commissioner Motee Sladen and her husband retired from organizing this mammoth relief operation, comprising 150 Salvation Army officers and relief workers in Belgium, Holland, France, Germany, Poland, Czechoslovakia and Austria, in 1948. She was awarded the Order of the White Rose of Finland for her work after the Russo-Finnish War, and in 1975 the Finnish Consul was present at her funeral, where the band played 'Finlandia'.

1. Motee Sladen, 'The unknown road', *The War Cry* (15.6.1940).
2. Motee Sladen, 'Salvation Army overseas relief', BBC Overseas Broadcast to Finland (22.3.1946).

3. Anon. (probably drafted by Hugh and Motee Sladen), 'The Salvation Army European Relief Correspondence Training Course', *European Relief Study Papers*, nos. 1 and 2, Salvation Army International Heritage Centre, London.

See also obituary, *The Times* (8.4.1975); and Mary Batchelor, *Catherine Bramwell-Booth* (Tring, Lion, 1986); Stanley and Kathleen Preece, *The Lost Is Found* (Caron, 1990*).*

<hr>

SNOWDEN, ETHEL ANNAKIN

(1880–22.2.1951)

SOCIALIST; FEMINIST PACIFIST; TRAVELLER; SPEAKER AND WRITER FOR INTERNATIONAL RECONCILIATION

Father: Richard Annakin, builder, Mayor of Harrogate, JP
Mother: — ('my noble and heroic mother')

Eventually a Quaker by convincement

In 1900 young Ethel Annakin, a student teacher in Liverpool, was converted to socialism by the Radical Temperance preacher Dr Aked, on hearing his sermon 'Can a man be a Christian on £1 a week?' Thereafter she combined school teaching with Temperance campaigning in the slums and with public speaking for the Independent Labour Party. In 1905 she married Philip Snowden, the Labour Party's expert thinker on finance, who became one of the first Labour MPs in 1906 and who was converted by Ethel to the justice of women's campaign for the vote.

Ethel Snowden was a convinced Christian pacifist. 'I believed with all the intensity of conviction that evil could not be wholly destroyed by evil . . . Militarism by militarism.'[1] During the First World War she therefore took the unpopular side, resigning, with other leading suffragists, in protest against the refusal of Mrs Fawcett and her supporters to back the Women's International Congress at The Hague in April 1915.[2] Even more courageously, she ran the gauntlet of police bans and violently hostile crowds as she constantly traversed the country, addressing huge meetings of the Women's Peace Crusade in favour of a negotiated, just and lasting peace.[3]

Between January 1919 and January 1921 Ethel Snowden went on an extraordinary, gruelling 'pilgrimage', including Berlin, Zürich, Geneva, Stockholm, Paris and Petrograd, in order to 'at least attempt to restore good feeling between the nations'.[4]

> Elected to the Labour Party's women's section of the National Executive . . . [she] went to Berne and to Vienna in various attempts to re-establish a united Socialist International. She went to [Soviet] Russia as a member of an official TUC/Labour Party committee of inquiry. She went to the short-lived Social-Democrat Republic of Georgia . . . *The Manchester Guardian* described her in 1922 as 'internationally the best-known British woman'.[5]

Ethel Snowden wrote reports home on the appalling consequences for German and Austrian children of Britain's part in the continued Allied Blockade; and she tried to intervene personally on behalf of Austrian and Hungarian prisoners of war still stranded in Siberia. While scathingly condemnatory of Britain's attempt to defeat Bolshevism by military means, she also dared to call a terrorizing, totalitarian spade a terrorizing, totalitarian spade when writing of the Bolsheviks' *coup d'état* and secret police.[6] (She was never elected to the Labour Party National Executive again.)

She took up the cudgels for the pathologically hated Jews: 'The outrageous anti-Jewish propaganda which is being conducted all over the world is a disgrace to our modern civilization.'[7] She faced much aggressive hostility from anti-British nationalists, both in Germany and in an Ireland still occupied by the Black-and-Tans, feeling shocked and ashamed of her country's policies and actions and promising to publicize them in Britain. Her approach in all this was expressed in her declaration: 'I want to shake hands with everybody . . . who is willing . . . to help to mend a broken world.'[8] She became 'one of the finest speakers of what the Americans call the "inspirational" type'.[9]

Ethel Snowden's credo in 1922 reads tragically at the beginning of the twenty-first century but still has relevance for us:

I believe that the system called Capitalism will have to give place some day to a collectivist internationalism which shall secure life and the fruits of the earth to its populations in proportion to their needs . . . Such things as are fundamental to life itself – land, minerals and means of communication – should not be at the disposal and under the control of a small number of private persons . . .[10]

A stable internationalism can be built only upon a universal recognition of partnership in the [war] guilt which has laid the world so low . . . *total disarmament by all the nations* is the only rational solution of the problems of peace and war. Such action may have to be gradual; it must certainly be taken in concert . . .

It may be that men and women will have to wade through oceans of suffering before they recognize modern warfare for the organized filthiness it is.[11]

1. Mrs Philip Snowden, *A Political Pilgrim in Europe* (London, Cassell, 1921), p. xi.
2. See Appendix I.
3. See entries for MARGARET ASHTON, SELINA COOPER, MAUDE ROYDEN and HELENA SWANWICK; and Jill Liddington, *The Long Road to Greenham* (London, Virago, 1989), ch. 6.
4. Snowden, *op. cit.*, p. x.
5. Colin Cross, *Philip Snowden* (London, Barrie and Rockliff, 1966), p. 168. See also Snowden, *op. cit., passim.*
6. See Mrs Philip Snowden, *Through Bolshevik Russia* (London, Cassell, 1920), pp. 7, 8, 11, 63, 141, 153 and 188.
7. Snowden, *A Political Pilgrim in Europe*, p. 181.
8. *Ibid.*, p. 163.
9. Mary Agnes Hamilton, *Remembering My Good Friends* (London, Cape, 1944), p. 114.
10. Snowden, *A Political Pilgrim in Europe*, p. 143.
11. *Ibid.*, pp. 271–4.

See also obituaries for Ethel Snowden, *The Times* (24.2.1951); and by Emmeline Pethick-Lawrence, *Manchester Guardian* (24.2.1951).

———

STARR, LILIAN
(later **UNDERHILL**)
(1886–1977)

MISSIONARY NURSE IN NORTH-WEST FRONTIER/AFGHANISTAN

Father: Reverend T. R. Wade, missionary in Peshawar
Mother: Anna, née Blake, Zenana medical missionary

Anglican

Born and brought up in the Himalayas and with an unusual knowledge of the language (Pushtu) and customs of the Pathans, Lilian Starr, having trained as a nurse at Norwich Hospital and in London, went out to join the Church Missionary Society's Afghan Mission Hospital in Peshawar in 1913. In 1915 she married the missionary doctor there, Vernon Starr, of whom it was said he was a man always overworked, often tired, but always optimistic and cheerful. On 17 March 1918 Dr Starr was murdered by mistake by an Afridi who had seen him at the door of the operating theatre with blood on his hands and believed that Dr Starr had murdered the patient, his kinsman.[1] Lilian Starr was then sent to do war service in the Indian Military Hospital in Cairo, nursing Indian troops. She had always wanted to continue working in Peshawar, however, and in 1920 she was permitted to return.

Lilian Starr's workload consisted of tending difficult maternity cases as well as male patients needing cataract operations, treatment for tetanus, gunshot wounds (from inter-family feuds), and amputation after gangrene had set in. The hospital staff continued their seven-day working week, sometimes in temperatures of 120°F, for years, despite their almost total lack of success in Christian conversion.

In 1923 Lilian Starr volunteered for a rescue mission to find an English girl kidnapped by Pathans who had just murdered the girl's mother in outrage that her father, a British officer, should have interrogated the Pathans' womenfolk concerning stolen guns. An intrepid traveller, who had already trekked by pony to Ladakh in Lesser Tibet during the preceding year, Lilian Starr was dressed as a Peshwari woman and succeeded in leading a group of 'loyal' North-West Frontier tribesmen across the frontier, where the writ of the British army did not run, to secure the girl's safe release. She was awarded the Kaiser-i-Hind medal and the life-saving medal of the Order of St John of Jerusalem.[2]

In 1924 Lilian Starr married Lt Col. G. E. C. Underhill of the First Punjabis. In 1928 she reported to the Joshi All-India Commission on child marriage:

> In Kashmir . . . many girls aged eleven or twelve are brought in labour to our hospital. They are often *in extremis* and quite unable to bear living children without the skilled operation of caesarian section. Undoubtedly many do not reach us and die in labour.[3]

Lilian Starr left India in 1929. She 'was perhaps the last of the great missionary characters of the Frontier'.[4]

1. An alternative version of events was that Dr Starr had been murdered in revenge for the conversion of a Muslim boy: see Basil Mathews, 'An appreciation' in Lilian Starr, *Tales of Tirah and Lesser Tibet* (London, Hodder and Stoughton, 1923), p. 17.
2. See Starr, *op. cit.*
3. Eleanor Rathbone, *Child Marriage: The Indian Minotaur* (London, George Allen and Unwin, 1934), p. 32.
4. Obituary, *Daily Telegraph* (7.1.1977).

For an account of mission and other hospitals in the Indian sub-continent during the first half of the twentieth century, see Alice Wilkinson, *A Brief History of Nursing in India and Pakistan* (Madras, Trained Nurses' Association of India, 1958).

STEPHENSON, ELSIE
(22.11.1916–16.7.1967)

RED CROSS NURSE IN AFTERMATH OF WAR

Father: Henry Stephenson, farmer, died of flu 1918
Mother: Ethel

Anglican

After failing her School Certificate and returning home to help her widowed mother, Elsie Stephenson still persevered in her determination to become a nurse. Having trained at West Suffolk General Hospital, Bury St Edmunds (1935–37), and done extra study in public health, she became an exemplary health visitor before joining the British Red Cross Civilian Relief group to work in the Middle East early in 1944.

Thousands of refugees – Poles, Greeks, Maltese and Yugoslavs, most of them destitute and sick women and children – had been arriving at camps around Egypt since 1942. On arriving in the desert in 1944, Elsie Stephenson had to train quickly with UNRRA on how to purify water, combat typhus, cook on mobile field stoves and disinfect individuals and whole villages of vermin. She then spent six months in Khatatba refugee camp in the desert, which served over 15,000 refugees. Whenever she came across a likely girl or woman with any background in nursing or literacy, she would enrol her as a charge nurse to help in achieving the impossible. At the end of 1944 she moved on to help in liberated Yugoslavia, where she met Dr KATHERINE MACPHAIL.

After a brief furlough in Britain at the end of the war, Elsie Stephenson joined Mobile Hospital no. 5 of the British Red Cross Civilian Relief as Senior Sister serving the needs of displaced persons, including concentration camp survivors, in the snow of Bad Münder, north Germany. 'Many of the patients in the hospital were broken people, in spirit, in mind, in body.'[1] Many of them could not bring themselves to accept care from German doctors or nurses. Elsie Stephenson's first duty was therefore to build trust again from scratch. She visited every ward to say goodnight to the patients before going off duty; she was with every dying patient in their last moments. 'Elsie's work, like that of all other relief workers at that time, was to put the lid back on Hell and to help people live normal lives again.'[2] Despite her horror at the revelations of Nazi Belsen, she went next to Berlin in 1946 to head the child welfare team there.

In 1947 and 1948 Elsie Stephenson was sent on many international advisory missions by the Red Cross, but first she advised on building up nursing and welfare services in the American Zone of Germany. The morale of German Red Cross nursing staff was at a low ebb after the Nazi party had appropriated the charity and tried to 'Nazify' it. Elsie Stephenson reminded the pale, overworked nurses in hungry, bombed-out Germany of their country's proud earlier record in the history of nursing: of Pastor Fliedner and the deaconesses at Kaiserswerth who had inspired Florence Nightingale. She talked to them as an equal: 'daily we can learn, and I am sure that you will agree that in nursing we never cease learning.'[3] Oberin [Sister] Tobroth of Marburg spoke for all of them, touchingly grateful for being reintegrated into the universalist principles of Red Cross nursing: 'We have . . . to thank you for the friendly statement concerning the inclusion of the German Sisters in the world-wide circle of all Sisters, and helping them take part in the general work.'[4]

Elsie Stephenson in Berlin, 1946 (From Sheila Allan, Fear Not to Sow, *The Jamieson Library, 1990)*

Elsie Stephenson continued to work for Red Cross and World Health Organization advisory missions on the training and establishment of nursing and welfare sevices throughout the world. She made strenuous visits to Singapore, Sarawak and Brunei, as well as to many countries in Eastern Europe. A Fellow of the Royal Society of Health, she also set up the first degree in nursing studies and directed it at the University of Edinburgh between 1956 and 1967. She died prematurely of breast cancer at the age of 51.

Her definition of a nurse was: 'A listener, a doer, someone who tries to understand the physical, mental and spiritual needs of man from infancy to old age.'[5]

1. Sheila Allan, *Fear Not to Sow: A Life of Elsie Stephenson* (Newmill, Cornwall, The Jamieson Library, 1990), ch. 5.
2. *Ibid.*
3. *Ibid.*, ch. 8.
4. *Ibid.* See also entry for ELAINE HILLS-YOUNG.
5. Allan, *op. cit.*, ch. 1.

STEWART-MURRAY, KATHARINE, DUCHESS OF ATHOLL, DBE
(6.11.1874–21.10.1960)

CHAMPION OF VICTIMS OF FASCISM AND STALINISM

Father: Sir James Ramsay, Bart
Mother: Charlotte, née Stewart, from an Indian army family

Church of Scotland

An aristocratic Conservative and Unionist, a loyal army officer's wife, an anti-feminist, an imperialist opposed to Home Rule for Ireland or for India,[1] who saw the 1920s miners' strike as a problem for the Chancellor of the Exchequer Stanley Baldwin rather than for the miners, the Duchess of Atholl might at first appear nothing more than a feudal-minded reactionary. But to the amazement of political allies and opponents alike, she evolved into a crusading, radical humanitarian force to be reckoned with, and sacrificed her own political career in the process. '[The] fire which smouldered in her small body . . . burned through party loyalties, social conventions, hereditary prejudices and landed her in strange company.'[2]

The first intimation that there was a vigorous, independent-minded humanitarian tendency in the Duchess appeared already in 1912 when she was invited by the Scottish Office to join a committee investigating medical and nursing services in the Highlands and Islands. On discovering such services to be woeful or lacking altogether, and, instead of decent health provision, 'overcrowded houses with endemic TB, undernourished children, inadequate hospital accommodation and overworked doctors',[3] her committee urged the setting up of an adequately funded Highlands Central Authority to remedy the situation. In 1917 she turned her attention to the education of Scottish tinkers' children, recommending the provision of better winter housing and the installation of an educational inspector to see that the children had at least part-time schooling, recommendations that were not implemented until the 1940s.[4]

Katharine Stewart-Murray, Duchess of Atholl, c. 1925 (Courtesy of Blair Castle Archive)

Elected the first woman MP for Scotland in 1923 (for the Conservative and Unionist Party, representing the constituency of Perth and Kinross of which her husband the Duke was Party Branch President), the Duchess of Atholl soon found herself sent to Geneva as the woman member of Austen Chamberlain's delegation to the League of Nations. On the one hand she struggled successfully 'to secure the continuance of the rescue work on behalf of Armenian women and children at Aleppo, which was being carried on 'by a very fine little Danish lady Miss Jeppe',[5] but on the other she blocked an irrigation project in the Armenian Republic of the Soviet Union, though she did agree to feasibility investigations. The Duchess became identified at the beginning of the 1930s with hostility to the Soviet Union. Her book *The Conscription of a People* (1931), which took almost all its facts either from official Soviet documents or from the sworn statements of refugees, was one of the first, if not *the* first substantiated indictment of Stalin's *Gulag* system of forced labour camps with their freezing, underfed 'ragged, lice-infested prisoners'[6] – an indictment all too easily thought by the Left to be invalidated by the Duchess's class position.

In 1933, influenced both by the Russianist Sir Bernard Pares and by her reading of translations from *Mein Kampf*, the Duchess of Atholl was convinced that the greatest threat to Britain, to European democracy and to humane civilization now came less from Stalin than from Hitler. She personally published the more alarming passages from *Mein Kampf*, concerning his unapologetic, aggressive expansionism, that had been omitted from a sanitized English translation.[7] She now found that many of those who had endorsed her criticisms of Stalin were wilfully blind to the criminality and threat of Hitler, and she was dropped as one of the three Presidents of the Christian Protest Movement, which wanted to focus only on the persecution of religion in Russia. She also found herself losing support among her personal as well as her political acquaintances.

Undeterred, in 1936 the Duchess went with ELEANOR RATHBONE,[8] with whom she now began to make common cause against Hitler, on a fact-finding parliamentary delegation to Czechoslovakia, Yugoslavia and Romania, where she was swiftly educated about the virulent anti-Semitism and fascist sympathies there that were hostile to the embattled democratic and liberal forces in central and eastern Europe. The 'great lesson of our trip had been the danger faced by Europe as a whole'[9] and the need for Britain to stand by the democratic forces. The Spanish Civil War now challenged the British government precisely on this issue. Together with Eleanor Rathbone and ELLEN WILKINSON, the Duchess of Atholl set up an All-Party Committee for Spanish Relief. With the other two non-Conservatives and Dame RACHEL CROWDY, she visited Barcelona and Madrid, which was then being shelled: 'I found myself thinking most of the plight of the children.'[10] She broadcast appeals for help for them; in direct consequence of her sympathy for Republican Spain, she was hauled before a body called the National Citizens' Union (founded to oppose independence for India) and 'arraigned': she was dropped as their Vice-President. She then worked to provide asylum in Britain for 4,000 Basque children, many of whose parents had been killed, imprisoned or disappeared in their flight as refugees in France. Helped by the Salvation Army, the Friends' Service Council, the Trades Union Congress and the Save the Children Fund, the Duchess was tireless in speaking and raising funds. In June 1938 she published her immensely successful *Searchlight on Spain*, which spelt out the long-planned fascist support for Franco from Italy and Germany. While she was in Vienna and Budapest early in 1938, speaking on behalf of international peace and for the League of Nations, her 'views on Spain had not gone unnoticed in [her] constituency'.[11] She had been attacked by a Catholic for being anti-Franco, but she was temporarily permitted to express her own views on foreign policy. In April 1938 the Prime Minister Neville Chamberlain withdrew the Party whip from her. Next, she was accused of singing 'The Red Flag' at a meeting in Glasgow where she appealed for relief for Spanish children. In fact she did not know the tune or the words and had already left the hall, but she was dropped as the Conservative candidate for the 'safe' seat of Perth and Kinross nonetheless. It was even spread about in the Commons that she was a Communist! She then stood as an Independent against a local laird, and was supported on her election platform, which stressed the urgent need for collective security with France and Russia against Hitler, by the Dean of Chichester, VIOLET BONHAM CARTER, Eleanor Rathbone and Winston Churchill, among others. Nevertheless she lost: 'It was a blow . . . and I inflicted on tolerant friends that evening performances of Beethoven's Waldstein and Appassionata Sonatas.'[12] Early in March 1939 – just a fortnight before Hitler's invasion of Czechoslovakia – she gave personal asylum to a refugee from Prague who had earlier had to flee Vienna: 'When I returned home and told Ilsa what had happened, she sobbed in my arms.'[13]

Later that year the Duchess travelled to southern France to see off thousands of Spanish political prisoners embarking with their families for exile in Mexico. In the Second World War she grieved desperately over the betrayal of the Poles, and wrote an account of the Warsaw Rising. Her last cause was to publicize the fate of returned Soviet prisoners and countless other east Europeans suspect to Stalin and locked in tightly sealed trucks for their repatriation east to forced labour in the *Gulag*. She also took on an immense load of case-work supporting east European refugees who had reached Britain. From 1944 until her death she was the Chairman of the British League for European Freedom, which made her, instead of a 'Red' in the eyes of Conservatives, a 'reactionary' in the eyes of the Left. But 'behind her demure exterior she had a nerve peculiarly sensitive . . . to cruelty and oppression . . . [and] cruelty was cruelty by whomsoever committed'.[14]

The Duchess of Atholl was a braw fighter and her own woman; it is impossible to categorize her with the simple political label of Left or Right. Her humanitarianism determined her stand, and once convinced, she was immovable, no matter how isolated she was then forced to be. 'She was small and rather hawk-like, high-principled and very sincere, . . . highly strung and intense, [she] was one of the most dedicated and interesting women to sit in the Commons.'[15]

1. The Duchess's wariness about India could hardly have been unaffected by the fact that both her maternal grandparents had been murdered during the Indian Mutiny.
2. Mary Stocks, 'Katharine Stewart-Murray, Duchess of Atholl, public servant', in the *Dictionary of National Biography, 1951–1960*.
3. Duchess of Atholl, *Working Partnership: Being the Lives of John George, 8th Duke of Atholl and of His Wife Katharine Marjory Ramsay* (London, Arthur Barker Ltd, 1958), p. 70.
4. *Ibid.*, pp. 102–5. She was also concerned ten years later about the educational and safety needs of canal boat children, whom she visited on behalf of the NSPCC in 1928 and whose cause she, along with Ellen Wilkinson, took up in Parliament until it was eventually addressed in the Education Act of 1944.
5. *Ibid.*, p. 149.
6. *Ibid.*, pp. 184–5. The Duchess also publicized the deportation of ethnic Germans within the Soviet Union (in her pamphlet *Out of the Deep*) and the appalling famine on Stalin's orders in the Ukraine: see p. 188–9 and 197.
7. *Ibid.*, p. 201.
8. The Duchess had already made common cause with Eleanor Rathbone in 1930, on the issue of enforced genital mutilation of Kikuyu girls in Kenya, as well as elsewhere in British Africa: see *ibid.*, pp. 176–8. She was appalled by the consequences for maternal ill health and mortality in childbirth.
9. *Ibid.*, p. 207.
10. *Ibid.*, p. 212.
11. *Ibid.*, p. 217.
12. *Ibid.*, p. 230. The Duchess was a gifted musician and had earlier shown promise not just as a pianist but also as a composer, especially of songs.
13. *Ibid.*, p. 231.
14. Stocks, *op. cit.* See also Duchess of Atholl, *The Tragedy of Warsaw and Its Documentation* (32pp.; London, John Murray, 1945).
15. Pamela Brookes, *Women at Westminster: An Account of Women in the British Parliament 1918–1966* (London, Peter Davies, 1967), pp. 42 and 122–3.

See also *The Spectator* (23.7.1937); obituary, *The Times* (22.10.1960); and the political biography of the Duchess by S. J. Hetherington, *Katharine Atholl, 1874–1960: Against the Tide* (Aberdeen University Press, 1989).

A collection of her papers is held at Blair Castle, Blair Atholl, Pitlochry, Perthshire PH18 5TL. They are listed by the Scottish Record Office, Reference N.R.A. (S)980; requests for access should be sent to Blair Castle.

STOPES, MARIE D.Sc.

(15.10.1880–2.10.1958)

PIONEER OF BIRTH CONTROL

Father: Henry Stopes, engineer and brewery architect
Mother: Charlotte, née Carmichael, Shakespearian scholar and suffragist

Brought up Christian, turned to belief in reincarnation of the exceptional soul

---

To exclude Marie Stopes from this book because of her undeniably 'difficult' personality would be perverse. As she herself wrote: 'What chains of slavery are, have been, or ever could be so intimate a horror as the shackles on every limb, on every thought, on the very soul of an unwillingly pregnant woman?'[1] A virgin who hymned her fantasies of the joy of married sex in *Married Love* (1918), a childless woman who told women how to be 'wise parents' (also in 1918), Marie Stopes had the courage of her vanity and the pertinacity of her exceptional aggressiveness. Hence it was she who contributed 'more than any other single person to freeing women from the threat of unwanted pregnancies',[2] thus allowing women the essential pre-condition for deciding what to do with their lives.

Marie Stopes's own driving motivation was sexological and eugenic. She wanted wives to be enabled to enjoy heterosexual intercourse – which had to be intercourse without fear of impregnation – and she wanted the Empire to breed a superior, white 'race', unimpeded by excessive numbers of the poor and therefore medically under par. However there was also a streak, at least, of humanitarianism in her, strengthened by the pitiful letters she increasingly received from desperate working-class wives:

> I cannot go out to work becaus of the children, . . . they do not have enough to eat and I cannot get boots for them to wear . . . do you think it would be best if I leave my Husband and go into the workhouse until the children have grown up a bit so that we don't have any moor?
>
> *(pregnant 27-year-old wife of farm labourer*
> *on £1. 7 shillings a week)*[3]

Marie Stopes responded by giving the writer not only contraception pamphlets but money for children's boots. Helpful and sympathetic to people she did not know, Marie Stopes replied to all the people who appealed to her, men and women alike, equally and without blame, as victims of total ignorance and inhibition. (Her relations with the people she *did* know were almost uniformly catastrophic.) She always knew she was right and therefore her form of showing solicitude for human suffering or frustration was 'to put it right – in her own way'.[4]

A distinguished Doctor of Science specializing in palaeobotany and the structure of coal, Marie Stopes insisted on bringing an adult, scientific attitude to human reproduction and its control. Her approach, however, would not be confined to a few intellectual Malthusians but would reach millions of people through her unapologetic, punchy style.[5] Helped by her moneyed husband, the aviationist Humphrey Roe, she opened the first birth control clinic (for married women only) in the British Empire in March 1921 in Holloway, North London, and was not afraid to antagonize the closed shop of the medical profession by employing nurses and midwives rather than doctors to examine and advise the women patients. In

Marie Stopes with nurses at the Mothers' Clinic, Holloway, London, c. 1928

1923 and 1924 she fought a Roman Catholic convert, Dr Halliday Sutherland, through the courts. He had alleged that she was 'experimenting' in a medically harmful manner on women of the slums; she sued him for libel and although she lost the court case before reactionary judges, the huge national publicity did a lot of good for public knowledge of the possibility of contraception – and public opinion would, in turn, fuel the successful campaign for state support.

In 1918 contraception had been a taboo subject throughout the British Empire, with leading doctors warning that it could cause sterility and even insanity; just twelve years later, in 1930, the British Ministry of Health Memorandum 153 allowed birth control information to be given out at maternity and child welfare centres; the memorandum was usefully publicized by Marie Stopes herself in her paper *Birth Control News*. Although pressure from the Women's Co-operative Guild (see MARGARET LLEWELYN DAVIES), the 'new', social feminism of ELEANOR RATHBONE, the women's section of the Labour Party (see DORA RUSSELL) and other private family planning clinics (see HELENA WRIGHT) had also contributed greatly to this historic *volte-face*, it was Marie Stopes's unashamed crusade that had done most to inform the majority of people in Britain that birth control was not only desirable but possible. In theory at least, it would be possible after 1930 in Britain for 'every child to be a wanted child'.[6]

1. Marie Stopes's appeal to President Woodrow Wilson (September 1915) in support of Margaret Sanger, quoted in Ruth Hall, *Marie Stopes: A Biography* (London, André Deutsch, 1977), p. 117.
2. *Ibid.*, p. 307.
3. *Ibid.*, p. 179.
4. Mary Stocks, obituary for Dr Marie Stopes, *Family Planning* (January 1959). See also Mary Stocks, *Still More Commonplaces* (London, Peter Davies, 1973), ch. 3, for her vivid personal reminiscences of Marie Stopes.
5. See Marie Stopes, *Wise Parenthood* (1918); *A Letter to Working Mothers: On How to Have Healthy Children and Avoid Weakening Pregnancies* (1919); *Radiant Motherhood* (1920); *Contraception, Its Theory, History and Practice* (1923); *Mother England* (letters to Marie Stopes, edited by her; 1929); *Birth Control Today: A Practical Handbook for Those Who Want to Be Their Own Masters in This Vital Matter* (1934); etc.
6. See also Ruth Hall, *Dear Doctor Stopes – Sex in the 1920s: A Selection of Letters Written to Marie Stopes* (London, André Deutsch, 1978); and Lesley Hall, *Hidden Anxieties: Male Sexuality 1900–1950* (Cambridge, Polity Press, 1991). Obituary testimonies in *The Times* (3.10, 7.10, 8.10 and 16.10.1958).

STRUGNELL, ELEANOR
(31.1.1887–8.6.1993)

MISSIONARY TEACHER; SOCIAL
WORKER AMONG CHILEAN
INDIANS

Father: William Strugnell, gardener
Mother: Elizabeth, née Atkins, 'in service'

Anglican

Eleanor Strugnell in Chile in the 1930s

After qualifying as an elementary teacher, Eleanor Strugnell was employed as a private governess and teacher before finally persuading her parents to allow her to leave home and train as a missionary. At the age of 33 in 1920 she was accepted by the South American Missionary Society and sailed for Argentina to run a girls' orphanage in Alberdi. Six years later she was sent to Chile, where she spent the whole of the rest of her 106 years. In addition to Spanish, she learned the language of the Araucanian (Mapuche) Indians. She taught at local missionary schools and evangelized for basic hygiene as well as for the Gospel as she crossed the wild countryside every summer on horseback, living with the Indians. 'Race and class were no barrier to her.'[1]

In 1941, at the age of 54, she married elderly Canon William 'Daddy' Wilson, a retired medical missionary and a veteran successful campaigner for native land rights. Together they travelled the country by bullock cart loaded with medical supplies, Bibles, and a battery-powered magic lantern projector with which to show slides illustrating both health education and Christian teaching. 'They had no bullocks, so . . . if a community wanted a visit, they had to provide the ox-power. This they willingly did, and "Granny" and her husband were always on the move, always in constant demand.'[2]

After her husband's death in 1958 when she was 71, Eleanor Strugnell concentrated on prison visiting and on work among the elderly. In her eighties she started teaching English at the University of Temuco. When she had finally given up horse-riding, at 90, she would ride pillion on the back of her students' motor bikes in order to continue visiting remote regions. She continued to be active until she suffered a severe stroke at 98. 'She was a missionary of the old school, unassuming and willing to do anything.'[3]

Eleanor Strugnell's whole life in Argentina and Chile was devoted to the exploited poor and downtrodden, long before the British middle-class conscience had heard of the 'Third World'. She deserved the name by which she was known throughout South America: 'Granny Struggles'.

1. Douglas Milmine and Rebecca de Saintonge, obituary, *Independent* (15.6.1993).
2. *Ibid.*
3. Rt Rev. Douglas Milmine, former Bishop of Paraguay, quoted in obituary, *Daily Telegraph* (30.8.1993).

STURGE, MARY

(1862–14.3.1925)

PIONEER MEDICAL AND SOCIAL
REFORMER

Father: Wilson Sturge, Quaker businessman,
Mayor of Birmingham and peace
campaigner
Mother: Mary, née Lloyd, Quaker
philanthropist

Quaker

Dr Mary Sturge represents all those
women doctors whose humanitarianism
found expression 'only' in their general
practice in one restricted region: in Mary
Sturge's case, Edgbaston, Birmingham.
She started as a pioneer woman medical
student who had to struggle for qualification, first at Mason Science College,
Birmingham (1880–86), and then at the
London School of Medicine for Women,

Mary Sturge, MD (From British
Medical Women's Federation
Journal, *June/July 1925)*

permission to study at Birmingham Men's Medical School having been refused her.
She qualified in 1891 with honours and worked in the Women's Hospital, Euston
Road, the Clapham Maternity Hospital and the North Eastern Fever Hospital,
before starting general practice in Birmingham. She was also anaesthetist to the
Birmingham and Midland Hospital for Women (1895–1905) as well as its visiting
consultant physician until her own last illness.

In 1907, together with Sir Victor Horsley, Mary Sturge published *Alcohol and the
Human Body*, one of the first attempts to treat factually and scientifically the medical
aspects of alcohol abuse. It went through six editions and sold tens of thousands of
copies. She also testified for the BMA on the danger of medicated wines to the
Select Committee of the House of Commons on Patent Medicines.

Birmingham had thousands of very poor families and Mary Sturge believed in
doing all she could to relieve personally those she knew as 'a gift from one citizen
to another':[1]

> I have never known her to refuse assistance to a needy case, and not only did
> she help with money, but she gave of her vitality and sympathy as well. Indeed
> the time came, when, for fear of over-taxing her strength, I restrained myself
> from mentioning a case of monetary difficulty or one of a seeming injustice in
> her presence. Curiously enough, although she was often imposed upon by those
> who knew of her kind-heartedness, she never grew indifferent or cynical . . .
> [She] preferred to be defrauded rather than to turn away anyone in need.[2]

At the end of her working life Dr Mary Sturge was one of the founders of the
Taylor Memorial Home giving hospice and respite care for women suffering from
the last stages of inoperable cancer. The Medical Women's Federation's memorial
to her was the endowment of a bed there.

Dr. Mary Sturge was, above everything else, a lover of humanity. No condition of life was too poor or insignificant for her to be interested in and to help, and no great movement for the alleviation of distress was too important or too far-reaching for her to assist and forward if possible . . . 'these people are more unfortunate than we are, it is our duty to help'.[3]

At the large, loving, memorial gathering after her premature death '[one] after another rose and testified to her goodness, her lavish generosity, indomitable energy and fearlessness, her sympathy, wisdom, uprightness and single-minded devotion to [that] duty'.[4]

1. Mary Sturge, quoted by Dr Elizabeth Moffett in *British Medical Women's Federation Journal* (June/July 1925), p. 14.
2. Dr Rose Molloy, *ibid.*, pp. 16 and 17.
3. *Ibid.*, p. 17.
4. Dr Amy Sheppard, *ibid.*, p. 15.

See also obituary, *British Medical Journal* (28.3.1925).

STURGE, SOPHIA
(1849–17.1.1936)

ANTI-MILITARIST SOCIAL REFORMER

Father: Joseph Sturge, Quaker campaigner against slavery in the West Indies, peace campaigner
Mother: Hannah, née Dickinson, Quaker

Quaker, first by birth and later by reconvincement

An ardent, gifted young Victorian gentle-woman, allowed only to live at home or travel with friends, Sophia Sturge had felt all the frustrations of her class and gender. Her rebellion in religious terms took the form of leaving the Society of Friends for Anglicanism. Her politics became increasingly radical and her strong commitment to Home Rule for Ireland led her at last, at the age of 37, to visit Ireland and see whether there was anything she could do, however small, to serve its people wronged by her own country for so long. It was when she first saw a starving baby while travelling in Donegal in 1887 that she resolved to found

Sophia Sturge, painted in 1917 by Mr Deller, the Dartmoor conscientious objectors camp artist (From William Hughes, Sophia Sturge: A Memoir, George Allen & Unwin, 1940)

some new cottage industry in Ireland to provide a livelihood for the desperate peasant families. She spent the following year herself learning the craft of basket-making from a teacher of the blind and then researching all the details of the necessary equipment, tools, different methods of production both in Britain and on the Continent, as well as costing and marketing. In autumn 1888 she settled in Letterfrack, Connemara, to embark on what her family considered a totally quixotic scheme. Sophia Sturge stayed in Ireland for seven years, including the famine winter of 1890, and oversaw the establishment of a new trade that gave hope as well as money to the local boys and girls.[1] Called home by family circumstances in 1896, she had to face the fact that the enterprise could not survive without her and that emigration to America was taking all her most skilled young pupils. In 1899 she started a new attempt – toy-making – in Ballycastle, Antrim and in the most desolate islands of the Hebrides.[2]

Henceforth Sophia Sturge's chief humanitarian commitment would be in the field of the prevention of war and the mitigation of its cruelties. She supported EMILY HOBHOUSE as a maligned 'pro-Boer' in the Boer War and interceded successfully against the death penalty for a defeated Boer captured while trying to save a wounded comrade. Between 1904 and 1914 she studied and publicized the cause of establishing international justice and preventing wars by means of arbitration. Passionately in agreement with Norman Angell's attack on warfare, *The Great Illusion*, Sophia Sturge redoubled her efforts to have the prevention of war discussed in British universities and schools. In the last days of July 1914, now 65 years old, she helped organize the distribution of half a million leaflets in the streets of London, urging Britain not to yield 'to the war madness'. She failed, but, travelling back to Birmingham the day that war was declared, she immediately planned measures to help the German 'enemy' civilians now stranded in Britain. She urged Stephen Hobhouse to get the Society of Friends to found an 'Emergency Committee for the assistance of Germans, Austrians and Hungarians in distress'.[3] All 'enemy' males were soon interned and Sophia Sturge not only sent books, gardening and handicraft tools and materials to the men imprisoned on the Isle of Man but also concentrated on getting a safe passage home for their destitute wives and children, if they were German, or collecting money, clothes and Christmas presents for them if they were English and could not be repatriated to Germany. Naturally Sophia Sturge was a signatory of Emily Hobhouse's Christmas Letter to German Women and a supporter of the British Committee of the Women's International Congress at The Hague in 1915.[4]

As soon as conscription became law early in 1916, Sophia Sturge, soon once again to become a Quaker, felt compelled to help the war resisters. She visited army camps where she had heard that conscientious objectors were being brutally treated:

> I can give you no idea of what it was like to go into that cell, with the four bare walls and only three planks about three inches from the ground for a bed, and the one man lying on the stone floor . . . He said 'If I disobey orders . . . I shall be put in a dark cell with irons on.' . . . I said to the guard, 'You will be kind to these men; they are not cowards.'[5]

Her particular concern was to support those conscientious objectors who had agreed to do alternative, non-military work of national importance and about whose severe conditions she became the national expert. So many reports of abuses at Dartmoor had reached her that she determined to go and live on Dartmoor herself in 1917, offering hospitality, books, food, and even tea-parties on the moor, to the weakened, underfed men.[6]

After the war, now aged 70, Sophia Sturge went to Holland to help organize relief work for the defeated 'children of hunger'. She spent much of 1920–30 continuing her internationalist talks on the League of Nations and on the prevention of war through arbitration at countless public meetings and in secondary schools up and down the country. In 1933 she took a girl medical student, a refugee from Hitler, into her home. Her last Christmas message, when she was 87, read:

> This illness is hard to bear. The pain, however, has made me long that the many prayers that are being put up at this time shall be that men of science may work for the relief of suffering, rather than for the inventions of war that cause it.[7]

1. William R. Hughes, *Sophia Sturge: A Memoir* (London, George Allen & Unwin, 1940), ch. 2.
2. *Ibid.*, ch. 3.
3. See entry for KATE COURTNEY.
4. See Appendix I.
5. Hughes, *op. cit.*, pp. 136–7.
6. *Ibid.*, ch. 6; see also Jo Vellacott, *Bertrand Russell and the Pacifists in the First World War* (Sussex, Harvester, 1980).
7. Obituary, *The Friend* (February 1936). See also 'Great social and peace worker', obituary, *Birmingham Gazette* (18.1.1936).

SWANWICK, HELENA, CH
(1864–16.11.1939)

ANTI-MILITARIST

Father: Oswald Sickert, painter
Mother: Helena, illegitimate daughter of a
*   Cambridge astronomer and an Irish singer*

Freethinker

No one has better described how it felt to be an unheeded, derided Cassandra[1] during the First World War than Helena Swanwick, already a veteran of countless women's suffrage meetings where hostile rowdies had subjected her to jeers, eggs, mud and even stones.

But whereas then there had been unquenchable hope and buoyant comradeship, there was now a rending pity, a horror of black darkness, and in my brain . . . something like a monotonous bell for ever tolling: 'Wicked! Wicked! Wickedly silly! Cruel! Silly! Silly! Silly!'

Helena Swanwick (From The Common Cause, *1913. Courtesy of the British Library)*

   . . . That many of the best men in every country should forswear their culture, their humanity, their intellectual efforts . . . to wallow in the joys of regimentation, brainlessness, . . . the primitive delights of destruction! For they did.

This brought me as near despair as I have ever been . . .

It was lonely in those days. I felt that men had dropped their end of the burden of living, . . . while they played this silly, bloody game of massacring.[2]

Helena Swanwick was convinced of two things: Germany was not solely responsible for the First World War, and 'smashing' Germany would only make it strengthen itself for a return blow. Exposing herself once more to abuse and even violence – and she was always afraid of crowds – Helena Swanwick, a freethinker, entered the void left by the 'moratorium in Christianity'[3] and addressed hostile crowds up and down the country, advocating a negotiated end to the war. She supported the Women's International League (WIL) from its inception (being elected first Chairman of its British Section),[4] and she was also on the National Executive of E. D. Morel's dissident Union for the Democratic Control of Foreign Policy, whose letters were opened and phones tapped.[5] Some of these meetings were violently broken up, sometimes by soldiers, sometimes by drunken mobs incited by the 'Kill-the-Hun' press, until no hall would provide them with a platform. The most horrible mob of all she found to be 'a mob of undergraduates or medical students'.[6]

Helena Swanwick knew that the Treaty of Versailles had broken the terms of the Armistice and was a 'peace to end peace'. She had helped the WIL in Britain to organize the dispatch of a million rubber teats for the blockaded German babies whose mothers were too weak with hunger to breastfeed, and then gone to the international WIL Congress in Zürich in 1919, where women delegates from both the victorious and the defeated Powers joined hands to dedicate themselves to peace. But there they learned of the Versailles Treaty, worse than anything they had expected. That women's Congress was the first political group in the world to spell out the Treaty's fatal, even unethical, misjudgements in their (ineffectual) cable to President Wilson and the other victorious negotiators in Paris:

By guaranteeing the fruits of the secret treaties to the conquerors, the terms of peace tacitly sanction secret diplomacy, deny the principle of self-determination, recognize the right of victors to the spoils of war, and create all over Europe discords and animosities, which can only lead to future wars . . . By the demand for the disarmament of one set of belligerents only, the principle of justice is violated, and the rule of force is continued . . . By the financial and economic proposals [i.e., reparations] a hundred million people of this generation in the heart of Europe are condemned to poverty, disease, and despair, which must result in the spread of hatred and anarchy within each nation.[7]

In 1920 and 1921 Helena Swanwick made several depressing visits to Ireland to see for herself the results of British armed intervention there. She collected photographs of devastated areas and had lantern-slides made to use at meetings all over the country addressed by herself or ELLEN WILKINSON, AGATHA WATTS or ANNOT ROBINSON.

They did more than any words could do. Audiences that were cool before, broke out into cries and groans [at] the ruined homes of Tuam, the roofless cottages of a whole street in Balbriggan, the wrecked shops and creameries and town halls of Cork and Mallow, the paralysed old women being rescued. 'Why, it's like Belgium!' was the commonest of all the remarks one heard.[8]

For the rest of the 1920s Helena Swanwick felt ever more 'lonely in a world [she] could not understand'.[9] She tried to help bring that world to its senses through her work for non-governmental peace organizations, through her own speeches at the League of Nations Fifth Assembly in 1924 as one of the Labour government's delegates, and through her editing of the enlightened, radical monthly *Foreign Affairs* (1925–28). An absolute pacifist, she had no sympathy with oppressed nationalists or revolutionary Communists who postponed their pacifism until victory was theirs. Grieved, though not at all surprised, by Hitler's successful capitalization on the oppressive Treaty of Versailles, she had to watch, impotently, the approach of the Second World War. Rather than witness the massacre of the children of Germany and Britain in the 'carpet bombing' raids that she foresaw, she took her own life on 16 November 1939.

1. Cf. Sybil Oldfield, 'England's Cassandras in World War One' in Oldfield (ed.), *This Working-Day World: Women's Lives and Cultures in Britain 1914–1945* (London, Taylor and Francis, 1994).
2. Helena Swanwick, *I Have Been Young* (London, Gollancz, 1935), pp. 241–2 and 247.
3. *Ibid.* p. 254.
4. See Appendix I; Jo Vellacott, 'Anti-war suffragists', *History*, **62** (October 1977); G. Bussey and M. Tims, *Women's International League for Peace and Freedom 1915–1965* (London, Allen and Unwin, 1965; republished as *Pioneers for Peace*, 1980); and Anne Wiltsher, *Most Dangerous Women: Feminist Peace Campaigners of the Great War* (London, Pandora, 1985).
5. See H. Swanwick, *Builders of Peace: The Union for Democratic Control of Foreign Policy – A History* (London, Swarthmore Press, 1926).
6. Swanwick, *I Have Been Young*, p. 295. See also report of the Kingsway Hall meeting (13.5.1915), chaired by Helena Swanwick, to hear Jane Addams's report on her deputation to the German Foreign Minister, in *Towards Permanent Peace* (London, WIL, June 1915), p. 18.
7. Quoted in S. Oldfield, *Spinsters of This Parish: The Life and Times of F. M. Mayor and Mary Sheepshanks* (London, Virago, 1984), pp. 217–18.
8. Swanwick, *I Have Been Young*, p. 336.
9. *Ibid.*, p. 355.

Helena Swanwick's later writings include: *Labour's Foreign Policy: What Has Been and What Might Be* (14pp.; London, Fabian Tract no. 227, 1929); *Collective Insecurity* (London, Jonathan Cape, 1937); and *The Roots of Peace* (London, Jonathan Cape, 1938). See also obituaries for Helena Swanwick in *Manchester Guardian* (18.11.1939); and *Girton Review* (Lent Term 1940).

T

TATE, MAVIS, JP, MP
(17.8.1893–5.6.1947)

ANTI-NAZI RESCUER; POST-WAR
INSPECTOR OF BUCHENWALD

*Father: Captain Guy Weir Hogg, sometime
Sheriff of St Helena*

Mavis Tate (From The Star,
18.11.1941)

Vivacious and striking, a qualified pilot and a progressive juvenile magistrate, Mavis Tate wore her Conservatism, rooted in family tradition,[1] with a difference after being elected MP for West Willesden in 1931 and later for Frome in Somerset. Instead of wanting to keep flogging, she was on the committee that recommended abolishing it; instead of keeping divorce procedure difficult, she tried to ease it; instead of maintaining silence on the question of abortion, she raised it, especially on behalf of poor women driven to backstreet abortionists and for girls who had suffered rape. She sided with the Labour stalwart ELLEN WILKINSON and with the Independent MP ELEANOR RATHBONE on the justice-for-women issues of equal pay, equal eligibility for pensions and the abolition of the 'marriage bar' for women teachers or civil servants.[2]

In May 1934 Mavis Tate personally carried out the dramatic rescue of political hostages in a Nazi concentration camp. On learning from the socialist Reichstag deputy Gerhard Seger, who had escaped from the infamous Oranienburg camp, that his wife and child were being held at another camp, Rosslau, near Dessau, Mavis Tate flew to Berlin, spent a week negotiating with people close to Hitler and persuaded them that the release of the woman and child would be positive propaganda for Germany. All three were flown back to Britain at German expense.[3] In May 1940 Mavis Tate was one of the 33 Conservatives who defied her Party whip and voted against the government, leading to the resignation of Neville Chamberlain and the choice of Churchill as war-leader of a Coalition government. 'It was not easy.'[4] In 1943 she had one notable back-bencher's victory: she persuaded the government to compensate civilian war victims of both sexes at the same rate, instead of paying single women 7 shillings less than single men. As well as being a most conscientious constituency MP and JP, she visited children's hospitals and juvenile remand homes and, posing as a woman worker's mate, 'Mary Smith', she inspected conditions for women workers in wartime aircraft factories.

In 1945 Mavis Tate was the only woman member of an all-party delegation of British MPs who volunteered to visit liberated Buchenwald. She was incredulous with horror at what she saw and suffered both physically and mentally ever after: not only did she contract a virulent virus infection at the camp but she was affected by acute clinical depression, which, combined with many difficulties in her private life, contributed to her gassing herself in 1947. It was said of her afterwards by her many shocked, grieving friends, who had always thought of her as exceptionally vital and even gay-spirited, that she was a woman of rare courage and great generosity of heart. They praised her devotion to righting the wrongs which the majority accepts, and her willingness to fight for anyone who needed help.[5]

1. Pamela Brookes, *Women at Westminster: An Account of Women in the British Parliament 1918–1966* (London, Peter Davies, 1967), p. 100. Mavis Tate's cousin was the Conservative MP Sir Douglas Hogg, later Lord Hailsham. Her second husband was Captain H. B. Tate of the Tate and Lyle sugar business.
2. Olive Banks, *The Biographical Dictionary of British Feminists*, vol. 2 (New York University Press, 1990), pp. 199–201.
3. See article on Mavis Tate in *The American Hebrew and Jewish Tribune* (November 1934).
4. *Hansard*, CCCLXXXV (25.11.1942), col. 756, quoted in Brookes, op. cit., p. 131.
5. See obituaries in the *Observer* (8.6.1947); *The Electrical Age* (July 1947); *Daily Herald* (6.6.1947); and *The Times* (6.6 and 11.6.1947).

THOMSON, CLAIRE, MB

(1894–*c*.1966)

MEDICAL MISSIONARY, INDIA

Father: William Thomson, Scottish Presbyterian brewer, d. c.1896
Mother: Frances, née Pease, daughter of Anglican vicar, d. 1903

Protestant

No one could have been a later starter as a humanitarian pioneer than Claire Thomson; her wry, unpublished account of her first 40 years reads like a female version of John Wain's *Hurry On Down*.[1] Born into a relatively privileged home with a succession of nannies and governesses, she suffered from the bleak consequences of childhood bereavement, inadequate education and threatened blindness. In 1913 she failed her Matric in Latin, Maths and French; she failed as a teacher trainee, and then failed her first attempt at the entrance examination for St Andrews University. After a breakdown in health in 1916 she failed, understandably, to become a sturdy Land Girl in 1917, and then failed as farm housekeeper and farmshop manageress. After training as a Lady Almoner, she was sacked after her first year in the nicest possible way and felt completely shattered. She then tried abroad, staying with relatives she had never known in New Zealand and managing to be judged '*almost* as good as a Lady help' in the continuous cycle of her hostess's house-cleaning. A term and a half of teaching in north Queensland proved that she was no teacher, and she returned to England to work throughout the 1920s as a Lady Almoner.

Nevertheless Claire Thomson was nothing if not stubborn, and along the way she had picked up a diploma in social work after working in the Glasgow Gorbals, and her time staying in Women's University Settlements, where she met HILDA CASHMORE, had led to the beginning of a lively concern for other people.[2] At the

Dr Claire Thomson with Indian women at the sinking of a new well (By permission of the British Library, MSS EUR D1102, Thomson Papers)

age of 36 she decided to enrol as a medical student at King's College, London, and promptly failed chemistry and physics. She hated dissecting and midwifery – babies were born in spite of, not because of, her – and she failed her first attempt at Finals surgery. When she finally qualified at the age of 41, she was terrified and always kept a list of antidotes for poisons in her knicker leg in case she was caught in a relevant emergency.

It was only on the declaration of war on 3 September 1939 that Claire Thomson vowed to try to become a medical missionary. Interviewed by the Society for the Propagation of the Gospel (SPG), she made no secret that she was 'not much good medically or spiritually' as she offered to go to India for a year at her own expense. Eight weeks later she was in Bihar, without a word of Hindi. And then everything changed. The desperate situation of her tribal and *harijan* Christian patients forced a huge responsibility upon Claire Thomson, and she found that even she could do something for them. She never forgot the first child she saved from tetanus. In 1940 she was in a jungle hospital 30 miles from Ranchi, totally isolated by the rains. She suffered sixteen bouts of malaria in as many months. She cycled to most deliveries, being asked for only after complications had already set in, and whenever there was a swollen stream she would wade across, carrying her cycle. 'She crosses big or little rivers by day or night without fear' was the farewell tribute to her there. She had to fight tuberculosis and leprosy as well as endemic gastro-enteritis; she examined her patients' stools for hookworm by the thousand.

In 1944 she was sent back to Britain on furlough and worked as a locum in Middlesex, where she met the inspiring doctor MARJORY WARREN, pioneer of geriatrics. The SPG now insisted that she do the minimum six months' missionary training at the college in Selly Oak; she did it, aged 52, and not surprisingly found the ambience schoolgirlish.

On her return to India in July 1945 Claire Thomson was 'the woman with the white hair who bicycles' once more. She also ran dispensaries in a large rural area east of Poona, driving a Land Rover packed with equipment and medicines whenever the height of the rivers allowed. She had to combat endemic plague and typhoid and was deeply depressed by the prevalence of acute malnutrition in the village children for whom she organized supplementary feeding programmes, as well as by the often fatal lack of hygiene. Average life expectancy was under 30. 'I knew that many of the fine upstanding girls at High School and Teacher's Training College would in a few years be again living in a village, often as a teacher.' How could she help them both to survive and to help others? She produced leaflets in English and Hindi and then her first book, *Better Health: Illnesses We Need Never Have*,[3] on such essentials as building safe wells and proper latrines, washing hands after defecating and before eating, and basic hygiene in childbirth. The book was translated into seven or eight regional languages and was followed by her *Improving Village Health: A Handbook for Rural Workers*.

Claire Thomson now realized that she wanted to concentrate on preventive medicine through health education. She joined the Christian Medical Association of India, which united all Protestant medical endeavour there. However, she was then told she was not qualified for this work, since she had never done a course in tropical medicine. Back she went to the London School of Tropical Medicine and, full of trepidation, took the diploma course at the age of 62. Fascinated by her visits to abattoirs and sewage farms and having found her métier at last, this time she did not fail. Back in India, between 1957 and 1964, she concentrated on popularizing preventive medicine in the villages. To do this she crisscrossed the length and breadth of India by train, visiting every medical centre large or small, promoting the cause of preventive health education. One such centre was Ludhiana, where the doughty spirit of Dame EDITH BROWN urged her on from the grave.

It was India and Indians – 'an amazingly generous people' – who gave Claire Thomson the joy of knowing she could be of use, even with her 'sparse medical knowledge'. On her final return to England at the age of 71, a wave of misery came over her, realizing that the happiest time of her life was gone.[4]

1. Dr Claire Thomson's memoir is held in the India Office, British Library, MSS EUR D1102. All quotations in this entry are taken from it.
2. She was also influenced by her childhood memory of her mother carrying a gypsy woman's large bundle for her up a hill.
3. Published by SPCK (India) (Madras, 1952).
4. I am grateful to Pat Barr, *The Dust in the Balance: British Women in India 1905–1945* (London, Hamish Hamilton, 1989) for introducing me to Dr Claire Thomson.

— ◆ ◆ —

THOMSON, MARGARET HENDERSON, MBE, MB, ChB
(1902–17.6.1982)

MEDICAL AID TO CIVILIAN WAR VICTIMS

Father: George Alexander Hunter, Edinburgh solicitor
Mother: Margaret, née Robertson

Church of Scotland

The sole testimony to the heroic humanitarianism of Dr Margaret Thomson (MB, ChB 1926, Edinburgh) comes from the *Daily Herald* (3.7.1943), concerning her actions during the Second World War in the Pacific when she was 41. The *Daily Herald* quoted the *London Gazette*'s citation (2.7.1943) that 'for her resolution and disregard of self, her sacrifice and admirable courage', she had been awarded the MBE. As reported in the *Daily Herald*, Dr Thomson, who was attached to the

Malayan Medical Service, had first comforted the distressed women and children fleeing Singapore by ship. Their ship had then been dive-bombed by the Japanese and she had had to swim for hours before she was picked up by a lifeboat containing shocked and wounded survivors. She insisted on taking an oar to help row the undermanned boat, despite being badly wounded in the thigh herself. The lifeboat's passengers having been rescued by the Dutch and taken to Senajang island, Dr Thomson then took charge of all the wounded and sick on the island, even performing life-saving operations with the crudest surgical instruments and inadequate medical supplies. She organized the evacuation of Senajang island to nearby Senkep island, where she knew there was a hospital; her own wound having turned septic, she herself had to be carried there by stretcher. She recovered in time to accompany and tend the evacuees still having to flee the Japanese army, first by sea to Sumatra and then on their long land trek before the advancing invaders.

Very little more is known about her. She was captured by the Japanese, who had already interned her husband, and was a prisoner of war in Changi camp until August 1945.[1]

In 1949 Dr Thomson was registered as a medical practitioner at the RRI Experiment Station, Sungei Buloh, Selangor, Malaya. The last official references to her are on the Scottish Medical Register, as practising first from Little Daugh, Ruthven, Huntly, Aberdeenshire, in the 1960s, and then living and farming in Huntly itself until 1982.

1. See entries for JOSEPHINE FOSS and Dr CICELY WILLIAMS.

THORNDIKE, SYBIL, DBE, CH, Hon. D.Litt.
(4.10.1882–9.6.1976)

TRAGIC ACTRESS; PACIFIST CAMPAIGNER

Father: Canon Arthur Thorndike
Mother: Agnes, née Bowers, daughter of shipping merchant

Christian humanist

It was Sybil Thorndike's husband Lewis Casson who first opened her eyes to the issues of social justice and peace. Until she met him, she had been totally absorbed in succeeding in the world of the theatre; he introduced her in 1908 to the causes of women's suffrage, socialism and anti-militarism. 'Your acting won't be much good', he told her, 'if you don't think about the world in which we live and the conditions of the people.'[1]

The first play with a contemporary humanitarian impact in which she acted was Galsworthy's *The Silver Box* in 1909. Once she joined Lilian Baylis at the Old Vic in October 1914, Sybil Thorndike continued the tradition of Emma Cons and Lilian Baylis of unofficial social work visiting in the grim Waterloo Road area.[2] She also carried on acting at the Old Vic throughout the First World War despite the birth of her fourth child, Zeppelin raids on London and the bombing of Waterloo station during a performance of *King Lear* when she was the Fool. Both Sybil Thorndike and Lewis Casson lost brothers in the war; deepening that horror was Casson's guilt and depression over his own role as an officer in the Royal Engineers in the preparation of gas missiles. The war converted both of them to pacifism. 'The horror, tragedy and utter folly of . . . war weighed on [Lewis Casson's] mind, and he saw little hope for the future.'[3] It was at that point (October 1919) that he produced Euripides' *The Trojan Women* – the 'most intense and sustained experience of suffering in all Greek tragedy'[4] in its confronting of the pitiless brutalities of war – to mark the founding of the League of Nations Union. Sybil Thorndike played the old Queen Hecuba, now an enslaved prisoner, lying prone on the earth, mourning the dreadful deaths of her husband and all her children and recognizing the total futility of the Trojan War: 'We have been slaughtering our hecatombs for nothing.'[5] An old apple-woman, who had a free seat, came up to her and said, 'Them Trojans was just like us. We've lost our sons and 'usbands in this bleedin' war, 'aven't we? So no wonder we was all cryin'. That was a real play, that was, dearie.'[6]

Sybil Thorndike as Shaw's St Joan (National Portrait Gallery. Photograph by Bertram Park, © Rosalind Thuillier)

In March 1924 Sybil Thorndike became Bernard Shaw's St Joan, a character she played over 200 times, for the last time in 1941. It was her greatest part; she acted that most human of heroines who was also a passionate, idealistic revolutionary who refused to recant, even at the price of the stake. Joan was one of those who, as Cordelia said, 'with best intent, incurr'd the worst'. Or as Shaw himself put it in the Epilogue, 'a Christ [needing to] perish in torment in every age to save those who have no imagination'. To Sybil Thorndike, Joan was another Abraham Lincoln.[7] When the 1926 General Strike closed the London theatres, including *St Joan*, the Cassons, alone among their friends, were on the side of the strikers.

In 1928, after playing EDITH CAVELL in one of the last silent films (Herbert Wilcox's *Dawn*), Sybil Thorndike toured South Africa with Lewis Casson, fiercely opposing the demand that they never play to a mixed audience by playing to African-only audiences when possible instead. When Paul Robeson acted Othello in 1929 Sybil Thorndike asked to be auditioned for the part of Emilia: the production was a breakthrough in race relations. But this was not her only cause: throughout the 1930s

> she became much in demand to speak for any sort of cause in which her broad humanity could be used to gain followers . . . She spoke at [MURIEL LESTER's] Settlements in the East End, she spoke to miners' political gatherings in Wales, she . . . pleaded for India's independence, and above all she spoke for the cause of pacifism.[8]

In 1931 she was created a Dame by the Labour government. In 1938 she joined VIOLET BONHAM CARTER, ELEANOR RATHBONE and ELLEN WILKINSON in cabling Hitler, petitioning him, in vain, to commute the death sentence for treason on the German pacifist Liselotte Herrmann.[9]

Sybil Thorndike's last great humane role in the theatre was written specially for her, the teacher Miss Moffat in Emlyn Williams' *The Corn Is Green*; she played it to packed houses for a year till the London theatres closed at the outbreak of the Second World War. The Cassons then took Shakespeare and other classics to tour the mining valleys of Wales during the war; they had never had such rapt audiences. At the end of the war Sybil Thorndike toured the British Zone of Germany and was taken to see both the children who would survive Belsen and those who would not. She said she would never get over the experience. It was a tribute to her real-life rôle as a humane cultural icon that her name was found after the war on the Nazis' black list for automatic arrest after their expected victory over Britain.[10]

It was agreed by all who knew her that Sybil Thorndike's greatest character was herself. Irene Worth summed her up as 'one of the very few artists who, having been blessed with a great gift, has repaid the debt by living up to it as a human being'.[11] Her love of life and of everyone living it was unquenchable; at 90 she would ask eagerly: 'When's the next Memorial Service?'[12]

1. Sheridan Morley, *Sybil Thorndike: A Life in the Theatre* (London, Weidenfeld and Nicolson, 1977), p. 37.
2. Elizabeth Sprigge, *Sybil Thorndike Casson* (London, Victor Gollancz, 1971), p. 106.
3. *Ibid.*, pp. 127–8.
4. Brian Vickers, *Towards Greek Tragedy* (London, Longman, 1973), p. 91.
5. Euripides, *The Trojan Women*, lines 1253–4.
6. Sprigge, *op. cit.*, p. 129. A slightly different version is given by their son John Casson in *Lewis and Sybil: A Memoir* (London, William Collins, 1972), p. 64.
7. Casson, *op. cit.*, p. 122.
8. *Ibid.*, pp. 201–2. Cf. Sybil Thorndike's tributes to the inspiration of Maude Royden and the steadfast moral courage of Vera Brittain.
9. See S. Oldfield, 'German women in the resistance to Hitler' in S. Reynolds (ed.), *Women, State and Revolution* (Oxford, Basil Blackwell, 1986), pp. 90–1.
10. See 'Nazis' black list discovered in Berlin', *Manchester Guardian* (14.9.1945).
11. Sprigge, *op. cit.*, p. 268.
12. Casson, *op. cit.*, p. 339.

TILLARD, VIOLET
(1874–19.2.1922)

NURSE; CHAMPION OF CONSCIENTIOUS OBJECTORS; INTERNATIONAL FAMINE RELIEF WORKER

Father: — Tillard, army man of Huguenot ancestry

Quaker by convincement

It was said after Violet Tillard's death that it 'would be good for the world that her name should become memorable'.[1] Why?

Tall, slender, delicate, reticent, graceful, Violet Tillard looked too much like a 'nice', quiet lady to be recognized by her opponents as the committed subversive she really was. A professional hospital nurse for ten years, she was inspired by

CHARLOTTE DESPARD to work for the Women's Freedom League in 1908 and was promptly imprisoned for eight weeks in Holloway for trying to present a suffrage petition to 10 Downing Street. On her release she organized WFL caravan tours throughout East Anglia and south Wales, and even journeyed to Australia in 1910 to win Commonwealth support for suffrage for British women. Her courage, sympathy, selflessness, determination and 'almost daredevil gaiety'[2] were by-words among her colleagues in that much mocked cause. From 1912 to 1914 she was in Dublin, supporting the striking Irish transport workers.

A pacifist in the First World War, Violet Tillard channelled all her energy into helping conscientious objectors. She was appointed co-treasurer, with ADA SALTER, of the No Conscription Fellowship's Maintenance Committee, handling the money donated (much of it from the sisters MARIAN and Edith ELLIS) to the families of the imprisoned men. Corder Catchpool recorded that his remembrance of her in 1916 was

Violet Tillard (From The Friend, *10.3.1922)*

of inspiration in personal contact, and of strong, quiet leadership in common counsel . . . Violet Tillard was the first, except one member of my own family, to greet me on my release from prison, and I shall never forget her welcome.[3]

Her care for individuals is seen in this letter to Bertrand Russell, acting Chairman of the NCF (19.1.1918):

There is a man in Wandsworth called Gardner who is pining for a message from you to generally 'buck' him and the others up. Do you think you could spare five minutes to write one? I hate to trouble you, but it won't be the same for them if anyone else does it – . . . Of course one realises how easy it is to feel isolated and forgotten.[4]

On 23 May 1918 she herself was on trial under the Defence of the Realm Act for refusing to give the police the name of the printer of the March *NCF News*, 'an undesirable publication'.[5] She served 61 days in Holloway, where she refused 'to obey those prison rules which she felt to be immoral and enforced with the object of degrading prisoners'.[6]

In 1919 Violet Tillard went to defeated Germany with the Quaker mission that was being master-minded by JOAN FRY. She was needed as a nurse to combat the epidemic of tuberculosis among the hungry population of Berlin. In December 1919 she applied formally to join the Society of Friends, though with misgivings that 'one who joins the Society as an adult should be a much better person than I am'.[7] From 1920 to 1921 she was still in Germany, concentrating on the student feeding programmes, especially in the University of Tübingen, where, like Joan

Fry, she was made an honorary member of the Students' Union, and where the richer students were taxing themselves to help the poorer ones. German students then were sleeping in rags, on straw, living on crusts of bread or one meal of potatoes or cabbage a day. They collapsed in lectures, and did not have the strength to write their examination papers. *Quäkern*, or eating from Quaker food aid, was essential to the survival of many young people.

In October 1921 Joan Fry had a wire from Friends in Russia asking for Violet Tillard to be sent there to help them organize relief in famine-stricken Buzuluk.[8] Like MARJORIE RACKSTRAW and EVELYN SHARP, and every famine relief worker after her, she had to learn to make herself swallow her own minimal food ration while seeing and hearing the cries of the starving. A fellow worker reported of her:

Three girls sitting on a bed (From Friends' War Victims' Relief Committee, Russia Album, no. 128)

'Till' now has charge of supplies and she is a level-headed person who says that we must consider ourselves as machines which can only give maximum service by being kept in [working] condition. But we bring in our own flour . . . rather than take any bread out of the country.[9]

Violet Tillard's hitherto unpublished letters convey something of what she was trying to do with a temperature outside of -30°F: housekeep for 20 to 30 aid workers, nurse those who had gone down with typhus, establish feeding kitchens throughout the 50-mile radius district, visit reception centres for starving children and hospitals for sick children in order to ascertain their most urgent needs:

One feels horrible to live in such good conditions when the people are literally starving at our doors – a boy of sixteen lies dead a few yards away . . . Some of these people come into our kitchen to beg before they give up. On Christmas Day 114 died in Buzuluk; on the 26th, 355, on the 27th, 212. 509 of these were children. It isn't so harrowing to see them lying dead. They suffer no more. It is the doomed shadows one sees around the streets and in the homes that are most horrible.[10]

Despite the dehumanizing, numbing statistics, she still responded to people as individuals: 'there is a dear old woman [here] who bakes and washes and has to be restrained from working day and night . . . I am very thankful for having come. We are a very harmonious family here . . . Holmes is a treasure.'[11]

But the strain was almost insupportable nevertheless and she was clearly working beyond her strength:

Yesterday I was in one of the Receiving Homes – In one big dreary room are children, sometimes a hundred, sometimes more; all along one side runs a long platform on which crouch little bundles of misery; here they live day and night –

no beds, no other coverings, not room for all to lie down, no clean clothes. The only thing one could do to improve this place would be to be able to give to each child an outfit of new clothes, so that it could be washed and put on them . . . The only cheering thing is that in every Home one finds that the death rate has gone down very much because of our food. I have been to two of the Homes for Sick Children . . . in one of which the sister in charge has made wonderful efforts – the children were only two in a bed but again there were absolutely no bed clothes . . . We are getting a lot of clothes out and a big sewing school here is going to make children's clothes . . . Some cases of sheets would be extremely useful . . .

8 January 1922. Conditions get worse and worse. I enclose a list of drugs very much wanted in the hospitals in the district which are practically without any . . . I went to a hospital the other day where 227 patients lay in their own filthy lousy rags on the beds, one half of the ward being taken up by hospital staff also suffering from typhus . . . In a Children's Home I saw yesterday sixty-four children had five outdoor garments among them . . . sewing cotton urgently needed.[12]

By the time that letter reached Quaker Headquarters in London, Violet Tillard was dead. She had been called to the Pavlovka district, 40 miles down the rail track, where three relief workers were ill with typhus. She had had to sleep on the vermin-infested floor before starting to nurse her three patients night and day; she pulled them through, but succumbed herself. The Soviet representative on the International Relief Executive wrote on hearing of her death: 'The Russian nation will forever preserve in their memory the heroic aid that was rendered by the Quakers to them in the year of their extreme adversity.'[13] And her fellow Quaker Barratt Brown wrote: 'She united a deep hatred of all evil institutions with a quiet and tender regard for human beings.'[14]

1. John Graham, *Conscription and Conscience* (London, G. Allen and Unwin, 1922), p. 185.
2. Muriel Matters (later Porter), unpublished manuscript memoir of Violet Tillard, especially in her WFL days, written 22.2.1930, held in the Suffragette Fellowship Collection, Museum of London.
3. *The Friend* (10.3.1922).
4. NCF papers, Friends' House Library Archive.
5. *The Tribunal* (25.7.1918), p. 4.
6. *The Tribunal* (15.8.1918), p. 2.
7. Violet Tillard, unpublished letter, in Friends' House Library Archive.
8. See entry for RUTH FRY; Michael Asquith, *Famine: Quaker Work in Russia* (Oxford University Press, 1943), pp. 18–22 and 54–7; Richenda Scott, *Quakers in Russia* (London, Michael Joseph, 1964), ch. 18; John Ormerod Greenwood, *Quaker Encounters*, vol. 1: *Friends and Relief* (York, William Sessions Ltd, 1975), pp. 244–7.
9. Arthur Watts, manuscript, in Friends' House Library Archive.
10. Violet Tillard, manuscript letters to Ruth Fry (30.12.1921 and 8.1.1922), in Friends' House Library Archive.
11. *Ibid.*
12. *Ibid.*
13. *The Friend* (10.3.1922).
14. *Ibid.*

V

VAUGHAN, JANET,
DBE, FRS, MD
(18.10.1899–9.1.1993)

SCIENTIST

*Father: William Vaughan, public school
headmaster
Mother: Madge, née Symonds, daughter of
the art historian J. A. Symonds*

Humanist

Janet Vaughan decided very young to
become a doctor in order to fight the
results of poverty and injustice.

> How anyone could do medicine in
> those days and not become a socialist I
> find hard to understand! It was so
> obvious that so much illness and suf-
> fering was due to poverty. What I hated
> most was the people's acceptance: . . .
> 'it was God's will.' I hated God's will
> with a burning hatred.[1]

Janet Vaughan

After practising as a newly qualified young doctor, encountering deficiency diseases,
malnutrition and childbirth endured in appalling slum conditions behind London's
Euston station in the 1920s, she turned to a life of scientific medical research. She
focused first on blood diseases and experimented to ascertain the therapeutic effect
of extract of liver on pernicious anaemia, a disease especially prevalent among
underfed child-bearing women. She co-wrote a bulletin on the importance of iron
in infant nutrition and a textbook on anaemia in 1935. By that time she had also
married David Gourlay, a conscientious objector in the First World War who had
worked with Friends' War Victims' Relief in France and who was now promoting
international travel as a means to greater cross-border understanding. He was a
very supportive husband who understood the depth of her commitment to medical
research. By then they had two young children.

The terrifying and growing strength of fascism in Europe caused Janet Vaughan
to become passionately involved in raising funds for the Committee for Spanish
Medical Aid during the Spanish Civil War. At the end of that war she and her
husband gave refuge to the defeated Republican Communist Director of the
Barcelona blood bank Dr Duran-Jordan. He had pioneered the use of stored
anticoagulated blood during the Civil War and passed on his techniques to Janet

Vaughan. She in turn set up an *ad hoc* medical committee in her own home in 1938 to discuss future necessary arrangements

> for blood storage and transfusion in case of war, how to collect donors, what sort of bottles to store it in, how to transport it and we wrote a memorandum – a group of utterly self-appointed people – about providing London with blood.[2]

Three days before war started she received a telegram from the Medical Research Council: 'Start bleeding.'

Not only did Janet Vaughan run the most efficient blood transfusion depot in wartime Britain, at Slough, she also pioneered plasma for wound shock, essential after the evacuation of Dunkirk, and the transfusion of blood into the bones of patients too badly injured for intravenous injection.[3] After being sent out to India to investigate and report on medical education and services there, she returned to wartime Britain to research the treatment of starvation, with a view to the plight of civilians in occupied Europe and of British prisoners of war about to be released. She was sent into liberated Europe to test injections of protein hydrolysate on those who had suffered starvation. Not finding any cases of starvation in Brussels hospitals, she decided to go on into Belsen in May 1945, without clearing it first with the Medical Research Council and even though she and her team had not been inoculated against typhoid. Once in the camp she found it impossible to inject people so traumatized by brutal treatment that they believed all injections must be lethal. 'What I saw there was past understanding.'[4] As she had foreseen, the protein hydrolysate proved impossible to swallow or digest without flavouring; she found her solutions of milk powder far more effective for those with any chance of survival. That discovery was to aid the recovery from starvation of countless civilians in Holland, where she went next, as well as prisoners of war from Norway and the dreaded Japanese prison camps. 'Her success in Belsen caused the War Office to alter completely the preparations then being made for the release of starving British prisoners in the Far East.'[5] Among the latter was her old friend and fellow student at Somerville College, Oxford, Dr CICELY WILLIAMS.

After the war Janet Vaughan was reunited with her husband and young daughters; supported by her fellow scientist DOROTHY HODGKIN, she was elected Principal of Somerville. There she researched bone-seeking radio-isotopes to investigate whether strontium-90 and plutonium were carcinogenic if incorporated into the skeleton ('I considered myself too old to worry about developing the cancers').[6] At the age of 70 she published her book *The Physiology of Bone* and four years later *The Effects of Irradiation of the Skeleton.*

> She was the senior scientist of a trio of British women doctors (the others are Dr Alice Stewart and Professor Patricia Lindop) who devoted their lives to understanding the effects of radiation on victims, and from time to time demonstrating the official underestimates of the damage.[7]

In her eightieth year she was elected FRS on the strength of her most recent research.

Janet Vaughan was a human being who 'overflowed with energy and enthusiasm . . . She wrote fast and she spoke fast, as if she could hardly keep up with the torrent of her ideas . . . [In her private life] she was boundlessly generous and kind' to the end.[8]

1. Janet Vaughan interviewed by Polly Toynbee in Leonie Caldecott, *Women of Our Century* (London, Ariel Books, BBC, 1984), p. 11.
2. *Ibid.*, p. 117.
3. See Douglas Starr, *Blood: An Epic History of Medicine and Commerce* (New York, Alfred A. Knopf, 1998), pp. 84–92.
4. Polly Toynbee, appreciation of Janet Vaughan, *Guardian* (13.1.1993). See also W. R. F. Collis on Janet Vaughan's work there, 'Belsen Camp: a preliminary report', *British Medical Journal* (9.6.1945), p. 815.
5. Anne Symonds, in *Independent* (23.1.1993).
6. Caldecott, *op. cit.*, p. 124.
7. Anthony Tucker, 'Vital nuclear detective', obituary for Dame Janet Vaughan, *Guardian* (11.1.1993). See also Helen Wadsworth, in L. Bindman, A. Brading and T. Tansey (eds), *Women Physiologists* (London and Chapel Hill, NC, The Portland Press, 1993), pp. 31–5; and M. Owen, 'Janet Maria Vaughan', *Biographical Memoirs of Fellows of the Royal Society*, **41** (1995), pp. 499–514.
8. Evelyn Irons, obituary, *Independent* (12.1.1993).

W

WALKER, JANE, CH, MD, Hon. LLD

(24.10.1859–17.11.1938)

PIONEER OF THE TREATMENT AND
PREVENTION OF TUBERCULOSIS

*Father: John Walker, wealthy Yorkshire blanket
manufacturer*

Nonconformist by birth, later Anglican

Dr Jane Walker

Encouraged by her liberal-minded father, Jane Walker studied medicine when it was almost impossible for a woman to do advanced study in the subject in Britain. She took the degree of MD at Brussels in 1890, having first studied at the London School of Medicine for Women, and at Dublin, Edinburgh and Vienna. She qualified in midwifery and in surgery, and specialized at first in the diseases of women and children in the East End of London. Her studies abroad, particularly visiting the Nordrach Colony in the Black Forest in Germany, had revealed to her the advantage of the open-air treatment for patients with tuberculosis, as opposed to confinement in warm, stuffy rooms. Disregarding general scepticism and even hostility, she therefore opened the first open-air sanatorium in Britain at Downham Market, Norfolk, in 1892, later transferring to Nayland, Suffolk. It became a model for such treatment both in Britain and abroad. At first Jane Walker took paying patients, but three years later she added a department for the working-class poor and in 1912 a children's section. In 1916 she had to open a ward for tuberculous soldiers. Among her other innovations, she introduced occupational therapy for her long-term patients.

Jane Walker recognized that it was necessary not only to cure tuberculosis, but to prevent it. She therefore spent much of her life stressing the importance of improving the standard of living of the mass of the population and abolishing overcrowded, insanitary slum housing, insisting on the medical necessity of the state's ensuring adequate nutrition for the poorest and weakest in the community.

It was natural therefore that politically she stood with the Labour Party . . . Liberty and opportunity for the development of the inherent powers in every human being were the aims for which she strove . . . in foreign affairs her sympathy was with the right of small nations to retain their freedom.[1]

A woman of apparently inextinguishable energy and immeasurable breadth of interest, Jane Walker was a leading suffragist who co-founded the British Federation of Medical Women; she published books and articles on the nursing of tuberculosis and maternal health as well as on many social questions; she was a member of the Agricultural Wages Committee for Suffolk, Treasurer of the Association of Moral and Social Hygiene and of the Open Door Council (concerned with tackling the prostitution of girls and women); she also read omnivorously and was a patron of music and modern painting – all this besides being medical supervisor of the Nayland Clinic and a leading Harley Street consultant. She did not stop working as a doctor until a few days before her death at 79. '[No] one in distress ever came to her without her planning some way or other of helping them . . . She was a "Beloved Physician".'[2] 'She inspired her patients, not only to get well but to "live".'[3] Full of humour and eagerness to think well of humanity, '[a] lovable friend was Jane Walker, who could swear at you at one moment and grasp your hand in real and eternal friendship the next'.[4]

1. Lady Florence Barrett, obituary for Dr Jane Walker, *British Medical Journal* (26.11.1938), p. 1120.
2. Dr Albert Mansbridge in *The Times* (18.11.1938).
3. Dr Louisa Martindale, obituary for Dr Jane Walker, *Medical Women's Federation Review* (January 1939), p. 21.
4. Barrett, *op. cit.*

See also obituaries in *Daily Telegraph* (18.11.1938); and *Manchester Guardian* (8.11.1938). See also *Medical Women's Federation Newsletter* (July 1951), pp. 17–20; (October 1951), pp. 62–3; and *The Lancet* (26.11.1938).

WARD, BARBARA, DBE
(23.5.1914–31.5.1981)

ECONOMIST; INTERNATIONALIST;
ADVOCATE OF GLOBAL JUSTICE

Father: Walter Ward, Quaker solicitor
Mother: Teresa, Catholic

Roman Catholic Christian Socialist

Barbara Ward

The 'only economist who is also a great moralist' was how Taya Zinkin described Barbara Ward.[1] Highly educated in France and Germany as well as at Oxford, the young Barbara Ward was converted to lifelong socialism by the Great Depression. From the age of 25, when she first became assistant editor on *The Economist* in 1939, throughout the Second World War (which she saw as being essentially a moral conflict), right up until her death in 1981, she not only advocated the equitable redistribution of the world's wealth, but also spelt out how it could be done. In broadcasts, articles, speeches and book after book with titles so clearly intelligible that they might be seen as 'simple Truth miscall'd Simplicity',[2] she urged that 'distribution should undo excess, / And each man have enough'.[3] Her most important writings are: *The International Share-Out* (1938); *The Rich Nations and the Poor Nations* (1962); *Why Help India? India and the West* (1963); *Nationalism and Ideology* (1967); and *Only One Earth: The Care and Maintenance of a Small Planet* (with René Dubos, 1972), in which she outlined how there could be development in poorer nations without their having to replicate the terrible mistakes of the 'developed'. 'The problem is how we can develop the two-thirds of humanity who live in conditions of increasing degradation . . . without damage to the earth.' She was 'a global visionary . . . [who] called for a second Marshall Plan'[4] from North to South as early as 1980. Barbara Ward wanted to pull the British and the Americans, in particular, out of their 'inward-looking preoccupation and selfishness . . . [and help create instead] a saner, less wasteful and fairer way of life for this planet'.[5] As a Catholic, her influence with the Vatican was quite remarkable for a woman, and her legacy lived on in the work of her friend Inge Thorsson, the Swedish economist and special adviser to the United Nations on disarmament for development.[6]

1. 'Economist with a conscience', *Guardian* (2.10.1961).
2. Shakespeare, Sonnet 66: 'Tired with all these, for restful death I cry'.
3. Shakespeare, Gloucester in *King Lear*, Act IV, scene 1.
4. Obituary, *Daily Telegraph* (1.6.1981).
5. Robert Nowell, 'Barbara Ward's last cry for world justice', *The Times* (27.7.1981).
6. See Sybil Oldfield, *Women against the Iron Fist: Alternatives to Militarism 1900–1989* (Oxford, Basil Blackwell, 1989), pp. 221–4. See also 'Outstanding contribution to economic thought', obituary for Barbara Ward, *The Times* (1.6.1981), and 'In tribute to a modern saint', *The Observer* (7.6.1981).

WARREN, MARJORY WINSOME, CBE, MRCS, LRCP
(1897–5.9.1960)

PIONEER OF GERIATRIC CARE

Father: — Warren, London barrister, lay preacher

Humanist

*Dr Marjory Warren (from Gerontologica Clinica, **3** (1), 1961)*

The untouchables to whom Dr Marjory Warren reached out were the old: apparently senile, immobile, demented, incontinent, incurable and in general past praying for. She found them locked up together by the hundred in a former workhouse, the Isleworth Poor Law Infirmary, when it became attached in 1935 to the West Middlesex Hospital where she was Deputy Medical Director. She described such infirmaries with their miserable history of minimal care, going back to the Poor Laws of 1834 and even of 1601, as 'ill-assorted dumps . . . large wards . . . devoid of any signs of comfort or interest'.[1] At best she found the chronic sick and elderly infirm lying 'warm, fed and clean, tucked up tight in rows of white quilted beds until death . . . released them. Dr Warren was not satisfied with this state of affairs.'[2] 'Her inquiring mind became preoccupied with the prodigal waste of human life in chronic hospital wards, and . . . she settled down to take a fresh and unbiased look at a traditional "problem".'[3] '[She] looked at something all of us had taken for granted for years and saw it in a completely new light.'[4]

The first thing Marjory Warren did was to examine each of her 714 elderly patients, discovering not just their medical condition but also their detailed personal and social history. She was then able to discharge 200 relatively healthy patients to live in residential homes and send 150 to have psychiatric treatment, leaving 350 chronically ill under her care. Then she got to work. She introduced armchairs, wheelchairs, additional railing for stairs and corridors, lower beds, lockers, earphones for radios, bright coloured curtains and bedspreads, drug therapy, physiotherapists, speech therapists, chiropodists, occupational therapists and almoners, while she herself invented a bed board to help patients stand after long bed rest, a shuffle board to help arthritic patients walk, and three- and four-legged walking sticks with rubber ferrules. She also became a champion of artificial limb-fitting for the elderly, not just for single but even for double amputees. She advocated treating the elderly sick neither in acute, general mixed wards nor in segregated, 'chronic' institutions, but in special geriatric wards within general hospitals. In order to prevent depression setting in, she insisted on a positive, even enthusiastic, approach by her staff and hopeful commitment to their own rehabilitation by the patients themselves. She was tall, auburn-haired, vigorous and dynamic; when 'she entered one of her wards, everyone in it redoubled their efforts and activities'.[5] She was convinced that 'the maximum activity an individual can perform [was] the most beneficial step he [or she] could take to . . . recuperation'.[6] She made it mandatory for patients to eat, drink and dress themselves, if necessary by using special knives and forks and Velcro fastenings. 'Nothing that a patient can do for himself should be done for him.'[7]

The result of Marjory Warren's determined, many-pronged onslaught, fortunately not noticed at first by the authorities, given the Second World War, was nothing less than a revolution in the lives of the elderly sick. Patients long despaired-of regained their independence and even their own personalities and minds. They were no longer helpless, imprisoned, silent sufferers but in many cases could return to a fulfilling life in their own homes. 'Although old age could not be cured, for very many patients she found it possible to make life not only worth while, but even useful once more.'[8]

Marjory Warren was thus 'the guiding light and the great leader' of a new branch of medicine: geriatrics. She was the principal architect of the *British Medical Association Report on the Care and Treatment of the Elderly and Infirm* in 1947, which established the basic principles for such care still practised today. As Secretary of the International Association of Gerontology and writer of many articles, in both English and French, on the physical, mental and social care of the elderly, she was able to share her innovatory therapeutic experience worldwide. When she was killed at the wheel of her car at the age of 62, colleagues and patients were stunned by their loss.

> Future generations of old people in illness, of the lame and the halt, and of those who bring them the benefits of a more enlightened age of medical and social care, will never know the full extent of the debt they owe to this great pioneer.[9]

'[She] was quite fearless in putting forward views which she considered right and did not hesitate to take a lead in righting wrongs however unpleasant the task might be.'[10]

1. Dale Matthews, 'Dr Marjory Warren and the origin of British geriatrics', *Journal of American Geriatrics*, **32** (1984), p. 254, quoting Marjory Warren, 'Geriatrics: a medical, social and economic problem', *The Practitioner* (157) (1946), p. 384.
2. *The Almoner* (November 1960), p. 353.
3. Dr G. F. Adams, 'Memorial Address for Dr Marjory W. Warren, CBE' at St Pancras Church (1.10.1960), reprinted in *Gerontologica Clinica*, **3**(1) (1961).
4. Obituary, *The Lancet* (17.9.1960), p. 657.
5. Matthews, *op. cit.*, p. 256.
6. *Ibid.*, p. 257.
7. *Ibid.*, p. 258.
8. *The Almoner, loc. cit.*
9. Adams, *op. cit.* See also obituary in *British Medical Women's Federation Journal* (1960); and Marjory Warren's own seminal articles in *British Medical Journal* (February 1943), p. 822; *The Practitioner* (157) (1946), p. 384; and *The Lancet* (January 1946), p. 841.
10. *The Lancet* (24.9.1960), p. 712.

WARRINER, DOREEN, OBE
(16.3.1904–17.12.1972)

RESCUER OF REFUGEES

Father: Henry Warriner, landowner and estate manager
Mother: Henrietta Beatrice, née McNulty

Humanist

'[We] were held together by Doreen Warriner.'[1] 'We' were a collection of British individuals who had gone to Prague in 1938 to do what they could for the stream of refugees from the Sudetenland after the Munich agreement between Britain and Hitler. Doreen Warriner, then 34, was already launched on a distinguished academic career. Educated at Malvern Girls' College and St Hugh's College, Oxford, where she had gained an outstanding First in philosophy, politics and economics, she had been awarded her PhD in economic history from the University of London in

Doreen Warriner, c. 1939 (Courtesy of her nephew Henry Warriner)

1931 and, after further research awards, had been made an assistant lecturer at University College. On 13 October 1938 she had been supposed to leave for the US to work on her Rockefeller Fellowship. Instead, she flew to Prague. 'I had no idea at all of what to do, only a desperate wish to do something.'[2]

Very quickly she realized that the people most immediately in danger of concentration camp and death were the Sudeten German Social Democrat leaders who had resisted Hitler. By 9 November 1938 she had helped William Gillies and

David Grenfell of the British Labour Party (together with the Swedish trade union movement)[3] to get the necessary money and both Polish and British visas for nearly 250 leading Social Democrats to flee Prague via Slovakia and Cracow. But that still left about 100,000 defeated refugees, possibly 90 per cent Czech and 10 per cent German Social Democrats, and the latter in particular could neither return to the Sudetenland nor remain in Czechoslovakia. Doreen Warriner visited them bedded down on straw with their families in freezing empty castles or schools or village halls.

> To me it was a revelation to see their faces . . . no hope came . . . Yet hope arose from [their] comradeship . . . The sort of socialism that I had known in England had been intellectual and rather spiteful in tone . . . In Russia three years ago I had wanted to see socialism as something alive, but it was fatalistic and abstract, and on the stations there were still the wire cages used to deport kulaks.[4]

But here were men and women who had risked and lost everything to testify to their anti-Nazism. Where could they go now? At the end of November 1938 Doreen Warriner was given the responsibility for administering the *News Chronicle* British Committee Refugee Relief funds for the various stranded refugee groups in Prague: the Zionists, the Reich German and Austrian Socialists, and the Sudeten Liberals and Communists. On 9 December she wrote a letter to the *Daily Telegraph* spelling out that it was not relief in the guise of blankets or chocolate that was needed from Britain but British visas. She was not popular, but she 'had felt bound to say something on behalf of the people [without money or connections] who could not push'.[5] The Lord Mayor's Relief Fund wanted her sacked from the *News Chronicle* Committee. On 14 December she accompanied a group of 150 women and children across the German frontier and into Poland before they could rejoin the 250 men already allowed in to Britain. But it was a bleak Christmas for the thousands of Sudeten German socialists still stranded.

On 4 January 1939, however, it was announced that Robert Stopford of the Treasury had negotiated a British loan to the Czech government of which £4 million was a gift to aid emigration; 5,000 Sudeten families would have earmarked funds to cover transport and resettlement in Canada to work on the railways or on farms. Then began a nerve-racking race against time: could the families be got out of Prague before Hitler marched in? 'I had all along been convinced that Czechoslovakia's semi-independent existence could not continue long . . .'[6] On 29 January 1939 Doreen Warriner flew to London to put the case for urgency for about 600 families and, after near-despair, it was agreed that formalities were to be speeded up. Back in Prague, 'We worked from eight in the morning until ten at night; . . . on the night before a transport [we] would go on till two or three in the morning.'[7] But the British Government then decided that the men should be sent out first; it would be cheaper if their families waited in Czechoslovakia until the men had reached Canada, thus eliminating the cost of temporary maintenance in Britain. Hitler, however, did not wait. On 13 March he issued his ultimatum to the Czechs. Doreen Warriner thus found herself responsible for over 700 refugee women and children without British visas. The next day was spent on tenterhooks awaiting the necessary British government go-ahead until at last 500 women and children were got out. That still left over 200. On 15 March the German army invaded. Doreen Warriner grabbed every passport and visa she could lay hands on and told the refugees thronging her building that they must hide, the Gestapo were on the way. Over the next few days she organized the feeding and shelter of the 240 distraught people, trying not to let the Gestapo find them and organizing false passports where necessary. The Gestapo threatened her for protecting Communist *Dreck*. Finally, when it was clear they were about to arrest her as they had her Jewish helper, she left with one of the last Czech refugee trains crossing Poland at the beginning of April 1939. 'Doreen refused to let go once she got her teeth into a thing. But it wasn't easy.'[8]

Immensely forthright and intelligent as well as blessed with exceptional courage and humour, Doreen Warriner managed to keep morale around her high even in desperate times. A brilliant improviser, she was not above bribing a Polish consul with postage stamps or stealing a General's visiting card that might come in handy when seeking an audience on behalf of 'her' refugees. In 1941 she was awarded the OBE for her stalwart voluntary work for the thousands of Sudetenländer.

Between 1944 and 1946 Doreen Warriner served as chief of the UNRRA food mission to Yugoslavia. Her academic work thereafter focused on attempting to solve the economic problems of underdeveloped countries; she wrote the first report on progress in land reform for the United Nations in 1954. A long-term optimist, she 'believed in the possibility of good news'.[9]

1. Jean Rowntree, 'A winter in Prague', unpublished family paper (1988), p. 1.
2. Doreen Warriner, 'Winter in Prague' (written June 1939), *Slavonic and East European Review*, **62** (2) (April 1984), p. 210. Introductory note says that this 'is a document showing what one determined and courageous woman could achieve, without any large funds and faced by enormous difficulties'.
3. David Grenfell was a Labour MP, and William Gillies the International Secretary of the Labour Party, whose links with Swedish trade unionists enabled many Sudeten socialists to be given asylum later in Sweden.
4. Warriner, *op. cit.*, p. 214.
5. *Ibid.*, p. 217.
6. *Ibid.*, p. 220.
7. *Ibid.*, p. 222.
8. Rowntree, *op. cit.*, p. 16. Note also Eleanor Rathbone's accolade from Prague in 1939 on Miss Warriner working away at refugee visas and transport arrangements: 'extremely competent, an indefatigable worker, though very overtired': Mary Stocks, *Eleanor Rathbone* (London, Gollancz, 1949), p. 261.
9. Jean Rowntree, supplementary obituary for Dr Doreen Warriner, *The Times* (30.12.1972); there was also an obituary in *The Slavonic and East European Review*, **51** (1973), pp. 292–3.

See also entries for TESSA ROWNTREE and MARY BAKER PENMAN. And see the British Library catalogue of Doreen Warriner's magisterial and hard-hitting publications on the necessity for land redistribution in the Middle East, Latin America and India, especially *Land and Poverty in the Middle East* (London, Royal Institute of International Affairs, 1948); *Land Reform in Principle and Practice* (Oxford, Clarendon Press, 1969).

WATSON, ELIZABETH SPENCE
(1838–1919)

ANTI-MILITARIST; INTERNATIONALIST

Father: Edward Richardson, Quaker businessman,
Newcastle
Mother: Jane, née Wigham, Quaker social
reformer

Quaker

Elizabeth Spence Watson, c. 1890
(From Percy Corder, The Life of
Robert Spence Watson, *Headley*
Bros, 1914)

Elizabeth Spence Watson's life exemplifies the continuity of morally courageous humanitarian endeavour by British women from the early nineteenth century into the twentieth. Her parents had supported the campaign against slavery and the Corn Laws; both she and her mother later risked the social obloquy entailed in supporting Josephine Butler's campaign to repeal the Contagious Diseases Acts (1870–84). Her marriage to the lawyer Richard Spence Watson, a radical Liberal, led to her giving hospitality to persecuted European reformers such as Peter Kropotkin and Sergius Stepniak, to explorers and poets and local miners' leaders and schoolteachers – all sorts and conditions of men.

The great test of Elizabeth Spence Watson's moral courage came during the Boer War, when she and her husband were extremely unpopular active members of the local Stop-the-War Committee. Her husband, an anti-Imperialist Liberal, was dismayed to discover the self-indulgent chauvinism of his own political party, of the capitalist press and of the vast majority of the British people, who, he said, 'can be as cruel and tyrannical as any despot'.[1] A huge crowd, numbering thousands of angry, bellicose Gatesheaders, actually marched on her house at night, booing, yelling, hissing, hooting and making death threats against her husband and her guest Cronwright Schreiner, the anti-war husband of Olive Schreiner. In the event, because of the police presence outside her gate, only a few stones shattered one of her windows.[2]

The First World War was also a great grief to Elizabeth Spence Watson, and again she took up the unpopular cause of the innocent 'enemy' victims and of those opposed to the great patriotic war. Now aged 77, she, like KATE COURTNEY and MARY SHEEPSHANKS, gave refuge and support to local persecuted German 'aliens' and their families; and she counselled hundreds of young conscientious objectors who would not undertake either direct or indirect military service and were sentenced to imprisonment. '[Their] punishments and imprisonments she felt most keenly, in all their afflictions she was afflicted.'[3] It was said of her after her death in 1919:

> She was one of the bravest spirits I have known, and the memory of her witness to the Light within remains a precious possession for those who share her ideals, and an incentive to continual effort for their realization in the sure belief that only through the ultimate triumph of such ideals can the world's salvation come.[4]

1. Percy Corder, *The Life of Robert Spence Watson* (London, Headley Bros, 1914), p. 280.
2. Cronwright Schreiner, *The Land of Free Speech: A Record of a Campaign on Behalf of Peace in England and Scotland in 1900* (London, New Age Press, 1906), ch. 10: 'The land of free speech', pp. 151–7.
3. Herbert Corder, *Elizabeth Spence Watson* (leaflet; London, Loxley Bros, 1919), quoted in *The Friend* (7.3.1919).
4. *Ibid.*, p. 4.

— ∙—

WATT, MARGARET ROSE ('MADGE'), OBE
(1868–31.11.1948)

FOUNDER OF BRITISH WOMEN'S INSTITUTES AND ASSOCIATED
COUNTRY WOMEN OF THE WORLD

Father: Henry Robertson, Canadian QC
Mother: Bethia

Presbyterian

On 30 July 1932 Einstein wrote an Open Letter to Freud asking: 'Is there any way of delivering mankind from the menace of war?' Freud answered:

All that produces ties of sentiment between man and man must serve us as war's antidote . . . All that brings out the significant resemblances between men calls into play this feeling of community, identification, whereon is founded, in large measure, the whole edifice of human society.[1]

Mrs Alfred Watt, a Canadian doctor's widow, without money, prestige or influence, but a brilliant rural sociologist[2] and orator, had already grasped these fundamental principles in the First World War and decided to apply them to women, above all to the millions of rural women worldwide, so that they could see their 'significant resemblances' one to another. Working from her experience of country Women's Institutes in rural Canada, especially British Columbia, she inspired the founding of a similar movement in Wales and England in 1915, ostensibly to improve food production, especially fruit and vegetables, as part of the war effort. But her vision went much deeper and wider than that.

She understood the needs of country women and knew their isolation, ap- preciated their longing for a wider sphere of activity, sympathized with the sense of frustration that assailed many who were capable of a much bigger career than was afforded them by the management of a household.[3]

Having seen the success of Women's Institutes in Canada and Britain, Mrs Alfred Watt, a committed anti-militarist,[4] went on after a long struggle[5] to establish Associated Country Women of the World in 1929. 'She envisaged linking the whole world in an association composed of rural women whose interchange of knowledge and experience would be of mutual advantage and would lead to an international understanding by which chances of friction between nations might be lessened.'[6] She herself travelled tirelessly across the world, speaking to hundreds of meetings of countrywomen in France, Germany, Belgium, Holland, Denmark, Norway, Sweden, Finland, Estonia, Latvia, Canada, the USA, New Zealand, Australia, Ceylon and Palestine, not to mention throughout the UK and Eire; and wherever she spoke there sprouted increased membership and enthusiasm. She chaired three world congresses of the Association in Vienna, Stockholm and Washington. Between 1929 and 1948 she was President and then Hon. President of the Associated Country Women of the World, of which Lady HOWARD became Vice-Chair. Both women were dedicated to work for international peace and shared a commitment to campaign against 'soil banditry', vowing to transmit the soil to succeeding generations, naturally enriched rather than over-exploited, artificially modified and impoverished.

> Mrs Watt was a short, squat woman with a fine leonine head, rather short white hair and, frequently, a fierce look . . . Her fine dark brown eyes shone with life and vigour . . . She was so charged with . . . contagious enthusiasm that her audiences forgot that she was small and stout, and did not think of her in terms of age. For she had an ability to infect other people with her own enthusiasm which really did amount to genius . . . Disappointments, snubs, rebuffs, recoiled from her sturdy little figure and left her still standing, rather aggressively – and still talking! Often enough her adversaries gave way, with bad grace, in sheer self-defence, because, short of liquidation, there seemed no method of disposing of her.[7]

Her ideals for her worldwide movement of countrywomen were articulated by Dr Ruby Green Smith of Cornell University:

> To cultivate international understanding and friendship; to create appreciation of talents and achievements of the People in all countries; to study their varied contributions to culture, and the beauty and wealth of One World.
>
> To maintain the highest ideals of home life; to share growing knowledge of home-making at its best: to place service above comfort; to let international neighbourliness supplant hatreds.
>
> So to guide children that their minds may be clear, their spirits happy, their characters generous, and their good-will so genuine that Peace on Earth, for which the people yearn, will come to pass.
>
> To pledge allegiance to righteousness in relations between countries: and to build a better civilization, through fidelity to the United Nations, with abiding faith in its promises of more abundant life for all Peoples.[8]

1. Otto Nathan and Heinz Norden, *Einstein on Peace* (New York, Avenel Books, 1981), pp. 188 and 199.
2. She had graduated BA with first class honours from the University of Toronto in 1889, and then was the first woman in Canada to gain her MA, in 1890.
3. Obituary, *The Times* (1.12.1948).
4. She was a signatory on the British Committee of the Women's International Congress at The Hague in April 1915: see Appendix I.
5. See Mrs Neve Scarborough, *History of the Associated Country Women of the World* (London, 1953), pp. 5–7.
6. *The Times, loc. cit.*
7. Scarborough, *op. cit.*, p. 8.
8. Quoted in entry 'Margaret Rose Robertson' in *Modern Pioneers, 1909–1959* (British Columbia Women's Institute), p. 26.

WATTS, AGATHA
(8.7.1861–28.6.1923)

PEACE WITNESS IN THE FIRST WORLD WAR AND IRISH CIVIL WAR

Father: William Jackson, Quaker tea merchant
Mother: Agatha

Quaker

Until 1914 Agatha Watts had lived the 'normal' life of a devoted wife and mother of seven children born between 1886 and 1901, all her energy going into the struggle to overcome poor health and financial worries and, with her Quaker builder husband Challacombe Watts, to rear their six sons and a daughter. But on the outbreak of the First World War she became a public citizen. She gave herself utterly to the rejection of all enmity, whether towards individuals or towards another nation, and to resistance to every aspect of war-making. Supported by her husband, she made their Manchester home a place of guaranteed sympathetic refuge for the wives and mothers of interned 'aliens'; she also made it the headquarters for those working with the No Conscription Fellowship and held weekly Sunday evenings there for 'Jews and Gentiles, Catholics and Protestants, all sorts and conditions of men and women who were suffering for their pacifist faith'.[1] Agatha Watts also testified to her deeply unpopular pacifism outside her home: 'Whenever a speaker was needed for a difficult meeting, she went and gave her message so fearlessly, and with such conviction, that she always commanded attention and respect.'[2]

All her children shared their parents' values. Her elder sons and daughter served with the Friends' War Victims' Relief Committee in France; all the sons of military age were conscientious objectors; one son, Arthur, was imprisoned twice, once for refusing to submit a Quaker pamphlet to the censor. (Her eldest son was interned in Norway in the Second World War and was later a worker for the Resistance there.) Agatha Watts spent herself to exhaustion supporting the families of men imprisoned for refusing military service and in helping to establish the Manchester branch of the newly formed Women's International League, again an unpopular cause in wartime.

After the First World War Agatha Watts felt most addressed by the brutal wars in Ireland, waged first between the British Army and the Irish and then between the Irish themselves. Although she knew she had an incurable disease, she volunteered to be part of the Women's International League delegation to Ireland in October 1920, returning in 1921 and 1922 to try to strengthen the few beleaguered, isolated Irish pacifists, especially the women, and to reconcile those, so much more numerous, inflamed with righteous enmity:

> She travelled throughout the length and breadth of the land, pleading with everyone she met for patience and understanding, and forbearance in attempting the solution of a problem that appeared well-nigh hopeless . . . 'Everywhere we went, among strangers in race and experience, and sometimes utterly among strangers in outlook, Mrs Watts would waste no time in preliminaries, but speak so directly from her heart to that of her hearers that the most hostile softened and seemed at once to love and trust her.'[3]

It was also in 1922 that she learned that her son Arthur had fallen victim to typhus while heading the Quaker famine relief team in Buzuluk, Russia, where VIOLET TILLARD had served and died. Agatha Watts crossed Europe to reach him and nursed him back to recovery.[4] Three months later, she was dead.

1. *Society of Friends London Yearly Meeting Proceedings* (1924), p. 177.
2. *The Friend* (20.7.1923), p. 559.
3. *Society of Friends London Yearly Meeting Proceedings*, op. cit., p. 177. See also Ethel Snowden's tribute to 'saintly Mrs Watts' in Ireland in her *A Political Pilgrim in Europe* (London, Cassell, 1921).
4. Arthur Watts, always a passionate champion of the working class, eventually settled in the Soviet Union at the end of the 1920s and helped to build a huge steel foundry there.

WHATELY, MONICA
(1891–12.9.1960)

FEMINIST; INTERNATIONALIST; ANIMAL RIGHTS HUMANITARIAN

Father: Capt. Reginald Pepys Whately

Roman Catholic

Monica Whately first distanced herself from her conventional Catholic family background when she went to study politics and world affairs at the newly established London School of Economics. She was one of the very first members of the Catholic Women's Suffrage Society before the First World War, and later helped to form St Joan's Social and Political Alliance. Immediately after the war she helped in famine relief operations in Poland. A left-wing socialist member of the ILP, she was a Parliamentary Labour Party candidate in 1929 and 1933 and defeated Sir Oswald Mosley in the London County Council election in Limehouse in the early 1930s. She was an equality feminist, and 'her beauty, energy and great sense of humour'[1] were all assets to the Six Point Group,[2] which operated on a shoestring from her London flat. Her unapologetic, assertive feminism alienated her from some of the more conservative elements in the British Labour Party: 'I have over and over again been threatened with excommunication owing to my fight for the complete emancipation of women,'[3] and her political radicalism plus feminism alienated her from the Catholic Church.[4] In 1932 she was part of a fact-finding delegation that also included ELLEN WILKINSON and V. K. Krishna Menon, sent to India by the India League.[5]

Monica Whately was an outspoken (and early) critic of Nazism, visiting Germany in order to try to help persecuted Jews and socialists and campaigning, in vain, for a boycott of German goods. On behalf of the Six Point Group she wrote to leading British women including VIRGINIA WOOLF in 1935, appealing for their support in interceding on behalf of German women held hostage in concentration camps for their Communist husbands.[6] Her humanitarian detestation of all human cruelty also led her to champion the animal prey of blood sports, and animal victims of vivisection.

After the Second World War Monica Whately visited South Africa 'where the colour bar distressed her beyond measure and the treatment of women in prison above all'.[7] She also made a point of travelling behind the Iron Curtain to Poland, Russia and Czechoslovakia to insist on the possibility of psychological disarmament and the necessity for peace and goodwill between different systems and beliefs.

1. Hazel Hunkins-Hallinan in *WFL Bulletin* (23.9.1960).
2. The Six Points were political equality, occupational equality, moral equality, social equality, economic equality and legal equality: see Dorothy Evans, *The Six Point Group: A Brief Account of Its National and International Work*, pamphlet, in Women's Library, London. Vice-Presidents of the Six Point Group included Vera Brittain, Violet Bonham Carter and Winifred Holtby.
3. Monica Whately, letter to Emmeline Pethick-Lawrence (end October 1947), in Six Point Group papers, Box 526/C7, Women's Library, London.
4. 'As her enthusiasms took her further and further afield the [Catholic] Alliance did not always see eye to eye with her and her membership lapsed': *Catholic Citizen* (15.10.1960). She died a practising Catholic, however.
5. She co-published, with Ellen Wilkinson and V. K. Krishna Menon, *The Condition of India: Being a Report of the Delegation Sent to India by the India League* (London, India League, 1932; 534pp.).
6. See letter (7.6.1935) pasted into Virginia Woolf's third scrapbook for *Three Guineas*, Monks House papers, B16g, University of Sussex Library. Monica Whately had just published a leaflet *Women behind Nazi Bars* (London, British Non-Sectarian Anti-Nazi Council, 1935).
7. Obituary, *Guardian* (15.9.1960).

‑‑

WILKINS, HONOR
(*c.* 1907–*c.* 1977)

MEDICAL MISSIONARY DOCTOR IN INDIA

Father: — Harvey, architect, Anglican
Mother: —, Baptist

Nonconformist Christian

Inspired as a girl by the missionary explorers in the Gobi desert, Mildred Cable and Francesca French, Honor Harvey studied medicine in order to become a medical missionary. She trained at the Royal Free Hospital and reflected that after university she had 'become much more broad in my mind . . . much more really interested in the humanitarian side of relieving suffering in places where they needed it very much'.[1] One such place was Orissa, among the tribal Kond Hill people whom she went out to serve in 1932 with her husband, a fellow medical missionary who had been brought up in India by missionary parents. Together, they fought the ignorance, ill health and poverty of their patch of India. Their first wards in the jungle hillside were whitewashed former cowsheds. Throughout their time in India they had no electricity, and only kerosene for light and sterilizing. Gradually they built a laboratory, a dispensary, a surgery, an operating theatre and a gynaecological ward. Honor Wilkins ran a women's clinic – with time off to have three babies herself. She also started varied vegetable gardens and kept a small herd of dairy cows in order to have milk for the orphan babies in their hospital. The Wilkins' greatest joy was the success of cataract operations. Their greatest misery was witnessing the Bengal famine of 1943, when they saw the desperate people picking individual rice kernels off the rail tracks.

Honor Wilkins worked as the anaesthetist for all her husband's surgical operations, which included patients suffering from mauling by bears, tigers and leopards. Malaria was the background of everything they did; 80 per cent of the children had enlarged spleens. She and her husband stayed in India for sixteen years, treating dysentery, hookworm, leprosy, cholera and venereal disease. They took an increasingly liberal and relaxed attitude to their patients' religious beliefs and practices, accepting their animism and hoping only that Christianity might be able to free the hill people from some terrifying superstitions. When they saw Catholic priests parading the Virgin Mary and other Christian images around on chariots, they recognized that this was exactly the right thing to do within a Hindu context. They left India reluctantly, and only in order to be able to keep in touch with their own children at school in England. What the Indian people gave them in friendship made them feel, just as Dr CLAIRE THOMSON had felt, that they had received at least as much from India as they had managed to give. The hospital they founded is still in existence, funded in part by War on Want.[2]

1. Transcript of taped interview with Drs Gordon and Honor Wilkins (1964), Mss Eur R129/1–2, Transcript T129, held in the India Office Library, British Library.
2. I am grateful to Pat Barr, *The Dust in the Balance: British Women in India 1905–1945* (London, Hamish Hamilton, 1989), for introducing me to the work of Dr Gordon and Dr Honor Wilkins.

WILKINSON, ELLEN, MP
(8.10.1891–6.2.1947)

SOCIALIST; ANTI-FASCIST CRUSADER

Father: Richard Wilkinson, former textile worker, insurance clerk
Mother: Ellen, née Wood, dressmaker

Methodist

Born to an unemployed cotton operative at a time when there was no unemployment allowance, maternity welfare or child benefit, Ellen Wilkinson never forgot her mother's life, battling against cancer in a crowded, cold, terraced house in Manchester but nevertheless having the spirit to be active and positive whenever the pain receded.[1] She too was to grow up a battler, not for her own family but rather for all the families of the British poor, and indeed for the underdog in Europe, India and Africa. Her short lifespan engaged with a particularly grim period of cyclical mass unemployment and Depression, interrupted twice by world war.

Ellen Wilkinson

Converted to the faith of the young ILP by the socialist orator KATHARINE GLASIER, 16-year-old Ellen Wilkinson ardently embraced the Party's socialist programme, including the abolition of child labour under the age of 14, a legally enforced eight-hour working day, state provision for the aged, sick and disabled worker and for widows and orphans, the abolition of indirect taxation, taxation to extinction of all unearned incomes, and work for the unemployed.[2] Katharine Glasier convinced her that she too could and must give her life to inspiring people to 'make life better, to remove slums and underfeeding and misery'.[3]

'Red Ellen', 'small in body, but great in heart',[4] was the outstanding spokeswoman, alongside ELEANOR RATHBONE, during the 1920s and 1930s for humanitarian causes at home and abroad, whether her forum was the House of Commons or, during her political wilderness years (1931–35), political journalism.[5] When 'mining villages became virtually famine areas'[6] during the tragic miners' strike of 1926, Ellen Wilkinson, a new, young Labour trade union MP, became Chairman of the Women's Committee for Relief of Miners' Wives and Children. She also electrified the House by showing the rope and hook or 'guss' that Somerset miners had to wear between their legs as they hauled tubs of coal along the underground tunnels, in places little more than nine inches high. She then took up the individual human tragedy of a destitute mother of four, the wife of an unemployed worker drowning in debt, who was actually sent to prison for three months for attempting suicide: 'Attempted suicide should be taken off the list of crimes.'[7] In 1932 she went on a fact-finding mission to India, where she visited Gandhi in jail and reported back attacking British repression there and urging his immediate unconditional release.[8]

Ellen Wilkinson was one of the first politically conscious people in Britain to be alive to the threat of European fascism:

> Many years before the Fascist danger was officially recognised she was associated with Socialist and democratic forces ready to go underground on the Continent. [Already at] the end of the twenties . . . [she] was always ready not only to advise but to help. [For the] German underground movement, Spanish Republicans, and Italian anti-Fascists . . . the men and women of the European Resistance movement, she [became] a symbol.[9]

A 'doer as well as a writer',[10] Ellen Wilkinson personally visited the Saar just before the 1935 plebiscite and helped in the relief and rescue of children there orphaned by Nazi terror.[11] She also helped set up the Legal Commission of Enquiry in Britain into the burning of the Reichstag and was labelled 'a red-haired agitator' by the Nazis in consequence. Not surprisingly, she was an outspoken anti-appeaser, a member of Eleanor Rathbone's Parliamentary Committee on Refugees (to many of whom she gave temporary shelter in her own small flat) and also a glowing champion of the Republicans in the Spanish Civil War, whom she visited in April 1937 with RACHEL CROWDY, Eleanor Rathbone and the Duchess of Atholl (STEWART-MURRAY), and again in December 1937, with Clement Attlee among others, returning home to tour Britain appealing for funds, food and medical aid for Spain.[12]

In 1939 Ellen Wilkinson wrote *The Town That Was Murdered* about the human wretchedness in her constituency, Jarrow, blighted by 80 per cent unemployment after the collapse of its shipyard. She had already walked much of the way with the deputation of 200 desperate hunger marchers from Tyneside to Westminster, where they were forbidden to present their petition at the bar of the House; she then presented it herself and bombarded the President of the Board of Trade to intervene effectually to re-establish industry in the stricken town.[13]

During the Second World War Ellen Wilkinson wore herself out as Parliamentary Secretary for Home Security, i.e., for civilian protection from the Blitz. She visited bombsites immediately after a strike and air-raid shelters not only in London but all over Britain, never taking shelter or adequate rest or food herself. Appointed Minister of Education after the Labour landslide victory in 1945, she dedicated herself to raising the school-leaving age to 15 and to making further and higher education accessible across the class divide. But she also wanted to change the *spirit* of British education. She herself had known at first hand crowded, harsh, joyless elementary classrooms where she, a bright, eager child, had hated school and where her 13-year-old boy pupils had actually been caned for being too interested in her lesson to remember to sit up straight, hands folded. Her greatest humane testament is her credo for education:

> Everything to do with children must have room to grow . . . Schools must have freedom to experiment, and variety for the sake of freshness . . . Laughter in the classroom, self confidence growing every day, eager interest instead of bored uniformity, this is the way to produce the Britons who will have no need to fear the new scientific age, but will stride into it, heads high, determined to master science and to serve mankind.[14]

1. See Ellen Wilkinson's chapter in Margot Asquith (ed.), *Myself When Young by Famous Women of To-day* (London, Frederick Muller, 1938); and Betty Vernon, *Ellen Wilkinson 1891–1947* (London, Croom Helm, 1982), pp. 1–4.
2. Vernon, *op. cit.*, p. 14.
3. Asquith, *op. cit.*, p. 414.
4. Clement Davies, MP in the House of Commons, quoted in *The Times* obituary tributes (7.2.1947).
5. Ellen Wilkinson's journalism can be found most often during the 1930s in *Time and Tide*, but also in the *Daily Herald*, *New Statesman*, *News Chronicle* and later in *Tribune*, which she co-founded.
6. Vernon, *op. cit.*, p. 89.
7. *Ibid.*, p. 99.
8. See entry for MONICA WHATELY.
9. F. A. Voigt (former Berlin correspondent of the *Manchester Guardian*), *Manchester Guardian* (7.2.1947).
10. Vernon, *op. cit.*, p. 158.
11. See Ellen Wilkinson's pamphlets *The Terror in Germany* (n.d. but written 1933) and *German Relief: Feed the Children* (?1933).
12. See Vernon, *op. cit.*, pp. 162–71; and Pamela Brookes, *Women at Westminster* (London, Peter Davies, 1967), pp. 117–18.
13. See Brookes, *op. cit.*, p. 124.
14. Ellen Wilkinson, Foreword to *The New Secondary Education* (London, HMSO, no. 9, 1947), quoted in Vernon, *op. cit.*, p. 221.

See also obituary tributes to Ellen Wilkinson in *The Times* (7.2.1947); *Manchester Guardian* (February 1947); and *Daily Herald* (7.2.1947).

━━

WILLIAMS, CICELY, CMG, FRCP
(2.12.1893–13.7.1992)

DISCOVERER OF KWASHIORKOR; SURVIVOR OF CHANGI; WORLD EXPERT IN MATERNAL AND INFANT HEALTH

Father: Rowland Williams, plantation owner in Jamaica, Director of Education
Mother: Margaret, voluntary community health worker

Christian

Cicely Williams grew up in Jamaica deeply influenced by her parents' commitment to Jamaicans. As she pointed out in her eighties: 'You haven't got to wait for Chairman Mao to say work for the people.'[1] The dead of the First World War included so many young male doctors that Oxford University at last opened its medical school to women students, among the first of whom was Cicely Williams.

Dr Cicely Williams (Cover photograph of Ann Dally, Cicely: The Story of a Doctor, *Gollancz, 1968)*

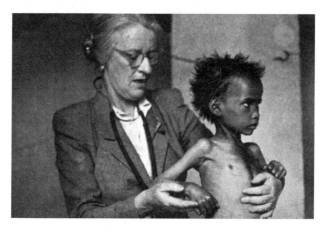

She struggled with some of the examinations but was a first-rate clinician from the moment she actually began to practise medicine among the women and children in the East End, where she realized that 'the care of the *whole* child . . . including the family and especially the *mother,* . . . was essential to child health' (my emphases).[2] It was not easy in the depressed late 1920s for women doctors to obtain hospital posts in Britain, and she had no capital with which to start up her own GP practice. She made one application after another to serve in the Colonial Health Service, having spent one year in malaria-infested Greece and having already obtained the Diploma of Hygiene and Tropical Medicine. Finally, in 1929, she was sent to the Gold Coast (now Ghana). There she worked herself to exhaustion, concentrating on maternal and infant health, doing mass vaccinations against smallpox and treating hundreds of patients for scabies, yaws, ulcers, malaria and dysentery single-handed.

It was in the Gold Coast that Cicely Williams made her first momentous discovery. Sickened by the huge number of small children suffering from swollen feet, distended bellies, reddish hair and flaking skin: a disease she could not identify, let alone cure, she began to perform post-mortem autopsies on the day of a child's death, and every time she found an enlarged, fatty liver. Eventually she concluded that the disease that killed so many toddlers in West Africa was not vitamin B1 deficiency, nor, as the medical world then believed, pellagra (niacin deficiency) but blood protein deficiency in the diet after weaning, which could be rectified. Hence she called the disease what the African mothers themselves called it, *kwashiorkor,* weanling disease.[3]

In 1938 Cicely Williams was transferred by the Colonial Office from West Africa to Singapore. Once again she concentrated on maternal and infant health, this time meeting new tropical diseases such as beri-beri. There she waged a ferocious battle against artificial milk, especially sweetened condensed milk, which, as a substitute for breast milk, she pointed out, actually killed babies.[4] She also intervened whenever she could against the selling of young Chinese children, including young girls sold into prostitution.

When the Japanese invaded Malaya in December 1941, Cicely Williams was conducting a child health survey in the Sultanate of Trengganu on the border of Thailand. Faced with capture by the Japanese, she trekked for eleven days through jungle, by river and over mountains to reach the railway line and, finally, Singapore, arriving a few weeks before it also fell to the Japanese.[5]

The chaotic period in Singapore before and after the British surrender 'was a terrible show'.[6] Cicely Williams saw evacuated and deserting British and Australian soldiers looting and pushing women and children out of the way to get shelter for themselves during the bombing raids, and crowding women and children off the last boats that were getting away. She soon found herself stranded, the only doctor in a children's ward of 50 sick children under 6: twenty sick war orphans, 40 orthopaedic children and ten mentally handicapped; she had to go from one wounded, screaming, terrified infant to the next all night during the intense shelling and machine-gunning. 'Bits of metal seemed to be flying about everywhere. So I picked up the babies in armfuls and put them under beds with three or four mattresses.'[7] She was ordered by the remaining British authorities to evacuate what were by now over 100 sick children, first to a former prison and then, orders changed, to the Dental Hospital, where she found all the children simply dumped on the floor. 'There were the children and there was the floor and that was that. Every thing to do, no one to do it and nothing to do it with.'[8] She commandeered some milk and boiled it up on the bunsen burners in the dental department. The water supply failed and she was ordered to move all the children again, this time to the Sepoy Lines Maternity Block, where she and the few remaining nurses scrubbed floors, sluiced latrines and washed the babies. Then the Japanese ordered them to move yet again, this time to a former mental hospital. It was almost more than she could bear. In desperation she gave what babies she could to be adopted as she herself went down with acute dysentery and was interned.

At first, conditions at Changi prisoner-of-war camp were bearable; many of the women supported each other well and although there was obvious malnutrition and extreme anxiety and depression, Cicely Williams found it therapeutic to be able to do some doctoring of her fellow prisoners, to work on her research notes on the deficiency disease of rickets, and to negotiate with the commandant on the prisoners' behalf, although 'it often made me shake in my shoes to be yelled at and to have revolvers waved about . . . [The] bowing business was a perfect farce. I never felt it was worth worrying about and used to bow to the Nips front, back or side.'[9] On 10 October 1943, however, Cicely Williams was arrested by the Japanese Gestapo, the Kempeitei, and accused of spying. 'I was very very frightened and horrified at the prospect of being . . . tortured.'[10] Imprisoned in a cage a few feet square, the only woman with three men, she had to endure hours of interrogation, weeks of near-starvation and deliberate humiliation, though not physical torture.

> The first few weeks in the Kempei prison were so horrible that one felt nothing could ever make life normal and wholesome again . . . It was horrible to see men taken out and savaged by the Nips, to see them injured and wretched and only able to crawl, to know that we might all be faced with mass executions – one often prayed for any sort of early ending to it . . . When I was first transferred to the small cell with three men in it I felt for a time that it was simply unbearable . . . and then luckily I found out that I could do something for Jackson who had . . . had a terrible time. His hands and back needed a lot of massage . . .[11]

Released back to Changi internment camp after three months, she was greeted as follows:

Welcome back Cicely. We're a much happier Camp today than we've been since last October. Oh so often have we talked of you – hoped for you – prayed for you, dreamt of you and now at last you're free and we're happy. You'd be flattered if you knew how enormously relieved we all are to-night. We missed you a lot . . . Rest yourself and *eat plenty*. (Emphasis in the original)[12]

In her statement to the police (2 September 1945) after the Japanese surrender, Cicely Williams paid tribute by name to the tortured British men prisoners she had known, who, amazingly, had

maintained their detachment and dignity . . . I also recall with pride and gratitude the courage and loyalty of many of the Chinese and Eurasians [in Changi] and the unfailing kindness and consideration which I received from all nationalities. Even occasionally from some of the Japanese.[13]

It might seem that, having survived so much and now needing to recuperate from severe weight loss, as well as from complex post-Changi diseases, Cicely Williams had done enough for one life. Instead, she worked to better the health of the poorest mothers and children, worldwide, for another 40 years. In 1948 she was appointed the first Head of Mother and Child Care at the UN's World Health Organization in Geneva.[14] Throughout her life she had the greatest respect for the mothers of the world who managed 'to care for their children in spite of poverty, frequent infections and inadequate nutrition'.[15] In a paper on public health from a global perspective she said: 'We worry a great deal about the persons we want to liberate from political tyranny, and we ignore those we could and should liberate from the tyrannies of dirt, ignorance, and hunger.'[16] As for herself, 'she used to say she felt she was . . . mother to millions of babies'.[17]

1. *Evening Standard* (3.12.1976), p. 21.
2. Ann Dally, *Cicely: The Story of a Doctor* (London, Gollancz, 1968), p. 21. See also the later biography of Cicely Williams by Sally Craddock, *Retired – Except on Demand: The Life of Dr Cicely Williams* (Oxford, Green College, 1983).
3. See Dally, *op. cit.*, chs 3 and 4; and Hugh Trowell, 'The beginning of the *kwashiorkor* story in Africa', *Central African Journal of Medicine*, **21** (1) (January 1975), p. 21: '[She] wrote the first comprehensive description of the "Deficiency Disease in Infants" in the Gold Coast Annual Report, 1931–2.' Note also Cicely Williams' respect for traditional herbal medicine in West Africa, which used spasm-relaxant drugs that could cure tetanus and pneumococcal meningitis, untreatable in Europe: Dally, *op. cit.*, pp. 77–9.
4. See her talk 'Milk and murder' given in Singapore in 1940: Dally, *op. cit.*, pp. 95–102.
5. See unpublished typescript 'Retreat from Trengganu', in Cicely Williams papers, pp/CDW/B2/14, held in the Contemporary Medical Archives, Wellcome Institute History of Medicine, London.
6. See unpublished typescript 'The fall of Malaya', in Cicely Williams papers, above.
7. *Ibid.*
8. *Ibid.*
9. Unpublished typescript 'Personal notes', in Cicely Williams papers, above.
10. Unpublished typescript 'Prison night', in Cicely Williams papers, above.
11. *Ibid.*
12. Pencil-written piece of card, signed 'Sheila', in Cicely Williams papers, above.
13. Cicely Williams papers, above.
14. See obituary 'Dr Cicely Williams', *The Times* (18.7.1992), for her work in more than 70 countries, teaching that 'medicine must be both preventive and curative and continuity of care is essential'.
15. Obituary, *Guardian* (21.7.1992).
16. C. Williams, 'Kwashiorkor', *Journal of American Medical Association*, **153** (1953), p. 1280, quoted by P. Farnes, 'Women in medical science', in G. Kass-Simon and P. Farnes, *Women of Science: Righting the Record* (Bloomington, Indiana University Press, 1990), p. 280.
17. Obituary, *Daily Telegraph* (20.7.1992).

WILLIAMS, ETHEL M. N.,
JP, MD, DPH
(1863–1948)

PIONEER PAEDIATRICIAN; PACIFIST
INTERNATIONALIST

Father: Charles Williams, country squire,
Cromer, Norfolk
Mother: Mary Elizabeth, descendant of
William Harvey

Anglican

Dr Ethel Williams, c. 1930 (Courtesy of Wellcome Institute Library, London)

Coming from a Norfolk country gentry family, Dr Ethel Williams was perhaps an unlikely person to become a determined feminist, social reformer and pacifist, on top of being that pioneer phenomenon, a woman doctor in late Victorian England. After studying at Norwich High School for Girls and Newnham College, Cambridge, Ethel Williams had to go to Vienna and Paris in the late 1880s for her clinical hospital training. She eventually graduated as MB and MD in London by 1895. After working in Clapham and Blackfriars, she moved to the north-east of England in 1896 to serve the poorest women and children of Newcastle.

At first she had to face huge prejudice and scepticism, both from male doctors and from potential patients, as the first woman GP they had ever seen; but after a year her fame began to spread as her remarkable personality became known. On realizing that infant mortality under the age of 1 in the poorest part of Newcastle was three times the national average, she personally undertook to pay for daily milk for these babies. Her first woman partner was DR ETHEL BENTHAM, and eventually Ethel Williams' practice became the largest in the whole of the city. 'It is no exaggeration to say that she completely revolutionized medical practice as it was then understood.'[1] Her own criterion for a good woman GP was patience, 're-inforced by real affection for one's patients'.[2] She saw herself as 'Mother's help and chief cook and bottle washer to families in distress . . . I have never been able to use the slapping and setting on a cold stone method of treatment.'[3]

Not many years after establishing herself as a woman doctor, Ethel Williams could be seen processing up Northumberland Street, Newcastle, wearing a sandwich board for the much mocked cause of women's suffrage. She also participated in the 1907 'Mud March' in London, when police forced the women demonstrators to walk in the flooded gutters. In 1910 she supported a woman candidate for election in Tyneside, saying

> She hoped that Miss Burnett would not go on to the Council in too quiet a spirit. Fighting was good, and the interests of women and children, housing

reform and the care of the tuberculous, were things that were worth fighting about.[4]

Ethel Williams and her lifelong companion Frances Hardcastle (mathematician and descendant of the astronomer Herschels) were the leaders of the National Union of Women's Suffrage Society in the north-east. They both felt conscientiously driven to break with Mrs Fawcett in April 1915 over the issue of the Society's position regarding the war, becoming supporters, instead, of the Women's Congress at The Hague. Ethel Williams applied to the Home Secretary, in vain, to attend the Congress.[5]

Even more radically, Ethel Williams testified publicly to her unpopular pacifism by chairing the north-eastern convention of the No Conscription Fellowship in October 1916 which 'unanimously pledged itself to support the dependents [sic] of C.O.'s and to work for the repeal of the Military Service Acts and a settlement of the war by negotiation'.[6] In May and June 1919 she

A starving child, Vienna, 1918 (From Ethel Williams, 'A visit to Vienna' in Towards Peace and Freedom, *Zürich Congress of the Women's International League for Peace and Freedom, London, 1919)*

was in Vienna investigating the health situation of its undernourished babies and children, suffering from the continued Allied blockade. Her report was balanced but devastating:

> people were not dying from starvation . . . There has been neither cholera nor plague . . . and practically no typhus or smallpox . . . [But the] increase of tuberculosis is appalling . . . almost all the children under two . . . were rickety. In the poorer parts of Vienna I saw no children of two and three walking the streets at all: those I saw were being carried by their mothers, miserable little morsels of humanity. The [older]children one saw . . . were white-faced, anaemic, with sunken discoloured eyes, and nothing but skin and bone . . . The stunted growth is most remarkable . . . there were outbreaks of scurvy and osteomalacia [softening of the bones resulting from lack of calcium] . . . I saw . . . little children unable to stand or walk, sitting with crooked backs and twisted limbs like little sad white-faced chimpanzees. The picture of that Out Patient Department is burnt into my mind . . . There was no playing, no laughing, no child was running about. Life for them had become a thing to be endured.[7]

Ethel Williams attended the third international Congress of the Women's International League for Peace and Freedom in 1921, also in Vienna, where she was voted on to the committee for Peace Mission work to initiate intensive peace work in frontier districts between France and Germany where hatred on both sides was endemic, making lasting peace impossible. In 1926 she retired from general practice, largely in the hope of being able to give more time to pacifist and similar work, serving both the WIL and the League of Nations Union.

In the 1930s Ethel Williams was a JP especially concerned with the Juvenile Bench, a passionate gardener ('Snow was lying thinly but Dr Williams did about two hours' digging'[8]), an offerer of hospitality to persecuted Jewish refugees, and a concerned, scientific speaker on the effect of the Depression on the nutrition and health of the families of the unemployed.[9] In her eighties, during the Blitz, she signed up for a postgraduate refresher course at a Hammersmith hospital in case she could help with civilian casualties. After the Second World War, she naturally supported the United Nations Association.

'Great woman, great life, great friend.'[10]

> She held strong political views. I never knew to what party she gave her loyalty, but I think it would be fair to say that she was always a 'left' politician. To those who needed her, and to the under-dog, her ready sympathy was always available . . . In time of need she could be counted upon to give herself without any reservation or qualification to whose whom she cared for.[11]

'One of the North's most remarkable women . . . [She] was always willing to lead where others faltered and pull out the extra ounce of strength.'[12]

1. Professor Grey Turner, transcription of his Presentation Address to Dr Ethel Williams (7.10.1946), held in Williams papers, Contemporary Medical Archives Centre, Wellcome Institute for the History of Medicine, London.
2. Ethel Williams, 'Thirty odd years in General Practice', *British Medical Women's Federation Newsletter* (1926?), p. 53.
3. *Ibid.*, pp. 54 and 56.
4. *Shields Daily News* (22.10.1910), quoted in Patricia Hollis, *Ladies Elect: Women in English Local Government, 1865–1914* (Oxford, Clarendon Press, 1987), p. 16.
5. See Introduction and Appendix I. 'Much struck with Dr Ethel Williams, Newcastle, strong, fine face – elderly – wish she lived in London' Kate Courtney wrote in her *War Journal* on meeting her at the latter's home where they co-founded the British Section of the Women's International League (3.10.1915).
6. *Tribunal* (5.10.1916).
7. Ethel Williams, 'A visit to Vienna' in *Towards Peace and Freedom: Report on The Women's International Congress, Zurich* (London, August 1919), pp. 10–11.
8. Obituary, *Journal of the Medical Women's Federation* (April 1948), p. 33.
9. See Ethel Williams, 'The effects of the world economic crisis on physical condition', Presidential Address to the MWF, Sheffield (May 1934), published in *Medical Women's Federation News-Letter* (July 1934), pp. 18–24.
10. Sir Angus Watson, quoted in Amy Landreth, 'A doctor who had to kill prejudice', *Newcastle Daily Journal* (8.10.1946).
11. Turner, *op. cit.*
12. *Newcastle Daily Journal* (1.2.1948). A university women's hostel was named after her at the University of Newcastle upon Tyne in 1950.

See also Nigel Todd, 'Ethel Williams, medical and suffrage pioneer', *N.E. Labour History*, Bulletin, no. 30 (1996), for Ethel Williams' startling manifestation in July 1917 as secretary of the Newcastle Workers' and Soldiers' Council, a British version of a 'soviet' created to mobilize a peace movement in 1917. The Special Branch intervened.

WILSON, FRANCESCA
(1.1.1888–4.3.1981)

INTERNATIONAL RELIEF AND
REFUGEE RESCUE WORKER

*Father: Robert Wilson, Quaker
businessman
Mother: Laura, née Wallis, Quaker
converted to Plymouth Brethren*

Quaker

My urge to do relief work was not
high-minded and RUTH FRY, who
interviewed me [for Friends' War
Victims' Relief], rightly sensed that
my motives were selfish. I began without dedication or any desire (except
the vaguest) to do good. I wanted foreign travel, adventure, romance, the
unknown.[1]

Francesca Wilson (From June Horder (ed.),
Francesca Wilson: A Life of Service and
Adventure, *privately printed, 1993. Courtesy of
Dr June Horder)*

Thus wrote Francesca Wilson about her own initial motivation, insisting on her
lack of altruism as a 26-year-old in 1914. In 1944 she wrote again about the impulse
to be a relief worker, again identifying the wish for adventure, but by then needing
to add

> a spirit of adventure is not a bad thing provided there is something else. Specialist
> qualification, organising powers, gift of improvisation, linguistic talent, all these
> things are necessities, but not enough. Those who go out to relieve the sufferings
> of the starving, the diseased and the uprooted, and to bring healing to sick minds,
> must have a gift for service and something that one can only call charity – [2]

She herself had had no social work experience, no medical or nursing training. She
did have linguistic talent and she did have a gift for attaching herself creatively to
groups of wretched, uprooted people and for helping them to make something
constructive from the ruins of their lives. What she found hardest to do was
administer 'humdrum emergency'[3] relief on a mass scale:

> [organizing] milk canteens, soup-kitchens, distributing dry rations and
> clothing . . . Perhaps that was why the work in Russia in 1922 was so
> overwhelming and so dreary. When famine is killing millions one cannot stop
> to rescue . . . a few dozen lost children.[4]

Nevertheless, Francesca Wilson stayed with the job, wherever she might be sent
by the Friends' Relief Services, 'always in the margins of war and of chaos'.[5] In
the First World War she went from a hostel for French evacuees in Savoie (where
she first encountered Dr KATHERINE MACPHAIL) to Serbian refugees in Corsica,
whose language, culture and crafts so fascinated her that her 'welfare work was
humanised by understanding, respect and admiration'.[6] Then, after a short time
working in post-war newly constituted Yugoslavia, she assisted Dr HILDA CLARK

and EDITH PYE as an interpreter in starving Vienna, a city of the dead (1919–22).[7] In Murcia in southern Spain in 1937, she was plunged into a nightmare:

We were in a vast unfinished building . . . no windows or doors . . . the floors had not yet been divided into rooms and formed huge corridors, which swarmed with men, women and children of all sizes and ages on a few straw mattresses. The noise was terrific, sick people groaning, women shouting . . . They surged around us telling us their stories, clinging to us like people drowning in a bog.[8]

She had encountered a few thousand of the 100,000 who had just fled Franco's Italian-backed army in Malaga, many of whom had lost children when strafed from the air on the flight. Having started a desperately needed children's hospital for typhoid victims in Murcia, she later founded a farm colony for Spanish orphan boys and a summer camp for bombed-out families. 'Only once or twice in my life have I felt such a bond between myself and a community.'[9]

Between 1939 and 1940 Francesca Wilson was in Hungary, trying to organize the transit of Poles fleeing the Nazis; she found herself also pulled into underground work, trying to help Czechs with false identity papers escape to join the French army. At one point she was arrested on the Romanian border and was terrified because what she was doing was illegal.

At the end of the Second World War she joined UNRRA and was sent to help set up camps for displaced persons in France, Germany (at Dachau), Austria and Yugoslavia. By this time she had, not surprisingly, worked out some of the ground principles of relief work: the need for co-ordination between foreign relief missions to prevent rivalry and duplication; the need for maximum co-operation with local administrators of social services; the prioritization of transport links to ensure that appropriate relief in kind reaches its destination as fast as possible; the need to recruit relief workers willing to work anonymously and without recognition; the need to enable refugees to work at agriculture and trades as well as to start their own schools, libraries, youth clubs and choirs in order to fight depression.[10]

Francesca Wilson did not only go abroad to succour the victims of war, revolution and famine; she also took a stream of young refugees, including Nikolaus Pevsner and Nikolaus Bakhtin, into her own home: 'any house that Francesca owned, however spacious, ended up crowded from cellar to attic with deserving, delightful people, the owner's territory having shrunk in no time to a more or less poky bed-sittingroom.'[11] She herself insisted to the last that she had achieved very little and almost nothing when compared with the nurses and doctors.

When I think of the appalling tasks undertaken by Dot Newhall, Sanitary Inspector for the Serbian Relief Fund, when she nursed typhus victims in Serbia in 1915, catching it herself retreating through Albania. Worst of all on the heels of the Serbs recovering their homeland in 1918, when she had to clean up the stinking corpses left in the drains of schools and hospitals, I am awed into silence.[12]

1. June Horder et al., Francesca Wilson: A Life of Service and Adventure (privately printed, 1993), ch. 10: 'Relief work', p. 105.
2. Francesca Wilson, In the Margins of Chaos (London, John Murray, 1944), Appendix, p. 280.
3. Horder, op. cit., p. 107.
4. Ibid., p. 108.
5. Wilson, op. cit., p. viii.

6. Horder, *op. cit.*, p. 107.
7. Wilson, *op. cit.*, pp. 138–9.
8. Horder, *op. cit.*, p. 173.
9. *Ibid.*, pp. 110 and 127.
10. See Francesca Wilson, *Advice to Relief Workers Based on Personal Experience in the Field* (pamphlet; London, John Murray and Friends' Relief Service, 1945); and Appendix to Wilson, *In the Margins of Chaos*, op. cit.
11. Elsie Duncan-Jones, obituary, *Newnham College Roll Letter* (January 1982), pp. 61–3.
12. Horder, *op. cit.*, p. 111.

See also Francesca Wilson, *Aftermath: France, Germany, Austria, Yugoslavia 1945 and 1946* (West Drayton, Penguin, 1947); *They Came as Strangers: The Story of Refugees to Britain* (London, Hamish Hamilton, 1959); *Rebel Daughter of a Country House: The Life of Eglantyne Jebb, Founder of the Save the Children Fund* (London, Allen and Unwin, 1967).

WOOLF, VIRGINIA
(25.1.1882–28.3.1941)

WRITER; PACIFIST

Father: Leslie Stephen, writer, editor of the Dictionary of National Biography
Mother: Julia, née Prinsep, later Duckworth

Humanist

It might seem incongruous to include in this dictionary an experimental novelist popularly assumed to be quite removed from ordinary life. But it is a fallacy to think of Virginia Woolf as unconcerned by the injustices and cruelty of the first half of the twentieth century. In fact she was pilloried for her 'out-of-date' humanistic feminism in *Three Guineas*, where she demanded open and equal access to education and employment irrespective of gender, race or class, while her lifelong pre-occupation with killing competitions, and how to prevent or end them, has only recently been paid serious attention.[1] For Virginia Woolf, thinking was her fighting, and, as she wrote during an air raid in the Battle of Britain, 'Unless we can think peace into existence we – not this one body in this one bed but millions of bodies yet to be born – will lie in the same darkness and hear the same death rattle overhead.'[2]

Already at the end of the First World War, Virginia Woolf was trying to 'think peace into existence' by struggling with the psychological explanation for warfare. She wrote in her diary (27.8.1918): 'The reason why it is easy to kill another person must be that one's imagination is too sluggish to conceive of a succession of days which are furled in him and have already been spent.' Thereafter she was to attempt in her fiction to unfurl that succession of days by '[digging] out beautiful caves'[3] of memory behind her characters: her antidote to the unimaginative, collective hatred behind war.

Mrs Dalloway (1925) is, among many other things, the first English anti-war novel after the 'Great War'. The heroine's alter ego Septimus is living his last day on earth, unable to bear the clinical depression of delayed shellshock; believing that the basic truth about our species is that we 'tear each other to pieces', he impales himself on the railings beneath his window.

Virginia Woolf's feminism entailed a repudiation of all patriotism that validates tribal killing for the 'fatherland': 'why should I kill women? . . . Why should charity cease as the Channel boat starts?'[4] On 2 October 1935 she attended the Labour Party Conference at Brighton: 'Tears came to my eyes as [the pacifist] Lansbury spoke.'[5] She felt that she must call her next work (*Three Guineas*) 'The Next War', connecting her essay on women's contribution to civilization with the prevention of war by means of an analysis of the essential and *recurrent* nature of fascism; it was clear to her that fascism always fuses misogynistic, racist anti-humanism with masculinist militarism.[6] The tragedy was that just when she was writing her own humanistic, anti-militarist feminist credo in *Three Guineas* in 1935–38, it was already too late to repair the political and economic disasters that had produced European fascism a decade earlier and that would, in turn, insist on 'the next war'. At first she indicted the male need to dominate, including to dominate women, as the root cause of war; but by the end of her life she saw this 'Hitlerism' as deep in the psyche of *both* sexes. Women must free themselves from the need for power over men – whether husbands or sons – and in so doing free men from their compensatory need for the gun.[7]

It took all the spiritual courage Virginia Woolf possessed to speak out against the sacred causes of 'our country' and 'our fighting men', even in the run-up to war, saying, 'As a woman I have no country. As a woman I want no country. As a woman my country is the whole world.'[8] And even though, at enormous inner cost, she renounced her total pacifism when confronted by the Nazis' drive to conquer the world, to the very end of her life her imagination worked on how we may, finally, conquer our human weakness for the righteous extermination of other humans. The gritty, humorous resistance to Hitler's *Blitzkrieg* on civilian targets in the cities of Britain revived her faith in human beings[9] and enabled her to make her last novel *Between the Acts* a hymn of reverence for life, including both the life of the natural world and the life that is in art.[10]

1. See Alex Zwerdling, *Virginia Woolf and the Real World* (Los Angeles and Berkeley, University of California Press, 1986); Sybil Oldfield, *Women against the Iron Fist: Alternatives to Militarism 1900–1989* (Oxford and Cambridge, MA, Basil Blackwell, 1989; reissued New York, Edwin Mellen Press, 2000), ch. 5: 'The elegiac artist: Virginia Woolf'; Mark Hussey (ed.), *Virginia Woolf and War: Fiction, Reality and Myth* (New York, Syracuse University Press, 1992); Hermione Lee, *Virginia Woolf* (London, Chatto and Windus, 1996), esp. ch. 37: 'Fascism' and ch. 39: 'War', and S. Oldfield, 'Virginia Woolf and Antigone', *South Carolina Review*, **29** (1) (1996).
2. 'Thoughts on peace in an air-raid', first published posthumously in Britain in Virginia Woolf, *The Death of the Moth and Other Essays* (London, Hogarth Press, 1942).
3. Virginia Woolf, *Diary* (30.8.1923).
4. Virginia Woolf, first (unpublished) scrapbook for *Three Guineas*, Monks House papers, University of Sussex Library, B16f, p. 38.
5. Virginia Woolf, *Diary*, vol. 4.
6. Virginia Woolf's public anti-Nazism did not go unremarked: like VERA BRITTAIN, MARGERY FRY, STORM JAMESON, SYBIL THORNDIKE, ELLEN WILKINSON and her own husband, she was on the Gestapo black list.
7. See Woolf, 'Thoughts on peace in an air-raid'; and letter to Shena, Lady Simon (25.1.1941) in Nigel Nicolson (ed.), *Leave the Letters Till We're Dead: The Letters of Virginia Woolf*, vol. 6 (London, Hogarth Press, 1980).
8. Virginia Woolf, *Three Guineas* (London, Hogarth Press, 1938), ch. 2, p. 96.
9. See especially Virginia Woolf's letters to Ethel Smyth (11, 12, 20 and 25.9.1940), in Nicolson, *op. cit.*
10. See Oldfield, *op. cit.*, pp. 127–30.

WRIGHT, HELENA, MB, BS, MRCS, LRCP
(17.9.1887–21.3.1982)

BIRTH CONTROL PIONEER

Father: Heinz Lowenfeld, Polish Jewish entrepreneur
Mother: Alice, née Evens, daughter of a naval captain

Christian, later Spiritualist

Having qualified as MRCS and LRCP in 1914 and MB, BS in 1915, Helena Lowenfeld worked in the Great Ormond Street Hospital for Sick Children and in Bethnal Green Hospital, where she married the surgeon Peter Wright. They went as medical missionaries to China (1922–27), more as medical practitioners and lecturers than as evangelists. Forced to return to Britain by the invasion of the Japanese, Helena Wright stopped in Berlin, where she met Dr Graefenberg, the inventor of the 'dutch cap', the first internal contraceptive device; he alerted her to the medical importance, and possibility, of birth control.[1] Helena Wright, who herself had four young sons, shared his conviction that the twentieth century would be the century to allow women to control their fertility scientifically. She differed from the medically unqualified MARIE STOPES both in the accuracy of her medical contraceptive knowledge and in her tactical approach to achieving the desired revolution, an approach that was persuasive rather than combative and messianic, although personally she too could be a great arguer.

In 1928 Helena Wright was appointed Medical Officer to the poverty-stricken North Kensington Women's Welfare Centre in Telford Road, which had been opened four years earlier. She became Chairman of the Medical Committee of the National Birth Control Committee, originally set up by Margaret Pike, Lady Denman, Mary Stocks and others, and served for 30 years. 'Our object was to prevent overworked working mothers who already had too many children from having more.'[2] Under her leadership the Centre became a family planning 'training centre for doctors, midwives, nurses, and others, some from overseas' (against immense opposition from the medical establishment). She addressed the Lambeth Conference of Anglican bishops in 1930 and obtained limited approval of contraception for married women; in the same year she persuaded the Minister of Health to allow advice to be given in public welfare clinics.[3]

In 1948, together with Margaret Pyke, secretary to the British Family Planning Association, Helena Wright organized a conference that set up what was later to become the International Planned Parenthood Federation. Believing as she did in every woman's right to choose whether to bear a child or not, she had tried in vain to persuade the authorities to provide contraceptive services to women serving in the WRENS, WAAF and ATS during the Second World War and contraceptive advice to women in prison. Whether or not it was she who coined the family planning slogan 'Every child a wanted child', that was her great aim for the world. 'We have now got the agreement of over 100 countries that the voluntary control of fertility is the birthright of everyone.'[4] Clearly she was forcing her opponents to declare that they believed in the *in*voluntary fertility of women – not a comfortable proposition. She also dared to champion the provision of therapeutic abortion to terminate unplanned pregnancies, whether for married or unmarried women.

'Her wonderful clarity as a teacher and her courage and conviction, inspired her many pupils and wore down the resistance she met in every direction.'[5] 'Give women the choice and they will choose . . . I want to see every individual on earth having that choice and having it free' (Helena Wright, in 1972).[6]

1. Obituary, *The Times* (23.3.1982).
2. *Sunday Times* (11.9.1977).
3. Josephine Barnes, entry for Helena Wright in the *Dictionary of National Biography, 1981–1985*.
4. *Sunday Times, loc. cit.*
5. Obituary, *The Times*.
6. Barbara Evans, *Freedom to Choose: The Life and Work of Dr Helena Wright, Pioneer of Contraception* (London, Bodley Head, 1984), title page.

Y

YOUNG, MARY HELEN
(5.6.1883–February 1944)

NURSE; RESISTANCE HEROINE IN SECOND WORLD WAR

Father: Alexander Young, grocer's clerk, Aberdeen
Mother: Elizabeth Anne, née Burnett

Presbyterian?

Only 4 feet 11 inches tall, Mary Helen Young was thought at first to be too small to be accepted as a nurse. However, after a short time as a dressmaker, she left Aberdeen for London, where she completed her hospital training. In 1909 she went as a private nurse to France, and on the outbreak of the First World War she was one of the first nurses in Paris to volunteer for service at the Allied front. At one time she was working so close to the trenches at Courtrai that she suffered from the effects of mustard gas, which was to weaken her health for the rest of her life.

On the outbreak of the Second World War Mary Young was still in Paris, but she refused to flee to England in the face of the German invasion of France. Instead, 'she received into her house English people who had come to organise the resistance movement in France . . . She received radio messages from London. She could have been condemned to be shot.'[1] Arrested by the Gestapo in 1941, she was interned at Besançon civilian camp in eastern France and then released on account of ill health. She returned to Paris and, despite being under Gestapo surveillance, managed to continue with her Resistance work; she also helped British prisoners of war, including captured airmen, to escape. She was re-arrested in November 1943 and, although nothing could be proved against her by the Nazi occupation authorities, sent to the women's concentration camp at Ravensbrück in February 1944.

'She could smile, even in [that] hell. Right up to the very end nothing could break her . . . [She] always kept her chin up, as you say, and all of us liked her, the little Scotswoman, "Mees Young".'[2] Too weak to do the impossibly heavy slave labour, Mary Young fell ill and her white hair was her death warrant. Aged 62, she was gassed.

1. Anon., letter to Mary Young's sister Mrs Annie Sutherland, quoted in *The Press and Journal* (Aberdeen) (28.9.1945).
2. Simone Saint-Clair, fellow prisoner and Ravensbrück survivor, quoted in *The Press and Journal* (Aberdeen) (27.9.1945).

I am grateful to Fran R. Watson, Archivist, Northern Health Services, Aberdeen, for supplying me with this and other information about Mary Young. See also 'They gassed the second "Cavell"', *Daily Herald* (27.9.1945).

British Committee of the Women's International Congress

THE HAGUE, April 28th, 29th, and 30th, and May 1st, 1915

OBJECTS:

1. To demand that international disputes shall in future be settled by some other means than war.
2. To claim that women should have a voice in the affairs of the nations.

Executive Committee.

Miss BONDFIELD.
Mrs. CHARLES BUXTON.
LADY COURTNEY OF PENWITH.
Miss ISABELLA O. FORD.
Miss LILIAN HARRIS.
Miss M. H. HUNTSMAN.

Mrs. PATRICK LAWRENCE.
Miss EMILY LEAF.
Miss EVA MCLAREN.
Miss CATHERINE E. MARSHALL.
Mrs. OUTHWAITE.
Miss A. MAUDE ROYDEN.
Hon. Mrs. ROLLO RUSSELL.

Miss ROYDEN.
Mrs. ALFRED SALTER.
Miss SOPHY SANGER.
Mrs. SWANWICK.
Miss PICTON-TURBERVILL.
Miss T. WILSON WILSON.

Chairman:
Miss KATHLEEN D. COURTNEY.
Hon. Treasurer:
Mrs. MINA B. HUBBARD ELLIS.
Hon. Secretary:
Miss CHRYSTAL MACMILLAN.

Local Committees:

BIRMINGHAM.
DUBLIN.
EDINBURGH.

LIVERPOOL.
MANCHESTER.
NEWCASTLE-ON-TYNE.

Office Address: QUEEN ANNE'S CHAMBERS (Room 37, Sixth Floor), 28 Broadway, Westminster, London, S.W.

GENERAL COMMITTEE.

Mrs. G. F. ABBOTT.
Miss M. C. ALBRIGHT.
Miss A. M. ALLEN.
Miss MARGARET ASHTON.
Mrs. J. BAKER.
Miss MARY B. BAKER.
Lady BARCLAY.
The Hon. Lady BARLOW.
Mrs. S. A. BARNETT.
Miss ROSA M. BARNETT.
Miss ETHEL M. BARTON.
Miss EMILY BEHRENS.
Miss E. BELL.
Mrs. PERCY BIGLAND.
Miss L. M. BOILEAU.
Miss MARGARET BONDFIELD.
Mr. ALFRED BOOTH.
Mrs. ISAAC BRAITHWAITE.
Mrs. JOHN A. BRIGHT.
Miss F. BROCKWAY.
Mrs. T. STEWART-BROWN.
Mrs. VINCENT BROWN.
Mrs. H. BUNAN.
Mrs. CHARLES BUXTON.
Mrs. HAROLD CHESSON.
Mrs. ALICE CLARK.
Mrs. HELEN BRIGHT CLARK.
Mrs. N. F. CLOTHIER.
Mrs. STANTON COIT.
Miss MARGARET COLBECK.
Lady COURTNEY OF PENWITH.
Miss K. D. COURTNEY (Chairman).
Miss E. LAIRD COX.
Miss ALICE CROMPTON.
Mrs. THOMASSON-CARTER.
Mrs. ALBERT J. CROSFIELD.
Mrs. DIMON DAVIES.
Miss LLEWELLYN DAVIES.
Mrs. C. DESPARD.
Miss CHARLOTTE C. J. DRAKE.
Miss CHARLOTTE LEEDS.
Mrs. J. E. ELLIS.
Miss MARIAN E. ELLIS.
Mrs. MINA B. HUBBARD ELLIS (Hon. Treas.).
Mrs. MARGARET FLORENCE.
Miss ELIZABETH FORD.
Miss I. O. FORD.
The Hon. Mrs. FRANKLIN.
Miss JEANETTE L. FRANKLIN.
Miss JOAN MARY FRY.
Miss LUCY GARDNER.
Miss ALISON GARLAND.

The Hon. VIOLET GIBBS.
Mrs. MONA GIRVEN.
Mrs. BRUCE GLASIER.
Miss EVA GORE-BOOTH.
Mrs. JOHN U. GREEN.
Mrs. WALTER GREG.
Mrs. M. A. HAMILTON.
Mrs. AGNES H. HARBEN.
Miss FRANCES HARDCASTLE.
Miss LILIAN HARRIS.
Mrs. C. V. HAWKER.
Miss J. W. HILLS.
Mrs. NEWNHAM HOARE.
Miss EMILY HOBHOUSE.
Mrs. J. A. HOBSON.
Miss WINIFRED HOLIDAY.
Miss DOROTHEA HOLLINS.
Mrs. ALFRED HOLMES.
Mrs. H. W. HORVILL.
Miss M. H. HUNTSMAN.
Miss RACHEL S. JEFFERY.
Mrs. ALFRED J. KING.
Dr. E. KNIGHT.
Miss ETHEL C. KNIGHT.
Mrs. SUSAN LAWRENCE.
Miss EMILY LEAF.
Mrs. CARVELL-LEWIS.
Miss MARY MACARTHUR.
Lady MUIR MACKENZIE.
Mrs. MCKENZIE.
Mrs. EVA MCLAREN.
Miss CHRYSTAL MACMILLAN (Hon. Sec.).
Miss EVA MACNAGHTEN.
Mrs. MARSH.
Miss CATHERINE E. MARSHALL.
Mrs. FRANK MARSHALL.
Miss LOUISE E. MATTHAEI.
Miss E. CAMERON MAWSON.
Miss FRANCES H. MELVILLE.
The Hon. LILY MONTAGU.
Miss LUCY F. MORLAND.
Lady OTTOLINE MORRELL.
Mrs. FELIX MOSCHELES.
Miss HARRIET C. NEWCOMB.
Miss HELENA NORMANTON.
Miss NORAH O'SHEA.
Mrs. OUTHWAITE.
Miss VIOLET PAGET.
Miss SYLVIA PANKHURST.
Miss HELEN PERL.

Mrs. G. H. PERRIS.
Miss CAROLINE E. PLAYNE.
Mrs. ARTHUR PONSONBY.
Mrs. THOMPSON PRICE.
Miss E. M. PYE.
Miss EDITH RATCLIFFE.
Miss JULIET RECKITT.
Mrs. GERTRUDE RINDER.
Miss EDITH A. ROBERTS.
Miss JANET ROBERTSON.
Miss E. G. REEVE.
Miss A. MAUDE ROYDEN.
The Hon. Mrs. ROLLO RUSSELL.
Lady MARGARET SACKVILLE.
Mrs. ALFRED SALTER.
Mrs. SANGER.
Miss SOPHY SANGER.
Miss OLIVE SCHREINER.
Mrs. ARTHUR SCHUSTER.
The Hon. Mrs. SCOTT.
Mrs. JULIA SCURR.
Mrs. SHANKS.
Miss EVELYN SHARP.
Miss PHOEBE SHEAVYN.
Miss MARY SHEEPSHANKS.
Mrs. PHILIP SNOWDEN.
Mrs. STANBURY.
Mrs. STRICKLAND.
Miss SOPHIE STURGE.
Mrs. H. M. SWANWICK.
Miss S. J. TANNER.
Miss JOYCE TARRING.
Dr. BARBARA TCHAIKOWSKY.
Miss MINNIE B. THEOBALD.
Dr. HENRIETTA THOMAS.
Mrs. K. THOMASSON.
Mrs. TIEDEMAN.
Mrs. CHARLES TREVELYAN.
Mrs. R. C. TREVELYAN.
Miss PICTON-TURBERVILL.
Muriel COUNTESS DE LA WARR.
Mrs. SPENCE WATSON.
Mrs. ALFRED WATT.
Miss ROSA WAUGH.
Mrs. ALEXANDER WHYTE.
Dr. ETHEL WILLIAMS.
Miss IRENE COOPER WILLIS.
Miss T. WILSON WILSON.
Mrs. W. E. WILSON.
Miss PHYLLIS WRAGGE.
Mrs. ZANGWILL.
Miss ALICE ZIMMERN.

(*Executive Committee.*)

Issued by The British Committee of the Women's International Congress, Queen Anne's Chambers (Room 37) 28 Broadway, Westminster, London, S.W.
Printed by the National Labour Press, Ltd., 74 Swinton Street, London, W.C.; also at Manchester.

British Committee of the Women's International Congress held at The Hague, 1915

286

Appendix I

British Committee of the Women's International Congress 1915

Entries in Dictionary marked *; others annotated where known

Mrs G. F. Abbott	National Union of Women's Suffrage Societies
Miss M. C. Albright	Birmingham Quaker
Miss A. M. Allen	Biographer and life-companion of Sophy Sanger*
Miss Margaret Ashton*	
Mrs J. Baker	Quaker, wife of Liberal MP, mother of Mary Baker
Miss Mary B. Baker [later Penman*]	
Lady Barclay	German-born suffragette, wife of internationalist barrister and MP
The Hon. Lady Barlow	Quaker convert, wife of pacifist Liberal MP
Mrs S. A. Barnett	First woman Poor Law Guardian, widow of Canon Barnett
Miss Rosa M. Barrett*	
Miss Ethel M. Barton	
Miss Ethel Behrens	Liberal Jewish suffragist, pacifist, convert to Quakerism
Miss J. Bell*	
Mrs Percy Bigland*	
Miss L. M. Boileau	Women's Freedom League activist, socialist
Miss Margaret Bondfield	Trade Union Leader, later Labour Cabinet Minister
Mrs Alfred Booth	President, National Council of Women
Mrs Isaac Braithwaite	American-born Quaker, co-Warden, Woodbrooke College
Mrs John A. Bright	Manchester Quaker suffragist
Mrs Fenner Brockway	Socialist pacifist, co-founder of NCF in 1915

Mrs E. Steward-Brown [i.e. Sadd-Brown]	Suffragette who attacked War Office 1912
Mrs Vipont Brown	Manchester Quaker, mother of Elfrida Vipont
Mrs De Bunsen	Middle East traveller, sister-in-law of Dorothy Buxton*
Mrs Charles Buxton*	
Mrs Barrow Cadbury*	
Miss Alice Clark	Historian of seventeenth-century women, Quaker, business director
Mrs Helen Bright Clark	Quaker suffragist, mother of Dr Hilda Clark* and Alice and Esther Clark
Mrs S. T. Clothier [née Esther Clark]	Somerset Quaker teacher
Mrs Stanton Coit	German Jewish-born Treasurer of IWSS, supporter of Ethical Church
Miss Margaret Colbeck	Aunt of Catherine Marshall*
Miss K. D. Courtney*	
Lady Courtney of Penwith*	
Miss K. Laird Cox	NUWSS
Miss Alice Crompton	Niece of Lydia Becker, Warden, Manchester University Settlement
Mrs Thornburgh-Cropper	
Mrs Albert J. Crosfield	Cambridge Quaker, social reformer
Mrs Dixon Davies	Beaconsfield Quaker, suffragist, sister of Mrs Crosfield?
Miss Llewelyn Davies*	
Mrs C. Despard*	
Miss Charlotte S. J. Drake	Supporter of Sylvia Pankhurst, lectured on birth control
Miss Charlotte Ellis	Leicestershire Quaker
Mrs J. E. Ellis [née Rowntree]	Yorkshire Quaker, wife of Liberal MP, mother of Marian Ellis*
Miss Marian E. Ellis*	
Mrs Mina B. Hubbard Ellis	Suffragist and geographer
Mrs Sargant-Florence	Artist pacifist suffragist, co-author of *Militarism v. Feminism*
Miss Elizabeth Ford	Artist sister/companion of Isabella Ford*
Miss I. O. Ford*	
The Hon. Mrs Franklin	Liberal Jewish suffragist, educationist, sister of Lily Montagu*
Miss Jeanette L. Franklin	Jewish Peace Society delegate, daughter of Hon. Mrs Franklin
Miss Joan Mary Fry*	

Miss Lucy Gardner	Ecumenicist, Quaker, co-founder of Fellowship of Reconciliation
Miss Alison Garland	Liberal Party activist, suffragist
The Hon. Violet Gibson	Daughter of Provost of Edinburgh, Sir James Gibson, Bart
Mrs Mona Ginever	
Mrs Bruce Glasier*	
Miss Eva Gore-Booth	Socialist feminist pacifist writer, companion of Esther Roper*
Mrs Jolan [Jean] U. Grave	Wife of French anarchist in Bristol
Mrs Walter Greg	Reformer of child labour, Cheshire suffragist
Mrs Walter Wilson Greg	Daughter-in-law of above
Mrs M. A. Hamilton	Socialist pacifist writer, later Labour MP
Mrs Agnes H. Harben	Wealthy socialist feminist
Miss Frances Hardcastle	Mathematician/astronomer, companion of Dr Ethel Williams*
Miss Lilian Harris	Economist/accountant, companion of Margaret Llewelyn Davies*
Mrs C. V. Hawker	
Mrs H. W. Hills	Socialist suffragist, later founder of early child guidance clinic
Mrs Newenham Hoare	
Miss Emily Hobhouse*	
Mrs J. A. Hobson	'The pudding lady', writer on vegetarianism, wife of anti-imperialist historian J. A. Hobson
Miss Winifred Holiday	Violinist, pacifist daughter of stained-glass artist friend of William Morris
Miss Dorothea Hollins	Utopian socialist 'peace crusader'
Mrs Alfred Holmes	
Mrs H. W. Horvill	Wife of Methodist journalist, member of Fellowship of Reconciliation
Miss M. H. Huntsman	Assistant Secretary, National Peace Council, since 1908
Miss Rachel S. Jeffrey	Midlothian supporter of NCF
Mrs Alfred J. King	Quaker factory reformer, first Englishwoman ski-racer
Dr E. Knight*	
Miss Ethel C. Knight	
Miss Susan Lawrence	Conservative converted to socialism, Poplar councillor, Labour MP
Miss Emily Leaf	Liberal suffrage worker, sister of Walter Leaf
Mrs Carvill-Lewis	
Miss Mary Macarthur*	

Lady Muir Mackenzie	Conservative suffragist, worked in India for education of girls
Mrs McKenzie	
Mrs Eva McLaren	Quaker suffragist, in local government
Miss Chrystal Macmillan*	
Miss Eva Macnaghten	Prominent in YWCA, supporter of NCF
Mrs Marsh	American-born Quaker
Miss Catherine E. Marshall*	
Mrs Frank Marshall	Liberal suffragist, mother of Catherine Marshall*
Miss Louise E. Matthaei* [later Lady Howard*]	
Miss E. Cameron Mawson	
Miss Frances H. Melville	Suffragist, theologian, Glasgow University administrator
The Hon. Lily Montagu*	
Miss Lucy F. Morland	Radical Quaker writer, teacher at Croydon High School
Lady Ottoline Morrell	Pacifist bohemian, wife of Liberal MP, mistress of Bertrand Russell
Mrs Felix Moscheles	German Jewish-born wife of internationalist pacifist painter
Miss Harriet C. Newcomb	Secretary, British Dominions' Women Citizens' Union
Miss Helena Normanton	WFL supporter, later pioneer woman barrister
Miss Norah O'Shea	
Mrs Outhwaite	New Zealand-born wife of radical MP, speaker on nationalization of land
Miss Violet Paget*	
Miss Sylvia Pankhurst*	
Miss Helen Peile	
Mrs G. H. Perris	Wife of internationalist foreign affairs editor
Miss Caroline E. Playne*	
Mrs Arthur Ponsonby	Pacifist daughter of Sir Herbert Parry, wife of Liberal pacifist MP
Mrs Thompson Price	
Miss E. M. Pye*	
Miss Edith Ratcliffe	Quaker Bible commentator
Miss Juliet Reckitt	Quaker suppporter of WFL, Hull
Mrs Gertrude Rinder	Records keeper for NCF
Miss Edith A. Roberts	Quaker by convincement, helped Armenian refugees in Syria
Miss Janet Robertson	Portrait painter

Miss E. G. Roper*	
Miss A. Maude Royden*	
The Hon. Mrs Rollo Russell [née Joachim]	National Peace Council member and suffragist
Lady Margaret Sackville	Edinburgh poet and anti-war writer
Mrs Alfred Salter*	
Mrs Sanger	Quaker, sister-in-law of Sophy Sanger*
Miss Sophy Sanger*	
Miss Olive Schreiner	Writer
Mrs Arthur Schuster	Manchester suffragist, wife of internationalist scientist
The Hon. Mrs Scott	
Mrs Julia Scurr	Supporter of Sylvia Pankhurst, Catholic socialist
Mrs Shanks	Supporter of UDC, wife of Glasgow City councillor
Miss Evelyn Sharp*	
Miss Phoebe Sheavyn, DLitt	University lecturer in English, Manchester suffragist
Miss Mary Sheepshanks*	
Mrs Philip Snowden*	
Mrs Stanbury	NUWSS Executive
Mrs Strickland	Congregationalist suffragist, Peace and Arbitration Society supporter
Miss Sophia Sturge*	
Mrs H. M. Swanwick*	
Miss S. J. Tanner	Quaker, niece of Priestman sisters, supporter of Josephine Butler
Miss Joyce Tarring	Suffragist daughter of liberal Judge, fed German children 1919
Dr Barbara Tchaikowsky	Radical doctor, supported Sylvia Pankhurst
Miss Minne B. Theobald	Theosophist, psychotherapist
Dr Henrietta Thomas	American Quaker, escort home of stranded German civilians
Mrs K. Thomasson	Quaker suffragist, daughter of John Bright
Mrs Tiedeman	Founder of Divorce Law Reform Union
Mrs Charles Trevelyan	Wife of Liberal MP who co-founded UDC
Mrs R. C. Trevelyan	Dutch-born wife of pacifist poet
Miss Picton-Turbervill*	
Muriel, Countess de la Warr	Socialist suffragist, sister-in-law of Margaret Sackville
Mrs Spence Watson*	

Mrs Alfred Watt*

Miss Rosa Waugh — Daughter of founder of NSPCC, wife of imprisoned CO Stephen Hobhouse

Mrs Alexander Whyte — Ecumenicist, pacifist, wife of Edinburgh Presbyterian preacher

Dr Ethel Williams*

Miss Irene Cooper Willis — Writer, cultural historian, worked for UDC, NCF

Miss T. Wilson Wilson — Quaker writer, her pacifist book for children burnt, 1918

Mrs W. E. Wilson — Quaker, sister-in-law of Mrs Isaac Braithwaite

Miss Phyllis Wragge — Writer of children's history textbooks, University of Durham administrator

Mrs Zangwill — Stepdaughter of Hertha Ayrton*, wife of Israel Zangwill

Miss Alice Zimmern — Classicist, pacifist suffragist writer

Appendix II

1st December, 1917

CopY OF THE ADDRESS
PRESENTED BY
THE ALL INDIA WOMEN'S DEPUTATION
TO
LORD CHELMSFORD
Viceroy and Governor-General of India,
AND
THE RIGHT HONOURABLE E. S. MONTAGU, M.P.
His Majesty's Secretary of State for India

MAY IT PLEASE YOUR EXCELLENCY,
RIGHT HONOURABLE SIR,

On behalf of the Women of India we welcome you to our land, Sir, and thank you for coming to investigate the position of affairs at first hand, and to consult about possible changes with representatives of our people. We beg you to accept our most sincere thanks for receiving us to-day in the midst of your crowded programme of engagements.

We have asked for a portion of your valuable time because the women of India have awakened to their responsibilities in the public life, and have their own independent opinions about the reforms that are necessary for the progress of India. Many organizations have been started by and for women during the past ten years, of which we have representatives here, such as the Women's Indian Associations, the Seva Sadan, the Mahila Seva Samaja, the Indian Women's University, the Women's Home Rule League branches, etc. We are in touch with the new outlook of Indian Women and we make bold, at this historic time, to lay before you Women's views concerning the necessary post-war Reforms, as we believe them to be the necessary complement to the views of our men.

The women of India understand and support the broad claims of their people for Self-Government within the Empire, and they press for its bestowal as urgently as do their brothers. They have in large numbers signed the petition organized by Mr. Gandhi in favour of the Scheme of Reform drawn up by the National Congress and the Muslim League. They have also held large ladies' meetings, taken part in processions and public meetings, and in many ways worked towards obtaining the measure of Self-Government suggested in this Scheme, and in the non-official Memorandum of the Nineteen Members of the Imperial Legislative Council, with the general terms of both of which they, through us, wish you to know that they are in agreement.

Our interests, as one Half of the people, are directly affected by the demand in the united Scheme (I. 3) that "The Members of the Council should be elected directly by the people on as broad a franchise as possible," and in the Memorandum (3) that "the franchise should be broadened and extended directly to the people". We pray that, when such a franchise is being drawn up, women may be recognized as "people", and that it may be worded in such terms as will not disqualify our sex, but allow our women the same opportunities of representation as our men. In agreeing with the demand of the above-mentioned Memorandum that "a full measure of Local Self-Government should be immediately granted," we request that it shall include the representation of our women, a policy that has been admittedly successful for the past twenty years in Local Self-Governments elsewhere in the British Empire. The precedent for including women in modern Indian political life has been a marked feature of the Indian National Congress, in which since its inception women have voted and been delegates and speakers, and which this year finds its climax in the election of a woman as its President. Thus the voice of India approves of its women being considered responsible and acknowledged citizens; and we urgently claim that, in the drawing up of all provisions regarding representation, our sex shall not be made a disqualification for the exercise of the franchise or for service in public life.

In order to fit ourselves and our children for future public responsibilities arising out of the foregoing considerations, it is absolutely essential that our educational system should be reformed. At present only one girl out of every hundred, and only thirteen boys out of every hundred, is educated. Mr. Gokhale recorded that only one out of every six Indian Villages possessed a school. All our young people are clamouring for knowledge, and the few schools we have are over-crowded. We bring the urgent necessity for immediate action in educational matters before you now because the granting of facilities for education is a section of Indian Administration definitely under the control of the Imperial Legislative Council and the Government of India, and it must be made as far as possible a uniform policy throughout British India.

We therefore ask (1) that the Government shall make a pronouncement in favour of Compulsory and Free Primary Education for Boys and Girls, and widely extended Secondary Education, and immediately set to work to bring this into being area by area, as is being done in several of the Indian States. (2) We ask that during the time elapsing before the completion of this reform, the Government shall immediately devote as much attention to the education of girls as is now given by them to boys and provide an equal number of school facilities for them, and thus remove the unwise differentiation which provides facilities for ten times as many boys as girls, a policy which defeats its own ends, as the uneducated wives of these boys later hold back their progress.

In order to supply teachers for this wide spread of education, we ask the Government to provide a largely increased number of Training Colleges for Indian Women Teachers and also to establish a number of Widows' Homes for this purpose, supplemented by the grant of scholarships to widows and those anxious to be trained as teachers. Several travelling scholarships should also be granted for specially promising teachers. We suggest that a system of grants should also be made to assist Associations which are now so widely attempting to continue the education of married women outside of ordinary school hours and curricula.

As a better physical standard is also an essential of Indian progress, it is necessary to have educational means by which to cope with the disastrously high rate of infant mortality and the high death-rate of young married women. We therefore press Your Excellency, and you, Sir, to urge the Government to establish more Medical Colleges for women and to institute short Maternity courses, giving certificates to duly qualified persons, in connection with local hospitals in the large towns throughout the country, and to encourage women to attend them by means of scholarships.

We deal with all these matters now, because, unless action is taken with regard to them, all other reforms will lose their full efficacy.

We request you with all the earnestness in our power to recommend the Imperial Government to initiate legislation on these lines, and so bring our country politically, educationally and physically upto the level of other parts of the Empire to which we are loyally devoted, and which we will serve more efficiently as we get better education and wider opportunities in the public life of the Motherland that we love so well.

We beg to be, Your Excellency,

Sir,

Your most obedient servants.

INDEX OF NAMES

INDEX OF PLACES

SUBJECT INDEX